A Concise History of the United States of America

Born out of violence and the aspirations of its early settlers, the United States of America has become one of the world's most powerful nations, even as its past continues to inform its present and to mold its very identity as a nation. The search for nationhood and the ambiguities on which the nation was founded are at the root of this intelligent and forthright book. Taking a broadly chronological approach, it begins in colonial America as the first Europeans arrived, lured by the promise of financial profit, driven by religious piety, and accompanied by the diseases that would ravage and consume the native populations. It explores the tensions inherent in a country built on slave labor in the name of liberty; one forced to assert its unity and reassess its ideals in the face of secession and civil war; and one that struggled to establish moral supremacy, military security, and economic stability during the financial crises and global conflicts of the twentieth century. Woven through this richly crafted study of America's shifting social and political landscapes are the multiple voices of the nation's history: slaves and slave owners, revolutionaries and reformers, soldiers and statesmen, immigrants and refugees. It is their voices, together with those of today's multicultural America, that define the United States at the dawn of a new century.

Susan-Mary Grant is Professor of American History at Newcastle University. She is the author of *North over South: Northern Nationalism and American Identity in the Antebellum Era* (2000) and *The War for a Nation: The American Civil War* (2006), and editor of *Legacy of Disunion: The Enduring Significance of the American Civil War* (2003) and *Themes of the American Civil War: The War Between the States* (2010).

D1262483

CAMBRIDGE CONCISE HISTORIES

This is a series of illustrated "concise histories" of selected individual countries, intended both as university and college textbooks and as general historical introductions for general readers, travelers, and members of the business community.

Series list continues following the Index.

For Peter

A Concise History of the United States of America

SUSAN-MARY GRANT

Newcastle University

CAMBRIDGE
UNIVERSITY PRESS

32 Avenue of the Americas, New York NY 10013-2473, USA

Cambridge University Press is part of the University of Cambridge.

It furthers the University's mission by disseminating knowledge in the pursuit of
education, learning, and research at the highest international levels of excellence.

www.cambridge.org
Information on this title: www.cambridge.org/9780521612791

First published 2012
Reprinted 2013

A catalog record for this publication is available from the British Library.

Library of Congress Cataloging in Publication data
Grant, Susan-Mary.
A concise history of the United States of America / Susan-Mary Grant.
    p.   cm. – (Cambridge concise histories)
Includes bibliographical references and index.
ISBN 978-0-521-84825-1 (hardback) – ISBN 978-0-521-61279-1 (paperback)
1. United States – History.   I. Title.
E178.G734   2012
973–dc23   2011031552

ISBN   978-0-521-84825-1   Hardback
ISBN   978-0-521-61279-1   Paperback

Contents

Figures

Tables

Acknowledgments

No general history of any nation can be accomplished without recourse to the work of other scholars and more detailed monographs on all aspects of that nation's development. In the case of the United States, one has a great wealth of scholarship to draw on. If the history of the land that became the United States of America is sometimes described as brief, its historians have more than made up for this in the depth of their analysis, the rigor of their research, and the extent of their enthusiasm. There are far too many of them to name individually, but the Guide to Further Reading at the end of this volume offers at least some indication of the range of their work, and the extent of my debt to colleagues on both sides of the Atlantic. This particular volume has benefitted from the insights afforded by those who commented on earlier drafts, to the work of Joy Mizan, to Cecilia Mackay for the pictures, and to Ken Karpinski at Aptara and the copyediting team at PETT Fox Inc for editorial expertise. Ultimately, however, it owes its existence to Peter J. Parish and its eventual appearance to the persistence, patience, and much appreciated encouragement of Marigold Acland at Cambridge University Press.

Introduction

The Making of a New World

Eventually all things merge into one, and a river runs through it. The river
was cut by the world's great flood and runs over rocks from the basement
of time. On some of the rocks are timeless raindrops. Under the rocks are
the words, and some of the words are theirs.

(Norman Maclean, *A River Runs Through It*, 1976)

Any historian of the United States working in Europe may easily lose
count of the number of times she is advised – by students, by colleagues,
by friends and family, by complete strangers – that the history she studies is a short one. The observation is frequently accompanied by a wry
smile; a short history, it is implied, therefore a simple history. And anyway, short or long, who needs to study it? Don't we all know it? Are we
not all thoroughly imbued, or infected, depending on one's perspective,
with American culture? Does it not permeate our lives through television, film, popular literature, the Internet? Are we not as familiar with
American culture, with American politics, as we are with our own? Perhaps even more familiar; perhaps there is no culture anymore, beyond
that refracted through American-dominated media and communications
networks. We live in the global village, and the corner store is a 7-11. Is
America not in the clothes we wear, the food we eat, the music we listen
to, and the Web we surf? America's history is already internationally
inscribed. It is not just in the political landscape of the East Coast, the
racially informed social landscape of the South, the reservation lands of
the Dakotas, the borderlands of Texas, Arizona, and New Mexico. It is
much bigger than that. It is a history frequently contorted through the
entertainment industry that is Hollywood, encountered in the heritage

industry built on Plymouth Rock, and, above all, commemorated first, in the national landscape at Valley Forge, Stone's River, and Gettysburg, and then the global one, at Aisne-Marne and Belleau Wood, near Omaha Beach, Normandy, and at Son My. Why go looking for America? Surely it is everywhere.

And yet America is also nowhere. America is vanishing. If we stare, or glare, at it long enough, it may disappear before our eyes. It is already slipping away into an Atlantic paradigm, that of the "Americas," in which the very invocation of America as the name of the United States is deemed potentially offensive to those who live proximate to the nation-state that has selfishly seized that signifier. Their lives, it is assumed, are subsumed by an imperialist superpower that casts its dark shadow over the borderland that separates the United States, *Los Estados Unidos*, from its neighbors to the south. Hundreds perish each year trying to cross this fatal *frontera*, to reach a New World whose shadow now extends into the Old. From the detonation of its atomic power over Japan in 1945 to the current "war on terror," do we not all live in the shadow of this superpower, a shadow now filtered through the floating fragments of the World Trade Center and rendered darker still by the retribution that followed that atrocity?

For those who fear the still further extension of the power of the last superpower, there may be hope. America's perceived cultural, military, and political dominance can be countered, negated, diminished, some assume, by denying it the name it took to itself. Through the power of language, it is anticipated, an imperial power will be brought down to size and forced to accept that it is not first among nations, *primus inter pares*, the "indispensible nation," as Secretary of State Madeleine Albright described it in 1998. It is portrayed instead as, in sociologist Michael Mann's phrase, an "incoherent empire," and in hues so dismal that one can only be grateful that its imperial and militarist ambitions have not achieved greater coherence. For others, the very lack of coherence and concomitant absence of a strong imperial impulse is a problem both for America and for a world in need of what historian Niall Ferguson perceives as a "liberal empire," a new "Colossus" driven as much by conscience as by commerce to effect global stability and security. For still others, more interested in America's internal constructs rather than its external impact, the United States is simply a nation among nations, with all the complexities and contradictions that accrue to the modern nation-state. Yet some would deny it even that status. Some would deny that America is even a nation at all.

In the upsurge of academic interest in nationalism that accompanied the end of the Cold War, the destruction of the Berlin Wall, and the disintegration of the Soviet Union, all of which prompted the reemergence of nationalist impulses long buried beneath an externally imposed overarching social and political ideology, the ethnic origins of the modern nation came under scrutiny once more. Yet no ethnic paradigm could accommodate the United States. A nation of immigrants could, at best, be described as a plural nation. At worst, it could be relegated to a category all of its own, a non-nation; a collection of competing *ethnies*, riven by racial, religious and linguistic wrangling, out of which only cultural confusion – certainly no coherent nation, let alone empire – could emerge.

As the debate continued, however, the idea of the United States as a civic nation, one held together by a civic nationalism, began to gain ground. In fact, this was little more than the application of new terminology to what some were perhaps more used to thinking of as the "American creed." Although the debate recognized that, from the outset, natives and nonwhites, women and non-Protestant religions were often relegated to the margins of an American identity predicated on an exclusive white ethnic core, nevertheless the emphasis turned increasingly to focus on its inclusive civic ideal. This ideal was predicated on the Declaration of Independence, the nation's founding document, its mission statement, its rejection of Old World values, the beginning of a New World republic.

That New Word republic today comprises more than 300 million people. It is the third largest nation on earth, both in terms of population and geography. Only China and India have (much) larger populations; only Canada and Russia are physically bigger. America's geographic and oceanic coverage, at 9,826,675 square kilometers (9,161,966 on land), is still twice that of the European Union. Bordered to the north by the Great Lakes and the St. Lawrence seaway, separating it from Canada, and to the south by the Gulf of Mexico and the Rio Grande (*Río Bravo*) River, separating it from Mexico, it occupies a geographical middle ground and, arguably, a national one, too.

This was not a land, however, that the population always took care of. America's abundance of natural resources, from silver to oil, gas, coal, timber, and fauna, was overexploited to the point of near-extinction of the buffalo (bison) herds on the Great Plains in the late nineteenth century. Deforestation, too, inevitably accompanied the nation's population and industrial growth over the centuries. A land that seemed limitless to early settlers too soon became a man-made, or degraded, landscape; however, since the same nineteenth century, the contrary impulse to protect that land emerged in the establishment of the nation's National Parks. Today, indeed, the National Park Service (NPS) is about much more than just land husbandry and natural resources. It is fundamentally about heritage, a contentious and potent political and cultural issue, one often fought over, with the battlefield sites that the NPS is responsible for as much the flashing point as the wilderness sites such as Yellowstone (the nation's first National Park) or Yosemite. Under the administration of George W. Bush, and partly in the context of the national security imperative, land that came under either NPS or Indian Nation jurisdiction was designated available for oil exploration and mining once again, thereby threatening to destroy a national landscape while simultaneously trying to defend it.

Before defense of the homeland became an issue, establishing that homeland was the main focus for America's peoples. For much of the nation's early history, populations and markets mainly functioned on a north-south axis, one aligned along the Mississippi River that runs through the middle of America from Minnesota in the north to the Gulf of Mexico. Settlers from the east seeking to reach the west coast along what became known as the Oregon Trail had, before the completion of the transcontinental railroad, to negotiate the Rockies, the mountain chain that runs from New Mexico up to Alaska. Today, with the wagon trains that traveled the Oregon Trail long gone, much of the nation's wide-open spaces remain relatively empty. The bulk of America's population – more than 80 percent – is urban. More than 80 percent of that population designates English as their first language, and 10 percent Spanish. Protestants remain in the majority, but only just, at some 51 percent. Of that population, the majority are still classified as white (almost 80 percent), almost 13 percent as black, some 4 percent as Asian, and some 15 percent as Hispanic. Sometimes Hispanic can be designated "white," which is why the figures appear to exceed 100 percent.

The question of ethnic designation is more than a census peculiarity, however. It goes to the heart of the question of American national identity, of what it means to be American and what the nation stands for. At less than 1 percent of the population, for example, Native Americans nevertheless comprise more than 2 million people, subdivided into hundreds of tribal units. Whether one is, or is not, "native" depends on a combination of genetic inheritance and cultural affiliation; some groups emphasize the former, others the latter. Similarly, whether one is deemed black or white tends to be geographically and/or linguistically determined. Hispanic covers pretty much everyone living, or coming from, south of the

Rio Grande, from a white perspective; and African American can appear no different from "Anglo" to those lumped together as "Hispanic."

African American, indeed, is one of the most context-sensitive designations of all. New arrivals from an African nation may encounter resistance from American blacks to their, possibly natural, assumption that "African American" automatically applies to them. Black and white in America represent descriptors derived as much from culture, heritage, and the history of slavery as from any objective genetic markers. African American almost automatically implies an enslaved ancestry. This brings its own set of problems and assumptions, of course, because not all African Americans were enslaved. The historian Barbara Jeanne Fields highlighted the contrary nature of contemporary cultural assumptions relating to race when she observed that in the United States, a white women may give birth to a black child, but a black woman cannot, at least as far as society is concerned, give birth to a white one. So white may create black, but not vice versa. Unless one turns to literature, in which case, as leading African-American author Toni Morrison contends, that is precisely what has happened. "Whiteness," she notes, required a black presence. Being American required something, someone to be positioned outside the nation, at least as it was culturally conceptualized. In this respect, concepts of "whiteness" and "blackness" (or "Africanism") functioned together, but for much of the nation's history it was hardly a relationship of equals.

Clearly, laying claim to an identity in the United States is, for the nation as for the individual, an endeavor fraught with difficulties and challenges but, increasingly, few political or cultural compromises. The once-compelling idea of the United States as a "melting pot" has over the years given way to, first, an emphasis on multiculturalism, and second, to ethnic and cultural (increasingly religious) distinctions that, some fear, are destabilizing the nation. Rather like the federal system itself, in which the states have been accorded varying degrees of autonomy over the course of the nation's history, so individual Americans sustain a sometimes uneasy balancing act between state and social identities and federal and national ones. Sometimes, as in the case of the American Civil War (1861–1865), this has broken down dramatically. At others, in periods of external conflict or crisis, internal divisions diminish – although they never disappear – in favor of a patriotism either promoted from the center, as during World War II, or derived from the grassroots, as was the case after 9/11 and in the ongoing "war on terror."

The link between warfare and American identity, indeed, is a complex one. Most nations have violent histories, and the United States is no exception. Yet understanding how a set of loosely connected colonies that relied so extensively on enslaved labor reached the point of coming together to overthrow a colonial power in the name of liberty, equality, and freedom requires an appreciation of the many and various contemporary impulses that led to this apparently contradictory position. Not the least of these was the early consolidation of the relationship between conflict and a New World identity that the colonists forged in relation to both indigenous natives and imperial power.

The land that became the United States became settled, in some cases only temporarily, by European migrants, missionaries, armies, and traders, driven there by the religious conflicts in Europe. From the beginning, therefore, conflict informed both the migration process and the attitudes of European outsiders to America's indigenous populations. Early propagandist efforts to persuade European monarchs and merchants that the "New World" promised profit in the cause of piety – there were natives to be converted and money to be made – established a deadly combination of the rapacious and the religious out of which conflict was, perhaps, inevitable. The martial origins of the nation were established, of course, in the ultimate colonial conflict, the American War of Independence, that forged the relationship between the nation and the concept of citizen service, between American nationalism and warfare.

That at least part of the story of the Revolutionary War was exaggerated after the event to suggest an enthusiasm not always in evidence at the time in no way diminished the enduring power of the myth of the "Minuteman" as an American martial ideal. This should not be exaggerated but nor should it be underestimated. In the United States today, veterans of America's wars comprise some 10 percent of the adult population. Ten percent, in the grand scheme of things, is not an overwhelming statistic, and hardly a universal troop movement. However, veterans, and through them the impact of warfare, has a powerful influence on American politics and society (and defense budgets), because as a group, veterans turn out to vote in a higher percentage (c. 70 percent) than the population as a whole (c. 60 percent).

In this context, it is unsurprising that one of the crucial threads in America's national story is the way in which the unity forged through warfare informed American national identity via the resultant emphasis on freedom or liberty as the fulcrum around which that identity was constructed. Yet even before the emergence of the nation itself, freedom in the "New World" had both positive (freedom to) and negative (freedom from) connotations. Freedom, as the contemporary slogan has it, is not free. And of course it never was. Freedom for the early European colonists impinged on already existing freedoms enjoyed by native nations. Freedom from monarchical rule, as the case of the loyalists during the Revolution made clear, was not the freedom all fledgling "Americans" sought, nor was it one they necessarily welcomed. Liberty was the animating principle of the American experiment, but it was a principle promulgated most vociferously by slaveholders. The Enlightenment, a process that Immanuel Kant described as the "emancipation of human consciousness," in the eighteenth century may have informed the American revolutionary impulse, but it did not translate into the emancipation of the American revolutionaries' slaves.

"We hold these truths to be self evident," the Declaration of Independence (1776) stated, "that all men are created equal, that they are endowed by their Creator with certain unalienable Rights, that among these are Life, Liberty and the pursuit of Happiness." For too long such "truths" only really held true for those who were either part of, proximate to, or had the potential to join the white, male elite whose perspective these truths had only ever partially represented. Although fully prepared to believe English radical Thomas Paine when he advised them that theirs was "the cause of all mankind," Americans interpreted Paine's message in the context of a republican ideology through which the promotion of equality and liberty went hand in hand with the defense of slavery. Facilitated by the development of markets and communications networks, the individual colonies could at least conceptualize a unified political and cultural whole. Achieving it was another matter. For some, liberty as the national ideal could only be achieved if it applied to all. For others, the nation's future would only be secure if some were permanently enslaved. By the middle of the nineteenth century, one truth was self-evident to Abraham Lincoln, struggling to hold the nation together during the Civil War. "We all declare for liberty," Lincoln observed, "but in using the same *word* we do not all mean the same *thing*."

The nation that emerged from the Civil War was one in which slavery had finally been abolished, but racial and ethnic distinctions remained as the means through which American identity was negotiated and refined, especially as the population expanded further west, fulfilling the nation's "Manifest Destiny" to achieve hemispheric hegemony. The persistence of, as well as the challenges to, Anglo-Saxon dominance in America on the eve of the twentieth century were exacerbated by concerns over racism, immigration, crime, and the city in a period that saw the United States dip a tentative toe into international waters in the form of a war with Spain. By this time, the generation that had fought the Civil War had reached political prominence. The experiences of their youth informed but certainly could not prepare them or the nation for the century to come, the so-called "American Century," which really began after World War II with the economic and, arguably, cultural global dominance of the United States.

Yet over the course of the "American Century," overshadowed as that was by the Cold War, and dominated, to a large extent, by the conflict in Vietnam, the idea of the American nation became nuanced. The national story of the civic nation with an ethnic core became one that emphasized the efforts of the excluded to challenge their exclusion. A renewed interest in America's cultural diversity became the means through which to complicate any lingering complacency about the reality of the civic ideal in the United States. At the same time, it highlighted the ways in which, in drafting the Declaration of Independence, America's founders had, as Abraham Lincoln argued, established an inclusionary premise through which all Americans, regardless of ancestry, could claim the nation "as though they were blood of the blood, and flesh of the flesh of the men who wrote that Declaration." In this context, too, the Atlantic world paradigm served not just to assuage international fears, but to stress the power of the civic ideal. It emphasized how permeable the nation's borders were not just to immigrants but to international influences – if not international influence as such – and how susceptible it was to shifting understandings of colonialism and postcolonialism, nationalism, sectionalism, warfare, identity, race, religion, gender, and ethnicity.

The imperative of making the civic ideal match or even approximate reality continues to confront America today, of course, and is a particularly problematic one in a nation of its geographic, demographic, and cultural complexity. Often more interested in how the democratic ideal has been exported, or imposed beyond the nation's borders, popular analyses of the United States sometimes underestimate the historical struggle to achieve that ideal within the nation itself. If the New World "Colossus" has frequently found itself in the paradoxical position of "dictating democracy" or "extorting emancipation" abroad in the later twentieth and early twenty-first centuries, its own history, be that from the 1860s or the 1960s, reminds us that it has frequently been forced to deploy similar processes at home. Less a paradox than a pattern, the sometimes uneasy balancing act between civic and ethnic, positive and negative freedom is hardly an unfamiliar one in a nation that seems to want for others what it sometimes struggles to achieve for itself. The challenges it faced, the choices it made, the compromises it reached are ones that all nations must contemplate; increasingly so in a world in which communication is all but instantaneous, in which all borders can be breached, and in which the challenges posed by immigration, religious intolerance, and racial and ethnic divisions continue to compromise the stability of the modern nation-state.

I

New Found Land

Imagining America

> Thus in the beginning all the world was *America*.
> (John Locke, *The Second Treatise of Civil Government*, 1690)

America was a land, and later a nation, imagined before it was ever conceived. Although the dreams and ambitions of its first human settlers can only be surmised, whether crossing the Bering Straits on foot or arriving by sea, early migrants to the North American continent came in search of a better life. Whether their original intentions were settlement or possible trade routes, whether they sought a new home or simply new resources to take back home, the lure of a New World proved a potent one. With the exception of the peoples that Christopher Columbus identified, wrongly, as Indians, the earliest migratory endeavors produced few permanent settlements. The continent's indigenous inhabitants were little troubled by the initially tentative forays of adventurous Vikings in the tenth and eleventh centuries, whose eventual settlements in Greenland were, although unwelcome, relatively short-lived, as quickly forgotten by the native tribes, perhaps, as they were by the world in general.

Absent external interference, therefore, the peoples that later comprised the many Native American ethno-linguistic and nationalist groupings of the modern period gradually developed what Jeremiah Curtin, a nineteenth-century folklorist, perceived as essentially primitive societies based on a combination of religious faith and consanguinity. As Curtin saw it:

The bonds which connect a nation with its gods, bonds of faith, and those which connect the individuals of that nation with one another, bonds of blood, are the strongest known to primitive man, and are the only social bonds in prehistoric ages. This early stage was the one in which even the most advanced group of Indians in America found themselves when the continent was discovered.

(Jeremiah Curtin, *Creation Myths of Primitive America*, 1898)

Despite the fact that he might as easily have been describing the bonds produced, and as frequently severed, by the religious turmoil and mon-archical machinations of fifteenth-century Europe as indigenous Amer-ican cultures, Curtin's views sound a discordant note today. Neither the idea of "primitive man" nor the notion that America was a continent just waiting to be "discovered" by Europeans forms part of the modern understanding of America's past.

Prior to their encounters with European peoples, the indigenous soci-eties of the Americas were, of course, both culturally and linguistically varied. Their actual population size remains a matter of debate, but was anywhere between 10 million and 75 million in total, of which 2 mil-lion to 10 million were within what is now the United States, at a time when the populations of Europe and Africa were 70 million and 50 million, respectively. Although there was a degree of interaction in the form of trade, travel, and – inevitably – warfare, the sheer size of the continent naturally encouraged the flourishing of a diverse range of set-tlements, cultures, and peoples. These ranged from the relatively stable but competitive agrarian political societies of the west coast, through the Hopewell peoples of what is now Ohio and Illinois, whose speciality was metalwork, to one of the most complex indigenous societies, that of the Cahokia who inhabited the Mississippi and Missouri floodplains. Nor were these static societies; like their European counterparts, they were subject to the forces of change, prompted by conflict and competition, by shifting agricultural patterns and expanding trading networks. Indeed, the parallels between indigenous American cultures and those European societies that eventually inserted themselves into their midst were perhaps more striking than their differences, both in terms of migratory patterns and, crucially, mythologies.

Native American creation myths take many forms, but in essence all tell a similar story; it is a story of origins and change, of metamorphoses, of human arrival in the world and of the transformations that made the human part of that world. Although absent the evocative trickster and anthropomorphic elements of their Native American counterparts, the European myth of American origins differs little from that indigenous pattern. The white European story of settlement, too, was ultimately one of grounding, of establishing not just a claim to the land, but an alignment with what was understood to be the spirit of that land. In the long term, that spirit would be accorded many titles – Liberty, Equality, Manifest Destiny – but for the earliest European settlers, simply making sense of the land itself, and of its aboriginal inhabitants, was the first step toward colonizing that land. This was the start of a process that would ultimately disinherit, if not entirely destroy, America's indigenous societies. It established in their stead a colonial culture predicated on Old World values informed by European, predominantly British, legal, political, religious, and social precedents that would, over the course of the following few hundred years, not only achieve independence from the British crown, but emerge as the single most powerful nation on earth.

This process began, of course, with the arrival in the West Indies in 1492 of the Genoese sailor Columbus, whose journey had been prompted by the shipbuilding and general oceanic navigational skills of one European power, Portugal. Just as trade and exchange underpinned much of America's indigenous culture, so material goods and changing patterns of consumption were the motivation for the burst of seagoing activity on the part of the Portuguese in the fifteenth century. Their interest in exploration was a by-product of a greater desire to acquire the spices, tea, silks, and, above all, gold around which international trade revolved. These goods had, up to then, been transported overland, from China to the Middle East and then to the Mediterranean, or, in the case of gold, from the Sahara through the northern tip of Africa to Europe. Control of much of this trade had rested with the Venetians and the Turks, and it was these middlemen that the Portuguese hoped to circumvent. In the process, Portugal acquired a stake in what would become one of the Atlantic world's defining economic and social features – the slave trade. In the context of a European world fast becoming accustomed to not just enjoying cups of tea but to having sugar in them, people – slaves – became as profitable as the luxuries they produced, as Portugal's sugar plantations on the Azores and Cape Verde Islands made clear. In short, Portugal's success with sugar, its finding a sea route around the southern coast of Africa, its establishment of trading posts on the continent's west coast, and, above all, the profits it accrued in all these endeavors prompted the other European powers – especially Portugal's most proximate neighbor, Spain – to seek a share of the action. It was to this end that Isabella of Spain directed Columbus to locate a westward route to the Indies.

Columbus's underestimation of the full extent of the globe – one not shared by many of his contemporaries – resulted in his relatively swift arrival in the Bahamas, and his belief that he had in fact reached the East Indies. It was this belief that prompted his inappropriate designation of the inhabitants he encountered as "Indians." How the "Indians" perceived Columbus is less certain, but what is undeniable is that his arrival inaugurated a period of exploration, acquisition, and conquest of the Americas on the part of several of the European powers in which the benefits of this encounter – the so-called Columbian exchange – were almost all on the side of the new arrivals. From the moment of first contact, it was clear that the European powers regarded the Americas as theirs for the taking. Indeed, Spain and Portugal argued over Columbus's discovery to such an extent that the Pope was forced to intervene. Via the Treaty of Tordesillas (1494), he divided their competing claims down the middle of the Atlantic. Portugal moved into Brazil while Spain set her sights on the rest of South America and the Caribbean.

At first, successful colonization seemed unlikely. Columbus's initial settlement on Hispaniola (now occupied by Haiti and the Dominican Republic) was a failure. In 1502, the last year when Columbus himself traveled to the New World, the Spanish explorer Nicolás de Ovando managed to establish a functioning outpost for Spain on Hispaniola at the same time as Italian explorer Amerigo Vespucci realized, as a result of his coastal travels, that what Columbus had encountered was a whole new continent, far larger, and far more populous, than Europeans could ever have imagined. It was not until Ferdinand Magellan's ships circumnavigated the globe between 1519 and 1520, however, that Europe gained a full appreciation of the world's size and some idea of the heterogeneous nature of its populations.

In the absence of hard evidence, imagination played a very large part in European reactions to the American continent, even before any European set foot on it; imagination, but also its opposite, an almost pathological inability to comprehend, let alone envisage any compromise with the lives of others. Yet it is important neither to exaggerate the effects of the Columbian exchange nor to bring the indigenous peoples into the historical frame simply that they might play the role of victim in a European-directed drama of greed-inspired genocide. Greed there was in abundance, certainly, but this alone does not account for the catastrophic demographic effects, for America's indigenous populations, of the first European-American encounter. Disease played a major part. The Arawak/Taino population of Hispaniola, estimated at 300,000 to 1 million in 1492, all but disappeared within the space of fifty years, whereas Mexico's population fell by as much as 90 percent in the sixteenth century. Yet although diseases such as smallpox, measles, or yellow fever wreaked havoc in the Americas, there is little medical evidence to suggest a particular indigenous susceptibility to European disease strains. Smallpox alone could prove devastating even in a population that enjoyed herd immunity to it. The death rate from that disease among white Union soldiers in the Civil War (1861–65) was around 38 percent – about the same as for Aztec society in 1520.

The danger for America's indigenous peoples in the sixteenth century was not solely the diseases carried from the Old World to the "New." The main problem was who carried them. Violence and virus worked in tandem, and to devastating effect, in the Americas after first contact, and continued to do so well into the late nineteenth century. Both emanated from a European environment that, although not inured either to conflict or contagion, was certainly familiar with both. The sixteenth century was a violent age, made more so by the religious realignments prompted by, first, the Protestant Reformation inaugurated by Martin Luther in 1517 and, later, England's version of it, ushered in by Henry VIII's Act of Supremacy (1534) through which he challenged the power of the papacy and established himself as head of the Church of England. When that, coupled with the inevitable greed for gold and all the power that it could purchase, moved across the Atlantic, the results were devastating. Competition and conflict were certainly not alien to the native populations of the Americas, but it was the relatively sudden burst of competitiveness among the European powers during what has been termed the First Great Age of Discovery that overwhelmed them. Inspired and threatened by the impact of Columbus's encounter in equal measure, the British and the French in particular sought to challenge Spanish dominance, in Europe as in the Americas.

The English were especially keen on undermining the power of Spain, and to that end sent Venetian explorer Giovanni Caboto (anglicized to John Cabot) to Newfoundland in 1497. His journey did a great deal for the European fishing industry, but England lacked the resources to follow up on Cabot's initiative. Further south, the Spanish had kept their eyes on the greater prize that the imagined wealth of the Americas offered. Naked greed, however, found it both convenient and, in the context of the Reformation, expedient to wrap itself in the banner of religion. So the Spanish *conquistadores* set out from Hispaniola in a New World echo of the crusades of the eleventh and twelfth centuries. Accompanied by missionaries, they marched under the sign of the cross to convert – or crush – the peoples they encountered. The most famous Spanish explorer of this period was, of course, Hernán Cortés, whose encounter with the Aztec civilization of central Mexico in 1519 was swiftly followed by a smallpox epidemic that facilitated his defeat of the Aztecs and the destruction of their main city, Tenochtitlán. The Incas in what is now Peru fared little better against Francisco Pizzaro a few years later.

Arguably, although the destruction of cities and their inhabitants was terrible enough, and the exploitation of indigenous peoples extreme even by the standards of Aztec civilization – sufficiently brutal to shock some Spaniards – it was the slow but inexorable erosion of New World cultures that not only defined the post-Columbian era, but set a precedent as far as European encounters with – and later within – the Americas were concerned. From the period of the earliest European exploration onward, the relationship between incomer and indigene was positioned on the cusp of contradictory impulses on the part of the Europeans. From an economic perspective, the indigenous peoples seemed ideal for exploitation. From a religious one, they were ripe for conversion. Europeans had little interest in acclimatizing themselves culturally to the environment of the New World, but nor had they thought through the implications of acculturating the indigenous populations to European norms. This uneasy juxtaposition of the non-European as both potential convert and alien "other" defined not just Spanish colonization efforts, but the colonization impulse as a whole across the Americas between the sixteenth and eighteenth centuries.

Additional developments within Europe itself must also be factored into the European impact on post-Columbian America. Not the least of these was the rise of print culture, which scholars perceive as one of the fundamental building blocks of the modern nation. The development of printing from the fifteenth century onward resulted in a wealth of words, woodcuts, and, crucially, maps being available to an ever-increasing percentage of the European populations. Within Europe itself, much of the early print culture proved the means of dissemination of clashing clerical perspectives, but images were as significant as words when Europeans looked across the Atlantic, images that helped them orientate themselves in that environment. As a human activity generally, but certainly in the age of European exploration, mapmaking often says more about the society producing the map than the landscape being mapped. Early maps frequently served a military purpose or, in the case of the Americas, functioned quite literally as treasure maps. One example is Battista Agnese's world map of c. 1544 with its clearly defined routes to the Spanish silver mines of the New World, its outline of Magellan's global circumnavigation, but its rather hazy depiction of the land to the north – the land that would, in time, become the United States of America (Figure 1.1).

Early maps of the Americas represented tangible representations of the extent, and limitations, of European geographical knowledge. They were also physical manifestations of the European imagination as far as the Americas were concerned. As Agnese's 1544 map reveals, North America really was an unknown quantity, *terra incognita*, in the sixteenth century. South America, by contrast, was portrayed as a landscape of economic opportunities, but a dangerous one. Such additional information as was available beyond early maps tended toward the sensationalist. Those publications that followed in the wake of Columbus's voyages presented images of the New World in which neither Spanish colonizers nor indigenous populations were presented in a particularly flattering light. Insofar as these images fed into the European imagination of the Americas, they revealed the stuff of nightmares. Many of them came out of the studio of Dutch-born engraver Theodor de Bry and his sons, who produced a multivolume study (1590–1618) of European-American encounters, illustrating such publications such as J. de Léry *Le Voyage au Brézil de Jean de Léry 1556–1558* (1578). A Protestant French minister and writer, de Léry had accompanied a colonizing expedition to Brazil that later settled near the indigenous Tupinambá tribe. What de Léry witnessed there shocked him, in particular how the Tupinambá "killed, cut up, roasted and ate some of their enemy." Rendered visually by de Bry, his description probably shocked his readers as well.

Although both de Léry's descriptions and de Bry's images of New World peoples were not consistently unsettling, and frequently focused on peaceful domestic scenes, de Bry's images of the European-American encounters were often brutally graphic, and especially graphic about Spanish brutality. He depicted the Spanish colonizers in much the same way as he would later portray the Tupinambá, as in the engravings that accompanied Bartolomé de Las Casas's *Short Account of the Destruction of the Indies* (1542) (Figure 1.2). In this case, the clue was in the title. De Bry's images for Las Casas's work were not drawn from an overactive imagination, but reflected the subject of at least some of the texts emanating from Europe's New World exploratory ventures.

Las Casas, a Dominican priest who had taken part in the violence on Hispaniola and in Cuba, wrote from the heart and from personal experience when he described the horrific treatment meted out to the natives by Spanish colonists. In turning against such behavior, Las Casas

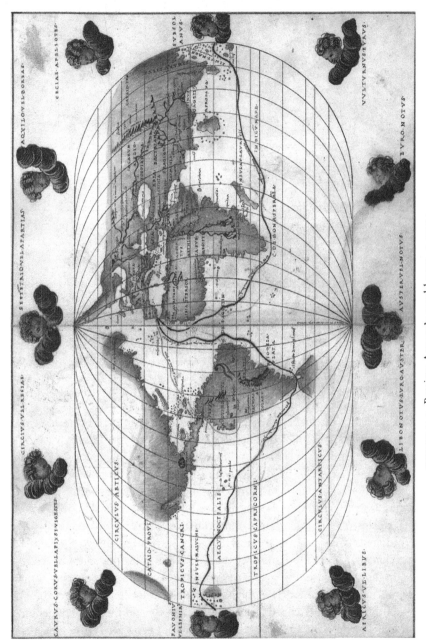

FIGURE I.I. Battista Agnese's world map, c. 1544.

FIGURE 1.2. Bartolomé de Las Casas' *Short Account of the Destruction of the Indies* (1542, 1552).

was ahead of his time. Yet his solution – which he later regretted – to the barbarities he had both witnessed and participated in before concluding that America's indigenous peoples deserved to be recognized, and treated, as equals was simply to replace one subject of exploitation with another – to replace native with African slaves.

The English at Home, and Abroad

Spanish cruelty toward natives in the early stages of European settlement in the Americas, although highlighted in the work of Las Casas, was not especially or unusually harsh within the context of the period. Those nations that sought to challenge Spanish dominance in the Americas, and particularly England, had little reason to feel superior to the Spanish, given that neither at home or abroad did they hold the moral high ground when it came to fulfilling their expansionist ambitions. Unfortunately for the indigenous natives in the Americas, late-sixteenth-century England's approach to the whole issue of expansion, colonization, and conquest was driven by a close-knit group of Protestant West Country aristocratic adventurers such as Walter Ralegh, his half-brother Sir Humphrey Gilbert, and his cousin Richard Grenville. Their views on English expansion could best be described as aggressive and their approach to other cultures intolerant. It was informed by what these men already knew – or thought they knew – about the Americas and about Spanish colonization efforts there. What they knew came from published accounts, including Spanish historian Peter Martyr Anghiera's *De Orbe Novo* (On the New World), which began publication in 1511. The first *Eight Decades* were published in 1530 but translated, at least partially, by Richard Eden in 1555 as *The Decades of the Newe Worlde or West India*. Yet before they turned to the idea of conquering a land across the Atlantic, one closer to home attracted their attention: Ireland.

In the English case, the infighting that ensued between Catholics and Protestants, ushered in by the Reformation and exacerbated by the monarchical instability that followed the early death of Henry VIII, carried over into English relations with Catholic Ireland. Ireland's inhabitants were frequently perceived as threatening alien "others," and as a consequence treated in a fashion distressingly similar to that experienced by America's natives more than three thousand miles away. The repercussions of this, for America's history, were profound. The Catholic Irish, potentially a threat to the Protestant supremacy, had long been pawns in the ongoing power struggle between Spain and England. With the ascension to the English throne of Elizabeth I (1558), efforts to bring Ireland under the rule of the Crown intensified. This need not necessarily have impacted on England's later American colonization activities, except for the fact that many of those sent by Elizabeth to impose her will in Ireland in the 1560s and 1570s were the same men who she would later send to extend her influence across the Atlantic.

For men like Gilbert, Ralegh, and Grenville, the Gaelic Irish were regarded as uncivilized barbarians whose loyalty to the Crown was suspect and whose system of government tyrannical. This justified not only the conquest of that island, but also the brutal methods employed in the process. On Gilbert's part, these methods included, according to contemporary witness Thomas Churchyard, the decapitation of Irish rebels so that the heads "should there bee laied on the ground by eche side of the waie ledyng into his own tente so that none could come into his tente for any cause but commonly he muste passe through a lane of heddes." In this way, Churchyard observed, Gilbert brought "greate terror to the people."[1] As far as both Ireland and America were concerned, it was a clear case of a quite literal vicious circle. Awareness of Spanish treatment of the indigenous populations of the Americas informed the English suppression of the Irish, and in turn their subsequent cruelty toward the Irish influenced their reactions to, and treatment of, the natives that they later encountered in the New World. In both cases, what they perceived as cultural inferiority on the part of the indigenous inhabitants provided the justification for extremes of cruelty in the service of "civilization." It also established a precedent. Over the next few hundred years, natives, blacks, Catholics, and, by extrapolation, the Catholic Irish in the New World would frequently be set apart from a society that, too often, defined itself through difference and reinforced the dominance of a white, Protestant ethnic core.

All this lay in the future. In the 1560s and 1570s, the suppression of the Irish was symptomatic of the instability of the English crown at this time, and itself absorbed resources that might otherwise have been devoted to more ambitious ventures further afield. When not wreaking havoc in Ireland, Gilbert found time to peruse the publications emanating from the New World, in particular French naval officer and navigator Jean Ribault's *The Whole and True Discovereye of Terra Florida* (1563), which emphasized the great wealth that might be found across the Atlantic. Ribault had, in 1562, led an expedition to the southeastern part of America with a view to establishing a settlement there for French Huguenots. In fact Ribault's initial efforts met with setbacks similar to those that the English would later face; internal squabbles, difficulties with indigenous natives and with the Spanish, and an overly harsh disciplinary structure for the colony. Ribault initially settled on one of the sea islands off the coast of South Carolina (Parris Island), but when he returned to France for supplies, the settlement floundered and soon dispersed, with many of the original settlers returning to France. It was not until several years later that Ribault succeeded in temporarily establishing a colony at Fort Caroline near what is present-day Jacksonville, Florida, but lost his life in the process, killed by the Spanish in 1565 when they, again, seized control of that part of Florida. Ribault's experiences, however, certainly influenced England's growing interest in American colonization. He had discussed the possibility of an American colonization venture with potential English backers and with Queen Elizabeth I herself. Naturally enough, Ribault's reports piqued Gilbert's interest. In 1578, he acquired a patent to colonize any part of the globe not held by a Christian monarch, and finally organized an expedition to Newfoundland in 1583. It might have seemed to the Irish, at least, that there was some justice in the fact that he was lost at sea on the way back.

Given that the recently knighted (1580) Sir Walter Ralegh had been an investor in Gilbert's ill-starred exploratory venture, it was perhaps inevitable that when Gilbert failed to return from the New World, Ralegh acquired a patent (1584) in his stead, which permitted him to establish dominion anywhere on the American coast. In the official language of the day, he was granted leave "to discover, search, finde out, and view such remote, heathen and barbarous lands, countreis, and territories, not actually possessed of any Christian prince, nor inhabited by Christian people" with a view to settlement.[2] A reconnaissance trip conducted in 1584 by Arthur Barlowe and Philip Amadas reached Roanoke Island, off the coast of North Carolina. Returning to England in the autumn of that year along with two of the indigenous natives and a bag of pearls, Barlowe's report promised a world more than suitable for settlement, a land of friendly and placid natives and unlimited natural bounties. "The soile is the most plentifull, sweete, fruitfull and wholesome of all the worlde," Barlowe reported, and the island boasted "many goodly woodes full of Deere, Conies, Hares, and Fowle, even in the middest of Summer in incredible abundance." "I thinke in all the world the like abundance is not to be found," he observed, "and my selfe having seene those parts of Europe that most abound, find such difference as were incredible to be written." The natives, too, proved more than welcoming, furnishing the expedition each day with "a brase or two of fat Bucks, Conies, Hares, Fish and best of the world," as well as "divers kindes of fruites, Melons, Walnuts, Cucumbers, Gourdes, Pease, and divers rootes, and fruites very excellent." The speed with which crops grew in this paradise amazed the Europeans; planting some peas they had brought with them, they were stunned to see them reach fourteen inches in ten days. The possibilities, clearly, were endless.

Barlowe's report, although it enthused about every aspect of nature and native that he encountered, did contain a few observations of a more ominous slant. If the natives seemed peaceful in the company of their visitors, they certainly were not pacifists. The Europeans were unable to meet the king of the island, Wingina, in person as he was recovering from a wound sustained in battle, and Barlowe acknowledged that their hosts "maintaine a deadly and terrible warre, with the people and King adjoining." He also reported the natives' marked enthusiasm "for our hatchets, and axes, and for knives." They would, he added, "have given any thing for swordes: but wee would not depart with any."[3]

It was hardly to be expected that the English would wish to relinquish any weaponry, then or in the future. One of the main attractions of the Roanoke Island, for Ralegh at least, had little to do with its natural abundance and everything to do with its proximity to Spanish settlements in Florida. Roanoke offered a useful base from which English ships could threaten Spanish dominance, and that was Ralegh's main ambition. Even before Barlowe and Amadas had returned, Ralegh had commissioned

Oxford geographer and friend Richard Hakluyt to produce a short work, never made public, intended to persuade Elizabeth I to support Ralegh's New World colonization schemes. Hakluyt had, two years previously, contributed to what was becoming a burgeoning literature on exploration in the Americas with his *Divers Voyages Touching the Discoverie of America and the Islands Adjacent unto the Same, Made First of all by our Englishmen and Afterwards by the Frenchmen and Britons* (1582). Now, with Ralegh's encouragement, he produced *A Particular Discourse Concerning Western Discoveries* (1584), which was really a polemic for English settlement in America.

In the context of an England concerned about both poverty and over-population, Hakluyt's argument struck a chord. England's population was on the increase in the sixteenth and seventeenth centuries: from 2.3 million in 1520, it rose to 3.75 million in 1603 and to 5.2 million in 1690, but its economy did not keep pace. Even when Hakluyt was writing, the ill effects of this were already becoming evident. We "are grown more pop-ulous than ever heretofore," Hakluyt observed, so many, indeed, "that they can hardly live one by another: nay, rather they are ready to eat up one another." The resultant unemployment, he concluded, produced individuals who either threatened the social order or who were, at the very least, "very burdensome to the common wealth." Prone "to pilfering and thieving and other lewdness, whereby all the prisons of the land are daily pestered," these social outcasts were destined either to "pine away" or to be "miserably hanged." Better by far, suggested Hakluyt, foreshad-owing what would become a standard defense of resettlement abroad, that this surplus population be put to use in establishing and maintaining English colonies in America. He had a fairly eclectic view of what skills and trades might be considered surplus. Colonization, he argued, would

minister matter for all sorts and states of men to work upon: namely all several kinds of artificers, husbandmen, seamen, merchants, soldiers, captains, phys-icians, lawyers, divines, cosmographers, hydrographers, astronomers, histori-ographers, yea old folks, lame persons, women, and young children by many means which hereby shall still be ministered unto them, shall be kept from idle-ness, and be made able by their own honest and easy labor to find themselves without surcharging others.

Missing from Hakluyt's list were the clergy, which was especially telling given that he preceded his description of all other benefits to accrue from colonization with the observation that it would, above all, serve "greatly for the enlargement of the gospel of Christ whereunto the Princes of the reformed religion are chiefly bound amongst whom her Majesty is principal." In short, it would spread Protestantism. In the process, it would spread liberty and rescue the indigenous peoples not just from the perils of heathenism, but from the "pride and tyranny" of Spain. "So many and so monstrous have been the Spanish cruelties," Hakluyt argued, "such strange slaughters and murders of those peaceable, lowly, mild, and gentle people together with the spoils of towns, provinces, and kingdoms which have been most ungodly perpetrated in the West Indies," that were "the Queen of England, a prince of such clemency" to rule in America to spread "humanity, courtesy, and freedom," then the natives would certainly revolt against the Spanish.

Hakluyt's main focus, however, was colonization's immediate material benefits for England. Settlement of America would, he pointed out, produce enormous economic gains in the form of "all the commodities of Europe, Africa, and Asia." It would, he suggested, "supply the wants of all our decayed trades," offer employment to "numbers of idle men," and, perhaps above all, "be a great bridle to the Indies of the king of Spain" as well as serving "greatly for the increase, maintenance and safety of our Navy, and especially of great shipping which is the strength of our realm." In case the Queen was not convinced by all this, Hakluyt stressed that England could not afford to "procrastinate the planting" because if she did not colonize America, other nations certainly would. Nothing less than England's honor was at stake.[4]

Fortunately, little in Barlowe's report – neither his descriptions of nature's bounties nor those of pliable if not wholly peaceful natives – directly contradicted what Ralegh, via Hakluyt, had told the Queen. Limited support was therefore offered Ralegh's scheme in the form of one ship of the line, the *Tyger*. In a sense, this set the tone for the whole enterprise, and it was a martial one. Although politically more stable by the 1580s, the Tudor monarchy under Elizabeth I was not flush with funds to direct toward American settlement. No English ship could afford to venture onto the high seas without some hope of acquiring treasure, in the form of Spanish prizes, in the process. It was for this reason that the Roanoke expedition, one supposedly intended to rescue the Roanoke natives from the threat of Spanish cruelty, was from the outset placed in the hands of a group of men whose apprenticeship in the colonization line had taken place in Ireland. Men such as Richard Grenville, Thomas Cavendish, and Ralph Lane certainly possessed the military expertise necessary for threatening the Spanish, but were less suited for diplomatic dealings with the natives of Roanoke alongside who they hoped to settle.

Accompanying these men of war when the expedition set off in April 1585 was a varied assortment of sailors, soldiers, and settlers, the painter John White, the mathematician Thomas Hariot, and the two natives who had accompanied Barlowe and Amada back to England the previous year, Wanchese and Manteo.

Although they made good time across the Atlantic, the expedition encountered problems on arrival when the *Tyger* ran aground and the supplies intended to support the new colony were spoiled. Nevertheless, under Lane's direction, a settlement was established and a fort constructed. Lane's initial reports were promising, and Wingina's people were, as before, both welcoming and generous with provisions, so the loss of the *Tyger*'s cargo was not, at first, the disaster it might have been. Whether it in fact caused more problems in the long run, or whether the settlers' total lack of ability to fend for themselves was intrinsic to the military nature of the endeavor, is harder to assess. What is certain is that these first settlers, as would be the case with future ones, exerted little effort toward becoming self-sufficient and relied almost entirely on the voluntary largesse of their hosts and, when that reached its limits, turned to violence to secure their survival.

At Roaonke, however, the violence was ultimately self-defeating. The English killed the goose that laid the golden egg. Lane murdered Wingina and then headed to England, just as Grenville, who had left Roanoke the previous year, was on his way back. Finding no sign of Lane or the colony, Grenville stationed a small body of men at the fort and then headed out to sea and to the prospect of seizing more Spanish ships. In July 1587, the artist John White arrived along with his family, the native Manteo, and more than one hundred prospective settlers. Leaving them there, White himself sailed with the fleet to England to secure supplies, arriving home just in time for his ship to be requisitioned as part of England's defense against the Spanish Armada (1588). On his return in 1590, he found the Roanoke colony deserted and the settlers, including his daughter and granddaughter, gone. All that remained was the word "Croatoan" carved into a tree. This was possibly a reference to the Croatan people, but whether the settlers had been rescued or murdered by them, no one knew. As far as the English were concerned, the fate of the "Lost Colony" of Roanoke could only be imagined.

This inauspicious beginning did not bode well for future English colonization efforts, but neither did it diminish the growing enthusiasm for the opportunities perceived to exist across the Atlantic. In naming the land Virginia, Ralegh had accorded it a validity it had not previously held in the English worldview. No longer *terra incognita*, Virginia became a place on the map, fixed in the English imagination as both location and potential property. In the English mind, it became, as Thomas Hariot would describe it, a "New Found Land" that, having been "found," could not then be forgotten. Hariot's study, *A Briefe and True Report of the New Found Land of Virginia,* first published in 1588 and then two years later with engravings by de Bry of illustrations by White, and translated into English by Hakluyt, was in every sense a composite view of the state of understanding of the New World in England when it was published. *A Briefe and True Report* offered a more measured assessment of the country and its population than many previous reports or propagandist works had provided and, even acknowledging the failure of the Roanoke expedition, sustained interest in the possibility of settlement in America (Figure 1.3).

Hariot's report spoke to a multiplicity of different agendas as far as American exploration and settlement were concerned. Above all, it sought to counteract what Hariot described as the many "slaunderous and shamefull speeches bruited abroad by many that returned from" the New World. For Hariot, it was a case of managing expectations:

Some also were of a nice bringing vp, only in cities or townes, or such as neuer (as I may say) had seene the world before. Because there were not to bee found any English cities, nor such faire houses, nor at their owne wish any of their olde accustomed daintie food, nor any soft beds of downe or fethers: the countrey was to them miserable, & their reports thereof according.

So far from miserable, Virginia was, Hariot stressed, a land of great natural promise, one both suitable for traders and settlers. He opened his argument with a reference to luxury goods. Silk worms in Virginia, he reported, were "as bigge as our ordinary walnuttes" and all that was needed was the planting of mulberry trees for a productive and profitable sericulture to develop. Development was the point. Hariot's observation that nature's bounty, whether that was in the form of wood, ore, fur, fruit or cereal crops, simply required the application of English labor, and not much hard labor at that, to become economically viable was more than an enticement toward profit; it was the basis on which the English justified their usurpation of the land from the indigenous people whose country it was. Turning to the subject of these people, Hariot reported that in "respect of vs they are a people poore, and for want of skill and iudgement in the knowledge and vse of our things, doe esteeme our trifles before thinges of greater value." Nevertheless, he considered

FIGURE 1.3. Title page of Thomas Hariot, *A Briefe and True Report of the New Found Land of Virginia : of the Commodities and of the Nature and Manners of the Naturall Inhabitants : Discouered bỹ the English Colonỹ There Seated by Sir Richard Greinuile Knight In the ỹeere 1585 : Which Remained Vnder the Gouernment of Twelue Monethes, At the Speciall Charge and Direction of the Honourable Sir Walter Raleigh Knight Lord Warden of the Stanneries Who therein Hath Beene Fauoured and Authorised bỹ Her Maiestie and Her Letters Patents* (London 1588, 1590). Newcastle University Special Collections.

them "very ingenious; For although they haue no such tooles, nor any such craftes, sciences and artes as wee; yet in those thinges they doe, they shewe excellencie of wit." It would be no great difficulty, he proposed, to show the natives the error of their non-English ways. Just as soon as they understood "our manner of knowledgeś and craftes to exceede theirs in perfection, and speed for doing or execution," he argued, "by so much the more is it probable that they shoulde desire our friendships & loue, and haue the greater respect for pleasing and obeying vs."[5] In short, conversion of the natives to European norms, both cultural and religious, seemed a real possibility.

White's illustrations for Hariot's volume reinforced the argument of the text. His images of America's Algonquin peoples were, of all those that had appeared, perhaps the most naturalistic and expressive. Yet for a readership more interested, perhaps, in the background against which these individuals were portrayed, it was his first image that would have resonated most strongly (Figure 1.4). What Hakluyt, Hariot, and others in the late sixteenth century were offering Europe was a new Eden in the New World. Some quite literally believed in its existence; Columbus, for one, continued to believe that a New Eden lay at the origins of the Orinoco River in Guiana (in present-day Venezuela). Almost exactly a hundred years later, Ralegh set off in the same direction, although he was seeking profit, not paradise – El Dorado, not Eden. Above all, it was the constant lure of the colony, the chance to start again in an imaginary version of the world before the Fall, that was being held out here. Hariot's *Report of the New Found Land of Virginia* was, metaphorically speaking, the Book of Genesis. Yet in White's illustration, Eve already has her hand on the apple. If Virginia was a new Eden, it was one from which the original inhabitants were about to be ejected.

By the 1580s, the Tudor monarchy under Elizabeth had achieved sufficient stability to contemplate an increase in foreign trade and exploration. The growth of a new enterprise, the joint-stock company, made financing such endeavors a more realistic proposition. The first such was the Muscovey (or Russian) Company, established in 1553 with a view to finding a northeast passage to the Indies. Its charter served as the basis for all future ventures, and it was through companies such as the Virginia Company of London, established as the London Company in 1606 (it became the Virginia Company in 1609), three years after Elizabeth's death, that future New World ventures would be conducted. Ralegh had already sold his rights in Virginia to one of London's foremost merchants, Sir Thomas Smith, and it was Smith and Hakluyt who drove England's

FIGURE 1.4. First plate (37–8) from Thomas Hariot, *A Briefe and True Report of the New Found Land of Virginia* (1590). Newcastle University Special Collections.

next main foray into Virginia. This was, however, a rather different type of settlement proposal. If the men whose hopes for profit from America had been chastened by the Roanoke experience, they were also restricted in terms of how to make colonization pay. With the ascension to the

English and Scottish thrones of James I (and VI), England could no longer be openly antagonistic toward Spain, nor look to Spanish prizes to furnish a return on any trans-Atlantic ventures. If profit was to be had, it was from the many plants, crops, minerals, and the promise of the land itself that the published works on Virginia had enumerated and mapped in such painstaking detail.

The Virginia Company, therefore, hoped to entice settlers who would pool their resources, both financial and in terms of labor, to colonize Virginia. Shares in the company were available to "adventurers," whose passage was paid by the company, or shares could be acquired simply by paying one's own way. The long-term plan was that the resultant profit would fund future settlers, some unemployed, some skilled trades, who would serve a form of what was called indenture. They would work for the Virginia Company for seven years and then be free to make their own fortunes in the New World. As far as the indigenous peoples were concerned, the Virginia Company, from the outset, was both wary of contact and, simultaneously, more ambitious about what could be achieved in terms of conversion to Christianity, in its Protestant form. The Virginia Company's intentions, its founders stressed, were not solely concerned with profit, but with souls. Although it had issued instructions to Captain Christopher Newport, in charge of the expedition, "not to returne without a lumpe of gold, a certaintie of the South sea, or one of the lost company sent out by Sir Walter Raleigh," they sought to put a more moralistic spin on the endeavor, and on their company's intentions. The "ends for which it is established," they emphasized, "beinge not simply matter of Trade, butt of a higher Nature."[6] In their publicized vision, at least, investors, Indians, and the indigent poor of England would all benefit from this latest New World venture.

With such high hopes sustaining them, the 104 men and boys who journeyed across on the *Susan Constant*, the *Godspeed*, and the *Discovery* under the leadership of Newport arrived at the southern headland of Chesapeake Bay in April of 1607. They did not stay long. Reconnoitering the shore, they were chased back to their ships by the locals. Yet Hakluyt had issued them with instructions for where best to establish their colony, and by the following month they had selected the site, sixty miles inland on the newly named James River, which they named Jamestown. From the first, the colony struggled. The indigenous Algonquians, ruled by Powhatan, were understandably suspicious and, at times, overtly aggressive, but that was not the greatest threat that the Jamestown colony faced. Its main problem in its first few years was starvation, which, given the natural abundance previously described by Barlow, Hakluyt, and Hariot and repeated in such promotional documents as Robert Johnson's *Nova Britannia: Offering most excellent fruites by Planting in Virginia* (1609), was the last thing its promoters had expected.

Johnson had promised an "earthly paradise" that was "commendable and hopeful every way," boasting an "air and climate most sweet and wholesome, much warmer than England, and very agreeable to our natures." Granted, he admitted the existence of "wild and savage people" who "have no law but nature," but these were, he assured the reader, "generally very loving and gentle" and would readily "be brought to good, and would fain embrace a better condition." Above all, Johnson reinforced the message brought back from previous voyages, that the "land yieldeth naturally for the sustentation of man, abundance of fish, both scale and shell: of land and water fowls, infinite store: of deer, kain and fallow, stags, coneys, and hares, with many fruits and roots good for meat." There were, in addition, "valleys and plains streaming with sweet springs, like veins in a natural body."[7] In the midst of such abundance, who could possibly want for anything?

The answer was simple enough, even if the reasons behind it were harder to understand. Although the English settlers had arrived with every intention of benefitting themselves and perhaps, depending on the degree of their religious convictions, aiding the benighted natives, in fact Virginia challenged the underlying superiority on which those expectations were based. At first, even though all did not exactly go as planned in the way of friendly natives and profitable planting, actual starvation was headed off by the efforts of Captain John Smith, one of the colony's original councilors appointed by the King. Smith not only secured the survival of the Jamestown colony in its first few precarious years, but gave America one of its most enduring founding legends. Smith's rescue by Powhatan's daughter, Pocahontas, furnished one of the earliest symbols of America's multiracial, *mestizo* possibilities when Pocahontas (or Rebecca, as the English chose to name her) later married another of the Jamestown settlers, John Rolfe. Smith was able to force the colonists to work and negotiated with the Powhatan Confederacy for additional supplies. It was when he left Jamestown in the autumn of 1609 that the situation deteriorated. Smith left behind some 500 settlers in Jamestown. By the end of what became known as the "Starving Time," the winter of 1609–10, there were sixty left.

As he later presented this horrific period in the colony's history, Smith himself had no doubts as to its cause. In his *Generall Historie of*

Virginia, New-England, and the Summer Isles (1624), Smith pretty much lifted, as he was prone to do, Hariot's earlier observations about the English abroad, but the fact was that nothing about the early Jamestown settlement suggested that Hariot's observation had been off the mark. Although he had earlier castigated the Algonquians for making "so small a benefit of their land, be it never so fertile," Smith discovered that the English settlers were no better at planting and, as events were to prove, far worse at living off the land. As later recounted by one of the surviving settlers, the problems that beset Jamestown after Smith's departure were caused by the colonists themselves. Finding themselves running out of food, their behavior turned desperate; so desperate indeed, that some of "the poorer sort" disinterred the corpse of a native and ate it. Another settler murdered his wife, "powdered her, and had eaten part of her before it was known, for which he was executed, as he well deserved." Whether "she was better roasted, boiled or carbonadoed, I know not," the writer commented, "but of such a dish as powdered wife I never heard of." The events of the winter of 1609–10 were, as described, almost "too vile to say, and scarce to be believed," but arose out of a "want of providence, industry and government, and not the barrenness and defect of the Country, as is generally supposed."[8]

Both support from the peoples of the Powhatan Confederacy and the arrival of supplies from England in 1610 and 1611 ensured that such extremes were never again experienced at Jamestown, but the colony still struggled to thrive. Relations between the settlers themselves came to be directed through the imposition of military discipline in the form of the *Lawes Divine, Morall and Martiall*, introduced by the governor, Lord De la Warr, and his deputy, Sir Thomas Gates. These prescribed death for a variety of crimes and misdemeanors, ranging from the simple theft of an ear of corn to blasphemy. Given how badly they treated each other, it is hardly surprising that the settlers' relationship with the Powhatan Confederacy took a turn for the worse after 1610. The story of early Virginia bore more than a passing similarity to the "Black Legend" of Spanish colonization in that respect, as in others. So far from a land full of natural promise, Virginia had turned out to be a deadly environment. It was one in which disease and sometimes hostile natives operated together, in a smaller-sale Chesapeake reverse version of the Columbian exchange, to undermine the Virginia Company's attempts to establish a lasting settlement, or rather a collection of mutually supporting settlements, in the New World. Although Smith and others believed that the difficulties had little to do with any "defect of the Countrie," in fact they were, in part, environmental. Despite the instructions issued by the company to the original settlers in 1606 that they should not "plant in a low or moist place," Jamestown was poorly sited for health, and especially deadly in the summer months. Yet the remarkable fact is that the high mortality rates, and the apparent inability of the colonists to extract sustenance, let alone wealth, from this land that had seemed to promise so much was not the end of England's early version of the American dream; it was only the beginning.

Despite all evidence from Roanoke and, later, Jamestown to the contrary, the idea prevailed in sixteenth- and seventeenth-century England that nature in the New World, if not unappreciated by its inhabitants, was certainly underexploited; that, in short, English settlers, as Hariot had suggested, could make more of it. The repercussions of this belief for the areas of English settlement were foreshadowed in a widely read work that was informed by Amerigo Vespucci's explorations at the start of the "age of discovery" – Thomas More's *Utopia* (1516). More, like Hakluyt, was concerned at the social conditions of his own time, in particular the poverty and resultant social unrest. In More's imaginary and somewhat intimidating island utopia, removing the surplus population to some distant mainland colony was a matter of course. "Such colonies are governed by the Utopians," the reader is advised, "but the natives allowed to join in if they want to. When this happens, natives and colonists soon combine to form a single community with a single way of life, to the great advantage of both parties." If, however, "the natives won't do as they're told, they're expelled from the area marked out for annexation."' Opposition to such exclusion, in More's semi-fictional universe, would result in conflict. His Utopians "consider war perfectly justifiable, when one country denies another its natural right to derive nourishment from any soil which the original owners are not using themselves, but are merely holding on to as a worthless piece of property."[9]

Nearly 200 years later, on the cusp of the eighteenth century, English intellectuals were still contemplating these moral and practical conundrums. When philosopher John Locke proposed, in *The Second Treatise of Civil Government* (1690), that "in the beginning all the world was America," he did so in the context of his broader discussion of property and the nature of possession. It was labor, he argued, that both conferred value upon land and established the right to it. Without labor, land was worth nothing and, if unimproved by European standards, was simply open to all comers. "There cannot be a clearer demonstration of any thing, than several nations of the Americans are of this," he observed, "who are rich in land, and poor in all the comforts of life." Yet the first English settlers of the sixteenth and early seventeenth centuries had little interest in applying their labor to the New World, far less working alongside the indigenous population to create a new multiracial utopian society rich in the comforts of life. Their presence alone, in their minds, established a claim that they validated through their imaginary response to the New World and its peoples as approximating a state of nature. Following the initial forays into that world by explorers such as Columbus and potential settlers such as Grenville, it was, by the start of the seventeenth century, no longer the case that America was wholly an unknown land, *terra incognita*. Imagination, however, did transform it from an environment already populated into a blank canvass, a *tabula rasa* onto which a variety of European hopes and aspirations could be projected.

Such flights of fancy as the English indulged toward America in the early seventeenth century had, too, a distinctly gendered tone. America, specifically Virginia, named by Ralegh for the "Virgin Queen," was frequently described not just as an Edenic garden or virgin land, but as a metaphorical female virgin. Ralegh himself famously described Guiana as "a country that hath yet her maydenhead, never sackt, turned, nor wrought." This feminization of the landscape was neither specific to him nor to the south of the Americas, but was an intrinsic element in Virginia's appeal in early descriptive and, later, directly promotional literature. In part, this grew out of the rhetoric of colonization that looked to the New World not only as a land to be conquered by male explorers and adventurers, but as one potentially pregnant with material possibilities and capable of producing, in a sense, an heir to English ambitions in the form of a transplanted England. This was what Hakluyt was driving at when he described Virginia as Ralegh's "bride" and advised him that she would "shortly bring forth new and most abundant offspring, such as will delight you and yours, and cover with disgrace and shame those who have so often dared rashly and impudently to charge her with barreness."[10] It may hardly be surprising, in the context of Tudor England, that a fixation on fecundity might influence the language used to describe the New World, but there was more to it than that.

From the period of the earliest explorations of the Americas, but especially by the turn of the seventeenth century when England was looking to establish itself in America, there is no doubt that the possibilities offered by colonization captured not just the English but the European imagination. Through publications, prints, and performance, that imagination was offered several contradictory images of the New World and its inhabitants, themselves derived from the plethora of ideas and arguments about nature, nurture, social relations, and religion that informed the late-sixteenth- and early-seventeenth-century world. From Michel de Montaigne's essay "'On Cannibals" (1580), through Shakespeare's treatment of a "'brave new world/That has such people in't" in *The Tempest* (c. 1611), to Milton's later (1667) reference to Columbus's "discovery" of "the American, so girt/With feathered cincture, naked and wild,/Among the trees on isles and woody shores" in *Paradise Lost*, many of the issues attendant upon New World settlement were circulated and explored. As the English measured and mapped the American landscape, however, their reasons for doing so changed. For the promoters of the Virginia colony, it became crucial not to draw too clear a distinction between the brave new world of America and England. Whereas its unfamiliarity rendered it exotic and potentially attractive on such grounds, the Virginia Company recognized that would-be settlers, as opposed to investors, might be more interested in how easily the unfamiliar could be transformed into the familiar. Promotional literature, therefore, hinted that, with just a little effort, this new world would become an improved extension of the old and, with perhaps rather more effort, its "naked and wild" inhabitants could become English.

The earliest reports to emerge from the New World had consistently presented it as both foreign and potentially domestic, for obvious reasons. Just as one cannot describe a color one has never seen, neither could America be described without reference to Europe, or specifically to England. Although nature was more abundant there, it was nevertheless a nature the English would recognize. Hariot's *Report*, as well as detailing many unfamiliar herbs and plants, assured readers that Virginia also boasted "*Leekes* differing little from ours in England." Similarly, de Bry's rendering of White's images of the Algonquian peoples (Figure 1.5) juxtaposed them with images of Picts (Figure 1.6) so as "*to showe how that the Inhabitants of the great Bretannie haue bin in times past as sauuage as those of Virginia*" (emphasis in the original). The American present, in other words, was essentially the British past. Its inhabitants were exotic, certainly, but neither unusually or irredeemably so.

Following in Hariot's footsteps, although now with settlement as the prime motivation, it was not for nothing that Robert Johnson entitled his work *Nova Britannia*, and highlighted a landscape that differed from that of England only in degree, not in essence. Virginia, as he described it, was England writ large, with its "goodly oaks and elms, beech and birch, spruce, walnut, cedar and fir trees, in great abundance."[11] This

FIGURE 1.5. "A weroan or great Lorde of Virginia," from Thomas Hariot, *A Briefe and True Report of the New Found Land of Virginia* (1590) 41: "The Princes of Virginia are attyred in suche manner as is expressed in this figure. They weare the haire of their heades long and bynde opp the ende of the same in a knot vnder thier eares..." Newcastle University Special Collections.

was an England that had existed before deforestation and enclosures, in effect, an England of the imagination, transported in imagination across the Atlantic.

When the New World shifted from a source of potential profit to a place of possible settlement, everything changed. From simply observing the land and its peoples, the English moved to insert themselves into that environment, to align their ambitions, their aspirations, and their imaginations with the reality of America. And, as Roanoke and early Jamestown proved, that was no straightforward matter. Over the course of the decade following the "Starving Time," the Virginia Company reinforced and, to a degree, restructured the Jamestown colony. It introduced the "headright" system, whereby settlers were given land and a financial stake in the venture in a bid to stabilize the settlement. Those who had arrived prior to 1616 received one hundred acres, those after fifty, and additional acreage was accorded to those who held shares. The draconian *Lawes*, more martial than either moral or in any obvious sense divine, were, after 1618, replaced by a system more closely approximating that

FIGURE 1.6. Pict, from Thomas Hariot, *A Briefe and True Report of the New Found Land of Virginia* (1590) 68–9: "In tymes past the Pictes, habitans of one part of great Bretainne, which is nowe nammed England, wear sauuages and did paint all their bodye after the maner followinge. the did lett their haire gro we as fare as their Shoulders, sauinge those which hange vppon their forehead, the which the did cutt." Newcastle University Special Collections.

of English common law. Under the direction of Sir Edwin Sandys, appointed treasurer of the company in 1619, new settlers poured into Virginia, many of them drawn from the poor houses of English parishes. Finally, it seemed, at least one part of the promise of the New World was about to be fulfilled. It would be a safety valve for the increasing social pressures of the Old. Yet in the process, it introduced a whole range of new social pressures in the New.

The granting of land to settlers seemed straightforward enough, but it was far from that. The land itself was already occupied, and the new arrivals were not yet completely convinced of their legal right to acquire it. In the same year as Johnson's *Nova Britannia* appeared (1609), Robert Gray had, in another promotional tract, *A Good Speed to Virginia*, queried by "what right or warrant we can enter into the land of these Savages, take away their rightfull inheritance from them, and plant ourselves in their places, being unwronged or unprovoked by them." Johnson did not wholly avoid the question of how the English might "warrant a supplantation of those Indians, or an invasion into their right and possessions," either, and countered the accusation that "private ends" might be drawing settlers to America by stressing the need "to advance the kingdom of God, by reducing savage people from their blind superstition to the light of Religion."[12] Conversion as justification for colonization was certainly a persistent theme in English accounts of the New World from Hakluyt onward, conversion not just to Christianity, but to its Protestant variant. In 1583, Sir George Peckham, another Elizabethan adventurer and a confederate of Grenville and Gilbert, published *A True Reporte of the Late Discoveries of Newfound Land*, in which he managed to assert English claims to the New World in the face of both French and Spanish competition by suggesting that it was to England, specifically, that the New World looked for deliverance, "praying our ayde and helpe." Some three decades later, and much further south, on the Chesapeake, it remained the case that any aid on offer was not from incomer to indigene, which perhaps made the deterioration in relations between the two the more inevitable.

By the second decade of the seventeenth century, it was becoming clear that bringing the gospel to the natives had taken second place to taking the land, and indeed their very culture, from them. Foreshadowing an approach to America's indigenous peoples that would persist well into the twentieth century, the Virginia Company had issued instructions to Thomas Gates that he should acquire some native children to ensure that they were "brought up in your language, and manners." Failing that, Lord De la Warr was advised the following year, they should send some "three or foure of them to England" where they might be instructed in English ways.[13] Quite what this was meant to achieve in the long run remains something of a mystery, but it did reveal the start of a shift in attitude toward the Powhatan Confederacy. Later, after the death of Powhatan and the assumption of power by his brother, Opechancanough, an accommodation was reached whereby entire families, rather than just their children, were brought into the English colonies. The underlying impulse, however, to render the Indian invisible, as it were, was a portent of trouble to come.

Whereas Smith, while he remained unconvinced that natives and new-comers could readily merge into a brave new multiracial society, was nevertheless clearly fascinated by the variety of indigenous cultures that he encountered, those that replaced him in Jamestown were not so appreciative of native culture, and indeed increasingly suspicious of it. As the Virginia Colony became established in the New World, it sought to fulfill the promises held out by Ralegh, Hakluyt, Hariot, and Johnson – to create a new England in the new world, and to force both the land and its people into an English social, political, and religious mold. This had not been the founding intentions of the Virginia Company, but the reality, as distinct from the dream, of colonization, introduced many changes. Much of what eventually ensured Jamestown's survival lay beyond the company's control and had little to do with removing the indigent poor from England.

In the end, it came down to two valuable commodities in the seventeenth-century world: tobacco and slaves. Neither had figured in the Virginia Company's plans, and for many years the cultivation of tobacco was restricted in favor of other crops. This early battle against the evil weed was doomed to failure. Tobacco simply commanded too high a price, and would become the economic and, indeed, social boost that the colony needed. In 1619, the company first shipped some ninety "younge, handsome and honestly educated maydes" to Virginia as wives for the colonists. The expectation was that "wifes, children and familie" might make the men in Virginia "more settled & lesse moveable." The absence of family ties not only meant that Virginia would always be reliant on incomers from England to sustain the plantations, but those who did travel there, the company feared, did so only "to get something and then to returne to England."[14] The fortunate recipients of this early speed-dating enterprise paid for their wives' passage in tobacco. Yet tobacco needed land, and it needed labor, more labor than the colony was yet in a position to provide. The long-term solution to that particular difficulty arrived in the same year, 1619, when a Dutch trader brought the first Africans to the Chesapeake, and a whole new imaginative world opened up for America's earliest immigrants and for the land that their ambitions had led them to.

2

A City on a Hill

The Origins of a Redeemer Nation

For we must consider that we shall be as a city upon a hill. The eyes of all people are upon us. So that if we shall deal falsely with our God in this work we have undertaken, and so cause Him to withdraw His present help from us, we shall be made a story and a by-word through the world.

(John Winthrop, "A Model of Christian Charity," 1630)

The arrival of English women in Virginia in 1619 was designed to ensure the long-term stability of the settlement, to make it resemble more closely the world from which the English settlers, at least, had come. However, the introduction of African labor, which in time became the enslaved labor that would form the economic bedrock of the free-born English colonies, ensured that the society constructed in the New World would bear little resemblance to the world that the English and the Africans had left behind. Although one group arrived voluntarily and the other was coerced, both faced the challenge of constructing a new life in a new world. The arrival of the first Africans, too, highlighted the fact that the North American colonies were part of an emerging economic and social Atlantic world. So, too, was England, of course, but as the end-producer of the most obvious comestible commodities the New World had to offer – sugar, tobacco, cocoa – the actual processes, and personal costs of production were not as evident in the English communities from which Virginia's settlers came as they would be in the Americas.

The very existence of the Virginia Company signaled the rise of the new capitalist forces at work in this period, and in particular the emergence of a powerful merchant class that recognized the opportunities offered by the New World and had the ability to raise the venture capital that America's early "adventurers" had lacked. As the Virginia Company discovered, however, raising the money was perhaps easier than controlling the men in whose hands its investments lay. A broader range and higher rates of productivity were necessary to drive this early capitalist revolution, but productivity was notably lacking in the early Chesapeake with the exception of one crop – tobacco.

Although its initial quest for wealth in the New World had not gone entirely to plan, by the summer of 1620, the Virginia Company was optimistic about the future. While acknowledging "the many disasters, wherewith it pleased Almighty God to suffer the great Enemy of all good Actions and his Instruments, to encounter and interrupt, to opprese and keepe weake, this noble Action for the planting of *Virginia*, with Christian Religion, and English people," it reported that the colony "hath as it were on a sodaine growne to double that height, strength, plenty, and prosperity, which it had in former times attained." Echoing earlier reports, the Company denied rumors that "sought unjustly to staine and blemish that Countrey, as being barren and unprofitable" and stressed that Virginia was, in fact, "rich, spacious and well watered," a land "abounding with all Gods naturall blessings" and one "too good for ill people." The degree to which the Company's imagination had expanded by this time, both to accept the absence of obvious gold deposits and to accommodate the possibilities of the New World, was evident in its emphasis on Virginia as a one-stop-shop opportunity for England. Goods – furs, hemp, flax, wood – hitherto acquired at great expense from, among others, Russia, Norway, or Germany were readily available, whereas the "Wines, Fruite, and Salt of *France* and *Spaine*; The Silkes of *Persia* and *Italie*, will be found also in Virginia, and in no kinde of worth inferiour."[1]

Unfortunately, too much of this report was wishful thinking. Life on the Chesapeake continued to be a struggle. In the same month as the Company was singing Virginia's praises to potential investors, the colony's Governor, Sir George Yeardley, was complaining that new settlers arrived with insufficient provisions, necessitating his supporting them out of his own supplies. "I pray sir," he pleaded with Edwin Sandys, "give me both tyme to pvide meanes and to build and settell" before sending more colonists and, when more were sent, "send at least 6 monthes victuall with them" (Figure 2.1). Yet when Yeardley wrote, the colony had just brought in a fairly substantial harvest. For some, at least, Virginia was fulfilling its promise, but not in the direction intended by the Virginia Company, nor in a way that it could control. The instructions issued by

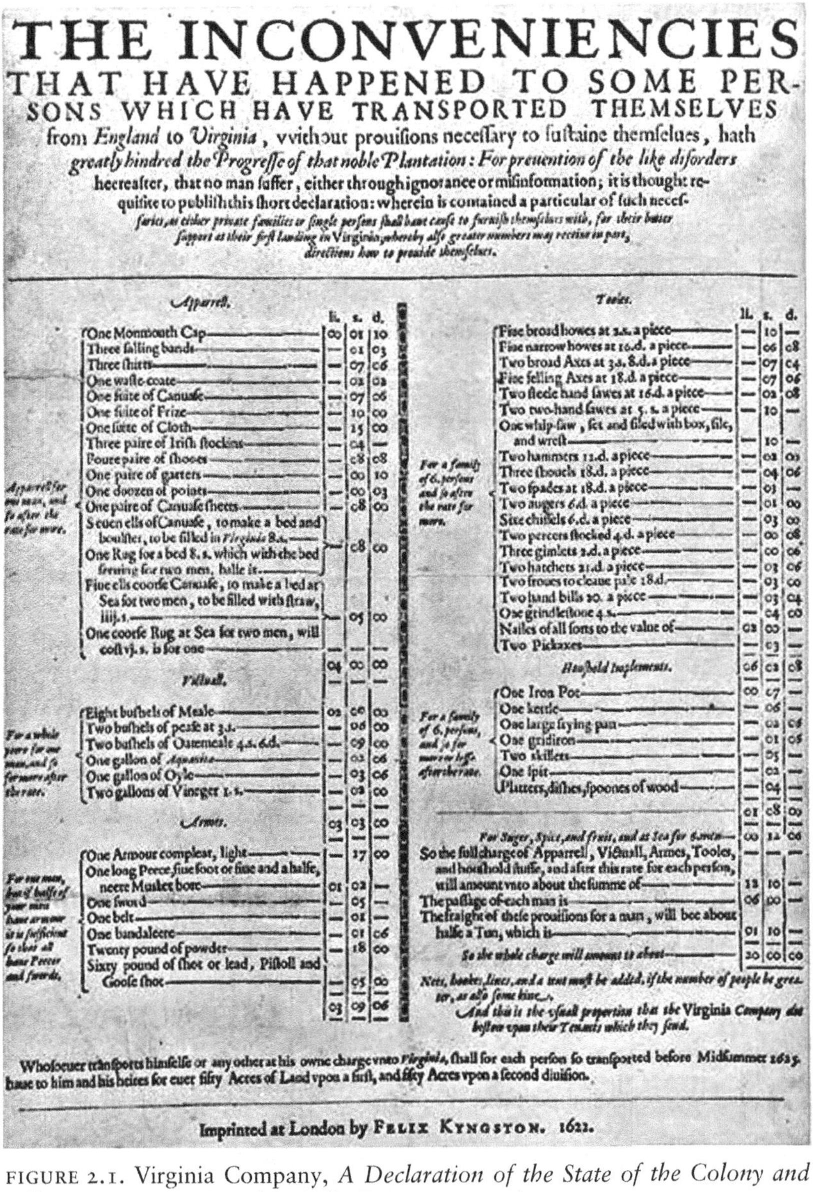

THE INCONVENIENCIES
THAT HAVE HAPPENED TO SOME PER-
SONS WHICH HAVE TRANSPORTED THEMSELVES
from *England* to *Virginia*, vvithout prouisions necessary to suſtaine themselues, hath
greatly hindred the *Progreſſe of that noble Plantation: For preuention of the like diſorders*
hereafter, that no man suffer, either through ignorance or miſinformation; it is thought re-
quiſite to publiſh this ſhort declaration: wherein is contained a particular of ſuch neceſ-
ſaries, as either priuate families or ſingle perſons ſhall haue cauſe to furniſh themſelues with, for their better
ſupport at their firſt landing in Virginia, whereby alſo greater numbers may receiue in part,
directions how to prouide themſelues.

(tabular list of provisions: Apparrell, Victuall, Armes, Tooles, Houshold Implements, with prices in li. s. d.)

Whoſoeuer tranſports himſelfe or any other at his owne charge vnto *Virginia*, ſhall for each perſon ſo tranſported before Midſummer 1625,
haue to him and his heires for euer fifty Acres of Land vpon a firſt, and fifty Acres vpon a ſecond diuiſion.

Imprinted at London by FELIX KYNGSTON. 1622.

FIGURE 2.1. Virginia Company, *A Declaration of the State of the Colony and Affaires in Virginia* (London: Felix Kyngston, 1622).

the Company the following year (1621), when Yeardley was replaced as Governor by Sir Francis Wyatt, emphasized the importance of "setting upp and upholding those staple Comodities w[hich] are necessarie for the subsisting and Encrease of the Plantation." They specifically sought to restrict the "excessive planting of tobacco" by, among other methods, prohibiting the colonists from wearing "any Gold in ther Clothes or any apparel of silke, until such time they have itt of the silk ether made by Silkewormes & raised by ther owne industry."[2] The colonists, however, were clearly less concerned with fashion than the Company hoped, and few on the Chesapeake heeded such advice.

Tobacco did not just purchase wives – who were initially valued at 120 pounds of tobacco, which retailed at three shillings a pound in 1619 – it offered a fast track to wealth in a period where tobacco, like other New World produce, found a growing market in Europe. Virginian tobacco, introduced to the colony by John Rolfe, was not considered to be as fine in quality as Spanish varieties, but it still commanded a high enough price to make it worth planting in place of corn or any of the other staples more necessary for sustenance. Yet beyond its pecuniary advantages, tobacco proved no better for the colony's health, indeed, than it was for the individual's. Although the idea behind the sale of wives, for example, was that it would induce the men engaged in this far-flung frontier venture to consider the benefits of family alongside that of fortune, it did not work out quite so neatly.

When women arrived in Virginia (Figure 2.2), the demand for them was high enough that their "bride price" swiftly rose from 120 pounds to 150 pounds of tobacco, placing them in the category of a commodity affordable only by the more successful planters. And the women themselves were unable to compete against what the Virginia Company critiqued as the colony's "overweening esteeme of theire darling Tobacco, to the ou'throw of all other Staple Comodities," and the market in wives, if it did not exacerbate this trend, did nothing to diminish it. The fact was that tobacco had become, by 1620, the standard unit of currency and would remain so for many years. Despite the Company's "extraordinary diligence and care in the choice" of wives for Virginia, and its expectation that the women concerned would marry "honest and sufficient men," the commercial-exchange element to the whole transaction undermined its domestic ambitions. Detailing the shipment of women that arrived aboard the *Tyger* in 1621, the Company made clear that economic concerns were paramount by noting that it expected "one hundredth and fiftie of the best leafe tobacco for each of them" but also that

BUYING WIVES.

FIGURE 2.2. Purchasing a wife (from E. R. Billings, *Tobacco: Its History, Varieties, Culture, Manufacture and Commerce*, 1875). This image highlights the commercial nature of the transaction by juxtaposing the woman, recently arrived from England, one assumes on the ship at anchor in the harbor behind her, with the hogsheads (barrels) and, beside her intended purchaser/husband, the bunches of tobacco that paid for her passage to Virginia. Photo: Wellcome Library, London.

"if any of them dye there must be a proportionable addition upon the rest."[3]

This commoditization of women highlighted the main problem facing the colony on the Chesapeake and reflected its attitude toward both goods and individuals from the outset. In its first few decades, it remained overly reliant on both the Powhatan Confederacy and on the Virginia Company itself for the basic means of sustenance and dependent on the constant influx of new arrivals from the poor houses and parishes of England for labor, most of which was put to work growing tobacco. The colony never managed to become either the self-sufficient reflection of English society or the New World gravy train supplying the home market that its promoters had hoped it would be. Jamestown remained a frontier town, hard-drinking, not particularly hard-working, under threat from outside attack and undermined by unrealistic expectations – both those of the Virginia Company and of the settlers themselves – of what was required for long-term success in Virginia. As one nineteenth-century history of Virginia described it, tobacco had a visibly detrimental effect on the colony:

The houses were neglected, the palisades suffered to rot down, the fields, gardens and public squares, even the very streets of Jamestown were planted with tobacco. The townspeople, more greedy of gain than mindful of their own security, scattered abroad into the wilderness, where they broke up small pieces of rich ground and made their crop regardless of their proximity to the Indians, in whose good faith so little reliance could be placed.[4]

Given that the good faith of the natives, while it may not have been assumed, certainly was exploited, it was perhaps inevitable that relations between colonist and native deteriorated, resulting in a massacre in March 1622, in which more than three hundred settlers perished. Even after this, the colonists still put tobacco production before self-preservation, unwilling to allocate men to the defense of the colony. In the year after the massacre, it was noted that in Virginia, there was still "noe Comoditie but Tobaccoe" and little attempt at all to plant those "staple Comodities" so necessary to the colony's future. In the following year, 1624, the Virginia Company's was declared bankrupt and Virginia became a royal colony. Its merchant-founders' dreams of New World riches had, quite literally, "vanished into smoke."[5]

The end of the Virginia Company did not mean the end of English settlement on the Chesapeake, or the termination of tobacco production there. Conveniently for the Jamestown colony, although the English Crown under James I and then Charles I was vehemently opposed to the consumption of tobacco, such opposition took the form of granting a monopoly to Virginia for its importation into England. The Crown thereby gained revenue as the inhabitants of London flocked in increasing numbers to the tobacco shops then beginning to appear across the city and to a new vice whose economic value eased its entry into English society. For Virginia, therefore, the demise of the company that had inaugurated the settlement meant little in practical terms. It was very much a case of business as usual, except in one major respect. As far as the native populations were concerned, the period after 1622 witnessed a clear shift not only in native-white power relations within Chesapeake society, but in white attitudes toward the "Indian."

John White's illustrations for Thomas Hariot's, *Briefe and True Report of the New Found Land of Virginia* (1590) had sought to stress the essential similarities between the Algonquian peoples and the British as a means of rendering the unfamiliar familiar. The Virginia Company sought to take this idea to its logical conclusion in its instructions regarding the indoctrination of native children, and later families, to English norms, to render the different domestic, in effect. By the mid-seventeenth century, however, an exclusive cultural dialectic was emerging, in which the unfamiliar became the exotic and, ultimately, the other. The Second Charter of Virginia (1609) had included – although in conclusion and almost as an afterthought – the importance of "the conversion and reduccion of the people" of Virginia "unto the true worship of God and Christian religion," but profit had always trumped piety on the Chesapeake.

By turns reliant on and destructive of the native populations, English settlers swiftly replaced the idea of conversion with the imperatives of conquest. Although the Virginia Company had, up to its demise, highlighted as crucial the transformation of the Algonquian into the Anglican, on the Chesapeake itself the process degenerated into one where cultural exchange became commoditization. With the white male settler the default dominant position in the colony, women, natives, and Africans occupied an uneasy middle ground in the transition from transient colony to fixed settlement. Whereas white women, in time, came to be seen as crucial components of the colonial project, neither natives nor Africans fitted easily into the evolving vision of a little England across the Atlantic.

The 1622 massacre, along with later attacks in 1644 and 1675, only reinforced the image of the "Indian" as treacherous savage, which, from a cynical English perspective, proved perfectly convenient. As John Smith recognized, many colonists regarded the massacre as "good for the Plantation, because now we have just cause to destroy them by all meanes possible." The secretary to the Virginia Company, Edward Waterhouse, was blunt enough about it at the time. The English "may now by right of Warre, and law of Nations, invade the Country, and destroy them who sought to destroy us," he enthused, "whereby wee shall enjoy their cultivated places, turning the laborious Mattocke into the victorious Sword (wherein there is both ease, benefit, and glory) and possessing the fruits of others labours."[6] Ultimately, Waterhouse concluded, "the way of conquering" the native populations "is much more easie then civilizing them by faire means," and he revelled in the opportunity not just to acquire "those commodities which the Indians enjoyed as much or rather more than we," but in the prospect of violent conquest. This, he asserted, could be achieved

by force, by surprise, by famine in burning their Corne, by destroying and burning their Boats, Canoes, and Houses, by breaking their fishing Weares, by assailing them in their huntings, whereby they get the greatest part of their sustenance in Winter, by pursuing and chasing them with our horses, and blood-Hounds to draw after them, and Mastives to teare them.... By these and sundry other wayes, as by driving them (when they flye) upon their enemies who are round about them, and by animating and abetting their enemies against them, may their ruine or subjection be soone effected.[7]

Assuming that some natives would be left standing after the English had done their worst, Waterhouse proposed that they "be compelled to servitude and drudgery" and provide the labor needs of the colony.[8] In fact, the natives proved an unreliable coerced workforce, but on the Chesapeake that turned out to be less of a problem than it might have been; there was, after all, a fallback option – African labor.

Race and Religion: The Chesapeake

The development of an economy and a culture constructed on the basis of unfree labor needs to be placed both in the context of labor, class, gender, religion, and race relations in Virginia in the seventeenth and eighteenth centuries and in comparison with other settlement projects in America in that period. Many, although not all, of the problems that had beset the Virginian venture were replicated elsewhere in America. For the native populations all along the eastern seaboard, from Florida to New France, the arrival of Europeans was an unmitigated disaster. Even if the Europeans in question stuck to the original plan of conversion rather than conquest, the diseases they carried with them effected irreparable damage among the New World populations. France's ambitions for North America in the seventeenth century were spearheaded not just by traders but by several Jesuit expeditions conceived as a means of extending both the political power of France and the spiritual power of Christianity over the Algonquian and Huron populations in the New World. The reports from New France, however, confirmed that since "the Faith has come to dwell among these people, all things that make men die have been found in these countries."[9] Yet "Faith" drew increasing numbers across the Atlantic in the seventeenth century, many of the settlers prompted not just by the desire to spread the gospel, but to secure a safe haven from religious persecution in their home countries.

The various waves of European exploration and settlement in the Americas in the seventeenth and eighteenth centuries were, to a great extent, simply part of the surging sea of faith that had engulfed the Old World in the sixteenth century. The long-term repercussions of the Reformation not only drove many Europeans to America, but influenced the societies they founded there. Although the British settlements came to dominate in North America, this dominance was neither foreordained nor, given their initial forays, all that likely. It was France and Spain that appeared to be the strongest European forces in the New World. Despite Spanish successes in driving out the early French Huguenot settlements in what later became South Carolina and Florida, and the difficulties faced by the French missions further north in New France, in the eighteenth century, France's influence gradually increased as Spain's declined. The discovery, in 1673, by French explorers Louis Joliet – both the city of Joliet in Illinois and the town of Joliet in Montana were named for him – and Jesuit missionary Jacques Marquette that the Mississippi flowed south to the Gulf of Mexico was the precursor to further French explorations along the Ohio Valley and into what would become Minnesota and settlements in Mississippi, Alabama, Michigan, and Louisiana. Yet as their mapping of river routes suggested, the French were more interested in trade than in settlement. By 1700, when the white population on the Chesapeake alone had reached some 90,000, the entirety of France's possessions, which stretched all the way from Québec to Louisiana, sustained only 25,000 French settlers – roughly a tenth of British settler numbers in North America as a whole by that point.

Numbers rarely tell the whole story, however, and the numerical strength of British settlers in early America disguised the chronic instability of many of those settlements they founded. By far the bulk of immigrants, both male and female, to the Chesapeake came as indentured servants who had to work off the cost of their passage. They did so in an environment that ushered many of them (some 30 to 40 percent of them) into an early grave, and offered a life expectancy into the mid-thirties, at best, to those who survived the initial "seasoning" period. Consequently, the white population of Virginia comprised an unusually high number of single men, widows, and, inevitably, orphaned children. Similar conditions prevailed in the second British colony to be founded on the Chesapeake – Maryland – although here the desire to escape religious persecution in England directly informed the settlement venture, distinguishing its ideals, if not its experiences, from its sister colony in Virginia.

Maryland began life as a proprietary colony. The land was granted to a single governor, or Lord Proprietor, in this case George Calvert, First Baron Baltimore, who had applied to Charles I for a charter to settle the area named for Charles's queen, Henrietta Maria. Calvert's death in 1632 meant that it was his son, Cecilius (Cecil) Calvert, the Second Baron Baltimore, who took charge of the founding of the colony. As a Catholic whose father had been persecuted for his faith, Cecil Calvert intended Maryland to be not simply a haven for Catholics, but a colony in which Catholic and Protestant might coexist peacefully. Naturally, the reality fell somewhat short of this. The history of early Maryland proved that, whatever its founder's ambitions, the reality of life as a colony was that 3,000 miles of ocean was not far enough if one wished to distance oneself from the religious and political machinations of the Old World, which too easily spilled over into the New. Although Calvert and the colony's rulers were Catholic, the bulk of the settlers who arrived – many, as in Virginia, as indentured servants – were Protestant, and the struggle between them for control, exacerbated as it was by the outbreak of the English Civil War in 1641, almost destroyed the colony.

Calvert's solution to the escalating violence and instability of the 1640s was two-pronged. First, he reached out to Virginian dissenters from the Anglican faith – Virginia was wholly Anglican and intolerant of alternatives as well as wholly Royalist and intolerant of parliamentarians – and encouraged them to settle in Maryland. He reinforced this message via his appointment of a Protestant governor, the parliamentarian William Stone from Virginia. Second, he emphasized the colony's position as protector of religious freedoms and formalized Maryland's position on toleration via the 1649 *Act Concerning Religion* (or Toleration Act). This noted that "the inforceing of the conscience in matters of Religion hath frequently fallen out to be of dangerous Consequence in those commonwealthes where it hath been practised," and announced that no resident of Maryland "shall from henceforth bee any waies troubled, Molested or discountenanced for or in respect of his or her religion nor in the free exercise thereof within this Province or the Islands thereunto belonging nor any way compelled to the beleife or exercise of any other Religion against his or her consent." A fine of ten shillings, the threat of prison, and a public apology was imposed against anyone who uttered "reproachfull words" against "an heritick, Scismatick, Idolator, puritan, Independant, Prespiterian popish prest, Jesuite, Jesuited papist, Lutheran, Calvenist, Anabaptist, Brownist, Antinomian, Barrowist, Roundhead [or]

Separatist." It was a fairly inclusive list for its day, even if it did exclude the Jewish faith by stipulating, above all else, both the acceptance of Jesus as the "sonne of God" and the doctrine of the Holy Trinity, on pain of death.[10]

Calvert's stance against religious intolerance, however, soon came under attack. Only six years after Stone became governor, an increasingly influential Puritan group in the colony sought to rescind the Toleration Act and reimpose laws restricting religious freedoms. This resulted in what has been termed the last battle of the English Civil War being fought on American soil, the Battle of the Severn (1655). The victory, in this case, went to Calvert's opponents, but it was short-lived. Within two years, Calvert had regained control of the colony. Yet although the Battle of the Severn was essentially a minor skirmish, both it and indeed the precedent of the Maryland colony itself highlighted two aspects of colonial life in America that would, over the course of the following century, cause increasing concern to the colonists: the importance of religion – specifically freedom of worship – to the New World, and the susceptibility of the colonies to the destructive forces of British, and European, political and religious conflict.

War in Europe brought war to America, and the struggle for survival in the New World, at least until its separation from Great Britain, took place within the broader context of conflicts not of the colonists' making, conflicts that many of them had come to America to avoid. Having arrived there, of course, the British settlers were more than capable of instigating colonial conflicts that had absolutely nothing to do with the home country, but everything to do with the their identity as freeborn Englishmen, an identity challenged, but ultimately reinforced, via their contact with the native "other." This was, to a great extent, the experience of the Chesapeake. Yet if one is looking for examples of the destructive but also, in national terms, constructive confluence of race and religion in America's early history, then one has to look further north, to a very different settlement venture, one driven by religious faith but defined by racial violence: New England.

Exodus: The Beginnings of a Bible Commonwealth

No aspect of the British settlement of the Americas has been invested with so much ideological and, over the course of America's development, nationalist baggage than the founding of the colonies that became

New England. The arrival of the *Mayflower* in 1620 may have brought only a hundred or so settlers to America's Atlantic coast, but an entire mythology, which persists to this day, was constructed on the small boulder that is Plymouth Rock. Writing in 1867, the politician Robert Winthrop acknowledged that the *Mayflower* was "consecrated in every New-England heart as the carrier . . . of the pioneer Pilgrim-band, which planted the great principles of religious freedom upon our shores."[11] As with the founding of Maryland, it was the religious schisms within England that prompted the founding of New England, and in this case, the clue was very clearly in the title. The Puritans who traveled to the New World between 1620 and 1642 were seeking nothing less than a new, improved England, at least in matters of religion.

Puritanism itself emerged in late-sixteenth-century England in response to what its adherents perceived as the dangerous persistence of Catholicism and "popish" ritual within the Church of England. It was never a single, coherent movement, however, more of an ideological banner beneath which both extreme and more moderate expounders of the faith could gather. What drew them together was the belief that the Church of England should be more closely aligned with the theological doctrine propounded by one of the leaders of the Protestant Reformation, John Calvin. According to Calvin, the individual soul was predestined either to salvation or damnation, and the former was achieved only by God's elect, termed "Visible Saints." Because it is hardly in human nature to deny human agency, the Puritans believed that a visibly good and, importantly, successful life, although it offered no promise of eternal bliss, might tip the balance in the direction of salvation.

For some English Puritans, reformation of the Church seemed a real possibility, but for those who landed in Cape Cod in 1620, the rot had already spread too far. Rather than reform the Church, they sought complete separation from it. These separatists, known to us – although not to their contemporaries – as the Pilgrim Fathers, had abandoned Scrooby, in Nottinghamshire, for Leyden in the Netherlands in 1608. A little more than a decade later, they returned to England, but only to set sail for the New World. After several false starts, they finally set off from Southampton in September 1620. Their intended destination was Virginia, but a winter storm landed them much farther north, far beyond the jurisdiction of the Virginia Company, and outside the patent originally awarded – and still valid, given that the Virginia Company still existed – by the English Crown. Aware of their unintended geographical position but uncertain of their legal one, the separatists agreed among themselves to devise a

FIGURE 2.3. Bradford Street, Provincetown, bas-relief sculpture depicting the signing of the Mayflower Compact. Photo: Peter Whitlock.

contract, the Mayflower Compact (Figure 2.3), by which they bound themselves

togeather into a civill body politick, for our better ordering & preservation & furtherance of [the] ends aforesaid; and by virtue hearof to enacte, constitute, and frame such just & equall lawes, ordinances, acts, constitutions, & offices, from time to time, as shall be thought most meete & convenient for [the] generall good of [the] Colonie.[12]

The significance of the Mayflower Compact as the first written document establishing a "just and equal" form of government in America certainly set the founding of what became New England apart from the many other colonies that comprised the future United States. Yet if necessity was the mother of invention in governmental terms, for all practical purposes there was little to set New England apart from her nearest English neighbors some 500 miles to the south. Although far from the Chesapeake, the Plymouth Colony's initial experiences bore more than a passing resemblance to those of Jamestown.

Some threat of violence was offered the new arrivals, but the native population of New England was in no fit state to offer any sustained resistance to the separatist settlers, because an epidemic, frequently identified as smallpox but possibly some variant of bubonic plague, had only recently (1616–19) wiped out up to 90 percent of the inhabitants between Cape Cod and Maine. Fortunately for the English, at least some natives had survived this devastation, because the *Mayflower*'s passengers were no more suited to the rigors of life in New England than Virginia's first migrants had been to the Chesapeake. This was inevitable, and not just because their motivation for emigration was religious. In fact, not all the settlers were separatists, and the merchant-backed voyage was, as had been the case for Jamestown, intended to produce a profit, hence the presence of tailors and a silk-worker, a printer and a shopkeeper among the passengers. Even those designated as farmers would have had little idea of farming as such, given that the term, in the seventeenth century, simply indicated a landowner. Nor would they necessarily have had any of those practical skills necessary for survival in a world that, as the colony's leader William Bradford pointed out, had neither "freinds to welcome them, nor inns to entertaine or refresh their weatherbeaten bodys, no houses or much less townnes to repaire too, to seek for succoure."[13] Again, in the seventeenth century, hunting, shooting, and fishing were the prerogatives of the aristocracy. It is perhaps unsurprising that half of the Plymouth settlers did not see the end of that first winter, while the rest were forced to turn to the locals for sustenance and support to ensure their survival.

The struggling settlers were fortunate in this respect in encountering two Algonquian natives who could speak English, the Patuxet Tisquantum (whom they named Squanto) and the Abenaki Samoset. Squanto had spent time in Spain and in London, having been seized by the English explorer Thomas Hunt a few years before the separatists set off for America in 1620. He had only just made his way back home the previous year, but in the interim his people had been wiped out by disease. Squanto helped the new colonists establish friendly relations with the local natives, who in turn aided them in planting. Out of this a second legend, and eventually a national holiday (although not fixed as such until 1863, during the Civil War), was born, when the following year native and newcomer celebrated the first Thanksgiving. For a decade after this, indeed, it seemed as if this struggling but ultimately successful colony might be the precursor of a very different kind of settlement venture.

Encouraged by reports from Plymouth, and growing increasingly despondent about the Church of England under Charles I, another group of Puritans under the leadership of Suffolk lawyer and landowner John Winthrop made the decision to abandon what they regarded as the Catholic corruption of the Old World and establish a "Bible Commonwealth" in the New. Under the auspices of another merchant company, the Massachusetts Bay Company, established in 1629, the Puritan exodus from England, the so-called Great Migration (1629–42) to Massachusetts, began. It was only the vanguard. During the following decade, more than 20,000 Puritans migrated to America and arranged themselves over five main areas of settlement, out of which three of the American nation's original thirteen states eventually emerged: Plymouth, *Massachusetts*, *Rhode Island*, New Haven, and *Connecticut* (Figure 2.4).

If the early settlers to the Chesapeake had been drawn to America in large part because of the natural bounty the land seemed to offer, for the Puritans, the flip side of that coin – the idea of America not as a new Eden but as an untamed wilderness – was almost as appealing. The combination of uncivilized natives and uncultivated land proved as irresistible as it was intimidating. It posed a challenge that the Puritan mindset was more than geared up to meet and maximize. Their response to this challenge would, the Puritans anticipated, establish the benchmark for Godly living, and a lesson for the world. Taking his text from the Sermon on the Mount (specifically Matthew 5:14), John Winthrop preached to his congregation on board the *Arabella*, en route to the New World, and a new beginning: "For we must consider," he told them, "that we shall be as a city upon a hill. The eyes of all people are upon us. So that if we shall deal falsely with our God in this work we have undertaken, and so cause Him to withdraw His present help from us, we shall be made a story and a byword through the world."[14] The Puritans sought to live up to the Biblical promise that neither "the light of the world" nor the "city on a hill" founded in its glow would ever be hidden. Winthrop's sermon on the sea was simultaneously an indictment of an old England that had succumbed to Satan and an inducement to the settlers of a New England to prove not merely that the Puritan path was that of the righteous, but that in choosing it the Puritans would, hopefully to the everlasting chagrin of their enemies, be proved right.

In social and economic terms, the Puritan settlements were certainly more stable than those founded on the Chesapeake. Although the threat of starvation hung over the settlers that first winter in Massachusetts, supplies from England secured the colony's survival. The environment was healthier, and the nature of the migration itself – family units, sometimes entire congregations arrived together – meant that the Puritans effectively brought the infrastructure of the mother country with them. They thereby ensured the growth of white society in New England, which grew to some 90,000 by 1700. Consequently, there was no need to import wives to

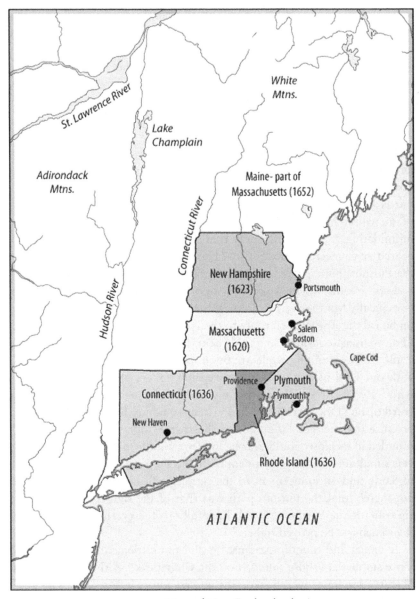

FIGURE 2.4. Map of New England colonies.

New England, there were far fewer single males or orphaned children, and women were considered to be the equals of men, at least spiritually. Socially, it was a different matter. For all practical purposes, stability was assured via a rigid patriarchal and ecclesiastical structure that was both inclusionary and exclusionary. God was head of the Church, the Church was the focus of social and family life, and the male was the head of the family. This arrangement was summed up in the contemporary observation that a "family is a little common wealth, and a common wealth is a greate family," and since "a family is not bound to entertaine all comers . . . no more is a common wealth."[15]

New England's legislative affairs also differed from those in both Maryland, which was the remit of one man, and Virginia, whose governor was appointed by the Virginia Company, and after its dissolution, by the English Crown. The Puritans organized their settlement according to the colony's original charter, which was interpreted via a General Court and by an elected governor. Yet this was neither equality nor democracy as understood today. Although the Protestantism preached by the Puritans encouraged individual interpretation of scripture, this was about as much individualism as the early Puritan settlements could take. Typically for a people who had suffered in an intolerant world, the new one the Puritans created was equally intolerant of difference or dissent. Both, naturally, arose soon enough.

It was perhaps inevitable that the emphasis placed on personal interpretation of scripture would produce alternative visions of the "city on a hill," and the Massachusetts Bay colony had barely unpacked before, in 1631, a minister with very different ideas from those espoused by Winthrop arrived in the colony – Roger Williams. Williams went even further than Calvert had in Maryland in his emphasis on religious freedoms (he included the Jewish faith), and in particular the need for a strict separation between church and any form of state. In a later publication, he set out his belief that "*God* requireth not an *uniformity* of *Religion* to be *inacted* and *inforced* in any *civill state*," but implicit in this stance was, of course, a denial that the Puritans themselves held any special spiritual directive, that they were, as Winthrop had argued, a uniquely chosen people who had been granted a "Covenant" with God.[16] With such views, Williams could hardly remain in Massachusetts Bay. As a result, the separate colony he founded, Rhode Island, became for the North what Maryland, to a somewhat lesser degree, was for the South: a haven for religious dissenters from all denominations.

Only a few years later, in 1634, an even more dramatic challenge to Puritan authority came in the form of Anne Hutchinson, whose outspoken disapproval of the Puritan leaders in Massachusetts led to what was known as the "Antinomian crisis" (antinomianism being the belief in justification through faith, direct communication with God). At Hutchinson's trial, in 1637, Winthrop charged her with having "spoken divers things as we have been informed very prejudicial to the honour of the churches and ministers thereof," and, he continued, revealing a fair bit about Puritan gender relations, "you have maintained a meeting and an assembly in your house that hath been condemned by the general assembly as a thing not tolerable nor comely in the sight of God nor fitting for your sex." Banished from Massachusetts for the crime of "being a woman not fit for our society," Hutchinson, too, left for Rhode Island.[17]

In the first decade of its existence, therefore, Winthrop's "Bible Commonwealth" was well on the way to establishing a reputation for being less than tolerant toward its own people. The apparent social stability that differentiated it from the Chesapeake was in many senses illusionary. Religion set New England apart, but at the same time tore it apart. In other respects, too, the similarities between these apparently extreme versions of English settlement in America were more obvious than their differences, and nowhere more so than in their relations with the Algonquian natives. Naturally enough, as dissenting groups moved out from Massachusetts to establish separate settlements, they encroached ever further onto native lands. This was not necessarily a problem for the Puritans. Conversion of the native peoples of New England was part of their remit.

The Puritan "errand into the wilderness" was undertaken not simply to secure personal salvation, but to aid what was understood to be a benighted people. And the Puritans were not wholly unsuccessful in their endeavors to convert the natives despite the fact that, conversion was not top of the agenda for the first few decades of their settlement. One contemporary account from 1632 praised their "loving, just and kind dealings with the Indians," whose "love and respect" for the Puritans had "drawne them to an outward conformity to the English."[18] Such "outward conformity," however, did not apply to all the New England native nations, and it had its limits. These were reached in 1637, when the Pequot tribe attacked some settlers in nearby Connecticut. The response on the part of the white settlers and their Narragansett allies was as cruel as it was comprehensive. They attacked the Pequot village at Mystic,

massacred most of its inhabitants, and sold the survivors into slavery in
the Caribbean.

Contemporary accounts by the Puritan leaders of the massacre provide
a sobering insight into the dominant white mindset of the time. "It was
a fearfull sight to see them thus frying in [the] fyer," William Bradford
recounted, "and [the] streams of blood quenching [the] same and horrible
was [the] stinck & sente ther of." Nevertheless, Bradford considered
the massacre and subsequent obliteration of the Pequot from the land
a "sweet sacrifice" and proof of God's support for the Puritan mission,
whereas John Mason, in charge of the Connecticut troops, enthused that
the massacre *"was the Lord's Doings, and it is marvellous in our Eyes!"*
(emphasis in the original). Writing to Bradford in its aftermath, Winthrop
expressed the hope that it had reinforced the recognition that the Pequot
"and all other Indeans" were the "comone enimie" of the white settlers.
It was a sentiment that Edward Waterhouse, 500 miles south on the
Chesapeake, would have recognized and doubtless concurred in.[19] Such
views, however, although influential, were not universal, and were to
some degree contradicted by men such as John Elliot, who founded the
first "praying town" – settlements of Christianized native peoples – in
Natick in 1650. For some, at least, the desire to convert the Algonquian,
and in the process to understand their society, was unencumbered by
an overt racial hostility even if it was driven by a cultural imperialism.
Unfortunately, exceptions like Eliot did rather prove the rule when it
came to native-English relations, and not just in New England.

The fact was, fear of, and sometimes open hostility toward, the native populations of the New World was a bond that united more than
just the Plymouth and Massachusetts Bay colonies. It was a defining
aspect of the British colonial endeavor in the Americas in the seventeenth
and early eighteenth centuries, one distinctly at odds with the "Indian
conversion" impulse that almost all colonial ventures had invoked as at
least part of their rationale for migration. It was not, however, particularly at odds with the reality of the seventeenth-century Atlantic world,
even if an oft-cited second rationale for British colonial ventures was the
gentle and constructive nature of these in contrast to the perceived cruelty
and destructiveness of the Spanish. Although, largely on the back of the
Puritan Great Migration to America and its self-defined mission to construct a "city on a hill," an influential mythology of "American excep-
tionalism" emerged, one that persists to this day, there was little that was
truly exceptional about colonial New England and almost nothing that

was distinctly American about it yet. The colonists' world, whether in Virginia or in Massachusetts, was very closely tied to that of England, and for New England, especially, it was less the "eyes of the world" that concerned them than the gaze of those they had left behind. It was to friends and family in England that their many letters were addressed, their colonial venture described and, up to a point, analyzed, and it was in London that they published their accounts – both harrowing and heartening – of all that America had to offer. They wrote themselves into the future nation's history even as they removed the Pequot from it.

In this respect the Puritans' sense of mission did distinguish them, even if only in their own minds, from other colonial ventures: from Virginia, where trade and tobacco dominated, as they also did in Maryland, whose laws on religious toleration were designed to provide a sanctuary, not produce a sermon, or from Pennsylvania, where the Quakers – whose version of Puritanism was banned in both Virginia and Massachusetts – and other nonconformist groups also sought a place of safety where they could practice their religion. It even set them apart from their nearest spiritual neighbors, the separatists of Plymouth, whose pilgrimage to the New World represented an attempt to escape from the corruption of the Old, not serve as a lesson for it. Certainly the Puritans wanted a New England, but they expected more than that. Out of New England, they anticipated, the New Jerusalem would arise. From their perspective, America was the Promised Land and they were the chosen people, but therein lay the problem. For a people so immersed in visions of the Apocalypse, danger was around every corner, and Satan lurked in every shadow. A people afraid of the preaching of one woman, or sufficiently unnerved by the Quaker beliefs of another, Mary Dyer, that they would put her to death, as they did in 1660, rather than tolerate her existence among them, were perhaps not likely to cavil at cruelty to the Algonquian peoples whom they failed to recognize as their equals in the first place. Their own community provided more than enough for them to fret about. The presence of natives was, for the Puritans, just another of the worldly trials with which they were burdened.

All this was not entirely as Winthrop had planned. He had anticipated a land that, if not exactly a *tabula rasa*, was certainly usefully vacant, a *vacuum domicilium*, for the very simple reason, as he put it, that "God hath consumed the natives with a miraculous plague, whereby the greater part of the country is left voide of inhabitants."[20] That God had not cleared out each and every native was not the main problem. The real challenge came from the land itself, from the New World environment over which the Puritans had so confidently expected to assert their authority, but which instead appeared to be exercising a pernicious influence on them. It came down to faith, and to the identity predicated on that faith. Both wavered in the New World in which the Puritans found themselves. Both faced a challenge that, their leaders feared, would undermine the foundations of their "city on a hill." Two decades into the Bible Commonwealth experiment, church membership had stagnated. Full membership was, of course, restricted to the "Visible Saints," those who had undergone a public conversion experience, but public testimonials were on the decline. By the middle of the seventeenth century, the Massachusetts synod had already compromised on the visibility of sainthood by permitting the offspring of the elect to be baptized, but the uneasy middle ground thereby created satisfied no one. In 1662, therefore, the synod came up with the idea of the "Half-Way Covenant," whereby the grandchildren of the first settlers could acquire membership in the Church. The implications of this decision, however, were more far-reaching than one might assume.

The Half-Way Covenant was a response not just to a wavering faith and declining church attendance, but to the gradual erosion of the traditional social and familial networks that the Puritans had brought with them from England. The tight-knit community structures, which were physical as well as spiritual, naturally broke down when the generation born in New England grew up and wanted their own land, both for economic survival and for the social status it afforded them. Although at first attempts were made to regulate the allocation of land specifically to prevent too wide a dispersal of the population as well as offer better defense against Algonquian attacks, this offered no solution to the growing needs of a growing population unthreatened by the scale of disease that still affected the Chesapeake. The original settlement patterns of townships comprising some 50 to 100 square miles of settlement structured around a central Meetinghouse with common land surrounding it for grazing livestock and growing crops (broadly, a variant of the pre-enclosure English pattern) gave way, over time, to individual family holdings of anywhere between 100 and 200 acres each. With individual property, of course, came a more individual perspective, the one thing that the early Puritans feared above all. Perhaps inevitably, with demographic dispersal and the increasing individualism that accompanied it came a more secular outlook, one at odds with the original vision that had driven the Puritan "errand into the wilderness." As the wilderness became tamed, so the vision faded.

It did not fade without a fight. Puritan ministers, especially after the halfway compromise had been effected, berated their congregations, via what were known as "jeremiads," with ever-increasing vigor over their moral and spiritual inadequacies, but this had been a theme almost from the start. As early as 1642, Governor Bradford had noted the moral decline of the Plymouth colony, the rise of "drunkenness" and "incontinencie betweens persons unmaried" along with a host of "things fearfull to name," all of which, he mused, "may justly be marveled at, and cause us to fear & tremble at the consideration of our corrupte natures." Why this was so had much to do with the Devil's influence but also, Bradford acknowledged, to the Puritan predilection for uncovering such lapses by making them "publick by due serch, inquisition, and due punishment."[21] Far worse, however, than moral declension were those cases of complete rejection of the Puritan mission via what was later termed, in the context of the British Empire, "going native." This was not a problem confined to New England. Turning one's back on white society and adopting – or being adopted by – one of the Algonquian nations was a crime punishable by hard labor in Connecticut and by death in Virginia. Both colonial ventures, on the Chesapeake and in New England, sought, with varying degrees of enthusiasm, to make the "Indian" English, but neither, in their wildest nightmares, could countenance the idea that the process might work the other way.

Indians, Indenture and Identity: Inventing a White Society

"Impress'd by New England writers and schoolmasters," observed one of America's greatest nineteenth-century poets, Walt Whitman, "we tacitly abandon ourselves to the notion that our United States have been fashion'd from the British Islands only, and essentially from a second England only." This, Whitman stressed, "is a very great mistake." Whitman was writing on the occasion of the anniversary, in 1883, of the founding of Santa Fé by the Spanish, but he was not simply flattering his audience when he suggested "that there will not be found any more cruelty, tyranny, superstition... in the *résumé* of past Spanish history than in the corresponding *résumé* of Anglo-Norman history." He knew that the "Black Legend" of Spanish colonialism still held sway in the late nineteenth century, just as he also realized that America's indigenous peoples seemed fated to "gradually dwindle as time rolls on," leaving, in the end, "only a reminiscence, a blank." He was perhaps wrong to ascribe the full responsibility for this to the Puritans, but in tracing the process whereby a racially exclusive mythology emerged from a multiracial reality, New England is as good a place to start as any.

In the case of New England, when the decline in the conversion impulse is married both to the practical effects of the Half-Way Covenant and to the dread that some colonists might prefer a way of life that was neither Puritan nor even obviously English, the evolving restrictive racial parameters of the Bible Commonwealth start to emerge. With the Half-Way Covenant, church membership became genealogically defined rather than faith-driven, and therefore closed not just to other immigrants, whether from Europe or Africa, but to the natives that the Puritans were supposed to be converting, thereby making explicit what had been implicit for quite some time: that there were ethnic and racial barriers to entry to that Bible Commonwealth, which to all intents and purposes was a white man's country. Just like the settlers on the Chesapeake, New England's Puritans struggled to accommodate the idea that Algonquian culture might peacefully coexist alongside English. In both cases, in Virginia as in Massachusetts, the open warfare between native and newcomer reached even more destructive levels in the later seventeenth century. In 1675, native uprisings occurred along the Potomac in Virginia and in southern New England closely followed, in Virginia, by a minor civil conflict within white society – Bacon's Rebellion.

In New England, the uprising that the colonists named King Philip's War (sometimes Metacom's Rebellion) was the result not just of increasing Puritan encroachment across the land, but of the shifting power relations within the native Wampanoag Confederacy after the death of both his father and his brother resulted in Metacom becoming Sachem (Algonquian leader, but not in the all-inclusive sense that the English understood it). Metacom was less welcoming of the English than his father had been, and more prepared to negotiate with others, such as the Narragansett, who had been allies of the English in the earlier Pequot War, with a view to combining forces against the Puritan settlements. The English were alerted to the danger by a man who, in a different context, could have helped bridge the native and English worlds, given that he belonged to both: the Christian convert John Sassamon. Sassamon had been raised by an English family after his parents' death, had fought alongside the English in the Pequot War, and attended Harvard College (founded in 1636). As is too often the case, however, being part of two worlds left Sassamon in a no-man's land between them both. Lines were being drawn in New England in 1675, and it was imperative to know which side one was on. Metacom may well have already been preparing

for war when John Sassamon was murdered, but the death, and resultant
trial and execution of three of his advisors for the deed, was the catalyst
for a conflict that was no minor skirmish but one of the most destructive
wars to take place on the American continent.

King Philip's war began in the summer of 1675 and raged across New
England for the remainder of that year and well into the next. Attacks on
the English frontier settlements were met by retaliatory raids by the colonial militias, including some against their former allies, the Narragansett,
who had attempted to remain neutral, in the winter of 1675–76. One
of the war's temporary casualties was one Mary Rowlandson, whose
account of her capture, *A True History of the Captivity and Restoration
of Mrs. Mary Rowlandson* (1682), became a best seller and, arguably,
launched the genre of the "captivity narrative" in America.[22] Rowlandson
interpreted her ordeal through the medium of the Bible, using the words
of the Psalms or extracts from the prophets the better to convey both
the horrors of her experience and her spiritual resilience. Her memoir
certainly fed the colonial fascination with and fear of the dangers of cultural contamination, but was ultimately reassuring, because Rowlandson
appeared to have emerged from her period of captivity among a people
she only ever referred to as "heathens," "barbarians," or "pagans" with
her essential Englishness and her Christianity not merely undiluted but
apparently reinforced. The same might be said of the war itself. The ultimate victory of the colonists over Metacom's forces in the late summer
of 1676 only enhanced the former's sense of cultural and martial superiority, and they readily interpreted it as yet another sign of God's support
for their settlement venture. Victory also enabled them, as they had done
after the Pequot War, to remove many of the surviving natives, including
Metacom's son, from the land, selling them into slavery in the Caribbean.

In demographic terms, New England's colonists recovered from the
war relatively speedily. What was never recovered was the hope for
peaceful Algonquian-English relations in New England. The brutality
of the war reinforced the racialized-religious discourse that had defined
that relationship from the outset, a distinction between nonwhite pagan
and white Christian that permitted colonists such as Mary Rowlandson
to make sense of the cultural gulf she recognized at the same time as it
prevented her from ever crossing it. Yet in removing at least some of the
natives from the land, and extending the possibilities for future white
settlement, English victory in King Philip's War also set the colonists on
the path to future conflicts, at first with the other European powers in
the New World – notably, in the case of New England, France – but,

ultimately, with Great Britain itself. Conflict, in short, would continue to define and refine New England's identity and, ultimately, that of all the American colonies over the next century. In that sense, King Philip's War was only the beginning.

Much farther south, in Virginia, Governor William Berkeley also had cause to contemplate what he described as the "infection of the Indianes in New England," one that he believed "has dilated it selfe to the Merilanders and the Northern parts of Virginia."[23] Contemporaneous uprisings against English settlements on the Chesapeake were, contrary to Berkeley's opinion, coincidental, but their repercussions were, if anything, more dramatic, exacerbated as tensions were by the unsettling reports from the north. As in New England, there were two main issues relating to colonial defense against the native threat, both practical in nature. The first was how, exactly, to identify who represented a threat. Neither in Virginia nor in New England were white racial attitudes so blunt or blinkered as to assume that the various native nations were interchangeable, but nor was it a straightforward matter for the English to ascertain which side any one of these was on at any given time. The second issue was, having identified the threat, how to meet it. Weaponry was neither cheap nor as plentiful in the colonial era as our contemporary image of America as a gun culture suggests. With the British Crown unwilling to commit the necessary expenditure to furnish the militia with the muskets they needed, Berkeley attempted, via a militia act in 1673, to raise local taxes to fund defense. Predictably, this was unpopular. Worse, it was not universally enforced.

In Virginia, therefore, the combination of the uprising of 1675 and the British lack of response to the danger the colonists faced proved a lethal cocktail for colonial stability. When the first attack came in the summer of 1675, the Virginian colonists not only pursued the Doeg natives responsible, but mistakenly also killed some Susquehannock, who lived in Maryland. The Susquehannock naturally retaliated, but others seized the opportunity to attack English settlements, so that by the spring of 1676, the settlers on the Chesapeake were embroiled in an undeclared war that they were convinced involved all the native nations along the east coast. As a result, they were soon engaged in another conflict, with each other. The uprising that became known as Bacon's Rebellion in part stemmed from a lack of faith in Berkeley's leadership at this time of crisis, but also from the unequal distribution of wealth and land in the growing colony. Settlers who had come to Virginia under an indenture were allocated the promised "headright" to purchase land once their period of servitude was completed. By the 1670s, however, the price of land had risen as that of tobacco had fallen, and few could afford, or even find, the land they wanted. This was more than a simple disjuncture between supply and demand. Landless freemen were perceived as a threat to the colony. As a version of the dissolute poor of England, their growing numbers produced a vision of social disintegration in Virginia. The solution arrived at, to deny the propertyless the vote, only exacerbated social tensions on the Chesapeake.

This was not a problem but an opportunity for Nathaniel Bacon, a recent arrival on the Chesapeake and a relatively wealthy man. Disenfranchisement was not his lot, and he had no difficulty either in locating or affording a substantial plantation upriver from the Jamestown settlement. Soon he was a member of the Virginia council. From this position he harassed Berkeley and the local natives alike, irritating the governor by his indiscriminate destruction of carefully cultivated relations with the tributary tribes. Yet Bacon garnered increasing levels of support in a colony already unsettled by the problems produced by a lack of available property and declining tobacco prices. His challenge for the leadership of the colony was predicated on the disaffection caused by the land shortage but pursued by mobilizing the resultant discontent against the local natives, specifically the friendly Occaeneechees. As Bacon's Rebellion gathered force, it turned on white society, resulting in the destruction, in September 1676, of Jamestown itself. It terminated only with the death, most likely from dysentery, of Bacon in the autumn of that year, and the subsequent trial and execution of those who had supported his rebellion.

The repercussions of Bacon's Rebellion were profound, both as far as English-native relations were concerned and for white society in Virginia. As with King Philip's War in New England, Bacon's Rebellion marked a transition point in white attitudes toward the Algonquian nations on the Chesapeake. This cannot wholly be ascribed to Bacon himself. Fear of and hostility toward the native populations had long been present – as the views of Edward Waterhouse in 1622 had made clear – but had been counterbalanced by men such as Berkeley who had consistently maintained that white settlement should not encroach on native land. All land north of the York River, in fact, had been denied to white intrusion via a 1646 treaty with the Powhatan Confederacy, but in the wake of Bacon's Rebellion, the line between Indian and white settlement became as blurred as that between friendly and hostile native. Although Berkeley was fully aware that there was a difference, in facing down Bacon's challenge he was pushed into a more extreme public position. When he advised the militia "to spare none that has the name of an Indian for they are all now our enemies," he may have been doing no more than asserting, for the benefit of his political opponents, his willingness to defend English settlement.[24] Unfortunately, the idea that no distinction need be applied in the case of the native nations was a sentiment that many of the English colonists concurred with. If all Indians were the enemy, then all bets were off, all land was available, and there were no limits to how far white society might expand.

Expansion, however, not only reinforced the emerging distinction between white and native society, but also established the parameters for the emergence of a white American identity itself predicated on the presence of nonwhite peoples. Bacon's Rebellion had revealed to Virginia's leaders how readily white society on the Chesapeake could implode. Equally, it had shown them how useful it was to have an external cultural "other" against which white society might be drawn together. Religion, in theory, was the bond that held New England together, and race, again in theory, served a similar purpose on the Chesapeake. It was never so clear-cut. Although geographically separated, and founded for a variety of different reasons and at different times, the various British colonial ventures in the New World, over the course of the seventeenth century, moved through violence toward a very similar position as far as the native nations were concerned. On the Chesapeake, the focus on tobacco drove the desire for land; in New England, the natural expansion of white society had the same effect. Tobacco, however, brought a whole new dimension to the development of white society in its intensive labor needs, needs that were not being met by immigration and indenture alone.

Clearly, given events between 1622 and 1676, Edward Waterhouse's notion of enslaving the natives to fulfill those needs was not a realistic proposition, at least not in the colonies. Neither Virginia's nor Massachusetts's leaders balked at the idea of Indian enslavement, but they preferred, for their own peace of mind, that such enslavement be in the Caribbean. Yet out of sight was not out of mind as far as slavery as a labor system was concerned. Servitude for life offered an obvious solution to the growing labor needs of the southern colonies, and at least part of the developing social needs of the northern ones. It was, after all, Massachusetts, not Virginia, that first formally recognized slavery in its legal code (in 1641), but it was in Virginia where the need for labor, especially after 1660, became sufficiently pressing that a permanent, and unalterable, labor force was sought. There was no supposition, however, that this need be racially defined.

Women had been commodities in the early Chesapeake, but this was not unusual in a world in which people had a value and immigrants a price. On arrival in America, servants were offered for sale, just as slaves later were. Under what was known as the "Redemptioner" system, poor people were given free passage on the understanding that friends or relatives would pay their passage on arrival. If this did not happen, they were sold, as were vagrants, children, and convicts, although the latter had a fixed-term indenture of fourteen years. When the first Africans arrived in Virginia in 1619, it was into this kind of world, so although they appear to have been "owned" by the then-Governor Yeardley, there is no indication that these were slaves in the later sense of slavery as it developed in America. In the early colonial period, blacks could own property as well as whites did. Yet along with the gradual cultural removal of whites from constructive contact with native society so, too, did slavery, along with the racial distinctions that would define its American variant, develop.

The laws that would come to define slavery were passed pretty much in line with the growth in the number of Africans in colonial America. In 1650, only some 4 percent of the North American population as a whole was black, and in the South the figure was 3 percent. This was at a time when the black population of the British Caribbean colonies was around 25 percent, but the numbers rose dramatically, and in a distinctly sectional direction. Compared to the British Caribbean, where by 1770 the black population comprised some 91 percent of the total, American numbers were never so large. By that year, the total black population in America was 22 percent, but for the southern colonies, it was 40 percent. It was, therefore, unsurprising that it was in the Chesapeake, the Carolinas, and later Georgia that slavery as a legal institution began to solidify.

In 1662, Virginia established the precedent that slavery would be a matrilineal institution; the children would take the legal status of the mother. Two years later, Maryland established the legal position of perpetual slavery, slavery for *Durante vita*, and Virginia, in 1667 and then in 1670, instituted two little tweaks to the legal position that revealed in which direction the colony was moving, racially speaking. In 1667, it was decreed that baptism into the Christian faith would not alter a slave's legal status. In 1670, it became illegal for any black to purchase a Christian or a white servant, this at a time when Virginia's black population numbered less than 2,000. A decade later, of course, that number had more than trebled, to some 7,000.

Over the next hundred years, slavery would come to be the economic bedrock of large parts of British colonial America, which given Britain's position as one of the main slave-trading European nations in the seventeenth century (by the mid-eighteenth she would dominate the trade) was perhaps not surprising. From tentative agricultural beginnings in general farming and domestic employment in both the Chesapeake and New England, with the further expansion of tobacco production on the Chesapeake, and the later (from the 1670s) cultivation of crops such as rice and indigo in the Carolinas (North and especially South) and Georgia, a comprehensive system of slavery began to take shape, and to shape those colonies in which it served as the mainstay of their agricultural production. In 1705, the Virginia House of Burgesses codified what was already becoming commonplace across the colonies: that "all negro, mulatto, and Indian slaves" comprised a form of "real estate" that could be bought and sold like any other, and on the back of this ruling, what became known as the South's "peculiar institution" was born.

Yet many of the elements that eventually defined American slavery were already in place by the mid-seventeenth century, and the clues to this reside not just in the statute books of the Virginia or Maryland colonies. Even at this early stage of the American nation's development, all the elements were in place that would set that part of the United States that became the South apart. In some respects, this process was more visible from Great Britain than in the colonies themselves. Tobacco did not arrive unaccompanied in England. The baggage it brought with it from the New World not only informed English views of the Americas, but fed back into the environment from which it had originated, influencing, as much as reflecting, an evolving ethnic awareness and a deepening racial divide separating white from nonwhite societies. Tobacco, in at least some of the iconography associated with it in the later seventeenth and throughout the eighteenth century, became a prize gained by England's conquest of Virginia; no longer simply a part of nature's New World bounty to be gathered or traded for with the natives, it was presented as a valuable commodity to be seized by superior English weaponry and, later, to be harvested by an unfree labor force. Tobacco, in effect, was presented as the ultimate product of racial imperialism. Some of the iconography associated with tobacco drew on long-familiar images of the New World. One in particular (Figure 2.5) invoked the capture, by John Smith, of the King of the Paspahegh (Pamunky), Opechancanough, which, in a simplified version (Figure 2.6), advertised not just the tobacco in question, but the shift in power relations on the Chesapeake.

FIGURE 2.5. From John Smith, *The Generall Historie of Virginia, New England and the Summer Isles* (London 1627).

The figure of Opechancanough, now visibly darkened in contrast to the original version (itself a reworking of an earlier John White portrait), presents a striking hybrid Native-African contrast with the white figure of Smith. No longer clearly Algonquian, nor self-evidently African, all

FIGURE 2.6. "Gaitskell's neat Tobaco at Fountain Stairs Rotherhith Wall."
Photo: Guildhall Library, London Metropolitan Archives.

that the viewer can conclude from the image is that Opechancanough is
not white; a potent, if inadvertent, comment on the state of affairs in the
colonies by the later seventeenth century. That is not all that has changed.
The background of the original has also been modified: where there were

trees and an open landscape, now a small church has been inserted, along with a ship; and where there were trees, now there is one, rather stunted, tobacco plant alongside Opechancanough's right foot.[25]

In essence, one tobacco advertisement summed up the dramatic changes that had taken place not just on the Chesapeake since Smith first set foot there, but in the British colonies as a whole over the course of the seventeenth century. The "New Found Land" was no longer so "new." European ships had brought European religion, European peoples and goods, and African peoples, all of which had altered forever the landscape and those who sought to live on it. The original vision, be it of New World wealth or a "city on a hill," had, by 1680, been transformed, and the original hopes for conversion of the native peoples abandoned. Nor was this the end of the transformative process. A century later, the British colonies would establish a wholly new nation, predicated on Enlightenment philosophy, constructed around civic principles that, in outline at least, had been fomented in Maryland's religious toleration, in New England's ambitious vision of a Bible Commonwealth, in Bacon's challenge to the Virginia elite. It would be all of these, and yet none of them entirely, because the development of this foremost civic nation of the modern world would, to a very great extent, be directed, and constrained, by the deep ethnic roots laid down in its formative years.

3

The Cause of All Mankind

From Colonies to Common Sense

The cause of America is in great measure the cause of all mankind.
(Thomas Paine, *Common Sense*, 1776)

Conflict, to a great extent, defined the colonial experience, and conflict would eventually destroy the colonial project and create the new nation that was America. Open warfare with the Algonquian nations helped the white settlers assert a separate identity from the aboriginal populations and established racial distinctions that would eventually divide white society from the African peoples brought to the New World. This was not racism as we would utilize the term today, but the assumption of ideas about race that would, in time, harden into a set of fixed racial and ethnic parameters themselves formed, at least in part, through warfare.

Warfare assured English settlers of their essential Englishness in an environment that called that identity into question and challenged it not just via English contact with the Amerindians, but by what they knew of other colonial efforts. The French in New France were more determined than the English to acquire native converts to the (in their case, Catholic) faith as well as to absorb them, absent their aboriginal culture, of course, into French norms. They frequently found that their efforts backfired. As one contemporary official, Jean Bochart de Champigny, observed, "[I]t happens more commonly that a Frenchman becomes savage than a savage becomes a Frenchman."[1] From an English perspective, this was a moot point. Before too long, they would be battling both French and native. For the English, it was through violence that they asserted their validity as freeborn Englishmen and upheld the values attendant on that status.

Ultimately violence would force them toward a new identity, derived from, but set apart from, that provided by their European origins. America as a political and cultural nation, a separate nation-state, may have originated in "Albion's Seed," but Albion's was the not the sole seed planted in the New World environment, and when all had germinated, a very different plant appeared.

By the late seventeenth century, Britain's colonial presence had expanded far beyond the Chesapeake and Massachusetts Bay. It comprised a mix of proprietary, corporate (joint-stock), and royal colonies. Three of them, Rhode Island, New Hampshire, and Connecticut, were effectively a form of Puritan Diaspora, founded or developed by individuals who had clashed with the Puritan hierarchy in Massachusetts and who hoped for greater religious freedom and economic opportunity farther afield. Rhode Island was directly the result of Roger Williams's having been banished from Massachusetts in 1635, to be joined later by Anne Hutchinson after her dismissal from Salem by John Winthrop. Further fallout from the "Antinomian crisis" caused Hutchinson's brother-in-law, John Wheelwright, and his followers to abandon Massachusetts in search of religious refuge in New Hampshire, which had sustained a small English settlement since 1623. In the case of Connecticut, there was disagreement but no outright hostility between the Rev. Thomas Hooker and Massachusetts's leaders, but Hooker nevertheless preferred to move beyond their jurisdiction, taking his followers to the Connecticut Valley in 1636.

Given their origins in mutual antagonism, there was little indication that the New England colonies would ever function together, but expansion brought its dangers, and with these a new, if relatively short-lived (to 1684), form of federal arrangement in the New World. To provide for defense against both native and European nations (the French and the Dutch), whose land the Puritan dissenters were increasingly intruding on, in 1643, the Massachusetts, Plymouth, New Haven, and Connecticut colonies organized together to form the New England Confederation (Rhode Island was not invited). Its main success, if it can be called that, was in the prosecution of King Philip's War in 1675–76. Yet even as these colonies were discussing defense, back in England, civil war was raging. For a time, emigration to the colonies slowed to a trickle. With the restoration of the Crown under Charles II (1660), a new era of colonial expansion dawned, but with it came an intensified and unwelcome interest in colonial affairs on the part of the now more secure English monarchy.

Prior to this, and not just because it was engaged in a civil war, Britain's involvement with her American colonies extended little further than breathing a sigh of relief that so many of the poor were finding their way to the Chesapeake and so many problematic Puritans had left for New England. In that respect, the colonies functioned as a kind of a safety valve for British society, whose less desirable elements could be safely shipped off to America, as well as to the Caribbean. In 1666, for example, it was with some satisfaction that the city fathers of Edinburgh, in Scotland, reported the removal of a number of "beggars, vagabonds and others not fitt to stay in the kingdome" to Virginia.[2] This really was a case of out of sight, out of mind. As far as the colonies went, Britain's sole concern, rarely expressed until European conflicts threatened it, was that English shipping be the main beneficiary of colonial trade. The English Commonwealth passed a Navigation Act to this effect in 1651, which Charles II promptly rescinded and replaced with his own, enhanced version in 1660. In the short term, this was good for English shipping (not British; ships and goods went via England and Wales only) and for New England's shipbuilding trade, because "English" ships included those constructed in the colonies. The longer-term prognosis was not so good as far as controlling said colonies was concerned.

This early and tentative attempt at trade protection was accompanied by an upsurge in colonial ventures after 1660. A raft of new English colonies – sometimes termed the Restoration colonies, to mark the period of their settlement – appeared in America (Table 3.1) All of these began as proprietary arrangements. The Carolinas were settled by a group of Lords Proprietors, including Lord Anthony Ashley Cooper, the future Earl of Shaftesbury, the Governor of Virginia, Sir William Berkeley, and Sir George Carteret. Both the latter were also appointed Lords Proprietors of New Jersey, which itself grew out of New York. New York, the future state, was formerly New Netherland, and had been settled by the Dutch. It was granted by Charles II to his brother, James, in 1664, after the English had gained control of it in the Anglo-Dutch war of that year. Lacking inspiration in the naming department, or perhaps simply determined to get his title everywhere, James (at that point the Duke of York) renamed its main city, formerly New Amsterdam, New York City. James made New York into a royal colony when he assumed the throne in 1685. By this time, its white population had doubled from 1664 levels, to around 20,000.

This new drive into America, as so many previous ones had been, was motivated by the search for profit as much as by the desire to expand

TABLE 3.1. *The Original Thirteen Colonies, in Order of Settlement*

Colony	Founded	Founders	Government
Virginia	1607	London (Virginia) Company	Joint-stock with a Royal charter, then Royal colony from 1624
Massachusetts	1620	Massachusetts Bay Company/Puritans	Joint-stock and then Royal colony from 1691
New Hampshire	1623	John Mason and Ferdinando Gorges; then John Wheelwright	Proprietary, then "Exeter Compact," then Royal colony from 1679
Maryland	1634	Cecilius Calvert (Second Lord Baltimore)	Proprietary
Connecticut	1636	Thomas Hooker Connecticut absorbed the New Haven and Saybrook colonies when it was granted a Royal charter in 1662	"Fundamental Orders" and later a Royal charter in 1662
Rhode Island	1636	Roger Williams	Charter (Long Parliament)
Delaware	1638	New Sweden Company/Peter Minuit, then William Penn (1703)	Swedish settlement, later purchased by Penn
North Carolina	1663	Lords Proprietors *Seven of the eight LPs sold their rights to the British Crown in 1729. Carteret (Earl Granville) did not.	"Fundamental Constitutions," separate governor from South, 1712, Royal colony from 1729*
South Carolina	1663	Lords Proprietors as for North Carolina	"Fundamental Constitutions," separate governor from North, 1712, Royal colony from 1729*
New Jersey	1664	William Berkeley and George Carteret	Proprietary, then Royal colony from 1702
New York	1664	James, Duke of York (later James II)	Dutch-owned, then Proprietary, the Royal colony from 1685
Pennsylvania	1682	William Penn	Proprietary
Georgia	1732	General James Oglethorpe	Royal Charter

English power and spread Protestantism. The latter impulse was somewhat doubtful in any case, given that James II was Catholic, but the religious alignment of the British Crown, as for the proprietors it supported, was not the main issue. For men like Berkeley, the Carolinas and New Jersey were simply investment opportunities. They had no intention of living there. Berkeley sold his share of the New Jersey proprietorship to English Quakers, who began to settle in the western part of the colony, whereas other dissenting groups, Congregationalists and Baptists, moved into the east.

Like New England, however, all was not harmonious in New Jersey. The purchase of the eastern part of the colony by a Quaker syndicate under William Penn in 1682 caused unease among those – mainly Scots – already settled there. New Jersey certainly provided a refuge of sorts for Quakers, one of the most persecuted of all the religious groups of the period, as the execution of Mary Dyer in Massachusetts in 1660 had shown. It was the fate of the Quakers, according to one of the first articles published in the Quaker journal *The Friend*, "to be misunderstood and misrepresented in a remarkable degree"; accused of being Jesuits or Deists, libertines or bigots, "there is scarcely a point of their doctrine or discipline which they have not been compelled to defend."[3] For this reason, Penn had always sought a more secure location for his "Holy Experiment." He found it when in 1681, Charles II granted him the land that he would name "Penn's paradise," Pennsylvania (Figure 3.1). The following year, Penn arrived in his proprietary paradise, to oversee the construction of what would become its foremost city, named for the Greek for "brotherly love" – Philadelphia. Penn later extended his experiment by purchasing the Swedish settlements on the Delaware River, which, in 1703, became a separate colony, Delaware. Pennsylvania was quick to attract Quaker settlers from England, where, by 1680, some 10,000 Quakers had been thrown into prison as punishment for their unorthodox beliefs, and many executed. Thousands came to America, attracted by Penn's assurance, set out clearly in his 1701 *Charter of Privileges*:

that noe person or persons Inhabiting in this Province or Territories who shall Confesse and Acknowledge one Almighty God the Creator upholder and Ruler of the world ? shall be in any case molested or prejudiced in his or theire person or Estate because of his or theire Conscientious perswasion or practice nor be compelled to frequent or mentaine any Religious Worship place or Ministry contrary to his or theire mind or doe or Suffer any other act or thing contrary to theire Religious perswasion.[4]

THE
F R A M E
OF THE
Government of Pennſilvania
IN
AMERICA, &c.

To all People, *to whom theſe Preſents ſhall come* :

WHEREAS **King Charles** the Second, by his Letters Patents, under the **Great Seal** of *England,* for the Conſiderations there-in mentioned, hath been graciouſly pleaſed to Give and Grant unto Me **William Penn** *(*by the Name of **William Penn Eſquire,** Son and Heir of **Sir William Penn** deceaſed*)* and to My **Heirs** and **Aſſigns** forever, *All that Tract of Land or Province, called* **Pennſilvania,** *in* America, *with divers great Powers, Preheminencies, Royalties, Juriſdictions and Authorities neceſſary for the Well-being and Government thereof*

Now know Ye, That for the *Well-being* and *Government* of the ſaid *Province,* and for the *Encouragement* of all the **Free-men** and **Planters** that may be therein concerned, in purſuance of the Powers aforementioned, I the ſaid **William Penn** have *Declared, Granted* and *Confirmed,* and by theſe Preſents for **Me,** my **Heirs** and **Aſſigns** do *Declare, Grant* and *Confirm* unto all the **Free-men, Planters** and **Adventurers** of, in and to the ſaid Province Theſe **Liberties, Franchiſes** and **Properties** to be held, enjoyed and kept by the **Free-men, Planters** and **Inhabitants** of and in the ſaid *Province* of **Pennſilvania** forever.

Imprimis, That the *Government* of this *Province* ſhall, according to the *Powers* of the *Patent,* conſiſt of the **Governour** and **Free-men** of the ſaid *Province,* in the Form of a **Provincial Council** and **General Aſſembly,** by whom all *Laws* ſhall be made, Officers choſen and publick Affairs Tranſacted, as is hereafter reſpectively declared ; That is to ſay,

II. That the **Free-men** of the ſaid *Province* ſhall on the *Twentieth* day of the *Twelfth* Moneth, which ſhall be in this preſent Year *One Thouſand Six Hundred Eighty and Two,* Meet and Aſſembly in ſome fit place, of which timely Notice ſhall be beforehand given by the **Governour** or his *Deputy,* and then and there ſhall chuſe out of themſelves **Seventy Two** Perſons of moſt Note for their *Wiſdom, Virtue* and *Ability,* who ſhall meet on the Tenth day of the Firſt Moneth next enſuing, and alwayes be called and act as the **Provincial Council** of the ſaid *Province.*

FIGURE 3.1. William Penn, *The Frame of Government of the Province of Pennsylvania* (London, 1682)

The settlement of Pennsylvania was the final British colonial venture of the seventeenth century. It would be several decades before Georgia was conceived and settled (1732), not as a refuge for religious dissenters but as an asylum for British debtors. By that point, the British colonies stretched from French Canada down the eastern seaboard to Spanish Florida. In structural, governmental terms, they were quite similar. Most were ruled by a governor, appointed either by the Crown or by the proprietor(s), and a legislature divided between a council (upper house) appointed by the governor, and an elected assembly (lower house). Only Rhode Island and Connecticut were the exceptions; in both colonies, the legislature elected the governor. For all practical, economic, cultural, religious, and social purposes, and the New England Confederation notwithstanding, there was little, beyond their links to Great Britain, to unite them, with one notable exception.

Print culture may have been the fulcrum of nationalism in the modern world, but it was not simply through the increasingly detailed maps, publicly disseminated propagandist tracts aimed at prospective immigrants, or travel accounts of the New World penned by individual adventurers such as John Smith or graphically illustrated by Theodor de Bry that America gradually came into focus. If one is searching for the animus of early American identity, one important clue lies in the rather more prosaic bureaucracy of colonization, of which Penn's *Frame of Government* was just one example. This was a land simply awash with the documentation of government, settled by people for whom the small print of contracts and charters, the subtle structure of their legal lives, really mattered – a lot.

The Puritans were especially keen on the control that a clearly worded charter could provide. The Great Migration was funded by a joint-stock company, the Massachusetts Bay Company, under the remit of a charter granted by the Crown. Unlike the London Company, however, the charter itself was in the possession of the original Puritan settlers who, via the "Cambridge Agreement" (1629), bought out those in the company not intending to emigrate and asserted their control over the governance and management of the colony under John Winthrop. Ten years later, in Connecticut, Thomas Hooker instituted the "Fundamental Orders" to govern the colony; one of the earliest written constitutions in the United States. In the same year (1639), New Hampshire instituted the "Exeter Compact" (modeled on the "Mayflower Compact") to govern that colony.

Further south, in the Carolinas, and with the help of philosopher John Locke, one of the Lords Proprietors, Sir Anthony Ashley Cooper, devised the "Fundamental Constitutions" to ensure the rule of a hereditary aristocracy in the Carolinas. Although this was not a success, and was soon replaced by the "standard" proprietary model for colonial management (a governor, a council, and an elected assembly), it revealed the extent to which the colonization project highlighted the whole question of government, social structure, race relations, religious freedoms, and political representation. The colonization experience moved the British colonists away from the traditional English ruling combination of Magna Carta, local and common law, and the courts. Indeed, given the apparently incessant scribbling and reworking of compacts and agreements during the colonial era, the eventual centrality of a written Constitution to the United States is hardly to be wondered at.

At the start of the eighteenth century, of course, no one anticipated the eventual unification of the British colonies, far less a single constitutional document to govern them. Nevertheless, the tensions inherent within colonial government, combined with the natural demographic and geographic growth of the colonies themselves, began to weaken the bonds between them and Great Britain, even if this did little, as yet, to strengthen the relationship between the various colonies themselves. One of the first clues to a future clash between the colonists and the "mother country" came only a few years after King Philip's War, and partly as a result of it, as the British crown, disturbed by reports from New England, sought closer control over the colonies. The efforts at controlling colonial trade, begun with the 1651 Navigation Act, were reinforced in 1673 via a Plantation Duties Act and, two years later, the establishment of the Lords of Trade and Plantations, a Privy Council committee whose remit it was to control colonial affairs. In 1684, the Massachusetts Charter was revoked as punishment for Massachusetts having flouted the trade restrictions. This was followed, in 1686, by the creation, under James II, of the Dominion of New England (Figure 3.2) under the overall charge of former New York governor, Edmund Andros. This brought together the colonies of Connecticut, New Hampshire, Plymouth, Rhode Island, Massachusetts, New Jersey, and New York, partly to ensure compliance with the Navigation Act, partly with a view to improving defense. James's efforts at colonial management were short-lived, of course, because the Glorious Revolution of 1688 removed him from the throne, to be replaced by William III (of Orange) and Mary in 1689.

The motto of the Dominion of New England, reproduced on its seal, proposed that "*Nunquam libertas gratior extat,*" which was an abbreviation of the quote *Nunquam libertas gratior extat Quam sub rege pio* ("Never does liberty appear in a more gracious form than under a pious king"). Yet the colonies were fast developing their own ideas of liberty, ideas that increasingly were at odds with monarchy and, it must be said,

FIGURE 3.2. Seal of the Dominion of New England (1686–89) in William Cullen Bryant and Sydney Howard Gay, *A Popular History of the United States*, Vol. III (1879): 9. Courtesy of the Library of Congress and the United States Diplomacy Center Exhibition at: http://diplomacy.state.gov/exhibitions/100935 .htm.

rather at odds with the idea of English-native cooperative subservience to monarchy that the image on the Dominion's seal suggested. It is important not to exaggerate this, nor ascribe republican ideology to what was not yet a republican age. Hostility toward certain policies implemented by the British Crown toward the end of the seventeenth century did not instantly and decisively translate into an ideological opposition toward all things regal in the eighteenth. Rather, the assertion of the "ancient" rights of freeborn Englishmen, as described in the 1689 Bill of Rights enacted by the British parliament and loudly trumpeted across England during the Glorious Revolution, found their echo in America. When confirmed reports of William's victory reached the colonies, popular uprisings ousted the governments of Edmund Andros (Massachusetts, but overall governor of the Dominion), Francis Nicholson (New York), and William Joseph (Maryland), but the impulse behind these was closely tied to events in Britain. In the case of Massachusetts and New York, those opposing the old regime did not act decisively until they were pretty sure a new one, in the shape of William and Mary, was in place.

The changing of the guard in England, in short, was simply replicated in the colonies in ways indicative of social and political schisms within these colonies, and followed the channels carved out by those that governed them. Opposition to the Dominion, and to the colonial elites who served as the British Crown's mouthpiece, was not necessarily an early indication of an anti-imperial position, which is not to say that it did not influence the future nation that America would become. James's defeat by William of Orange had longer-term repercussions for America than simply the removal of Catholics from positions of power in Massachusetts, Maryland, and New York. The Glorious Revolution ended all hopes for a Catholic resurgence in Britain, but also bequeathed a persistent anti-Catholic strain to the future American nation. It would be almost 300 years before America elected a Catholic president (John F. Kennedy in 1960); and it was in the colonial period that the assurance of the white Protestant ascendancy was formed, but it was formed in a monarchical context.

The Dominion of New England had attempted to limit, indeed eliminate, the rights of colonial assembly. These were restored under William and Mary, but only up to a point. In 1691, Massachusetts and, briefly, Maryland became a royal colony, with their governors appointed by the British crown and, in the case of Massachusetts, the franchise defined not by church membership but by property ownership. The rule of the "saints" thereby gave way to the rise of a new, secular elite, mainly merchants and landowners. This was the start of a trend. In the early decades of the eighteenth century, many of the colonies shifted from corporate or proprietary to crown control. Five did not: Pennsylvania, Maryland, Delaware, Rhode Island, and Connecticut. Yet even in these colonies, the royal reach could not be entirely avoided. Driven by a mercantilist mindset that perceived the colonies in much the same way as the Virginia Company had first viewed the Chesapeake – as a source of wealth, raw materials, and employment both in the colonies and at home – Britain had no cause, a century after the Jamestown settlement had limped into existence, to feel disappointed, but it was keen to protect its investment.

The creation, in 1696, of a Board of Trade extended the control over colonial products inaugurated, but hitherto loosely applied, in the Navigation Acts. By the mid-eighteenth century, virtually all the raw materials produced in British America fell under its remit. This was not necessarily bad for the American colonies. It assured them of a market in Britain. By 1720, for example, Glasgow, in Scotland, imported more than 50 percent of all American tobacco. It also opened up new markets via trade with other British colonies, notably those in the West Indies, and confirmed America's position as part of the lucrative "triangular" trade in goods and slaves that operated between Europe, the Caribbean, and West Africa. In the American case, New England replaced the European point of the triangle. New England ships took rum from Boston and Newport to Guinea, transported slaves from Africa to the West Indies, returned to America with the molasses and sugar required to make more rum, and thereby perpetuated the vicious cycle of sail and return in which people figured as the greatest source of profit. Britain's American colonies, in short, did not develop in isolation. England's religious and regal conflicts may have reverberated within them, but the kind of societies these colonies became were never just a distant echo of England.

After 1700, indeed, English immigration tailed off somewhat as that from other European nations rose. At the same time, the rise in importation of African peoples, combined with an increasingly ethnic definition of servitude within the southern colonies in particular, not only confirmed the trend toward a racially bifurcated society, but provided the economic and, crucially, cultural basis on which that society would develop. From the late seventeenth through early eighteenth century, colonial economic, social, religious, and political life increasingly began to be informed by two apparently contradictory concepts: liberty and slavery. Of course, they are not contradictory at all. The one cannot be fully understood absent the other and, in America's case, the one could not, in the end, be achieved without the other.

What, then, is the American?

In 1782, the year before the Treaty of Paris (1783) formally recognized the new nation that was the United States of America, French émigré John Hector St. John de Crèvecoeur published, in London, a series of essays under the title *Letters from an American Farmer*. In it he posed the question for which he later became famous: "What, then," he inquired, "is the American, this new man?" His answer has defined America's more positive public face since Crèvecoeur arrived at it. The American, he asserted, was a European, but with a difference. "*He* is an American," asserted Crèvecoeur, "who, leaving behind him all his ancient prejudices and manners, receives new ones from the new mode of life he has embraced, the new government he obeys, and the new rank he holds." The American was viewed as a conglomeration of national types, a "strange mixture of blood, which you will find in no other country," Crèvecoeur observed, proud of the fact that he "could point out to you a man, whose grandfather was an Englishman, whose wife was Dutch, whose son married a French woman, and whose present four sons have now four wives of different nations." America itself was a place where

individuals of all nations are melted into a new race of men, whose labours and posterity will one day cause great changes in the world. Americans are the western pilgrims who are carrying along with them that great mass of arts, sciences, vigour, and industry which began long since in the East; they will finish the great circle.... The American is a new man, who acts upon new principles; he must therefore entertain new ideas and form new opinions. From involuntary idleness, servile dependence, penury, and useless labour, he has passed to toils of a very different nature, rewarded by ample subsistence. This is an American.[5]

Given that non-English immigration did not really gather momentum until 1700, if we follow Crèvecoeur, then, it took less than a century, maybe a maximum of four fertile generations, or the single life span of an individual who had not exceeded by too much her allocated three-score years and ten, for the erratic mix of British American colonies not just to merge and achieve separate nationhood, but for the white people of that new nation to have acquired the quasi-mythic status of "western pilgrims" charged with fulfilling the destiny of humankind. The question arises, how was this possible? The question arises, indeed, was this possible?

Hindsight advises us that the American Revolution, or War for Independence, did end with the separation of Britain's colonies from the "mother country" in 1783. Not gifted with foresight, the colonists in the early eighteenth century were hardly preparing to declare independence in 1776, nor gearing themselves up for the war necessary to achieve it. Yet in some senses they were doing precisely that, because there were two dominant features to American colonial life: change and war.

The colonies were, if nothing else, societies in transition; almost perpetual transition. In part, this instability derived from the constant influx of new immigrants. Even within white society, colonial life – certainly on its frontiers – offered less opportunity for cross-cultural fertilization than

Crèvecoeur's later enthusiasm about the possibilities of inter-European exchange made it seem. In the period between 1700 and the colonists issuing the Declaration of Independence (1776), more than half a million immigrants arrived in the colonies. Of this half-million, approximately 100,000 arrived as indentured servants, and some 50,000 were deported convicts, the latter mainly from England and Wales (c. 35,000), but also from Ireland (c. 17,000) and Scotland (c. 2,000). The various groups that arrived – the Germans (c. 85,000), the Scots (c. 35,000), and the Irish (c. 108,000) – did not mix easily. So the colonies were certainly diverse, but the various groups that comprised this diversity tended to remain relatively homogenous in terms of their religion and their culture, rarely marrying outside these. Dwarfing all other immigrants, however, in numerical terms, and also absent the status variations within the European immigrant groups, were those who arrived from Africa, as slaves (c. 280,000), partly as a result of the dramatic fall in slave prices that followed the loss of the Royal African Company's monopoly of the African slave trade in 1697. The concomitant rise in the importation of slaves meant that the black population of the colonies soared from about 20,000 in 1700 to more than 350,000 in 1763. In this period, therefore, more than half of all immigrants who arrived in the British colonies arrived involuntarily, either as convicts or as slaves.

The world they entered was one frequently riven by conflict, mainly the natural overspill from the European wars of the period, conflicts that had European national origins, but recognized no European national boundaries. Between 1689 and 1763, the American colonies were participants in no fewer than four wars fought between Britain and France: the War of the League of Augsburg, which the colonists designated King William's War (1689–1697); the War of the Spanish Succession (Queen Anne's War, 1702–1713); the War of the Austrian Succession (King George's War, 1744–1748); and finally, and most decisively from the colonial perspective, the Seven Years' War (the French and Indian War, 1756–1763), terminated by the Treaty of Paris in 1763 and the removal of the French threat to Britain's colonial ambitions in America. It was against this background of almost constant conflict – and conflict that, as the different colonial names for them suggested, was perceived as intrusive and certainly was destructive – that Britain's American colonies developed. It was hardly a recipe for either social or imperial stability.

Instability and uncertainty, however, were intrinsic aspects of the colonial experience. Virtually all immigrants who were not members of the English governing elite – and that comprised pretty much the majority, male and female, black and white – entered a world of uncertainty, voluntarily or otherwise, when they arrived in the colonies. The response of at least some of them to this was astutely observed by England's earliest female playwright, Aphra Behn, toward the end of the seventeenth century. In her dramatic interpretation of Bacon's Rebellion in Virginia, one of her characters declares that this "Country wants nothing but to be People'd with a well-born Race to make it one of the best Collonies in the World." Instead, it was "Ruled by a Councill, some of which have been perhaps transported Criminals, who having Acquired great Estates are now become your Honour, and Right Worshipful, and Possess all Places of Authority."[6] This early definition of what would later be termed the "Log-Cabin Myth or the "American Dream," was, in the early colonial period, as Behn clearly understood, a source of unease, not enthusiasm. It was interpreted as opportunism, not optimism. Optimism, indeed, was in rather short supply in the British colonies at the start of the eighteenth century. Yet these colonies were about to experience a remarkable period of growth and development that would change their world, and their outlook, forever.

In 1700, the American colonies were poised on the cusp of the modern age. They comprised a combination of elements wholly in tune with the modern world as that is understood today but also attitudes that we would now designate as premodern. In the latter case, perhaps the most obvious, if also extreme, example was the Salem witchcraft trials of 1692, which might best be described as a premodern response to modern pressures and to the unsettled environment of Massachusetts at the end of the seventeenth century. The reality of the Salem settlers' lives was that they were coming under increased pressure from a monarch who, although a firm believer in the "divine right of kings," was undeniably human. The threat the colonists' reacted to, however, emanated from a very different power altogether, that of Satan. From a Puritan perspective, of course, a Catholic monarch might easily have been confused with the prince of darkness, but Satan was all too real in their minds in 1692 in a way that James II was not.

Belief in witchcraft and in magical intervention was, of course, common both in Britain and in the colonies in this period, and the hysteria that broke out in Salem in 1692 was a few years in the making. The first accused "witch," Goody Glover, was hanged in 1688. Leading Puritan minister Cotton Mather described the case in his *Memorable Providences, Relating to Witchcrafts and Possessions* (1689), which offers a glimpse into a world prepared to execute an innocent woman on the evidence provided by an emotional thirteen-year-old girl who had argued with her. This was a world whose response to external threat was to turn on itself. "Go tell Mankind," Mather urged in his pamphlet, "that there are Devils and Witches," and that New England "has had Exemples of their Existence and Operation; and that no[t] only the Wigwams of Indians, where the pagan Powaws often raise their masters, in the shapes of Bears and Snakes and Fires, but the House of Christians, where our God has had his constant Worship, have undergone the Annoyance of Evil spirits." Salem certainly harbored evil spirits, but these were a little more earthbound than ethereal.

In 1691, the stuff of children's nightmares became horribly real when witchcraft was identified as the cause of their fits, and a colored slave named Tituba accused, along with several white women, of being the source. By the following year, the entire situation had mushroomed out of all proportion. Neighbor turned on neighbor, and some evidently secular old scores were settled, until the governor of Massachusetts stepped in and dissolved the Salem court that had, by that point, tried well over a hundred people and condemned and executed fourteen women and five men for the crime of witchcraft. In the face of this mass hysteria, Cotton Mather's father, Increase Mather, also a leading Puritan divine, felt moved to condemn the entire business of "spectral evidence" in his treatise *Cases of Conscience Concerning Evil Spirits* (1693). Mather's message was reinforced in the later publication (Figure 3.3) of John Hale's *A Modest Enquiry into the Nature of Witchcraft* (1702). Hale, a minister in Beverly, Massachusetts, had proved quite robust in his prosecution of witches until his wife, Sarah, became one of the accused. At that point, he rather went off the whole idea; but then, so had most New Englanders by 1700.

The response to the Salem Witchcraft trials simply confirmed, if confirmation was needed, a more general reaction against elite ecclesiastical authority, which, in 1699, expressed itself in the founding of the Brattle Street Church in Boston, the first Church to dispense entirely with the idea that only God's elect could qualify for membership. By the mid-eighteenth century, and in the context of what was known as the "Great Awakening," a massive religious revival that began in New Jersey and upstate New York and spread throughout the colonies between the 1720s and 1760s, some of the more radical clergy had even dispensed with the notion of predestination altogether and preached salvation instead.

Change clearly was in the air, a change partly informed by and partly entirely at odds with Britain's colonial outlook. The mercantilist mindset

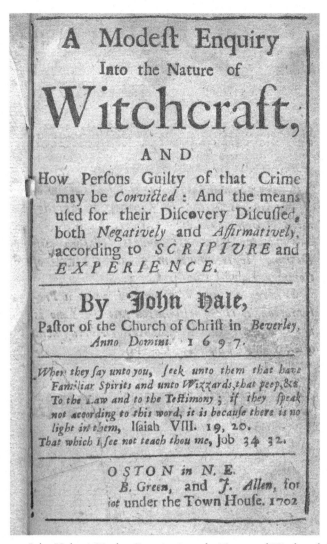

FIGURE 3.3. John Hale, *A Modest Enquiry into the Nature of Witchcraft* (Boston: Green and Allen, 1702).

that directed Britain's attitude toward its American colonies was not just concerned with colonial goods and the trading opportunities these afforded, but with the home population. Although immigration, except in the case of skilled artisans, was not openly discouraged after 1700, it was no longer positively encouraged, except, and especially after the 1718 Transportation Act, in the case of convicted felons.

Since the early colonial period, one of the draws for voluntary immigrants to the New World had been the promise of greater liberty, be that religious, social, or purely economic. For women, in particular, there seemed to be – and in the earliest years of settlement, there sometimes was – at least the possibility of living a life less limited by patriarchal rule. The extent to which this possibility was realized depended, naturally, on the colony, on the circumstances, and on the woman. The initial shortage of women on the Chesapeake gave those who did arrive a degree of power, which was both undermined and enhanced by the reduced life expectancies the region afforded. Being left a widow might mean financial freedom, but with it the attendant risk of not surviving long enough to enjoy it. In New England, the healthier environment produced its own burdens in terms of enhanced family size, which was wonderful, no doubt, but did rather restrict a woman's life to matters domestic. In short, a life beyond the kitchen or the nursery was the lot of only a very few.

The enhanced growth, economic, geographic, and demographic, of the prerevolutionary decades served only to eradicate the opportunities for female independence that had been present in the early colonial era. By the eighteenth century, by which time some 90 percent of American colonists derived their living from the land, most women's lives revolved around the family, the farm, and the field. Diaries from the period provide a glimpse into the lives of the literate, at least. One of these, Mary Cooper from Long Island, detailed a life of drudgery and almost constant toil. Christmas Eve of 1768 found her "tired almost to death," having been "drying and ironing my cloths till almost brake of day." On May 13 of the following year, she recorded "Much hard worke" that left her feeling "dirty and distrest." Two months after that (July 13), she reflected on the fact that it had been "forty years sinc I left my father's house and come here, and here have I seene little els but harde labour and sorrows, crosses of every kind. I think," she concluded, "in every respect the state of my affairs is more then forty times worse then when I came here first, except that I am nearer the desierered haven."

The precise cause of Mary's misery was not the ironing pile alone. A clue to what was worrying her appeared in her diary in August. "My hearte is burnt with anger and discontent," she confided, "want of every nessesary thing in life and in constant feare of gapeing credtors." Fear of poverty was compounded in her case, as in so many others, by the terror of disease. Smallpox, in particular, was a very real danger. When an outbreak occurred in Boston in 1721, Cotton Mather, for one, was willing to explore the possibilities of inoculation against the virus, but fifty years later, in Long Island, the practice was not yet widespread. It was with relief that Mary Cooper reported her daughter's recovery from the disease, but she acknowledged that she "frighted much about the small pox" in her diary entries for early 1771.[7]

Disease, debt, and debilitating physical labor defined the lot of many of America's white colonists in the eighteenth century. The New World's wealth was never evenly divided, and as the colonial population grew, expanding into the hinterlands of the first settlements and developing urban centers on the eastern seaboard, so the inequalities of life grew more apparent. Some of these inequalities were gender-based, some racial, some simply financial, many a reflection of the interaction of at least two of these components. For women, being 3,000 miles from Europe, in an environment where, as was the case in New England, women actually outnumbered men, counted for little in terms of the opportunities it afforded them. This was not an egalitarian world, even as the men in it increasingly debated the limits of authority and challenged traditional expressions of dominance, whether emanating from the pulpit, the political chamber, or the proprietary edicts that still governed some of the British settlements. In several important respects, America in the early eighteenth century was a world of challenge and change, but at the heart of its many transitions – religious, political, cultural, ideological – some things remained fixed. The male colonist may have been moving toward becoming "the American, this new man," but the "new principles" that Crèvecoeur ascribed to him did not yet include gender equality. The new woman would have to wait, for quite a while, as it turned out, in the case of some states.

Generalizations are, naturally, invidious, as there were enormous regional, social, and cultural variations across the Americas by 1700. The British colonies were placed, geographically but also in terms of trade, between two powerful European empires, those of France and Spain, both of which they had issues with, and in the midst of a country that was still home to at least some of America's aboriginal populations. Between 1700 and 1770, the population of these colonies soared from 265,000 to more than 2.3 million. It did so in the broader context of an overall population decline since 1600, because the rise of white, and black, society was paralleled by, if not always predicated on, the decline of the native populations. Estimates vary, but it has been proposed that only around 5 percent of the native population of New England in 1600 was still there by 1700. For that 5 percent, however, and for the other native nations in the interior, change was not what they had been seeking, but it was something they had to accommodate.

Pushed farther into the interior, and forced to compete not only with the white settlers but with other native groups for land and resources, many of America's aboriginal peoples, especially those in the South, simply vanished altogether over the course of the eighteenth century, absorbed into other tribes or wiped out by disease. In his historical account of the development of Pennsylvania and New Jersey and the impact this had on the Delaware, or Lenni Lenape ("original people"), one contemporary observer, the Quaker Gabriel Thomas, reported that "the Indians themselves say that two of them die for every one Christian that comes in here." Pennsylvania, in this period, was described by indentured servant William Moraley, who arrived in 1729, as the "best poor man's country in the world," but opportunity for some came at a high price for others.[8] For many white settlers, Moraley included, the "best poor man's country" proved to be no such thing. The streets of Philadelphia were no more paved with gold than any imagined urban utopia ever had been. For people such as the Lenni Lenape, it was far worse. Change for the native peoples was never for the better.

On one front there was continuity: conflict. This particularly affected New England. At the start of the eighteenth century, native-English conflict in the region was rather more complex than it had been several decades previously, during King Philip's War. Naturally enough, that particular armed exchange left both sides wary, and occasional, if relatively isolated, incidences of violence between them marred relations after 1676. Tensions were heightened, however, by the outbreak of another period of warfare between France and Britain, the War of the Spanish Succession (Queen Anne's War), which began in 1702. As its European name suggests, it was not France alone that Britain faced. In the war's opening year, Spanish forces, too, launched raids against British settlements, mainly in South Carolina, while British forces retaliated with assaults against Spanish missions in Florida.

In that year, in northern New England, the colonists faced an increasing number of raids by the Abenaki, who enjoyed good relations with the French. The more isolated settlements in Maine, New Hampshire, and Massachusetts were especially at risk. One of the most susceptible towns was Deerfield, Massachusetts, which experienced a number of minor attacks followed, in February 1704, by a larger-scale combined French and Abenaki raid that resulted in more than fifty of its inhabitants dead and another hundred of so taken into captivity. Yet even before the main attack on Deerfield, some of New England's leaders, at least, advocated extreme retaliatory measures against the Abenaki. One of them was Boston minister Solomon Stoddard, who advised Massachusetts' governor Joseph Dudley that the people of Deerfield were "much discouraged" by the events. His solution was that they should go on the offensive. If "dogs were trained up to hunt Indians as they do bears," he proposed, "we should quickly be sensible of a great advantage thereby. The dogs would be an extreme terror to the Indians," who, he pointed out, "are not much afraid of us." He reminded Dudley that such methods had proved effective in Virginia, and argued that the Abenaki should "be looked upon as thieves and murderers," who "do acts of hostility without proclaiming war." They were, he asserted, like wolves, and should "be dealt withal as wolves."[9]

Stoddard's advice was certainly informed by a white racialist mindset – he said nothing about the French, for example – but his concerns stemmed from no great feeling of superiority. They arose from fear. Caught between two warring European worlds, colonists like Stoddard naturally began to resent what were increasingly perceived as foreign conflicts, warfare that threatened their world but that should not have been part of their world. The fear was both physical and cultural. Loss of life was one aspect of it. Loss of the still living was another. In the aftermath of what became known as the Deerfield "massacre," many of the captured colonists managed, despite having to endure a forced march into New France (Quebec), eventually to return to Massachusetts. Some did not. One of these, Eunice Williams, was the daughter of Deerfield's minister, John Williams. To her father's dismay, Eunice chose not to return, married into the Mohawk (Iroquois people) tribe, and became a Roman Catholic. Eunice never entirely broke contact with her white family, but from the moment of her capture in 1704 she was, from their perspective, culturally, socially, and spiritually, lost to them forever.

In his account of events, *The Redeemed Captive Returning to Zion* (1707), Eunice's father certainly interpreted her loss as both cultural and Catholic threat to his faith and to the English way of life. Yet this was not his daughter's perspective. For Eunice Williams herself, although under circumstances she would not likely have chosen, colonial America certainly proved to be a land of opportunity. She succeeded in achieving what Crèvecoeur would later identify as a uniquely American identity. She left behind her "ancient prejudices and manners" and adopted new ones, and fully embraced "the new mode of life" that cultural exchange could offer. For her family, for most white settlers, however, this was not quite the opportunity they had anticipated, nor was it one that they welcomed.

From her brother Stephen's diary, in which he recorded every piece of news about and attempts to redeem Eunice, it is clear that as her family saw it, Eunice's forced apostasy, her rejection of Protestantism, was of greater concern, almost, than her decision to build a life and family among the Mohawk. The Jesuit-taught Mohawk's religion, more than their race, was the problem. Eunice's last visit to New England was in 1761. Some of her descendents returned to visit the graves of their white ancestors in 1837. By that point, of course, America was a separate nation. The borders with what was by then British-controlled Canada were closed. Only the native peoples of the region, legally separate from both Britain and the United States, could transcend them. White Americans had long since made their decision about what side they were on. In the end, contra Crèvecoeur, there would be no easy merging of peoples, cultures, and faiths in the New World; as Eunice was reported saying in 1713, on being urged to return to New England, *"zaghte oghte"* – this "may not be."[10]

'Tis Time to Part

As was the case for Eunice Williams and her extended family, both native and English, eighteenth-century America comprised a collection of parallel lives that developed in tandem but rarely touched. The development was rapid, however, both demographically and geographically (Figure 3.4). By the mid-eighteenth century, the growing population of the British colonies was on the move, extending far beyond the original colonial boundaries. By the time of the Revolutionary War, British America's geographic spread had more than doubled, from around 360,000 to more than 830,000 square miles. In part this growth resulted from the termination of Queen Anne's War. In the same year as Eunice rejected, once and for all, her English roots, the Treaty of Utrecht terminated the war that had removed her from her people. For Britain, this meant the acquisition of territory formerly controlled by France, and an opportunity to extend her settlements further inland from the eastern seaboard, up the coast into New Hampshire and Maine, inland into the Hudson Valley, south into the valleys between the Blue Ridge Mountains (of Virginia) and the Appalachians, and into the Piedmont region.

These settlements had little in common. New England as a whole was relatively homogeneous, in terms both of population and culture, compared with many of the other colonies, certainly compared to Pennsylvania or New York. Philadelphia, in particular, was attractive to

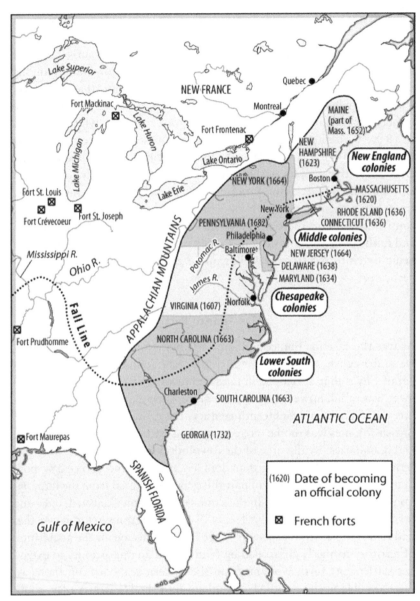

FIGURE 3.4. Map of colonies.

immigrants because, as a Quaker settlement, there was no military service requirement there, taxes were low, and it was relatively peaceful. As a result, a greater variety of immigrants, both in terms of origins and status, poured into Pennsylvania between 1720 and 1740. The southern colonies, those on the Chesapeake, the Carolinas, and Georgia, saw a massive increase in their slave population, but also tended to absorb a greater variety of English, Scots, Scots-Irish (from Ulster), and Irish, although, equally, many of these settled in the fast-growing urban seaports of Boston, New York, and Newport, or Philadelphia, which also attracted high numbers of German migrants. These towns represented four of the five major urban centers in colonial America, and it was notable even at that stage that they were in the North. Only Charleston, in South Carolina, was of comparable size. Purely in percentage terms, these seaport towns grew more slowly than the colonies as a whole. In 1720, they held around 7 percent of the population, and by 1770, only half that. Yet they would have a major impact on America's move away from Great Britain, positioned as they were between the colonial settlements and the European world. More so than in the rural areas, all humankind was in the urban seaports, and if common cause was going to be identified, it stood the best chance in their kaleidoscopic environments. They were the catalysts of revolution.

The elements of revolution, however, were scattered across the colonies, and so widely scattered that historians since the nineteenth century have been kept occupied in pulling them together. At its most basic, however, the gradual development of the idea later expressed in the Declaration of Independence, that "these United Colonies are, and of right ought to be Free and Independent States," cohered around the complementary concepts of liberty and slavery. These, in turn, emerged in the specific context of constant colonial conflict, of Britain's increasingly intrusive attempts to exert greater control over its American colonies, and in the broader context of a growing continental perspective among the colonists. At the same time, even as late as 1760, one of America's most famous Founding Fathers, the diplomat and scientist Benjamin Franklin, not only remained of the opinion that any union of the colonies against Britain was unlikely, but expressed it, consciously, from an English perspective. In discussing the state of affairs in "our colonies," Franklin, then in London, dismissed the idea that their growth "may render them *dangerous*." Britain's America colonies, he stressed, "are not only under different governors, but have different forms of government, different laws, different interests, and some of them different religious persuasions, and different manners." Moreover, he added, their "jealousy of each other is so great" that nothing "but the immediate command of the crown" could ever unify them, and then only imperfectly. Yet Franklin ultimately hedged his bets, adding:

When I say such an union is impossible, I mean without the most grievous tyranny and oppression. People who have property in a country which they may lose, and privileges which they may endanger, are generally dispos'd to be quiet; and even to bear much, rather than hazard all. While the government is mild and just, while important civil and religious rights are secure, such subjects will be dutiful and obedient. The waves do not rise but when the winds blow.[11]

For the colonists, the property and privileges they enjoyed comprised people as well as land. The growing opposition to what was perceived as unjust authority being imposed on the colonies took place in an environment in which certain types of authority were being more rigorously imposed within the colonies. The dynamics of this process were never driven by the simple juxtaposition of the morality of the New England sermon with the materialism of the southern slave code. Quite apart from anything else, slavery in this period was a northern urban as much as a southern rural reality. In terms of percentage of population, there were as many slaves in the northern towns as in the tobacco-growing regions of Virginia and Maryland. In New York alone, at the end of the seventeenth century (1698), some 35 percent of families owned slaves. By the early eighteenth century (1703), that figure had crept upward, to 41 percent. Between 1710 and 1742, in Boston, the white population doubled, but the slave population quadrupled to 8.5 percent of the population as a whole.

The winds of change that were blowing partly originated with Franklin himself, who managed to distil and disseminate some of the more philosophical concepts of his age both via his publication, under the pseudonym of "Richard Saunders," his collection of "Poor Richard's Almanacks," and in his general – and official – writings and correspondence. His Almanacks began publication in 1732 and appeared over the next quarter of a century. Selling around 10,000 copies per annum, they were the best sellers of their day. Juxtaposed with, for example, the harsh reality of indentured servant William Moraley's experiences in Pennsylvania, the fictional "Poor Richard" inhabited an America of the imagination, in which virtue was its own reward and hard work the road to riches. The unpleasant reality that, for some, no matter how hard they worked, success would never come, or for an increasing number of settlers in both

North and South the hard work in question was someone else's, did not impinge on Franklin's upbeat advice to his countrymen and countrywomen. Writing to his friend, London merchant Peter Collinson, Franklin suggested that aiding the unfortunate might constitute "fighting against the order of God and Nature, which perhaps has appointed Want and Misery as the proper Punishments for, and Cautions against as well as necessary consequences of Idleness and Extravagancy."[12]

Such sentiments were hardly unique to Franklin, or to the eighteenth century, yet they had a particular potency for colonial America. In part they achieved momentum in the context of what has been termed the "American Enlightenment," the absorption by the colonial elites of Lockean liberalist ideas of natural rights, liberty, and the social contract. Certainly Locke's writings had an influence once the colonists had made the decision to seek separation from Britain. Sections of his *Second Treatise on Civil Government* (1690) were echoed in the Declaration of Independence. How influential his ideas were in bringing about the decision that led to that Declaration, at least absent the other forces at work in the colonies, may be a moot point. Locke was, for America at least, a man for all seasons, as capable of advising the proprietors of the Carolinas on how best to retain hereditary privilege as he was at advocating natural rights in the *tabula rasa* that was, in his philosophy, both man and America. In that more general sense, Locke's ideas certainly jelled with a growing optimism and belief in opportunity in the later colonial period, one that Franklin both epitomized and encouraged. In some senses this harked back to the Puritans' original mission statement of their settlement venture as a "city on a hill." By the mid-eighteenth century, this idealized exemplar was increasingly located more broadly in the varied colonial landscapes of British America, although not yet aligned with "the cause of all mankind."

Discussions and debates over the potential for the perfectibility of man, nature and the New World certainly extended beyond the dinner-party conversations of the colonial elites. These reached a wider audience through sermons such as Boston minister Jonathan Mayhew's *A Discourse Concerning Unlimited Submission* (1750). Written on the anniversary, and to defend, the execution of Charles I, and reprinted several times on both sides of the Atlantic, Mayhew's argument addressed the question of how far "persons of a private character, ought to yield to those who are vested with authority." His answer was, not far at all if the authority in question was "*one* unreasonable, ambitious and cruel man" – the same point made by Franklin a decade later. In 1750, however,

Mayhew, no more than Franklin, was not yet advocating the throwing off of colonial shackles, because at that point, British authority was not obviously overbearing. For Mayhew, like Franklin, the important thing was that the colonists to "learn to be *free*, and to be *loyal*." At the same time, he reminded his congregation, and the broader audience beyond them, that "government is *sacred*, and not to be *trifled* with."[13]

Government in the colonies was, of course, taken very seriously indeed. In most cases, the basic rules were set down in the original colonial charter, or some carefully reworked version of the same, and power and authority divided and, it was hoped, balanced by a tripartite division that replicated the King-Lords-Commons arrangement of the British Parliament, post-Glorious Revolution, namely the Governor, Council, and Assembly structure. Although, as Franklin had noted, there were great differences between the colonies as far as legal and administrative affairs were concerned, this was not necessarily a cause for concern. Similarly, the law was neither uniformly imposed nor, indeed, understood insofar as it applied to the colonies in this period. This may not be surprising. Gabriel Thomas had considered it a point of honor for Pennsylvanians that there were so few lawyers or physicians among them, and hoped that the colony would "never have occasion for the Tongue of the one, nor the Pen of the other" because both were "equally destructive to Mens Estates and Lives," and Franklin, similarly, once had "Poor Richard" observe that "a country man between two lawyers is like a fish between two cats."[14] Clearly, some colonists believed that not every part of the Old World had made it, or ever should make it, across the Atlantic. This was a brave new world indeed that had no lawyers in it.

Such sly digs at the legal profession, hardly unique either to America or to the period, nevertheless hinted at the popular attitudes held by the colonists in the mid-eighteenth century, as well as at the divide between the urban and the rural in the colonial landscape. Of course there were lawyers to spare in the urban seaports and across the colonies: lawyers, merchants, traders in people and produce, a fledgling corporate and commercial class with the specialized knowledge and the working capital necessary to develop America's trade in the markets of Europe and Africa. This was a class for whom Britain's mercantilist policies were of greater concern than for the inhabitants of some of more inland settlements; a class whose own concerns, indeed, frequently took precedence. Yet between 1750 and 1776, the interests of the rural and urban populations, the farmers and the financiers, began to draw closer together. If not exactly singing from the same song sheet, increasingly they were participants in a developing debate, to which ministers such as Jonathan Mayhew contributed, over government, over authority in general, and, more specifically, over colonial management. The majority of colonists in the mid-eighteenth century probably did not have a copy of Locke's *Second Treatise of Civil Government* on their bedside tables, but in due course, they might have had Pennsylvanian lawyer John Dickinson's *Letters from a Farmer in Pennsylvania* (1768) or, later, Thomas Paine's *Common Sense* (1776). What prompted their sudden interest in this kind of reading matter comprised a complex combination of conflict and, paradoxically, the cessation of conflict.

Theoretically, the one thing that should have drawn the rural and urban populations of the American colonies together in the mid-eighteenth century was warfare, the persistent threat of warfare, and, specifically, the outbreak of the final war for empire of the eighteenth century – the Seven Years' War, or French and Indian War (1756–1763). Yet the one thing, oddly enough, that did little to foment colonial unity was the need for defense. Two years prior to the declaration of war by England on France in 1756, Franklin had devised a proposal, the Albany Plan of Union, that, he hoped, would draw the colonies together and simultaneously address the French and Indian threat by establishing an intercolonial confederation with tax-raising powers to finance a colonial army. Franklin later suggested that it was British opposition to what was perceived as too much devolved power that sank his plan, but in fact the colonial assemblies were no more enthusiastic about it. When war with France was officially declared, the extent of colonial divisions became obvious. It proved impossible to persuade the various assemblies to pull together against the French threat. Worlds unto themselves, the separate colonies perceived no common cause in opposition to the French and barely registered events beyond their own borders.

What finally began to draw the various colonial interest groups together was not warfare itself, but its longer-term impact. The effects of the French and Indian War were felt in both rural and urban areas. The rural settlements, particularly along the Pennsylvania and Virginia frontiers, had experienced the war directly, and devastated communities, widows and orphans, were the result. The urban seaports at first benefitted enormously from the war, mostly from the billeting of British troops there. Some 2,000 arrived in 1755, another 11,000 in 1757, and a further 12,000 the following year. The economic impact of this sudden and captive market was huge. It was not to last. Although the Seven Years' War officially ended in 1763, in North America the fighting ceased in 1760.

When it did, the British army disappeared as swiftly as it had arrived. The subsequent loss of lucrative military contracts impacted merchants and smaller retailers alike, in New England and on the Chesapeake, New York and Philadelphia, and the resultant economic depression was only exacerbated by the rise in taxes that the war had occasioned. Yet although the troops had left, leaving debt, inflated prices, and unemployment behind them, not all of them actually went that far. About 10,000 of the 25,000 British regulars sent to the colonies to engage the French remained in North America after the Treaty of Paris terminated the war, not in the colonies themselves, but close enough that the colonists were aware of their presence, and unnerved by it.

This was, therefore, not the best time for the British to start imposing greater economic control over the colonies, yet in some senses it was inevitable that they would try. For one thing, the French and Indian War had proved a costly victory – it had doubled Britain's national debt – which someone had to pay for. For another, the outcome of the war had left Britain in undisputed control over a vast amount of territory, with a population neither familiar with English political practice nor, in some cases, with the English language (Figure 3.5). It was natural that thoughts turned toward its future. It was perhaps also natural that the existing thirteen colonies would resent any changes to the status quo, and the British had already experienced a degree of opposition immediately after hostilities had ceased in 1760 when they attempted to stamp out black-market trading with the enemy and Boston lawyer James Otis had argued against their right to do so.

Indeed, any perceived interference in colonial affairs could produce a response seemingly out of all proportion to the interjection itself. In what became known as the "Parson's Cause" case, the Virginian lawyer Patrick Henry, engaged to defend the proposal that Anglican ministers, traditionally paid in tobacco, might be remunerated in cash instead, voiced the accusation that the British king had "from being the father of his people, degenerated into a tyrant, and forfeited all rights to his subjects' obedience."[15] What the king's tyranny amounted to was a veto of the "Two Penny Act" in Virginia. The tobacco harvest of 1758 had been poor. The cost of tobacco had risen, from two to six pennies per pound, and the Virginia Legislature sought to minimize the impact of this by paying the clergy in cash, but at the lower rate. It was, in the end, all about money. A very great deal of what followed in terms of colonial opposition to the Crown was also about money, but not all. Ultimately, that made all the difference.

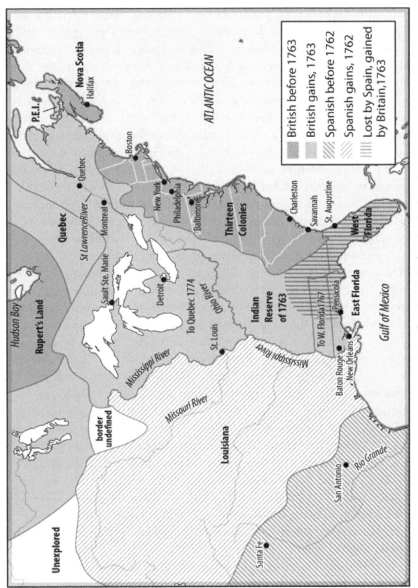

FIGURE 3.5. Map showing British gains in America.

Hindsight can, of course, be a significant barrier to comprehending the past. The series of colonial challenges to British authority after 1763 can too easily acquire a relentless momentum of their own as they progress, in strict chronological order, toward an inevitable outcome, the decision on the part of the colonies to seek separation from Britain. The Sugar Act and the Currency Act, both passed by Britain in 1764 as a means of raising revenue to pay for the French and Indian War, the Quartering Act and the Stamp Act of the following year, the Townshend Duties imposed in 1767, the arrival of British troops in Boston in 1768, the resultant "Boston Massacre" of 1770, and then the Tea Act of 1773 and the so-called "Intolerable Acts" of 1774, all frequently appear simply as signposts on a predetermined path at the end of which lay the First Continental Congress of 1774 and the opening salvo of the Revolutionary War on Lexington Green on the morning of April 19, 1775. Yet there was nothing inevitable about the road to revolution and, the rhetorical bombast of men such as Patrick Henry aside, no widespread sense, in 1763, that the British crown, then in the form of George III, was behaving in a manner likely to arouse the suspicions of Jonathan Mayhew or Benjamin Franklin.

The colonists were naturally concerned at the sudden interest in their affairs. Any attempt, by any government, anywhere and at any time in history, to raise taxes is likely also to raise objections. The American colonists were hardly unusual in their vociferous opposition to the increase of duties on imports via the Sugar Act, or to the attempt to control credit by banning the production of paper money in the colonies via the Currency Act, which exacerbated an already existing trade deficit in the colonial economy. Similarly, the billeting of troops in the colonies, under the remit of the Quartering Act of 1765, was regarded as intrusive, despite the fact that the merchants and traders of the urban seaports, only five years previously, had been dismayed to see these troops, and their pay, leave. Opposition to these measures tended to be fairly localized, both in terms of impact and response. Only the Stamp Act of 1765, another revenue-raising measure that specified special stamps should be affixed to all documents, from newspapers through legal documents down to playing cards, managed to upset everyone and produce anything approaching a united colonial reaction against it.

The Stamp Act Congress of 1765 summarized the colonial position in the first "Declaration of Rights and Grievances" (when the grievances in question did not abate, a second document of that title appeared in 1774). This emphasized colonial allegiance to the British Crown while simultaneously stressing that the colonies occupied something of an outlier position in parliamentary terms. In short, they could not be represented, but it appeared that they could be taxed without their agreement. This, the Congress asserted, was wrong. The "only representatives of the people of these colonies are persons chosen therein, by themselves," it stressed, "no taxes ever have been or can be constitutionally imposed on them but by their respective legislatures." The colonists managed to get the Stamp Act repealed, but it was a Pyrrhic victory. What the British gave with one hand they deftly removed with the other. The Declaratory Act (1766), which accorded the British parliament "full power and authority to make laws and statutes of sufficient force and validity to bind the colonies and people of *America*, subjects of the crown of *Great Britain*, in all cases whatsoever" (emphasis in the original), was imposed in its place.[16]

Although frequently pounced on as one of the first expressions of the "no taxation without representation" rallying cry ascribed to the American Revolution, the Stamp Act was not exactly a case of print culture by proxy fomenting American nationalism. In attempting to, quite literally, impose their stamp on the colonies, the British Crown certainly inspired a united opposition, but not a lasting one. Not that the problem went away; far from it. The Townshend Duties, named for the then-Chancellor of the Exchequer, of 1767 sought to impose duties on an increasing range of colonial imports, prompting James Otis's *Letters from a Pennsylvania Farmer* (1768), which furthered the argument against taxation. This argument took to the streets of Boston two years later when a mob sought to prevent British troops from enforcing the revenue laws, and five colonists were killed. Yet the "Boston Massacre," although the subject of what has become one of the most famous images of American opposition to the British (Figure 3.6), did not inaugurate a mass uprising against the British; but Boston's role in bringing about the Revolution was not over yet. When the conflagration came, its spark was, of all things, tea.

The famous "Boston Tea Party" of 1773 – a response to the Tea Act of that year, which, in seeking to prop up the flagging financial fortunes of the East India Company, threatened the profits of colonial merchants – was what brought the colonies and the Crown into direct conflict. Yet even the dramatic gesture on the part of the colonists of hurling tea chests into Boston Harbor need not have escalated into armed opposition to Britain but for the British reaction. The Coercive (Intolerable) Acts of 1774 sought to bring Massachusetts to heel, but instead prompted a unified reaction across the colonies against the British Crown. This was no longer simply about revenue raising or economic control, but about

FIGURE 3.6. Paul Revere, "The Bloody Massacre Perpetrated in King Street" (1770). Revere's engraving of an original by Henry Pelham was not the only visual rendition of the attack on the colonial mob by British troops, but it was the most widely distributed. It was designed for effect rather than accuracy and has been critiqued for, among other things, portraying a blue sky when the massacre actually occurred at night (the moon, top left, does indicate that the hour was late). Leaving aside the question of how Revere might have conveyed events that took place in the dark, the more interesting "tweak" in the image concerns the fallen colonial in the middle of the picture. This was Crispus Attucks, the first black colonial to die in the Revolutionary cause, but here revealingly rendered white.

control, period. The Coercive Acts closed the port of Boston, sought to bring the entire colony of Massachusetts under tighter royal control, effectively removed the threat of trial for royal officials by stipulating they be tried in England, and proposed a more rigorous enforcement of the Quartering Act. Tangential legislation that sought to formalize and extend the Province of Quebec (the Quebec Act) and that recognized Catholic dominance of the region only intensified colonial unease, indeed growing anger, at British policies.

It was against this background that the thirteen British colonies of North America finally made the shift from a collection of discrete jurisdictions barely communicating with each other in 1763 to an almost coherent body of individuals who, by 1776, were able to equate their quibbles with the British Crown with the "cause of all mankind." Yet they might never have done so had there not appeared, in 1776, an influential little pamphlet, composed by Thomas Paine and entitled *Common Sense*. Even after the First Continental Congress convened in Philadelphia in September 1774, as the colonists and the British moved toward open armed conflict in Lexington and Concord over the winter of 1774–75 and the spring of 1775, and the Second Continental Congress of May 1775 adopted its "Declaration of the Causes and Necessities of Taking up Arms," even then there was no universal move toward separation or a clearly articulated expression of what was at stake. Paine provided one.

Paine's pamphlet was brief, and its brevity ensured its impact. He cut through much of the ambivalence affecting not just the delegates to the Continental Congresses, but the more widespread uncertainty across the colonies between 1774 and 1776 as to their situation. To an extent, Paine flattered the colonists by suggesting that their fight against British oppression was "the cause of all mankind." Certainly his ideas were grounded in the more universal antimonarchical, republican rhetoric of the age. Yet they had particular resonance in a world comprising such a heterogeneous population of individuals who had traveled to America in search of profit or religious tolerance, opportunity or escape, some of whom had never intended to go there at all, but who nevertheless found themselves in this New World, forced, or willing, to make a new start in it. That was what Paine himself, the corset-maker from Norfolk, had done. In that sense, he knew his main audience, he exemplified it, but his message had a wider resonance.

For those in the urban seaports whose profits were threatened, whose trade was disrupted, Paine's arguments were undoubtedly persuasive. "Europe is too thickly planted with kingdoms to be long at peace," he observed, "and whenever a war breaks out between England and any foreign power, the trade of America goes to ruin, *because of her connection with Britain.*" For those on the frontiers, who had suffered so much during the various periods of conflict that had culminated with the French and Indian War, Paine's sustained attack on the rule of kings that had "laid . . . the world in blood and ashes" would hardly have seemed off the mark. "France and Spain never were, nor perhaps ever will be our enemies as *Americans,*" he wrote, "but as our being the *subjects of Great Britain.*" Only through separation from Britain could the colonies ever be secure. "Every thing that is right or natural pleads for separation," Paine urged his readers. "The blood of the slain, the weeping voice of nature cries 'TIS TIME TO PART.'" Yet Paine was doing much more than listing grievances long held, if not yet acted on, by the colonists. By addressing them as *"Americans,"* he was offering them not just a route out of empire, but a path to a new identity, an identity whose origins lay in warfare and whose future would be secured through it, an identity that, by the time Paine published *Common Sense,* the colonists were already trying on for size: that of a nation in arms.

4

Self-Evident Truths

Founding the Revolutionary Republic

I do not mean to exclude altogether the idea of patriotism. I know it exists, and I know it has done much in the present contest. But I will venture to assert, that a great and lasting War can never be supported on this principle alone. It must be aided by a prospect of interest or some reward.

(George Washington to John Banister, April 21, 1778)

"We hold these truths to be self-evident," announced the Declaration of Independence of 1776, "that all men are created equal, that they are endowed by their Creator with certain unalienable rights, that among these are life, liberty, and the pursuit of happiness." Inspiring words, yet they hardly reflected the reality of colonial America nor bore much relation to the nation's development once independence was achieved. Yet for America as a nation, this was a clear-cut case of, as the *The Rubáiyát of Omar Khayyam* has it, the moving finger "having writ/Moves on; nor all thy Piety nor wit/Shall lure it back to cancel half a Line,/Nor all thy Tears wash out a Word of it." Such ambitious sentiments, once having been set down in plain manuscript, could not be taken back.

America's Founding Fathers believed, in drafting the Declaration, that they were simply defending their decision to separate from Great Britain. In fact, what they had produced was a vision statement, one that would commit their immediate progeny, and the many generations following them, to make real an ideal that these colonists may have believed in but most certainly never lived up to. At its inception, the American nation encapsulated the paradox of slaveholders preaching liberty, a fact that haunts the nation to this day. At the same time, from the moment of transition from colonies to nation, America developed under a self-imposed injunction to marry principle with practice. Like Banquo's ghost at the federal feast, the specter of those words, "all men are created equal," and the accompanying assertion that this was a "self-evident truth" kept popping up at inconvenient moments to rattle the white republican cage.

In 1776, the reality of slavery in colonial America lent strength to Thomas Paine's argument in *Common Sense* that the colonies were, in some senses, enslaved by Great Britain. Slavery was never simply an abstract concept or a rhetorical device in eighteenth-century colonial discourse, but a way of life for a growing number of colonists. Yet neither was it a term that could be pinned down with precision. Both slavery and freedom, indeed, proved to be slippery concepts for the new nation. When, in the mid-nineteenth century, Americans were fighting each other in the Civil War (1861–65), the Union President Abraham Lincoln summed up the respective positions of North and South. "We all declare for liberty," Lincoln observed, "but in using the same *word* we do not all mean the same *thing*. With some the word liberty may mean for each man to do as he pleases with himself, and the product of his labor; while with others the same word may mean for some men to do as they please with other men, and the product of other men's labor."[1] It was the revolutionary generation, however, who really established this precedent, this paradoxical perspective on liberty that, almost a century later, Americans were still struggling with.

The inconsistencies inherent in the identity of the "freeborn Englishman" emerged in the colonies in the seventeenth and eighteenth centuries. White political ideologies – which revolved around twinned, but quite distinct, understandings of liberty – and black social reality rarely took cognizance of each other in this period. On the one hand, there was the republican position, which posited liberty as essentially a civic and social construct, dependent on an active and informed citizenship, which the state could defend but could also destroy. With voting rights increasingly removed from free blacks, there was little room for them within republican discourse. On the other hand, there was Lockean liberalism, which located liberty as an individual right, a universal right, the "cause of all mankind," which the state could cultivate but also curtail. With so many blacks enslaved, the whole notion of individual rights was nugatory for that demographic, too. The entire philosophical debate that lay behind separation from Britain consisted, in most respects, of whites talking to each other.

Between Britain and America there was a natural cross-fertilization of discussion and debate about liberty and arbitrary authority, over the role of the citizen and the rule of the state, over the balance of power between the government and the governed. Thomas Paine's opening argument in *Common Sense*, for example, set out the republican position. It essentially summed up the perspective of the English "Commonwealth men," such as John Trenchard and Thomas Gordon, whose views on state and society, and on the state of society, met a more receptive audience in the colonies than in their home country. With the groundwork already laid, Paine was preaching to the at least half-converted when he asserted that "[s]ociety in every state is a blessing, but government even in its best state is but a necessary evil; in its worst an intolerable one."

Trenchard and Gordon's series of essays, published as *Cato's Letters* in the *London Journal* and the *British Journal* in the early 1720s, championed republicanism and freedom of conscience. By the mid-eighteenth century, their arguments, and the *Letters* themselves, were widely circulated in the colonies. Their impact in 1776 was that much greater because of Paine's summation of a discussion that originally ran to 144 letters in a more readily digestible, pamphlet form, and because of the opportunity provided by the British colonial experience in America. It is, after all, easier to build from scratch than to renovate. What holds true for children and buildings might, some colonists hoped, be true for nations. Paine certainly thought so. "The infant state of the Colonies" was, he argued, what made the time right for independence, for the emergence of a new nation established on the principle of natural rights. "Youth," he assured the colonists, "is the seed time of good habits, as well in nations as individuals."

Yet by 1776, the colonies had not acquired especially good habits and had developed some appalling ones as far as race relations were concerned. Whether the white colonists discussed, and ultimately defended, these habits utilizing either the rhetoric of republicanism (Paine) or the language of liberalism (Locke), or a combination of both, they proved incapable of squaring the circle of natural rights and slavery. A fundamental tenet of their argument in defense of property was the right to define it in people; in short, to own slaves. The colonists could concur with Paine's critique of monarchy, namely that that men "who look upon themselves as born to reign, and others to obey, soon grow insolent; selected from the rest of mankind their minds are early poisoned by importance," yet miss completely the striking parallels with slaveholding in their own society.

Not all did. The author of the Declaration of Independence and future American president, Thomas Jefferson, certainly spotted the flaw in the republican argument; hardly surprising, given that he was so instrumental in framing its American variant in the first place. Yet for Jefferson, too, slavery held multiple meanings. In his response to the Intolerable Acts, *A Summary View of the Rights of British America* (1774), Jefferson critiqued what he described as "a series of oppressions" imposed on the white population of the colonies as indicative of "a deliberate and systematical plan of reducing us to slavery." This virtual enslavement was very different from the harsher reality of nonwhite chattel slavery in the colonies, the abolition of which, Jefferson asserted – more in hope than expectation – was "the great object of desire in those colonies, where it was unhappily introduced in their infant state."

Certainly several colonies had attempted, via their assemblies, to impose prohibitively high duties on African slave imports, and the British parliament had blocked any such attempt, but the motives of each side were not necessarily informed by any moral considerations. By preventing the abolition of slave imports, Jefferson declared, the British Crown had preferred the "immediate advantages of a few African corsairs to the lasting interests of the American states, and to the rights of human nature, deeply wounded by this infamous practice."[2] Jefferson placed too positive a spin on colonial behavior. The colonists wanted tax revenue, not the source of that revenue to cease. There was little evidence in support of Jefferson's belief, and a fair amount contradicting it, that the colonies wished to abolish chattel slavery.

This was not a theme that Jefferson relinquished readily. It was one he struggled with. Time and again he returned to it, in the Declaration of Independence, in his later *Notes on the State of Virginia* (1787). In the latter, he contemplated the "unhappy influence" that slavery had on the white population. "The whole commerce between master and slave is a perpetual exercise of the most boisterous passions," he asserted, comprising "the most unremitting despotism on the one part, and degrading submissions on the other." Slavery, Jefferson understood, had an enervating influence on the industry and economy of white society, but far worse was its destructive impact on the foundations of the new nation itself. Can "the liberties of a nation be thought secure when we have removed their only firm basis, a conviction in the minds of the people that their liberties are the gift of God?" Jefferson asked. It was a rhetorical question, and he knew it. "Indeed," he concluded, "I tremble for my country when I reflect that God is just: that his justice cannot sleep forever."[3]

The decision of the country in question not to abolish slavery at the same time as it abolished its colonial ties with Great Britain was not, then, entirely the fault of the man who drafted its Declaration of Independence. Indeed, in Jefferson's original version, the Declaration had a great deal more to say about slavery than its final draft suggested. In its first incarnation, the final and, from Jefferson's perspective, perhaps the most conclusive of all the heinous crimes that George III had perpetrated on the colonies was that he had "waged cruel war against human nature itself, violating its most sacred rights of life & liberty in the persons of a distant people who never offended him, captivating & carrying them into slavery in another hemisphere, or to incur miserable death in their transportation thither."[4] Jefferson's desire to devolve the blame for the slave trade onto Great Britain may have had much to do with the fact that it is difficult to preach liberty from behind an auction block, and the colonies were, when he put pen to paper in their name, seeking to argue their case not just before Great Britain, but in full view of an interested world audience.

That world audience included renowned author and critic Samuel Johnson, already well known in the colonies not just for his famous Dictionary but in part through the publication of his novel, *The History of Rasselas, Prince of Abissinia* (1759), which was published in America in 1768. As participants in the larger Atlantic world of commerce, consumerism, and print culture, much of which cohered around slavery and the slave trade, American colonists and the British alike were primed to peruse Johnson's later defense of the Intolerable Acts. This took the form of a pamphlet, "Taxation No Tyranny: An Answer to the Resolutions and Address of the American Congress" (1775), in which Johnson, contra Jefferson, argued that what he described as antipatriotic "prejudices" against the British Crown were no more than "the abortions of folly impregnated by faction." They were, he suggested, "born only to scream and perish." Even more memorable was the pithy sound bite, one that would be reiterated time and again until slavery in America was abolished, with which he concluded his main argument. "We are told," he observed, "that the subjection of Americans may tend to the diminution of our own liberties; an event, which none but very perspicacious politicians are able to foresee. If slavery be thus fatally contagious," he asked, "how is it that we hear the loudest yelps for liberty among the drivers of negroes?"[5] This was not a question that Jefferson could answer, although, goodness knows, he tried.

Whatever Jefferson believed, or hoped, many of his fellow countrymen had anything but abolition on their minds in the decades leading up to the Revolution. Late-eighteenth-century America was, as Britain was

FIGURE 4.1. Frontispiece for Phillis Wheatley's *Poems on Various Subjects, Religious and Moral* (London: A. Bell, 1773). The original engraving was by Scipio Moorhead.

too, largely dismissive of nonwhite cultures, was dismissive, indeed, of the very concept of culture being ascribed to any nonwhites. A case in point was the initial suspicion accorded America's first black, female poet, Phillis Wheatley (Figure 4.1). Wheatley, brought as a slave to America when she was a child and educated by her owners, the Wheatley family of Boston, published a volume of verse, *Poems on Various Subjects, Religious and Moral*, in 1773. Her work, however, required a preface in which a number of the great and the good white men of Boston, including the then-governor of Massachusetts, Thomas Hutchinson, confirmed, for the benefit of a skeptical readership, that the poems in front of them really were "written by PHILLIS, a young Negro Girl, who was but a few Years since, brought an uncultivated Barbarian from *Africa*." The men in question had the grace to acknowledge that Phillis had, since her arrival in the colonies, been laboring "under the Disadvantage of serving as a Slave in a Family in this town," a disadvantage that necessitated the verification of her intellectual and literary abilities by those whose gender and color accorded them the unquestioned acceptance that Phillis herself was denied.[6]

Phillis's lot as a slave in Boston, even had she not been singled out by her abilities, would have been significantly different from that of most slaves in the colonies on the eve of the American Revolution, the majority of whom, but certainly not all, lived in the south. The existence of slavery in Massachusetts may have been obscured by the gun smoke of the Revolution, but it was widespread enough in the early eighteenth century, still present well into the nineteenth, and cut across all sectors of society. It mainly concentrated in Boston and Newport, which was where most of the slave sales, both private and public, took place, to the dismay of Quaker abolitionist John Woolman who confided to his diary his distress at learning that slaves were being sold by a fellow Quaker. "I was desirous that Friends might petition the Legislature to use their endeavors to discourage the future importation of slaves," he confided, "for I saw that this trade was a great evil, and tended to multiply troubles." Yet Woolman feared that any such attempt would be pointless. As he realized, the colonies increasingly subscribed to "the idea of slavery being connected with the black color, and liberty with the white. And where such false ideas are twisted into our minds," he observed, "it is with difficulty we get fairly disentangled."[7]

Disentangling slave from free was particularly problematic in the northern towns, where slaves were employed in a wide variety of businesses as well as in the home, as waiters, coachmen, blacksmiths, hairdressers, and shoemakers, among many other roles. The urban environment also blurred the line between liberty and slavery. The assertion of free status by some who had been sold as slaves resulted in not a few court cases that highlighted the growing instability of the institution in the northern seaports. It was a rather different situation in the southern colonies. The ties that bound slavery to the northern colonies weakened as those in the south grew stronger. Consequently, the distinction between black and white too readily became synonymous with the difference between slavery and freedom. As colonial British America matured and stabilized, so the middle ground between slavery and freedom in the South constricted, leaving blacks less room for maneuver and committing whites to the maintenance of a slave system that, in economic terms, benefitted a relatively small number but, in social and cultural terms, increasingly defined the white way of life.

Despite the fact that, by 1776, Virginia was the most populous of the British colonies, with a fifth of the entire colonial population residing there, its capital, Williamsburg, sustained less than 2,000 permanent residents. With the notable exception of Charleston, South Carolina, the South in the colonial period did not develop urban centers of a size and population diversity comparable to Boston, New York, or Philadelphia. Slaves were consequently more crucial to the southern colonies, as they provided the agricultural expertise and the labor necessary for the development of the economy and society on the Chesapeake and in the rice- and indigo-growing regions of the Carolinas and, later, Georgia, after 1700. South Carolina sustained a strong Caribbean influence, but the other southern colonies increasingly imported slaves from, as Phillis Wheatley described her own origins, "*Afric's* fancy happy seat" rather than from the British Caribbean. This created a more bifurcated society in the South. Even in South Carolina, where the cause was not the importation of "non British" slaves but the tendency for wealthier slave owners to divide their time between their farms and Charleston. Black and white in the South, in short, increasingly led more separate lives than was the case in the northern towns, which exacerbated the tensions already inherent in the system.

If the urban seaports were, in the years leading up to the Revolution, increasingly dominated by a mercantile class, the southern colonies witnessed the emergence of a planter elite whose economic power was grounded in, and expressed through, the culture of consumption that permeated the Atlantic world. Their wealth, even if inherited, was frequently augmented by the profits from the slave trade, but the society they constructed was, perhaps in a deliberate denial of the harsh realities underpinning it, a self-conscious reflection of upper-class English culture transplanted to the colonies. This may not be surprising given that a great many of the wealthiest southern planters of the late-colonial period had been educated in England and continued to send their sons there for schooling. The southern elite, indeed, had much in common with the landed proprietors of England, as with the merchants of Liverpool and Glasgow in this period, whose stately piles and impressive town houses were constructed on the profits from slave labor. The difference was, they did not have to live proximate to the labor force in question. White southerners did, and this produced an extraordinary cultural complexity in the southern colonies and, in due course, in the post-Revolutionary and early-mid-nineteenth-century south that would define the region well into the twentieth century.

The wealth enjoyed by these planters was considerable by any standards. That of the so-called First Families of Virginia – the Carters, the Fitzhughs, the Lees, and the Randlophs – derived mainly from their substantial tobacco plantations, whereas in the South Carolina low country, the profits from the rice plantations swiftly transformed the colony into one of the wealthiest in British America and its main city, Charleston, into a thriving and conspicuously refined city. It was in many ways a privileged life, but never an entirely easy or secure one. White South Carolinians, by the mid-eighteenth century, still suffered from many of the problems that had beset the earlier colonists and were helpless in the face of diseases such as smallpox that periodically ravaged the colonies. Assuming the management of her husband's plantation on the Cooper River after his death in 1758, noted South Carolina planter Eliza Lucas Pinckney observed to a friend, "I find it requires great care, attention, and activity to attend properly to a Carolina Estate, tho' but a moderate one, to do ones duty and make it turn to account." To another she commented that a "great cloud seems at present to hang over this province," which was "continually insulted by the Indians" and simultaneously suffering from "a violent kind of small pox...that almost puts a stop to all business." It was in dismay that Eliza reported that many of her "people," by which she meant her slaves, "have died very fast even by inocculation."[8]

Eliza Pinckney may have been unable to cure her slaves' illnesses, but she did have confidence in controlling them. By the time she took over the Pinckney estate, South Carolina already had in place a series of laws designed to curb and control the slave population, laws that made clear, even as they attempted to contain, black opposition to chattel slavery. A brief but violent slave uprising near Charleston in 1739, the Stono Rebellion (named for the river where the slaves congregated), had fueled growing white fears of blacks in a colony where slaves comprised the majority. The fact that the rebellious slaves were Catholic hardly helped. As would be the case for all future massed slave rebellions, the Stono Rebellion was not successful. Those involved not killed by the militia were later executed or, following the pattern of treatment meted out to the Indian peoples of New England in the previous century, sold off to the West Indies. Smaller-scale uprisings in South Carolina and Georgia, combined with the growth in numbers of slave imports over the next few years, convinced the slave owners that tighter controls should be imposed on the black population, not just its slave component.

Consequently the "Act for the better Ordering and Governing of Negroes and other Slaves" (or Negro Act) of 1740 in South Carolina restricted slave movements without an owner's permission, made it illegal to educate slaves, and permitted the execution of rebellious slaves by their owners. The Negro Act in South Carolina was in no way out of step with developments in other colonies. After 1700, the shift from indentured servitude to slave labor gathered momentum on the Chesapeake, the rice-based economies of the Carolinas and Georgia became increasingly profitable, and a raft of restrictive legislation began to impinge ever more closely on black life and liberty. Yet if one colony exemplified not just the powerful attraction of slave-sustained profits, but the extent to which white liberty had become not merely entangled with but almost dependent on black slavery, it was Georgia.

Founded by English philanthropist James Oglethorpe to provide a fresh start for the English poor, Georgia was idealistic in conception. Oglethorpe sought to remove all sources of temptation from its first colonists – the temptations, one presumes, that had led them into penury and from there to Georgia in the first place. Alcohol and slavery were prohibited. Georgia would, its founder anticipated, be a colony of the clean-living, hardworking "deserving poor" of England. The poor in question, however, felt they were deserving of rather more leeway, and petitioned, as freeborn Englishmen, for the right to hold slaves. When Georgia became a crown colony in 1751, its new assembly lost no time in repealing the laws banning slavery and alcohol; by the eve of the Revolution, Georgia's main town, Savannah, was, like Charleston, a major slave-trading center (Figure 4.2) through which many black slaves passed en route to the rice plantations that would become their life and, in many cases, reduce their life span.

As the Savannah broadside shows, in 1774, on the very eve of the Revolution, the year the First Continental Congress met, the year that found Jefferson arguing for the rights of British America and Phillis Wheatley enjoying the fruits of her literary efforts, the slave trade flourished. Even as Jefferson asserted his belief that "God who gave us life gave us liberty at the same time," it was clear that white colonial life, not to mention liberty and the pursuit of happiness, was increasingly contingent on the denial of the last two and sometimes the first to the black population of the British colonies. In some sense, this was inevitable. From the period of earliest settlement, in the Chesapeake as in New England and most points between, a white, Protestant identity had been refined through contact with nonwhite, non-Protestant peoples. The

TO BE SOLD, on WEDNESDAY 3d AUGUST next,

By COWPER & TELFAIRS,
A CARGO

Of 170 prime young likely healthy

GUINEA SLAVES,

Just imported, in the Bark Friends, William Ross Master, directly from Angola.
Savannah, July 25, 1774.

To be Sold at Private Sale, any Time before the 18th of next Month,

THE PLANTATION, containing one hundred acres, on which the subscriber lives, very pleasantly situated on Savannah River in sight of town. The terms of sale may be known by applying to
July 21, 1774.   RICHARD WYLLY.

WANTED,

AN OVERSEER thoroughly qualified to undertake the settlement of a River Swamp Plantation on the Alatamaha River. Any such person, who can bring proper recommendations, may hear of great encouragement by applying to   NATHANIEL HALL.

THE subscriber being under an absolute necessity of closing his concerns without delay, gives this last publick notice, that all persons indebted to him by bond, note or otherwise, who do not discharge the same by the first day of October next, will find their respective obligations, &c. in the hands of an Attorney to be sued for without distinction. It is hoped those concerned will avail themselves of this notice.
                                                  PHILIP BOX.

RUN AWAY the 20th of May last from John Forbes, Esq.'s plantation in St. John's parish, TWO NEGROES, named BILLY and QUAMINA, of the Guiney Country, and speak good English. Billy is lusty and well made, about 5 feet 10 or 11 inches high, of a black complection, has lost some of his upper teeth, and had on when he went away a white negroe cloth jacket and trowsers of the same. Quamina is stout and well made, about 5 feet 10 or 11 inches high, very black, has his country marks in his face, had on when he went away a jacket, trowsers, and robbin, of white negroe cloth. Whoever takes up said Negroes, and deliver them to me at the above plantation, or to the Warden of the Work-House in Savannah, shall receive a reward of 20s. besides what the law allows.
                                                  DAVIS AUSTIN.

FIGURE 4.2. Broadside advertising a slave auction, Savannah, 1774. This broadside is revealing about the reality of slavery in the South on the eve of the Revolution. For Savannah, specifically, the general trend to import more slaves directly from Africa held; from c. 1755 to 1767, about 60 percent of slaves imported into Savannah originated in the Caribbean and about 25 percent from African countries. Between 1768 and about 1771, however, those arriving directly from Africa rose to 86 percent (the slaves advertised here were from Guinea). As well as advertising slaves for sale, this broadside also carries a "for sale" notice for a plantation and a job advert for a plantation overseer, the latter highlighting the absentee ownership problem on many plantations, the distance between owner and slave. Most tellingly of all, however, it carries a notice of two runaway slaves, Billy and Quamina, probably arrivals from Africa in light of the reference to "country marks" on Quamina's face. Library of Congress, Prints and Photographs Division. Reproduction Number: LC-USZ62–16876 (1–2).

trans-Atlantic nature of the elite colonists' lives, at least, informed the development of this identity even as it gradually undermined the English-ness on which not just racial distinctions but the Revolution itself was predicated. Liberty, as John Woolman had foreseen, became aligned with whiteness, slavery with blackness, but, crucially for the future American nation, only from a white perspective.

To Be or Not to Be

If certain truths seemed not to be as self-evident as all that to some of the white colonists, one was pretty obvious to the British: that liberty really was the cause of all mankind, and all mankind might well be prepared to fight for it. When the Revolutionary War broke out, the governor of Virginia, John Murray, the Earl of Dunmore, lost little time in declaring "all indented servants, Negroes or others . . . free, that are able and willing to bear arms." With freedom as the inducement, many of Virginia's slaves did not hesitate to join "Lord Dunmore's Ethiopian Regiment" to fight alongside the British. Equally, there were many free blacks who, inspired by the rhetoric of revolution, hoped to align with the colonial cause. Many had, after all, served in at least some of the colonial militias. Despite this, blacks were rebuffed by the main colonial force, the Continental Army, whose position as of October 1775 was that they would not enlist "Negroes, boys unable to bear arms, or old men unable to endure the fatigues of campaign."

Although Lord Dunmore's announcement raised the specter of slave rebellion, slaveholders, north and south, proved reluctant to accord official sanction to the arming of their slaves. Individual states, responsible for the raising and funding of their militia units, were sometimes dissuaded by the cost. Slaveholders could receive considerable compensation for the loss of their property – about 1,000 dollars, at a time when the monthly pay for a Revolutionary soldier was just under 6 dollars (or 40 shillings), and the cost of an individual slave could be between 100 and almost 400 dollars. As the war dragged on, however, and states struggled to meet the recruitment quotas for the Continental Army imposed by Congress, the whites-only policy broke down in many areas, notably in some of the New England states. It wavered in the southern states, whose legislatures hesitated to condone the raising of black regiments. Individual owners did sometimes send a slave to war in their stead, so that many blacks during the revolutionary war ended up fighting for liberty on two fronts: for themselves and for white society.

Freedom in revolutionary America always carried a price. In assuming that the ends justified the means in the case of the American War for Independence, the actual means have sometimes become subsumed in the myth, or myths, given that, as the founding "act" of the American nation, the story of the Revolution has naturally received more embellishment than many. In the process, reputations were made, even as sometimes race was lost. Boston Massacre casualty Crispus Attucks was the victim not just of British bullets but a postmortem whiteout by colonial illustrators. Other individuals fared better and were dragged center stage to symbolize events that involved entire communities. One of these was engraver and silversmith Paul Revere, whose rendition of an Anglicized Attucks proved such a powerful propaganda tool in the buildup to Revolution, and whose famous midnight ride to Lexington became the stuff of legend. Tellingly, it was a legend that really took form in Henry Wadsworth Longfellow's poem, "Paul Revere's Ride," written almost a century after the events it described took place and published at a time – in the middle of America's Civil War – when the nation was perhaps most receptive to this particular patriot's message, one expressed visually in any number of prints, paintings, and lithographs over the years (Figure 4.3).

Revere certainly made the journey portrayed on the night of April 18, 1775, to warn of the movement of British troops toward Lexington and Concord and the weapons' store there. He would hardly, however, have shouted the warning "The British are coming" later ascribed to him. In the first place, the British, in the form of regular troops, were already there, and had been since the Boston Tea Party. In the second, it would have been a nonsensical statement, because many of the colonists regarded themselves as British. The gap between truth and its semi-fictional representation, however, is, in essence, the divide between patriotism and nationalism in America. Colonial patriotism, in effect, clashed with English nationalism, but the white colonists did not overnight transform themselves into Americans, even if the postwar tales of the Revolution suggested that they had. Encapsulated in the legend of Revere's ride is the idea that the Revolution consisted of a spontaneous uprising of the American colonists acting in concert against British oppression. Nothing could have been further from the truth. Nevertheless, Revere's supposedly solitary ride carried with it the essence of events in the colonies in 1775 and 1776, the truth, from a colonial perspective, of Thomas Paine's injunction that it was time for Britain and its colonies to part. Revere's ride became a symbolic representation of an opposition to British authority that had been slowly building but that, in 1775, had not yet coalesced

FIGURE 4.3. Paul Revere's ride. Illustration from a nineteenth-century edition of Longfellow's poetry. Photo © National Archives, Washington, DC.

into a commitment to separation, far less an identifiable expression of American identity.

The process of becoming American was, as in some senses it always had been, one driven by and defined through conflict; conflict between the colonies and Britain, between the colonists and the native populations, and among the colonists themselves. This much was obvious at the time. The *Declaration of the Causes and Necessities of Taking up Arms* issued by the Continental Congress in 1775 acknowledged that much of the colonial experience had led to this point. It was bombastic, not to say overly optimistic, in some of its assertions: "Our cause is just," it proclaimed. "Our Union is perfect. Our internal resources are great, and, if necessary, foreign assistance is undoubtedly attainable." It was more realistic in its recognition that the colonies "had been previously exercised in warlike operation, and possessed of the means of defending" themselves. Constant contact with native tribes and the requirements of a frontier life certainly produced a population more familiar with warfare on their doorsteps than many European populations of the time.

The American belief in the importance of an armed citizenry, therefore, had its origins in the colonial period, as did the European assumption that almost all colonials would be natural marksmen. This idea was reinforced by reports from the colonies suggesting, as one Anglican minister did in 1775, that the weaponry produced in the colonies was "infinitely better" to that normally used in Europe, and that colonial gunsmiths were "everywhere constantly employed." The hunting of deer and turkey, he observed, had made "the Americans the best marksmen in the world."[9] Even so, military engagement with one of the strongest armies of the period, one likely to put up more of a fight than the average turkey, was not something to be undertaken lightly. The British population outnumbered the colonial by more than three to one, and Britain's naval as well as her land-based military capacities were formidable. Taking these on was a move fraught with both practical danger and moral and ideological uncertainty.

In the context of a national identity that was predominantly rooted in Englishness, in a conflict fought over the rights of Englishmen, what the colonists were being asked to do was to kill their fellow countrymen. This was unacceptable for some. For minister Ebenezer Baldwin, the Revolution was "a most unnatural War," an immoral war, in which "those of the same Nation, of the same common Ancestry, of the same language of the same professed Religion, and heirs of the same Privileges, should be imbuing their hands in each others Blood."[10] Increasingly, however, opposition to the British came to seem not simply natural but inevitable. When the smoke had cleared from those first shots fired at Lexington, a very different landscape was revealed, one in which both British oppression and colonial opposition were thrown into sharp relief, on which a multitude of hitherto half-formed ideas about independence, themselves fueled by rumbling grievances about British governmental behavior, started to solidify.

The perspective of Samuel Ward, formerly the governor of Rhode Island and one of the delegates to the Continental Congress, epitomized this sharpening of colonial thinking. Writing from Philadelphia to his brother, Henry, late in 1775, Ward offered his opinion that the British intended to "receive Us & our Posterity for their Slaves." He noted the widespread disapproval of the presence of "foreign troops" in the colonies, "English, scotch, irish, roman catholics, Hessians, Hanoverians," all of whom threatened both towns and trade. In the face of such threats, Ward argued, "every private View, Passion & Interest ought to be buried. We are embarked in one common Bottom [*ship*]. If She sinks We all perish; if She survives the Storm, Peace & Plenty (the offspring of Liberty) and every thing which will dignify & felicitate human Nature will be the Reward of our Virtue." Echoing Paine, Ward advised his brother that theirs was "not the Cause of the Colonies & of Britain only but of human Nature itself." For the colonies, specifically, however, suffering as they were under "a Ministry fit to serve a Nero," there was only one possible course of action, one decision to be made. "To Be or not to be," Ward declared, "is now the Question."[11]

Ward may have identified the question, but the affirmative answer he anticipated was neither guaranteed nor speedily forthcoming. It took eight long years before the war begun at Lexington secured the independence of the colonies via the Treaty of Paris in 1783, and a further five before their inhabitants could refer to themselves, with absolute confidence, as "We, the people of the United States." Those eight years of fighting tend to be foreshortened, as most wars eventually are in hindsight, into a series of vignettes, flash points in a struggle the outcome of which is known and the complexities of which are rarely commended to posterity. From a contemporary perspective, the battle for independence was all too often a case of one step forward and two steps back.

Absent any permanent or organized colonial force, the opening encounter between British regulars and the colonial militia at Lexington on April 19, 1775 was followed by a period of confusion as the colonists attempted to organize themselves. Yet many of the colonial troops who had gathered at Lexington, collectively known as the New England Army of Observation, soon went home again, lacking supplies and unable to set aside their farms or businesses to ensure that the British regulars were secured in Boston. Despite this, the popular imagery of the permanently prepared "Minutemen" as the elite of the colonial militia (Figure 4.4) holding the line against the British redcoats gained widespread credence. The Minuteman ideal, in fact, was little more than a New England militia affectation, designed to confer some distinction on what was, inevitably, a rapidly assembled makeshift force, frequently lacking sufficient munitions, certainly lacking uniforms. Nevertheless, this image of a new kind of citizen-soldier, although inflated in some respects, spoke to a deeper

FIGURE 4.4. Line of Minutemen being fired on by British troops in Lexington, Massachusetts, 1775 (John H. Daniels & Son, Boston, 1903). Courtesy of the Library of Congress Prints and Photographs Division (LC-DIG-ppmsca-05478).

and more permanent truth about the emergent American nation and the nationalism of the revolutionary era, its military dimension and its voluntary nature.

This fledgling American nationalism had a number of mutually reinforcing components, including the already widespread belief in colonial frontier martial efficacy and a militia system whose origins lay in England's twelfth-century version, the Assize of Arms (1181), under which all able-bodied freemen were required, at their own expense, to train for the public's protection. Whereas in Europe the idea of civilian service had been rendered obsolete by the rise of professional armies, in the context of colonial conflict, the citizen was society's first, and last, line of defense against attack. This was both economically and ideologically desirable. The alternative was to retain regular troops, funded by the colonies but loyal to the royal governor. In the context of colonial opposition to the Quartering Act (1765), a standing army was hardly desirable. A citizen who could, in an emergency, be transformed into a soldier and as quickly turned back again was both a cheaper and, from a colonial perspective, safer option. The citizen's service, however, could not necessarily be compelled. Self-interest might necessitate self-defense, but once the danger passed, so too did the need to arm against it. As one Pennsylvanian minister, Joseph Doddridge, recalled, members of the colonial militias "were soldiers, when they chose to be so, and when they chose laid down their arms. Their military service was voluntary and of course received no pay."[12]

By contrast, if mustered into the newly formed Continental Army, these former militia troops were at least paid, but this did not instantaneously transform them into a unified professional fighting force. A voluntary military tradition married to a myth of near-universal martial prowess proved an unstable basis on which to construct an army. Indeed, no single permanent army was ever successfully formed. The Continental Army and the state militias (sometimes designated as a Continental army) fought side by side or, on occasion, singularly failed to do so. George Washington noted with anger how at the Battle of Camden (1780) in South Carolina, the militia "fled at the first fire, and left the Continental troops surrounded on every side and overpowered by numbers to combat for safety instead of Victory."[13] If the militia could at times prove unreliable, nor was it the case that the thirteen colonies readily pulled together in their opposition to the British government. Rather, thirteen essentially quite separate revolutions took place, all pursuing a similar trajectory, eventually, but approaching the desired end-point from rather different directions and bearing somewhat different agendas.

Washington's position as general and commander-in-chief of the Continental Army resulted less from his military experience than from the fact he was a Virginian. Putting a Virginian in charge of an army primarily made up of New Englanders would, it was hoped, foster colonial unity. The fact that Washington was a conservative and a wealthy planter was, too, intended to allay conservative fears of radicalism. It turned out to be an inspired choice. When Washington was appointed in July 1775, the colonials had just come through what turned out to be the revolutionary war's bloodiest engagement – at least for the British – Bunker Hill (June 17), although the battle itself was on Breed's Hill, in Boston. Following the relative success of Bunker Hill, the war went downhill for the Americans. New York fell into British hands almost immediately and remained occupied for the duration of the war. Indeed, the British managed to seize every major American town in the course of the revolutionary war, and Washington lost more battles than he won, yet the colonists still emerged victorious, in no small part thanks to that one individual. Washington proved adept at balancing the various interest groups at play in the revolutionary war, which is not to say that the task did not, on occasion, drive him to distraction.

The end of 1776, only the second year of hostilities, proved to be a turning point. With Washington's success at the Battle of Trenton on December 26 – a feat achieved by his managing to get the Continental Army across the then-swollen Delaware River – colonial morale improved, at least up to a point. Washington was still pressing the Continental Congress for more regular colonial troops. The militia, he stressed, was "not to be depended on, or aid expected from 'em, but in cases of the most pressing emergency." Indeed, he fumed, "their lethargy of late and backwardness to turn out at this alarming crisis, seems to justify an apprehension, that nothing can bring them from their Homes." This was to prove a persistent theme for Washington. He could never be persuaded of the efficacy of a volunteer force. Indeed, he once observed, "America has almost been amused out of her liberties" by the credulous supposition that the militia were good for anything beyond furnishing "light parties to skirmish the Woods." Neither the militia nor "raw troops" were, in his opinion, "fit for the real business of fighting."[14]

The real business of fighting proved to be a struggle for the revolutionaries. All wars, of course, are miserable in their own way. The American way during the Revolution was to maintain an inadequate army. Congress never gave Washington the troops he needed, and failed to maintain, adequately, those he had. Short-term enlistments (three months was usual) ensured too frequent a turnover of troops, and state loyalties established almost constant dissension in the ranks. The Americans also overstretched themselves at the start. An abortive invasion of Canada over the winter of 1775–76 revealed both the limits of enthusiasm for the revolutionary cause beyond the British colonies and the terrible hardships that many of the colonial troops would have to endure over the next six years. As had been the case in camp following Lexington, supplies were scarce and disease endemic. The dreaded smallpox, spread by the movement of troops across the colonies, resulted in the first mass inoculation against this virus, on Washington's orders, among the colonial forces. No simple injection, however, could stem the constant ebb and flow of support for the Revolution. Washington's army, over the course of the conflict, fluctuated between 2,000 and 20,000 men.

Washington was, in almost every sense, an embattled leader, and a sense of the difficulties he faced come across clearly in much of the iconography associated with the Revolution, most notably that portraying the terrible winter of 1777–78 at Valley Forge, Pennsylvania (Figure 4.5), to which Washington had retreated following his army's defeat at Brandywine Creek in September of 1777 and the subsequent British seizure of Philadelphia. From there, Washington offered his gloomy prognosis to the Continental Congress "that unless some great and capital change suddenly takes place in that line, this Army must inevitably be reduced to one or other of these three things. Starve, dissolve, or disperse, in order

FIGURE 4.5. "Valley Forge, 1777." General Washington and Lafayette visiting the suffering part of the army. The Marquis de La Fayette was a French military officer who served with Washington. He was instrumental in the retreat from the Battle of Brandywine, and later in the negotiations that brought France into the war on the American side. He returned to America to confront Cornwallis at Yorktown. Painted and drawn by A. Gibert. Lithograph and publication by P. Haas. Washington, DC: Courtesy of the Library of Congress Prints and Photographs Division (LC-USZ62–819).

to obtain subsistence in the best manner they can; rest assured Sir," he stressed, "this is not an exaggerated picture."[15] Yet Valley Forge was not the low point it seemed. It was the darkness before dawn in America's national story. Washington's difficulties were matched by those of the British, whose lack both of supplies and coordination prevented their pursuing their military advantage to its conclusion. This did as much to drag the conflict out as any of the recruitment and retention problems Washington faced.

By the spring of 1778, colonial fortunes were starting to improve, largely because in the previous fall, the main British army, under the command of General John Burgoyne, failed in its campaign to seize control of the Hudson Valley, which would have isolated New England from the southern colonies. At Saratoga, New York, in October, Burgoyne surrendered, and the remains of his forces returned to Canada. More importantly, American success at Saratoga also garnered the colonies the foreign aid that the *Declaration of the Causes and Necessities of Taking up Arms* had confidently assumed would come. It did, in the form of the French, but not until it was obvious to France that she was backing the winning side.

Washington had no illusions about this. "I am heartily disposed to entertain the most favourable sentiments of our new ally and to cherish them in others to a reasonable degree," he observed, "but it is a maxim founded on the universal experience of mankind, that no nation is to be trusted farther than it is bound by its interest; and no prudent statesman or politician will venture to depart from it." With an eye to the future, he warned that America "ought to be particularly cautious; for we have not yet attained sufficient vigor and maturity to recover from the shock of any false step into which we may unwarily fall."[16] Yet in 1778, it suited all parties that France should aid the colonists. The French and British hardly needed much encouragement to declare war on each other, as they officially did in the summer of 1778. Spain soon followed suit. The suit she followed was French, rather than American. Spain never aided the American cause directly, but Britain's embattled position within Europe all added up on the American side.

It was not yet a case of it all being over bar the fighting. Washington's problems remained acute. The colonial combination of voluntarism and localism as far as defense went was, to his eternal frustration, a significant barrier both to the successful prosecution and the speedy conclusion of the war. He had attempted "to discourage all kinds of local attachments, and distinctions of Country [state], denominating the whole by the greater name of American," but, he reported, "found it impossible to overcome prejudices." Four years later, little had changed. By the end of 1780, Washington remained "most firmly of [the] opinion," as he advised Major General John Sullivan, "that after the States have brought their Troops into the Field, the less they have to do with them" the better. Trapped between the rock of British military might and the hard place of clashing state and individual ambitions, Washington struggled to merge the various parts of the colonial military machine into a functioning whole. As he commented to Sullivan, "[i]f in all cases ours was *one* army, or *thirteen* armies allied for the common defense, there would be no difficulty, but we are occasionally both, and I should not be much out if I were to say, that we are sometimes *neither*, but a compound of *both*."[17]

By 1780, this compound army had moved away from New England, the main battleground of the revolutionary war having shifted south. Inspired by reports of loyalist support and hoping that slavery might have created a weakened social system ripe for defeat, the British had headed for Georgia. The seizure of first Savannah (December 1778) and then Charleston (May 1780) was followed by the Battle of Camden, where the militia, as Washington complained, so conspicuously failed to distinguish itself. Yet, as soon as the British, under Charles (The Earl) Cornwallis, turned their backs, quite literally, as they headed into North Carolina, the colonists undid all that had been achieved, adopting a guerrilla style of warfare that was susceptible to sporadic setbacks but that proved impossible to defeat decisively. By the end of the summer of 1780, the British still held Savannah and Charleston, but that was pretty much all they held. In the spring of the following year, the French alliance, too, finally proved its worth. A combined force of French and American armies and the French navy succeeded in boxing in Cornwallis's force on the Yorktown peninsula, where Cornwallis surrendered on October 19, 1781.

Yorktown, although frequently understood as the conclusion of the American War for Independence, was not yet quite the end, but it was the beginning of the end, for the British, and, of course, the end of the beginning for America. British troops remained in the colonies, but on the defensive in a halfhearted way. In Paris in 1782, the various emissaries were already gathering to discuss the terms under which peace would be established and a new nation created. A contemporary political cartoon summed up the situation (Figure 4.6), graphically advertising the fact to the British that their former colonies now had the upper hand.

Articles of Faith

For both sides, British and colonial, the Revolution represented a new kind of conflict for which neither frontier fighting, on the part of the colonials, nor large-scale battles, on the part of the British regulars, offered much in the way of useful precedent. It was, fundamentally, a battle for hearts and minds as much as a direct military confrontation. This is no anachronistic phrase drawn from much later American wars. Sir Henry Clinton, one of the commanders-in-chief of British forces, fully recognized the need "to gain the hearts" as well as "subdue the minds of America."[18] The problem, however, was not on the British side alone. If Washington struggled to persuade Congress of the need for a more

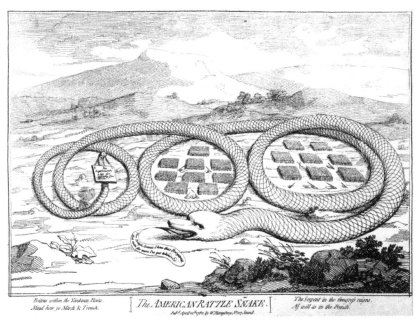

FIGURE 4.6. James Gillray, "The American Rattle Snake" (London: W. Humphrey, April 1782). The snake was a common motif for the colonies; it was used by Americans on their flag before the adoption of the stars and stripes. Previous cartoons, in particular an image from 1754, had portrayed the colonies in the form of a disjointed snake, and suggested that they "join or die." This one, that appeared when the Paris peace talks were underway, proposed that the colonies were now one, united body. The snake's tongue boasts: "Two British Armies I have thus Burgoyn'd,/And room for more I've got behind." Two of the serpent's coils surround representations of the forces of Burgoyne and Cornwallis; the third advertises "An Apartment to lett for Military Gentlemen." The verse below advises: "Britons within the Yankeean Plains,/Mind how ye March and Trench,/The Serpent in the Congress reigns,/As well as in the French." Courtesy of the Library of Congress Prints and Photographs Division (LC-USZ62–1531).

effective army, and his fellow countrymen of the need to join same, there were some who were never persuaded of the necessity for an army, for armed conflict with Britain, at all – the Loyalists.

Inevitably, given that the revolutionary war did result in the separation of the colonies from Britain, it is the growing momentum, and military successes, of the American patriot cause, not the arguments of those whose loyalties remained with Britain, that dominate the story. Numerically, of course, America's patriots were in the majority, even if Washington sometimes felt they were too often a silent, or at least an inactive, majority. Out of a population of some three million in the colonies at the time, only an estimated half a million aligned with the British cause. Theirs was an invidious position as the war progressed, because the Revolution was a civil war as much as it was one for colonial independence.

In some states, notably in the Carolinas in the latter stages of the conflict, loyalist militia group clashes with both the Continental Army and patriot militias produced the anarchy and violence that the loyalists had dreaded all along, as neighbor turned on neighbor in ways that had more to do with personal vendettas than the cause of independence. All states implemented oaths of allegiance, which combined the renouncement of the British Crown with a pledge of allegiance to the individual state. The penalties for nonconformity to the patriot cause were high, ranging from confiscation of property to exile and, sometimes, death. In the end, many thousands of loyalists – estimates vary from 60,000 to almost 100,000 – left the colonies for good, seeking refuge in Canada or in Britain.

The Loyalists, by virtue of backing what turned out to be the losing side, may have effectively written themselves out of America's national story. Yet their significance lies less in any military threat they offered to the ultimate achievement of American independence – frankly, not much, although some 30,000 fought on the British side – than in their role in helping clarify, and define, the cause for which the colonies were fighting – a separate American nation. The battle for the hearts and minds of that nation proved to be a brutal one. The experiences of the Loyalists not only highlighted the destructive power of what, some half a century later, would be described as the "tyranny of the majority" in the United States, but also the very real uncertainties that plagued that majority.

The Loyalists were no narrow elite wedded to a traditional way of life and social structure at odds with the youthful enthusiasm of the colonies. Loyalists came from all backgrounds, classes, and professions, although there were some discernible patterns to the loyalist demographic. Most notably, those already on the margins of the dominant white, British ethnic core – the Germans, Dutch, and Scots – and those with a strong religious identity – the Quakers, Methodists, and southern Presbyterians – tended toward the loyalist camp. What, Crèvecoeur had asked, is the American? The revolutionary war provided no definite answer to that question, although it did succeed in narrowing the options by identifying, up to a point, what the American was not.

The period of the Revolution was a liminal one for colonists and British, patriots and nationalists, black and white alike. The decisions made at that time were more complex than a simple choice between liberty and slavery, between being colonial subjects of Britain and independent Americans. In some cases, for slaves, for Loyalists, the choice was never wholly theirs to make. Washington would later, at the end of his presidency, highlight the voluntary nature of American identity, but voluntary patriotism, as he continued to stress throughout the revolutionary war itself, was never enough militarily, and possibly not enough ideologically. "I do not mean to exclude altogether the idea of patriotism," Washington observed, from the perspective of Valley Forge in the spring following his long, hard winter there. "I know it exists, and I know it has done much in the present contest. But I will venture to assert, that a great and lasting War can never be supported on this principle alone. It must be aided by a prospect of interest or some reward."[19]

What that reward was depended on the individual. For some, like Washington, it was an independent nation. For slaves, it was the prospect of freedom. For others, it was the opportunity to own slaves. The interests of the loyalists persuaded them that the only bond that held the colonies together was about to be broken, and tyranny would result. In their case, they were not far wrong. White Americans had always struggled to differentiate slave from free in colonial America. And they struggled to differentiate loyal from disloyal in revolutionary America, and were unwilling for that distinction to be wholly voluntary. With freedom of the press curtailed so as to mute opposition to the revolutionary cause, the colonists paved the way for later national laws that would seek to legislate for loyalty: the Alien and Sedition Acts of 1798. In the end, the idea of choice proved as constraining as it was liberating. Identifying who was welcome and who excluded from their emerging nation would exercise American minds from that nation's inception, and continues to do so to this day.

In the immediate aftermath of the Treaty of Paris (1783), there were more pressing, although not unrelated, problems to contend with. One of these was still military. In the summer of 1783, mutinous soldiers guarding the public offices in Philadelphia threatened violence when their back pay was not forthcoming. Fearful of the implications, Congress swiftly disbanded the Continental Army. This speedy transformation of the soldier back into the citizen again, however, could only ever be partially complete. Many men took from their military service permanent reminders of the cost of American freedom. That was one problem that the new nation would have to address.

Between 150,000 and 200,000 men served in the revolutionary armies – clearly not all at the same time, or Washington would have had an easier time of it. Of those, about a third were either killed or injured. There were around 25,000 service-related deaths, roughly one in ten of those who fought, a per capita equivalent of around 2.5 million today. Causes of death were typical for the wars of the period. Fewer than 10,000 died directly in battle, an equal number died of disease, and, of course, many revolutionary veterans died sooner than they otherwise would have due to wounds and diseases that produced persistent health problems. In 1818, Congress took steps to compensate surviving veterans via a pension act, the applications for which reveal the extent of injuries sustained. Yet the recipients of these pensions were only the tip of the iceberg of the Revolution's long-term physical impact. Its ideological impact was another matter entirely. In theory at least, service in the revolutionary armies provided a bond between individuals that would otherwise not have been forged. Washington's battle against local prejudices notwithstanding, the war might also have been expected to awaken some awareness of life beyond each separate state, a greater sense of the nation that was at issue. At the same time, the loyalty oaths implemented during the Revolution referenced not the new nation as a single entity, but each individual state. Although James Gillray's cartoon had suggested a newfound unity among the colonies, some contemporary commentators felt this to be, at best, a premature assumption.

Given the circumstances, the speed with which Congress disbanded the armies was not surprising, but it perhaps sent the wrong message and reinforced a sense that, now that the war was over, life could go on as it had before. Former army surgeon Benjamin Rush expressed his dismay at finding "a passion for retirement so universal among the patriots and heroes of the war." Those who had only recently laid down their arms, he maintained, "resemble skilful mariners, who, after exerting themselves to preserve a ship from sinking in a storm, in the middle of the ocean, drop asleep as soon as the waves subside, and leave the care of their lives and property, during the remainder of the voyage, to sailors, without knowledge or experience."

"The American war is over," Rush acknowledged, "but this is far from being the case with the American revolution. On the contrary," he reminded Americans, "nothing but the first act of the great drama is closed. It remains yet to establish and perfect our new forms of government; and to prepare the principles, morals, and manners of our citizens, for these forms of government, after they are established and brought to perfection."[20]

The focus of Rush's concerns was the framework of government in the new nation. This was a recognized problem. Indeed, it had been the root of many of Washington's military problems. The Continental Congress had drawn up Articles of Confederation between the states in 1777, but these conferred such limited powers on Congress as to be almost ineffective. Congress could, for example, suggest to each state a sum necessary for the maintenance of the revolutionary armies, but only the individual states could decide if they would pay it. If the Articles proved less than adequate for raising an army, they were certainly not up to the task of running a country, especially one as fluid and unformed as America was in the immediate postwar period. The fight for independence had left the former colonies in a parlous financial state, and the population itself, as is usual following any war, was on the move, expanding into the land that lay beyond the Appalachians, into the territories of Kentucky and Tennessee. Congress itself, indeed, could barely settle down, shifting from Philadelphia in 1783 to Princeton, Annapolis, and Trenton before pausing, briefly, in New York in 1785. In between moves, however, it did manage to establish some important regulations for the nation's geographic expansion in the form of the several land ordinances, enacted between 1784 and 1787.

The first of these (1784), which was drafted by Jefferson, conferred statehood on a territory once its population matched that of any of the original thirteen states (60,000). In the following year, under the Land Ordinance of 1785, Congress began to sell off land, reserving some to revolutionary war veterans and designating an amount to be set aside for schools. Under the terms of the Northwest Ordinance (1787), slavery was also banned from the territories. "There shall be neither slavery nor involuntary servitude in the said territory," it stipulated, "otherwise than in the punishment of crimes whereof the party shall have been duly convicted." If the Articles of Confederation failed in so many other respects, in this they were successful. The significance of these land ordinances cannot be overestimated. The precedent they established – that the territories were under the control of Congress, not individual states, and that out of them new states, "on an equal footing with the original States," would be created rather than existing ones expanded – established the very bedrock on which the nation, its geographic and its political form, would take shape. The legal wording of the Northwest Ordinance, with its emphasis on the rights of *habeas corpus* and religious toleration, would find its echo in the Constitution and in its first ten amendments (the Bill of Rights).

Yet it was one thing to bring the newly acquired territories under central control and quite another to forge their populations, and those of the original thirteen states, into a unified national body with a single national purpose. It was imperative that some means to do so be found, because the country was in financial and consequently social flux. America's farmers, overburdened with debt, and her merchants, denied access to the credit they had previously secured in Europe, were increasingly frustrated and, worse, increasingly prone to express that frustration physically. The most dramatic challenge to authority occurred in 1786 in Massachusetts, when a Continental Army veteran, Daniel Shays, sought to seize the federal arsenal at Springfield. "Shays' Rebellion," as it became known, was suppressed by the state militia. It had never posed a serious threat to law and order, but it did concentrate minds, especially those of men such as Benjamin Rush. Rush saw clearly the need both to improve the workings of the central government and, perhaps more importantly, to make the American population understand the significance of the new republic and accept the responsibilities necessary to "become good republicans."

A more diffuse sense that to be a nation one had to look, act, and sound like a nation already prevailed in the revolutionary era. The Continental Congress had, in fact, initiated the process of designing what would become the Great Seal of the United States (Figure 4.7) at the same time as it adopted the Declaration of Independence in 1776. Yet the new nation required more than the symbolism of an official signature to validate its existence. It needed, of course, military victory, which Washington provided, and a flag (the Stars and Stripes), which, the legends notwithstanding, Betsy Ross did not, but which was adopted in 1777. It needed, too, according to Rush, writing centuries before the idea of print capitalism as a nationalizing force would be proposed, to cultivate newspapers and, crucially, a reliable means of disseminating these. It needed to expand the post office.

In the current age of international, instantaneous communication, the profound significance of Rush's perspective in 1787 may easily be missed. Yet for the development of the nation, his was no trivial point. Newspapers, Rush asserted, constituted not simply "the vehicles of knowledge and intelligence" but the very "centinels of the liberties of" the nation, but it was the post office that represented "the true non-electric wire of government" and the "only means of conveying heat and light to every individual in the federal commonwealth." The Constitution concurred with Rush, empowering Congress to, among many other things of course, "establish post-offices and post-roads." The importance of communication to the new nation was later reinforced in the Post Office Act of 1792 and confirmed by a future Supreme Court Justice, Joseph Story, who in 1833 praised the United States' postal service for the efficiency with which it "brings the most distant places and persons . . . in contact

FIGURE 4.7. The Great Seal of the United States. The reverse is not used as part of the official seal, but does appear on the reverse of a one-dollar bill (along with the obverse seal). *E Pluribus Unum*: one out of many. *Novus Ordo Seclorum*: a new order of the ages is born, from Virgil, *Eclogues* IV, 5. *Annuit cœptis*: [Providence] approves our undertaking, from Virgil, *Aeneid*, IX, 625. The symbolism references the original thirteen colonies (thirteen stars, thirteen stripes, thirteen layers to the unfinished pyramid, thirteen arrows in the eagle's sinister claw, thirteen leaves and olives in its dexter claw). The date on the pyramid is 1776, the year of the Declaration of Independence. The "Eye of Providence" above the pyramid was a familiar element of Christian iconography in the eighteenth century. The final version of the Great Seal, after its design had gone through several committees, was undertaken by Secretary to Congress Charles Thomson. Photo courtesy of www.istockphoto.com.

with each other; and thus softens the anxieties, increases the enjoyments, and cheers the solitude of millions of hearts."[21]

Indeed, the very newspapers carried so efficiently, as Rush hoped, by the post office would not simply convey a sense of national belonging in the articles they published, but would reinforce it via the language in which these articles were written. If the British ethnic core of the colonial era had ensured its linguistic dominance, by the revolutionary period, Americans were receptive to the efforts of Noah Webster, whose spelling book of 1783 highlighted the ways in which English and American spelling and pronunciation were already diverging and who urged Americans to "act like independent beings," reminding them that they had "an empire to raise and support by your exertions – and a national character to establish and extend." Americans, Webster averred, had "been children long enough, subject to the control and subservient to the interests of a haughty parent."[22] Yet if the former colonies were to heed such advice, it was not simply that the spelling of the Articles of Confederation required modification. The very language of liberty itself had to be enshrined and codified at the heart of the American national enterprise.

When the Federal Convention met in Philadelphia in May of 1787, however, it was with the fairly modest intention of revising the Articles of Confederation. The decision to construct an entirely new Constitution grew out of the shared political ideas many of the delegates held, ideas rooted both in English precedent and in the recent revolutionary experience. The convention comprised members of the colonial elite, men who were aware, if not fearful, of the implications of events such as Shays' Rebellion, opposed the whole idea of standing armies, and had made their position on monarchy pretty clear. So, they were a group generally suspicious of an excess of democracy but, equally, determined to extend it, albeit in some controlled form, across the republic. The Founders' position was summed up effectively by New England clergyman Jeremy Belknap, who famously argued that it should "stand as a principle that government originates from the people; but let the people be taught . . . that they are not able to govern themselves." What the Founders sought, in short, was what is termed an indirect democracy, whereby citizens elect representatives rather than voting directly on all issues. The representatives on offer would, it was confidently assumed, be drawn from the elite. So a citizen's range of options as far as political representation was concerned would be limitless in theory and fairly limited in reality, and therefore safe in practice.

The political pattern the Founders traced was, and is, pretty convoluted. It was structured on the premise of a separation of powers, or "checks and balances," both horizontally, between the federal government and the state, and vertically between the various branches of government: the Executive (President), the Legislature (Congress), and the Judiciary (Supreme Court). The reasons for making sure that each part of government could keep a weather-eye on every other part, and that no one part could dominate lay in the Founders' ambivalent attitude toward human nature. Indeed, the symbolism of the Great Seal summed it up, because the eagle balances, in one claw, the olive branch of peace and, in the other, the arrows of war. This may be taken as a simple representation of any nation's preferred public position – desirous of peace and capable of conflict – but equally it reveals a distrustful, albeit arguably realistic, perspective on people and their relationship with power. Such was the view of the Founders regarding the masses whose rights they sought to extend. As far as political power went, the Founders could look several self-evident truths in the face and address them directly.

In other respects, the delegates who met at Philadelphia proved remarkably coy, not least where a different kind of power was concerned: that of the master over the slave. Their stringent belief in property was part of the difficulty here. Liberty and property were inextricably linked in their worldview, and because slaves were property, immediate abolition seemed not to be an option. The compromises on this issue effectively sidestepped the problem. By seeking a middle way between slavery's opponents and its defenders, the Constitution left the new nation on the fence and future generations with the task of deciding how, exactly, to get off it.

To accommodate slavery's critics, the Constitution stipulated that the "migration or importation of such persons as any of the States now existing shall think proper to admit shall not be prohibited by Congress prior to the year one thousand eight hundred and eight." In short, come 1808, the external slave trade would be abolished. In the meantime, escape to a state less receptive to slavery was not an option for slaves, because the Constitution, in deference to slavery's defenders, also ruled that "[n]o person held to service or labor in one States, under the laws thereof, escaping into another, shall . . . be discharged from such service or labor, but shall be delivered up on claim of the party to whom such service or labor may be due." This, the fugitive slave clause of the Constitution, made it clear that masters could pursue and recover any runaway slaves. Yet even this was insufficient for some of the southern delegates, who wanted to have their cake and eat it too. Although they regarded their slaves as property, they found it convenient to assert their humanity when it came to the business of representation. The native peoples were excluded from counting toward representation on the grounds of not being taxed, but slaves counted as three-fifths of a free person. The South, in short, could hold their slaves as property and still count them as people.

If the legislative language used in some of these clauses seems even more obtuse than usual, this was quite deliberate. Detailing the debates to a correspondent in London, Benjamin Rush had noted, somewhat caustically, that "[n]o mention was made of *negroes* or *slaves* in this constitution, only because it was thought the very words would contaminate the glorious fabric of American liberty and government. Thus," he observed, "you see the cloud which a few years ago was no larger than a man's hand, has descended in plentiful dews and at last cover'd every part of our land."[23]

Rush was, as usual, a prescient commentator. The Constitutional Convention had devised a framework of government that would prove – that still does prove – the extent of the Founders' political acumen, the dexterity of their thinking, and the flexibility of their vision for the new republic. The Constitution itself became one of the defining documents of American national identity, of American nationalism, remarkable in its enduring ability to accommodate the changing circumstances of American political and social life since 1787. Yet perhaps the Founders were a little too confident that their compromises on slavery would hold. Preceded as it was by the Declaration of Independence, which posited a more expansive version of liberty, the Constitution was not the sole document to define the emerging nation. As the delegates prepared to leave Philadelphia in mid-September 1787, the debate over the Constitution they had drafted was not yet finished, and the argument over the implications of the Declaration of Independence had only just begun.

5

The Last, Best Hope of Earth

Toward the Second American Revolution

We know how to save the Union. The world knows we do know how to save it. We – even *we here* – hold the power, and bear the responsibility. In *giving* freedom to the *slave*, we *assure* freedom to the *free* – honorable alike in what we give, and what we preserve. We shall nobly save, or meanly lose, the last, best hope of earth.

(Abraham Lincoln, *Annual Message to Congress*, 1862)

Benjamin Rush had described the conclusion of the Revolutionary War as only the end of the first act of the republican drama. The drawing up of the Constitution was, similarly, far from the last word on the new nation's administrative and political structure. Contemporary cartoons portrayed "America triumphant" (Figure 5.1), but with triumph came turmoil. Just as the removal of the French threat in 1763 had provided the colonies with the space to contemplate their perceived subservient position to the "mother country," so the exit of Great Britain from the American stage left the new republic with only itself to argue with. This was potentially problematic. Gouverneur Morris, frequently credited as the composer of those famous lines starting with "We, the people," had warned during the Constitutional Convention that this "Country must be united. If persuasion does not unite it, the sword will."[1] None of the Founding Fathers attempted to deny this, but they tried to be realistic. Not the least of the differences between the Articles of Confederation and the Constitution was the recognition that in the creation of a federal union, unanimity was not a viable option.

The agreement of all thirteen colonies had been required to amend the Articles, but only nine needed to sign on the Constitutional line for it to

AMERICA TRIUMPHANT and BRITANNIA in DISTRESS

EXPLANATION.

I America fitting on that quarter of the globe with the Flag of the United States displayed over her head, holding in one hand the Olive branch, inviting the ships of all nations to partake of her commerce, and in the other hand supporting the Cap of Liberty. II Fame proclaiming the joyful news to all the world. III Britannia weeping at the loss of the trade of America, attended with an evil genius. IV The British flag struck, on her strong Fortresses. V French, Spanish, Dutch, &c. shipping in the harbours of America. VI A view of New-York, wherein is exhibited the Traitor Arnold, taken with remorse for selling his country, and Judas like hanging himself.

FIGUREX 5.1. "America Triumphant and Britannia in Distress." Frontispiece, *Weatherwise's Town and Country Almanac* (Boston, 1782). Courtesy of the Library of Congress Prints and Photographs Division (LC-USZC4–5275).

come into effect. Some were prompt to reach for their pens. Pennsylvania and Connecticut ratified the document via majority decisions, and New Jersey, Delaware, and Georgia with unanimous ones. Other states hesitated. Massachusetts only narrowly conceded the Constitution's authority after a protracted debate. Other states had less of an issue with it but still checked the small print carefully before agreeing. When Maryland, South Carolina, and New Hampshire came on board, the Constitution had its required nine supporters. Unfortunately, two of the tardiest states, Virginia and New York, were also two of the most powerful. Without them, nine was not, in fact, enough.

The divisions and disagreements over the Constitution were not in any sense regionally informed. There was no North/South divide on this subject, as there later would be on so much else. Nor was it a wealth issue, although those who most strongly supported the new Constitution, like those who drew it up in the first place, were, as popularly described, "gentlemen of property and standing." Those who were more suspicious of its implications included smaller freeholders but also substantial landowners. In short, it had nothing to do with either state or status, but rather came down to two competing interpretations of government. The contending camps, Federalist (pro-Constitution) and Anti-Federalist, effectively clashed over the extent, and dangers, of centralized power.

The Federalists – men such as George Washington, Benjamin Franklin, the Virginian James Madison, Washington's former aide-de-camp Alexander Hamilton, and former president of the Continental Congress John Jay – believed in the power of the Constitution to protect American citizens from an excess of political power. The Anti-Federalists included revolutionary leaders such as Samuel Adams, Patrick Henry, John Hancock, and Richard Henry Lee. It was, of course, Lee's resolution in the Second Continental Congress that "these colonies are, and of right ought to be, free and independent states... absolved from all allegiance to the British Crown," which had inaugurated the process leading to this very impasse.

The Anti-Federalists were more skeptical of those Constitutional safeguards that their opponents assured them were in place. They were fearful that the rights of individual citizens would be subsumed by the greater economic interests and political influence of the merchant elites. Many white southerners suspected that such interests might also threaten their own. Those who wished slavery abolished saw the Constitution as too protective of the institution. Those who wished to retain it feared that the termination of the external slave trade in 1808 was the first step on the path to abolition. Some, like Virginia slaveholder George Mason, even managed to sustain both perspectives simultaneously.

For the Federalists, the Constitution offered the necessary protection both of and from government; for the Anti-Federalists, it was in some respects the sum of all their fears for the future of the nation. The Federalists, however, driven as they were by a sense of purpose rather than of panic, constructed a comprehensive case for the Constitution, one that the Anti-Federalists eventually found impossible to refute. The power of the written word, as had been the case in colonial America, proved crucial at this very early stage of what historians designate as the Early Republic. Three of the Federalists, Hamilton, Jay, and Madison, composed and published, under the *nom de plume* of Publius, what became known as the *Federalist Papers* in 1788. This series of eighty-five essays that originally appeared in the New York newspapers are, with justification, regarded today as the touchstone of America's political perspective. In them, the Federalist position was not just defined, but refined.

Unsurprisingly, given the colonial experience, many of the initial arguments put forward in the *Federalist Papers* concerned the baleful influence of warfare, and of foreign influence. Without a strong central government, a fully functioning Union, Hamilton argued in *Federalist No. 6*, Americans would be left dangerously "exposed" to the "arms and arts of foreign nations." At the same time, he was mindful of the danger "from dissensions between the States themselves, and from domestic factions and convulsions." "A firm Union," he stressed, "will be of the utmost moment to the peace and liberty of the States."[2]

Hamilton's coauthor, Madison, had his own ideas as to how this firm Union could be achieved and sustained. Whereas Rush had stressed the necessity of improving the "principles, morals, and manners" of American citizens to construct the republican edifice, Madison had a rather more robust take on human nature. Believing that the "causes of faction" were not an American problem specifically, but were "sown in the seed of man," he saw the new republic's expansion – both geographic and demographic – and Constitutional structure as the twin safeguards for its future. "Extend the sphere," he argued, "and you take in a greater variety of parties and interests; you make it less probable that a majority of the whole will have a common motive to invade the rights of other citizens; or if such a common motive exists, it will be more difficult for all who feel it to discover their own strength, and to act in unison with each other."[3]

Safety, for Madison, lay in numbers. Although couched in the language of political theory, he posited what was in effect a statistical security through which no individual would be left unprotected, but no group of individuals was likely to impose its perspective, be that religious, regional, or economic, on the whole. The Anti-Federalists were not convinced. Attempting to counter the arguments of the *Federalist Papers*, they warned that "in forming a constitution . . . great care should be taken to limit and definite its powers, adjust its parts, and guard against an abuse of authority." If one truth was "self evident, that all men are by nature free," it was argued, it followed that men should not "assume or exercise authority over their fellows." Instead, the "origin of society" lay not in authority but in "the united consent of those who associate" voluntarily.[4]

Although sometimes described, disparagingly, as "men of little faith," the Anti-Federalist perspective was simply that they placed their faith in the individual rather than in the institution, in the citizen rather than the Constitution, and wished to retain as much power as possible in the separate states rather than relinquish it all to a central government. Yet the Federalist faith proved, in the end, the more persuasive, possibly because it offered so much more. As James Wilson put it in the process of persuading his fellow Pennsylvanians to ratify the Constitution, "by adopting this system, we become a nation; at present we are not one. Can we," he asked, "perform a single national act? Can we do any thing to procure us dignity, or to preserve peace and tranquillity?"

Without the Constitution, Wilson warned, the "powers of our government are mere sound." Without it, America could neither be defended nor developed. Indeed, it would be unable to "remove a single rock out of a river." With the Constitution in place, however, rocks and rivers would be but the building blocks and conduits of a great nation. Wilson went further. In becoming a nation, he predicted, Americans would "also form a national character," and not just any national character, but one molded by the very Constitution then under discussion. Every nation, he asserted, "should possess originality," but America remained too influenced by the customs and habits of others. Its system of government would set it apart. Through it, Wilson promised, America might lead the world in "national importance."[5]

Such a prospect was hard to resist. Wilson's arguments helped bring Pennsylvania on board, as those of his fellow Federalists did in Virginia in June of 1788 and in New York in July. By the end of 1788, only North Carolina and Rhode Island were still struggling with the idea of the Constitution, but the viable majority had been reached. The Federalists had carried the day. As a contemporary cartoon (Figure 5.2) revealed, most of the "federal pillars" were in place, and if America was not yet a nation, "these United States" at least had a functioning form of government and would soon, under the national elections called for January of 1789, have their first president, the man who had secured their independence – George Washington.

The defeat of the Anti-Federalists over the Constitution was not the end of the matter. If they could not prevent its ratification, the Anti-Federalists were at least able to ensure its almost immediate modification. One of their persistent concerns about the Constitution as drawn up in Philadelphia was the absence of a Bill of Rights. Some of the Federalists questioned the efficacy of any such addition to protect individual rights much further than the Constitution already did, either then or in the future. In *Federalist No. 48*, Madison had specifically warned against according too much "trust to these parchment barriers against the encroaching spirit of power."[6] Nevertheless, in deference to Anti-Federalist concerns,

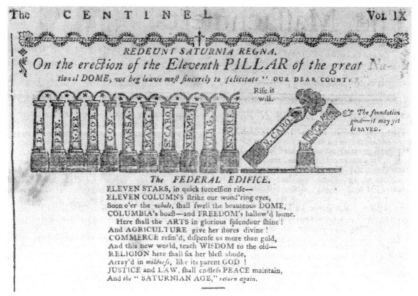

FIGURE 5.2. "The Federal Pillars," August 2, 1788. This is the third and final print in a series published in The *Massachusetts Centinel* on January 16, June 11, and August 2, 1788. The first was titled "United they stand – divided fall," and showed the Massachusetts column being guided by a heavenly hand into position next to columns representing Delaware, Pennsylvania, New Jersey, Georgia, and Connecticut. The second, titled "*Redeunt Saturnia Regna*" ("honored rules return," from Virgil's fourth Eclogue, like the motto on the Great Seal), included pillars representing Maryland and South Carolina, with Virginia being eased into place. This final woodcut, also titled "*Redeunt Saturnia Regna*," shows eleven pillars, including New Hampshire and New York, already in position, and reinforces the message of America as "freedom's hallow'd home" and the ratification of the Constitution as ushering in the return of the "Saturnian Age" (or Golden Age). The "divine hand" is in the act of straightening the twelfth pillar, representing North Carolina. By this point, only Rhode Island, as the illustration shows, was in danger of crumbling but, as the commentary makes clear, with "The foundation good – it may yet be SAVED." Print courtesy of the Library of Congress Prints and Photographs Division (LC-USZ62–45591).

the first Congress did pass such a Bill comprising ten amendments in 1791. Designed to curb any abuses of centralized power, these amendments protected freedom of speech, the press, and religion (Article I), established the right of citizens to bear arms in the service of the militia (Article II), and addressed general issues that had been hanging over from the colonial era, such as the quartering of troops and "unreasonable searches and seizures" (Articles III and IV). They also sought to ensure fairness in criminal proceedings by preventing individual citizens from being tried for the same crime twice, from testifying against themselves (hence the phrase "taking the Fifth"), or suffering "cruel and unusual punishment" (Articles V, VI, VII, and VIII).

Some of the amendments represented quite dramatic departures from the English precedents, notably the English Bill of Rights of 1689, that had informed the very notion of a Declaration or Bill of Rights in the first place. The English Bill of Rights, too, established freedom from monarchical (or centralized) authority, codified the right for Protestants to bear arms, and protected freedom of speech. The Americans, however, had not removed themselves from colonial control simply to replicate the forms and functions of English life and government. The strict separation between church and state established in the wholly secular vocabulary of the Constitution, and reinforced via the First Amendment, was the most significant deviation from traditional norms. In practice, of course, it did little to impair the influence of the mainly Protestant white elite that would come to dominate American political life.

Along with the passage of the Bill of Rights, America's first Congress took tentative steps toward quantifying who, exactly, the Bill might be protecting, and authorized the first official census for 1790. What this revealed was that the population of the United States, excluding the native peoples, comprised some four million individuals, of which slightly more than three million were classified as free and some 700,000 as slaves. Half of this population lived in the South, which was home to the bulk of the nation's slaves. Virginia remained the biggest state, with a population in excess of 700,000, almost twice that of the next largest state, Pennsylvania, with some 400,000 people. Rhode Island, which had yet to join the Union officially at the census date, was the smallest state, with a resident population of a little less than 70,000.

America's rate of growth was at first relatively gradual. In the decade following the first census, the population increased by about 1.5 million, and the number of slaves by slightly less than 200,000, and the decade following saw similar increases in terms of population. Landmass was another matter. In 1803, Jefferson finalized the "Louisiana Purchase," the acquisition of some 828,000 square miles comprising the French territory of Louisiane. Out of that timely – and, it must be said, bargain – buy, America would eventually create no fewer than fourteen states and Canada the provinces of Alberta and Saskatchewan. By 1820, therefore, both the land and its population had doubled in size from 1790. The number of slaves now exceeded 1.5 million, and no fewer than ten new states had joined the original thirteen (Vermont, 1791; Kentucky, 1792; Tennessee, 1796; Ohio, 1802; Louisiana, 1812; Indiana, 1816; Mississippi, 1817; Illinois, 1818; Alabama, 1819; and Maine, 1820).

The 1790 census had revealed that slightly more than 3 percent of Americans lived in towns or cities. By 1820, it was more than 7 percent; by 1860, almost 20 percent. In the 1840s alone, America's urban population grew from 1,843,500 to 3,548,000: a 92 percent increase. In the context of such rapid growth, places that had been little more than frontier towns in 1810 became booming cities. Cincinnati, for example, the smallest designated "urban place" in the 1810 census with a population of 2,500, had within a decade become a city and trebled its population. In only ten more years, it had entered the top ten of American cities, and by the time of the Civil War its population exceeded 160,000.

After 1830, the combination of immigration and natural increase meant that America's population growth was running at around 35 percent per decade. Immigration alone accounted for 1.75 million between 1840 and 1850; in the following decade, more than 2.5 million migrants arrived in America. By 1860, there were almost 32 million people, excluding those of the native tribes, living in the United States, and more than 10 percent of these – almost 4 million – were enslaved. This population was, by that point, divided across thirty-three states (Figure 5.3). The twenty-three that existed in 1820 had been joined by Missouri (1821), Arkansas (1836), Michigan (1837), Florida and Texas (1845), Iowa (1846), Wisconsin (1848), California (1850), Minnesota (1858), and Oregon (1859). Many of these new states were in the west, across the Appalachian-Allegheny mountain chain. By 1860, indeed, more than half of America's inhabitants were located in the west, and a great many of those that were not were looking in that direction.

Such dramatic increase might have exceeded even Madison's expectations, but it ushered in a whole new set of problems for a nation still finding its feet in a social, political, economic, and cultural sense. The Northwest Ordinance (1787) had sought to impose a degree of republican regulation on the westward movement of a mainly free white population. Yet Americans were not expanding only in a northwest direction. The lesser-known Southwest Ordinance of 1790 established a slightly different precedent, and sent a very different message. This legislation covering the Southwest Territory, which eventually became the state of Tennessee, was identical in all respects to that set out in the Northwest Ordinance three years previously, with one notable exception: it did not prohibit slavery. In effect, two parallel processes were inaugurated in

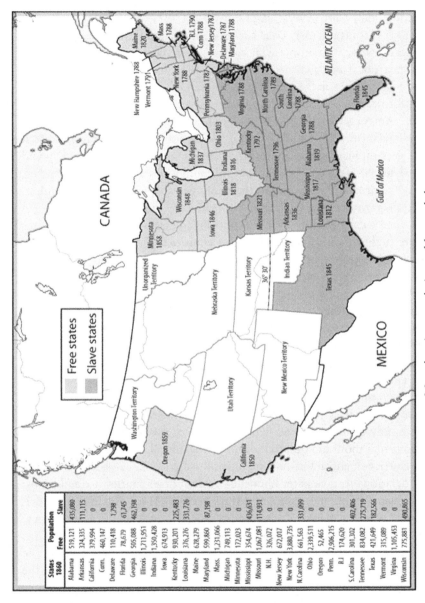

States 1860	Population Free	Slave
Alabama	519,121	435,080
Arkansas	324,335	111,115
California	379,994	0
Conn.	460,147	0
Delaware	110,418	1,798
Florida	78,679	61,745
Georgia	595,088	462,198
Illinois	1,711,951	0
Indiana	1,350,428	0
Iowa	674,913	0
Kentucky	930,201	225,483
Louisiana	376,276	331,726
Maine	628,279	0
Maryland	599,860	87,198
Mass.	1,231,066	0
Michigan	749,113	0
Minnesota	172,023	0
Mississippi	354,674	436,631
Missouri	1,067,081	114,931
N.H.	326,072	0
New Jersey	672,017	0
New York	3,880,735	0
N. Carolina	661,563	331,099
Ohio	2,339,511	0
Oregon	52,465	0
Penn.	2,906,215	0
R.I	174,620	0
S. Carolina	301,302	402,406
Tennessee	834,082	275,719
Texas	421,649	182,566
Vermont	315,089	0
Virginia	1,105,453	0
Wisconsin	775,881	490,865

FIGURE 5.3. Map showing populations of free and slave states.

these eighteenth-century land ordinances: one reflected a northern program for American expansion, and stressed liberty; the other, a southern variant that anticipated the extension of slavery. Given that they were parallel, they were never going to meet.

These contradictory constructions highlighted the fact that early America was, in many crucial respects, a nation without nationalism, at least not a nationalism driven from the center. The expectations of the Federalists notwithstanding, Americans of the Early Republican era conformed more closely to Anti-Federalist assumptions about social cohesion. America was a land whose population expressed an expectation of egalitarianism – for whites – even if social mobility did not always match the geographical variant in terms of speed and spread. What did spread were ideas, ideas emanating from the pulpit and the political chamber, disseminated and discussed in the many newspapers, books, pamphlets, and magazines of the late eighteenth and early nineteenth centuries.

America's population was well positioned in this respect. Literacy rates were higher than in some European countries. The estimates for New England suggest that at the time of the Revolution, approximately 90 percent of adults were literate to some degree. It may not be surprising, therefore, that this period saw the emergence and extension of a broad range of voluntary associations, private, professional (Figure 5.4), religious, and, increasingly, political, whose members, already familiar with town meetings and tavern debates, sought to work out the new national imperative on a local level.

This urge to form associations was an aspect of the new nation that drew comment. French visitor Alexis de Tocqueville, author of *Democracy in America* (1835, 1840), noted the American tendency to found "not only commercial and manufacturing companies" but also "associations of a thousand other kinds, religious, moral, serious, futile, general or restricted, enormous or diminutive." Americans, he observed, "make associations to give entertainments, to found seminaries, to build inns, to construct churches, [and] to diffuse books." This "principle of association" was, Tocqueville recognized, a crucial component in a democracy, in which the risk was that all "become powerless if they do not learn voluntarily to help one another.... If men are to remain civilized," he stressed "the art of associating together must grow and improve in the same ratio in which the equality of condition is increased."[7]

This was not an alien idea for Americans. Although a great many fraternal organizations and associations had their origins in the Early Republic, others, and particularly library societies and athenaeums, had

FIGURE 5.4. 'Massachusetts Mechanic Association' [n.d. Engraver Samuel Hill, 1766?–1804). One of the many professional fraternal associations in early America, forerunner of the labor unions, the symbolism of the Mechanics' Association not only suggests the proliferation of opportunities in the new nation, but reinforces the recognition of the role of the working man to the success of the Republic. Such associations expressed the absence of deference to elites, the importance of work as a civic virtue, and the economic, social, and political independence of the working man in a democracy. This particular certificate admits one Nathaniel Bradlee, a carpenter, to the Association in 1800. Incorporating national imagery (the eagle) it also invokes the Great Seal and its motto with the image of the industrious beehive, bottom center. The message is that via the various skills that the mechanic arts can offer, America will become a nation of plenty (the cornucopias flanking the two women emphasize this point). The Masonic imagery was typical for the period; there were Masonic Lodges in many American cities, and much of the symbolism of freemasonry was echoed in national iconography. Print courtesy of the Library of Congress Prints and Photographs Division (LC-USZ62–33263).

existed since the colonial period. The earliest was the Library Company of Philadelphia, founded in 1731 by Benjamin Franklin, but there were many others across most of the states, including the Redwood Library and Athenaeum in Newport, Rhode Island (1747), the Boston Athenaeum

(1807), and the American Antiquarian Society, founded in Worcester, Massachusetts, in 1812. Some of these institutions, a great many of which still exist today, grew out of preexisting social and cultural networks; in the Library Company of Philadelphia's case, that surrounding Franklin himself. Others were wholly new. All brought together a broad cross-section of like-minded individuals in pursuit of educational and intellectual advancement.

The Charlestown Library Society, in South Carolina, is just one example, founded in 1748 by a group of professional men, including several merchants, a schoolteacher, a printer, a distiller, a lawyer, a planter, and a wig-maker. In 1762, it described its function, in terms that Tocqueville later echoed, as the promotion of learning among its members "who are ambitious of approving themselves worthy of their mother country, by imitating her humanity, as well as her industry, and by transporting from her the improvements in the finer as well as in the inferiour [sic] arts." Although hardly a motivation that would have found much favor after the Revolution, in fact the driving forces behind that society, at least, provide some clue to what was exercising these literary self-improvement enterprises in the late eighteenth and early nineteenth centuries.

While America remained under colonial control, the members of the Charlestown Library Society held up the "gross ignorance of the naked Indian" and his "savage disposition" as a threat of what might befall any society not prepared to inculcate learning and the arts. Revealing a quite remarkable faith in the prophylactic power of print to "obviate this possible evil," it was precisely "to prevent our descendants from sinking into a similar situation" that, its members advertised, the library society had been formed in the first place.[8] The risks of "going native" may have been reduced in the years between the society's founding and the Early Republic, but the threat of remaining subservient to English learning and letters had replaced it.

This would develop into a perennial concern for Americans. Noah Webster had popularized the problem, and conveniently provided part of its solution, in his famous spelling book and, later, his *Dictionary* (1806). In the process of persuading Pennsylvania to ratify the Constitution, James Wilson had stressed that America's "national importance" might depend, in large part, on her taking the "lead in literary improvements." Yet when English critics sniped, as author and clergyman Sydney Smith did in 1820 when he asked "in the four quarters of the globe, who reads an American book?" Americans winced. "Our day of dependence, our long apprenticeship to the learning of others lands, draws to a close," America's foremost transcendentalist thinker, Ralph Waldo Emerson, asserted in 1837, in an address sometimes described as America's literary Declaration of Independence. Almost a decade later, however, the noted journalist and critic Margaret Fuller sounded a less optimistic note. Although "we have an independent political existence," she observed, "our position toward Europe, as to Literature and the Arts, is still that of a colony."[9]

Voluntary organizations and literary societies alike worked to draw the new nation out from under that shadow of colonialism. In that sense, as in others, they served an important nationalizing function. They were, in effect, democratic debating societies, loci for the meeting of like-minded Americans in pursuit of a variety of goals, professional or political, practical or entertaining, local or national. Yet this "principle of association" was not all positive. It had the power to divide as much as to unify, to undermine as well as reinforce the nation it exemplified. Via their many voluntary societies, Americans both created a form of Anti-Federalist idealism and simultaneously challenged the Federalist foundations of their nation. The various individual organizations did not do this alone, of course. The problem for America came when rather more overarching associative principles began to foment and solidify; principles that cohered around politics, around reform and, worst of all, around region.

At the outset, America was governed by one political perspective, that of the Federalists. Although opposition to the Federalist program certainly existed, an alternative political party did not. Politics, and indeed national sentiment, initially cohered around the first president, Washington. The practical business of constructing a working administration alongside a viable economic program fell to – or, more accurately, was seized by – Washington's ambitious former aide-de-camp and subsequently Secretary of the Treasury, Alexander Hamilton. Hamilton's reports on public credit (1790) and on manufactures (1791), while not as conceptually inspiring as either the Declaration of Independence or the Constitution, consolidated the achievements of the latter, at least. Hamilton's economic policies, the basis for a future (1830s) mercantilist program termed the "American System," stressed the importance of tariffs to protect the new nation's fledgling industries and trade and to provide for internal – mainly transport – improvements.

Not all agreed with Hamilton, however, most notably Jefferson, who resigned from Congress when Hamilton's bill establishing a national bank was passed. Jefferson had not been involved in the Constitutional debates, serving as he did as Minister to France between 1785 and 1789. That did not prevent his holding strong opinions on the direction the nation was taking. Jefferson's vision of the ideal republic was one comprising yeomen farmers, independently – or, in some cases, with slaves, although he never made that point – tilling their own little patch, secure from the impositions of all those things that Hamilton, rather more realistically, regarded as crucial for the republic: tariffs, internal improvements, banks – in short, the cash nexus. In an echo of Anti-Federalist concerns, Jefferson feared that, under Hamilton's program, the new nation would too quickly resemble the Old World from which it had fought so long and hard to escape.

Jefferson outlined his perspective in a letter to Madison: "I think our governments will remain virtuous for many centuries as long as they are chiefly agricultural," he observed. However, he warned, this would hold true only for "as long as there shall be vacant lands in any part of America. When they get piled upon one another in large cities, as in Europe," he warned, "they will become corrupt as in Europe." Agriculture, as he advised Washington, was America's "wisest pursuit, because it will in the end contribute most to real wealth, good morals and happiness." Hamilton thought it more likely to contribute to national bankruptcy. He was quite naturally stunned that a man so recently returned from Paris should wish to remain on the farm. America's financial future, Hamilton believed, lay beyond the simple cultivation of the land itself. It lay in commerce and industry, in urban growth and expanding markets, all under the control of Congress.[10]

This ideological fissure led to the emergence of the first united political opposition to the Federalists in the form of Jefferson's supporters, the Democratic-Republicans (a combination of their chosen title, Republicans, and their opponents' name for them, Democrats). Intended to pull the Union together, Hamilton's policies served to sharpen divisions between the merchant, industrial, and commercial interests, most closely associated with the northern states, and the slaveholding planter and farming interests, mainly located in the South, and to render them in political form. This in itself hardly threatened the republic, but other forces, over the years that followed, worked to deepen these distinctions of party as much as to minimize their differences. The clash between Hamilton and Jefferson, and by extrapolation between Federalist and Republican, really symbolized not just those issues exercising Americans in the Early Republic, but longer-term divisions that the nation needed to work out in the nineteenth century: between aristocracy and democracy, industrialization and agrarianism, and centralized power and states' rights. All had the potential to divide a nation only recently brought together.

Washington could not, of course, foresee how these contradictory constructions would play out, but as president, he was aware, as he had been as commander of the Continental Army, of the pressing need for some sense of national unity, both for national security and for internal stability. Shortly before leaving office, he had stressed to Patrick Henry that his "ardent desire is, and my aim has been . . . to keep the U States free from *political* connections with *every* other country, to see that they *may be* independent of *all* and under the influence of *none*. In a word," he declared, "I want an *American* character, that the powers of Europe may be convinced we act for *ourselves* and not for *others*."[11]

In 1796, Washington declined to stand for a third term as president, thereby establishing a precedent all future presidents followed, with varying degrees of enthusiasm, with the exception of Franklin D. Roosevelt during World War II. He had been planning not to stand even for a second term, but the threat of already apparent sectional divisions, outlined to him by both Jefferson and Hamilton, persuaded him to remain in office. "The confidence of the whole union is centered in you," Jefferson advised him. "North and South will hang together, if they have you to hang on." On this subject, Hamilton concurred. The "impression is uniform," he told Washington, "that your declining would be deplored as the greatest evil, that could befall the country at this present juncture."[12]

At some point, as all realized, the country would have to hang together without Washington. He left office in 1796, and it is a measure of how mixed his feelings were toward his presidency and the pressure on him to hold the union together that he began to compose what became his famous "Farewell Address" in 1792. In it, he reminded Americans of just some of the benefits, and many of the risks, attendant on forming the national character that he saw as so crucial for America's future. He highlighted the importance of "unity of government" as not only making Americans into "one people" but as "a main pillar in the edifice" of independence. It "is of infinite moment," he urged his fellow Americans, "that you should properly estimate the immense value of your national Union to your collective happiness." He emphasized that Americans were "[c]itizens, by birth or choice, of a common country," and "that country has a right to concentrate your affections." He encouraged them to position their "American" identity before that of their state, to place patriotism ahead of "any appellation derived from local distinctions." What America had achieved, he stressed, was the result of "joint counsels and joint efforts, of common dangers, sufferings, and successes."[13]

That Washington felt it necessary not just to make but to emphasize these points reveals the already widening gulf between the several regions of the United States even as early as the end of the eighteenth century. He saw this as partly produced by what he termed "the baneful effects of the spirit of party." In fact, the "geographical discriminations, Northern and Southern, Atlantic and Western," that so concerned him predated party politics, predated, indeed, the nation itself. Captain John Smith was way ahead of Washington here. In 1631, he recognized the potential for enmity between the Chesapeake and Massachusetts Bay colonies. Some, he noted, "would have all men advance Virginia to the ruine of New-England; and others the losse of Virginia to sustaine New-England." Foreshadowing Washington's warning more than a century later, Smith had commented that the competitive colonies in question might do better to concentrate on "strengthening each other against all occurrences." Of course they did no such thing. Even as the new nation debated its Constitution, Gouvernor Morris lamented the fact that "State attachments and State importance have been the bane of this country."[14]

Hindsight possibly lends a greater prescience to both Smith and Morris than they merit. Yet when Tocqueville visited the United States in 1830 he, too, concluded that the Union was weak relative to the states. The "Union is a vast body, which presents no definite object to patriotic feeling," he observed. The states, by contrast, were "identified with the soil; with the right of property and the domestic affections; with the recollections of the past, the labours of the present, and the hopes of the future." American patriotism, as Tocqueville saw it in the 1830s, was "still directed to the state and has not passed over to the Union."[15]

Confirmation of his perspective was provided by the disintegration of that Union in 1860. Americans, it seemed, failed to heed Washington's warnings. When he left office, America's first president left a predominantly rural population, fully in accord with Jefferson's ideas about moral and material stability. It was also a very youthful population. Some 50 percent of Americans in the late eighteenth century were under sixteen. Yet as the nation grew and urbanized, at least some of these children of the Revolution would survive long enough to see their national inheritance disintegrate. The expansion that the Federalists had so confidently believed would secure America's future, by the mid-nineteenth century, seemed poised to tear it apart.

Our Federal Union! It Must Be Preserved!

The election of America's second president, John Adams, in 1796 was unusual in having the president and vice-president belonging to different political parties. It was, unfortunately, less unusual in its sectional divisions, with voters in the northern states mainly supporting Adams and those in the southern and western states preferring Jefferson. This would become something of a pattern. As political parties themselves became the most prominent and influential of all the many organizations America sustained, so many localized conflicts were played out on the national level just as national battles moved down into the states. Supported by political societies, and having a publishing outlet in the proliferation of a partisan press, political opposition began to find its feet in American society. The 1796 election was also unusual in being the first, and last until 1824, time anyone from outside the southern states – indeed, from Virginia – held the executive office. Both of the northern presidents, John and, in 1824, John Quincy Adams not only came from Massachusetts but from the same family; they were father and son. Not until 1828, with the election of Andrew Jackson from Tennessee, did any other state produce a president.

Adams's presidency was in many respects a hiatus as far as America's political and social development was concerned. Several threads were picked up in those years that would skein out more obviously in the decades, indeed century, to follow, while others reached the end of their particular reel. By the time Adams left office, and Jefferson assumed it, in 1800, one of the threads fast fraying away was the Federalists themselves. The death of Washington in 1799 removed their most potent and popular symbol. What remained was a group of politicians whose disdain for "the people" was a little too apparent to assure them of future success at the polls. Americans quite naturally preferred Jefferson's version of them as independent, hardworking farmers, which of course a great many of them were.

The Federalist perspective was revealed at its most extreme as a result of an undeclared naval war (the Quasi-War) with France (1798–1800). This provided them with an excuse to attack political opponents at home under the broad banner of defending America from dangers from abroad. This early factional use of fear did the Federalists little good and, in the long term, did others a great deal of harm. The Alien and Sedition and the Naturalization Acts of 1798, although purportedly passed for America's protection, were more about depriving the Republicans of votes. The Sedition Act, in particular, removed anyone deemed "dangerous to the peace and safety of the United States," which too readily translated into "critical of the government." Naturally the Republicans invoked the Bill of Rights against the Federalists, but a problematic precedent was set by both Virginia and Kentucky, whose legislatures passed resolutions (or resolves) protesting the acts, using states' rights as the basis for their opposition. As Morris had realized, states' rights would indeed become the bane of the United States. Yet the larger problem for America lay beyond the states; in fact, it lay just offshore.

Although Washington had stressed the importance of America's keeping well clear of foreign entanglements – and on a diplomatic level she mostly did – in fact the new nation's development cannot be divorced either from events in Europe or from the forces impacting on the broader Atlantic world, and in particular on those parts of it most proximate to America. The strongest of these related to slavery. The United States, during Adams's presidency, was moving closer to that point when, under the Constitution, the external slave trade had to cease. Many Americans could not have cared less; they neither owned nor sought to own slaves; those who did care, however, cared a lot. They had good reason to.

In 1791, the slave uprising in Saint-Domingue led by the black leader François Dominique Toussaint L'Ouverture and the establishment, in 1804, of Haiti was not a development likely to cheer the souls of America's slaveholders. The thirteen years of bloodshed in what became Haiti sent a clear message to America about the dangers inherent in sustaining a slave society in a world in which slavery was coming under increasing attack both from abolitionists, white and black, and from slaves themselves. The events in Saint-Domingue, and indeed elsewhere in the Caribbean, in the early nineteenth century – the Easter Rebellion in Barbados (1816) and the Demerara Rebellion (1823) – naturally unsettled America's slaveholders, already aware of the potential for the violent overthrow of slavery in their own society.

At the same time, slavery had increased both in economic and social importance in the South in the decades following independence. The dramatic rise in global demand for cotton caused by the textile industries of England and New England alike expanded southern markets. The invention, in 1793, of Eli Whitney's cotton gin permitted the successful separation of seed from fiber in upland, or short-staple cotton, an innovation that made cotton production feasible across a much wider area than previously. As the number of slaves in the North declined, therefore,

FIGURE 5.5. A slave auction in the South, from an original sketch by Theodore R. Davis, published in *Harper's Weekly*, 13 July, 1861. Print courtesy of the Library of Congress Prints and Photographs Division (LC-USZ62–2582).

southern states such as Alabama, Georgia, Louisiana, and South Carolina saw massive increases in their slave population. Between 1810 and 1860, Georgia saw a fourfold increase; in South Carolina and Kentucky, the enslaved population more than doubled; in Alabama, the increase was almost tenfold. Given that the external slave trade had long since ended by this period, such increases were the result of the burgeoning internal slave trade. The slave markets of the South (Figure 5.5), in towns and cities such as Lexington, Kentucky, New Orleans, or Natchez that had previously traded slaves from Africa and the British Caribbean, now made their money by moving slaves from the upper South, from Virginia and Maryland, "sold down the river" to the more productive lands of the Deep South or the southwest.

And there was money to be made, no doubt. The closing of the external slave trade simply increased the value of those slaves America held. In the 1830s, a "prime field hand," by which was meant a young and healthy male slave, was valued at some 500 dollars. By the 1850s, his market value could be almost three or four times that. The internal slave trade as a whole, by the eve of the Civil War, turned over approximately 80,000 slaves and some 60 million dollars annually. The real cost, of course, was paid by the slaves themselves, trapped in this especially lethal variant of the cash nexus that Hamilton had placed so much faith in. Slaves who were traded were frequently separated from friends and family, most cruelly of all from their partners and children, and sent south either by steamboat or, chained together in what was termed a slave "coffle" and accompanied by armed guards, forced to march along routes such as the Nachez Trace that linked Natchez, Mississippi, with Nashville, Tennessee.

Such slaves endured a miserable transition between the smaller slave regimes of the upper South to the far larger, harsher, and impersonal slave plantations of states such as Mississippi. William Wells Brown, who had been born a slave in Kentucky but who escaped the institution and fled to freedom in the North and to a successful if stormy career as an abolitionist orator and author, described a process so common as to elicit little comment at the time, yet so cruel that the memory of it retains the power to unsettle America to this day: the sight of a "drove of slaves on a southern steamboat, bound for the cotton or sugar regions." No one, Brown recalled, "not even the passengers," paid much attention to the slaves, "though they clang their chains at every step." Detailing both the practical business of slave sales, where older slaves had their hair blackened so as to appear younger to prospective buyers, and the personal misery of the transactions, Brown's memoirs made horrific reading. In particular, he recounted how, on a trip down the river, "one woman who had been taken from her husband and children, and having no desire to live without them, in the agony of her soul jumped overboard, and drowned herself." It was hardly surprising that the slaves themselves described the slave traders as "soul drivers."[16]

As the Preface to his famous *Narrative*, published by the Boston Anti-Slavery Society in 1847, put it, on the subject of slavery, Brown had "been behind the curtain. He has visited its secret chambers. Its iron has entered his own soul." In many respects, however, the iron had also entered the soul of America. For the slaves concerned, slavery was, as sociologists incisively term it, a form of "social death."[17] Its repercussions, however, impacted not only the slaves, but also free black society and white, North and South alike. Slavery was a far more complex system than the simple exploitation of black labor by white owners on southern plantations. It was integral to the nation's economic and social structure.

Although some northerners did try to pretend that slavery was the South's "peculiar institution" (as in, specific to the South, rather than strange), this was self-delusion on a national scale. As one southerner commented, the "history of the wealth and power of nations is but a record of slave products."[18] America was no exception. Slavery was in the commodities Americans purchased, the goods they traded, the coffee they consumed. This much was obvious to Ralph Waldo Emerson, who highlighted the nation's complicity in slavery in his 1844 address commemorating its abolition in the British West Indies. "What if it cost a few unpleasant scenes on the coast of Africa?" he asked, given that this was "a great way off." Back home in America, slavery's realities could be avoided, by those in the North, at least, and if "any mention was made of homicide, madness, adultery, and intolerable tortures," Americans would simply "let the church-bells ring louder." So long as the sugar, coffee, and tobacco produced by slaves "was excellent: nobody tasted blood in it."[19]

As early as the second decade of the nineteenth century, however, those same church bells that muted slavery's realities in the North were sounding a louder and more discordant note in the South, and in Congress. A confluence of contemporary concerns made it increasingly difficult for the nation to keep avoiding that indecisive inheritance bequeathed it by the Constitutional Convention in 1787. On the matter of slavery, Jefferson famously pronounced, America had "the wolf by the ears, and we can neither hold him, nor safely let him go." A great deal of handwringing went on as far as slavery was concerned, not least by those, like Jefferson, who were seeking to remain balanced on the fence they managed to maintain in their minds between liberty as the ideal they lived up to and slavery as the reality they lived with.

The nation's expansion only exacerbated the problem. Expanding the geographical sphere, as Jefferson had done in 1803, did not, in fact, as Madison had hoped, ensure stability. Would this vast new territory be slave or free? Would the representative balance between the free and slave states in Congress, and specifically in the Senate, be maintained? In the opening decades of the nineteenth century, it was, although more by luck than judgment. Of the six newest states, three were from the lands covered by the Northwest Ordinance (Ohio, Indiana, and Illinois), and therefore free of slavery, and three from the South (Louisiana, Mississippi, and Alabama), and therefore slaveholding states. When, in 1819, the territory of Missouri, mainly settled by southerners and with some 10 percent of its population enslaved, applied for admission, however, that balance was threatened.

There was a solution to hand. Maine, which at that time was still part of Massachusetts, was also seeking admittance as a separate state that year. Yet Congress did not automatically grasp that particular straw, evidence in itself of how heated the whole matter was becoming. Instead, it was proposed, by New York representative James Tallmadge, that gradual manumission be made a requirement of Missouri's admittance. The House of Representatives was supportive. The Senate was not. Only some deft negotiation by Henry Clay of Kentucky ensured that both Maine and Missouri were admitted to the Union, free and slave, respectively.

The deal that Clay struck closed all lands acquired under the Louisiana Purchase lying north of 36°30′ to slavery. The sole exception was Missouri itself. It was a clever compromise, but it was also a clumsy one, through no fault of Clay's. It simply put off the evil day. Jefferson knew that. Writing toward the end of his life in 1820, he described how "this momentous question, like a fire bell in the night, awakened and filled me with terror. I considered it at once as the knell of the Union." The Missouri Compromise was, in his view, "a reprieve only, not a final sentence. A geographical line, coinciding with a marked principle, moral and political," he asserted, "once conceived and held up to the angry passions of men, will never be obliterated." He concluded on a bleak note. "I regret that I am now to die in the belief, that the useless sacrifice of themselves by the generation of 1776, to acquire self-government and happiness to their country, is to be thrown away by the unwise and unworthy passions of their sons," he bemoaned, "and that my only consolation is to be, that I live not to weep over it."[20]

Jefferson was being somewhat disingenuous here, passing the buck, and the blame, onto the generation that followed him, but he was right in his prediction. Slavery would sunder the Union. Slaves, excluded from the polity by virtue of their legal position under the Constitution, inhabited a halfway house between person and property, a construction that conferred considerable political power on their owners. It was only when this power began to threaten the Union, only when the politicians decided that the nation itself could no longer sustain this awkward balancing act, that the abolition of what was an increasingly anachronistic institution was contemplated in earnest.

The assertion of future president Abraham Lincoln in 1858 that a "house divided against itself cannot stand," that the American "government cannot endure permanently half slave and half free," seems a self-evident truth to twenty-first-century minds.[21] Yet the fact was, by 1858, the American nation had endured on precisely this basis for the best part of a century. As slave rebellions destabilized the Atlantic world, and the foremost slave-trading nation, Great Britain, moved to abolish slavery in her Caribbean colonies, the American South only became more strident in its defense of its "peculiar institution," apparently oblivious to the winds of change blowing in from both the Atlantic and the North. Of course, the South was not oblivious, but it was increasingly defensive.

This defensiveness comprised economic as well as cultural components. Alexander Hamilton had devised an economic program geared toward drawing the component parts of the United States together. Yet it could not succeed when the requirements of each part not only contradicted, but clashed with each other. Tariffs were a case in point. Indeed, in 1828, tariffs became the case in point, when South Carolina challenged the federal government over a tariff introduced that year. Put simply, the North wanted tariffs to protect its manufacturing development. The South did not, because they threatened the European trade in slave-produced commodities, especially, but not exclusively, cotton, which was the basis of its economy. South Carolina's threats to nullify what it termed the "Tariff of Abominations" of 1828, or to secede if it were imposed, offered a clear challenge to federal authority and highlighted the as-yet unsettled relationship between the individual states and the Union.

The then-vice-president, John C. Calhoun from South Carolina, set out his state's position, and his understanding of the right of nullification based on the Kentucky and Virginia Resolutions in his *Exposition and Protest* (1828). Although he stressed that South Carolina "would never desire to speak of our country . . . but as one great whole, having a common interest, which all its parts ought zealously to promote," he pointed out the impossibility of avoiding "the discussion of sectional interest, and the use of sectional language."[22] Over the next few years, there was plenty of "sectional language" uttered in Congress as politicians debated the specifics of tariffs and the broader issue of states' rights within a federal system.

The Democratic president, Andrew Jackson of Tennessee, had a reputation for supporting states' rights, but not, as it turned out, if these threatened the Union. He made his point forcibly at the annual Jefferson Day dinner in 1830 when he proposed the toast, "Our Federal Union! It Must Be Preserved." This was not at all what men like Calhoun wished to hear, so they simply did not listen. When a revised tariff was passed in 1832, Calhoun resigned from the Vice-Presidency and South Carolina adopted an ordinance nullifying the tariff acts of 1828 and 1832, making it clear that the state would secede if forced to comply.

The president was having none of that. Addressing South Carolina directly in December 1832, Jackson argued that "the power to annul a law of the United States, assumed by one State," was in his view "*incompatible with the existence of the Union, contradicted expressly by the letter of the Constitution, unauthorized by its spirit, inconsistent with every principle on which it was founded, and destructive of the great object for which it was formed.*" Any such attempt, indeed, was "TREASON," Jackson asserted. "Are you ready," he inquired, "to incur its guilt?"[23] The short answer, in 1832, was "no" – or, more accurately, "not yet." With federal troops in Charleston, and the other southern states moving back with some speed from the precipice toward which South Carolina was urging them, it was the only possible response. Yet what became known as the Nullification Crisis was an ominous portent. It invoked the specter of secession and disunion that, until 1865, was never fully laid to rest.

A House Divided

The period following the Nullification Crisis in America is usually accorded the title of "antebellum" (before war), reflecting the knowledge that, in 1861, the Civil War between North and South broke out. Consequently, the growing antagonism between these two sections tends to dominate assessment of the period between 1830 and 1860, highlighting the differences that divided them at the expense of those forces that worked to unite them. Contemporary observers sometimes also saw it that way. Tocqueville, for one, had arrived in the United States in the midst of the tariff turmoil, so it was perhaps unsurprising that he perceived "two opposite tendencies" in American life, "two currents flowing in opposite directions in the same channel," and that he located this tendency most strongly in the South. "The inhabitants of the Southern states," he observed, "are, of all the Americans, those who are most interested in the maintenance of the Union; they would assuredly suffer most from being left to themselves, and yet they are the only ones who threaten to break the tie of confederation."[24]

The first attempt, unsuccessful though it was, to sunder the ties of confederation occurred not in the South but in New England. The context was the War of 1812, an inconclusive conflict waged against Great Britain between 1812 and 1815 the most lasting legacy of which was America's national anthem, the Star-Spangled Banner. New England Federalists, unhappy at Congressional demands for troops, met at Hartford, Connecticut, in 1814 to debate the extent of Congressional prerogative, and concluded that a state might, under extreme circumstances, either refuse to comply with Congress or, in the worst case, remove itself from the federal compact. If this was the first blip of disunion on the federal radar, and the Nullification Crisis the second, then the secession of the southern states from the Union in 1861 may be regarded as completing a third-time charmed – or rather charmless – pattern. Yet it was not until the 1830s that any such pattern really began to emerge and, even then, no certainty that it would be the one the nation followed.

The Hartford Convention sounded a discordant note in a conflict that had, it was believed at the time, revivified national sentiment and drawn the United States closer together against a common and familiar enemy. Unfortunately, such unity was short-lived, not least because the War of 1812 had simply reinforced the fact that, dominant in the Western Hemisphere, and protected from Europe by 3,000 miles of ocean, America had no natural predator. It was the last time that any foreign power would physically compromise American domestic space until the terrible events of 9/11 in 2001. For Americans in the nineteenth century, the only danger they faced was from themselves. Not that they realized they were in any particular danger, given that the dissolution of the Union, although it took a violent form in the end, was effected via the persistent drip of divisive sectional disagreement rather than the full-scale drama of congressional North/South confrontation that had been the Nullification Crisis.

Andrew Jackson had faced down South Carolina in 1832 and held the Union together. This was not the least of the achievements of a man who lent his name to an era, but not everyone appreciated it. Despite the fact that the Age of Jackson was for a long time also known as the Age of the Common Man, Jackson did little to boost social or political mobility, and even at the time his authority was perceived as overly autocratic. The emergence of a new political party in opposition to the Democrats in 1833, the Whigs, inaugurated what is termed the "Second Party System" in American political history. In theory, and to a great extent in practice, this system served a unifying purpose, drawing Americans together under the banner of party rather than state or, indeed, slave ownership. Again, it proved relatively short-lived (1833–1856), and the reason for its lack of longevity was slavery. It survived by avoiding the subject. Increasingly, that proved impossible.

Not the least of the many associations that directed and influenced American lives after 1830 was the abolition movement. Initially it was not popular. Abolitionists were perceived as radicals, a disruptive force in a North seeking to distance itself from slavery altogether, and a potentially dangerous one in a South increasingly devoted to the protection of its "peculiar institution." Yet driven by the principle that, on this subject, it was perhaps better to be hated than ignored, the abolitionists persisted in their efforts to draw America's attention to the evils of slavery, and their persistence paid off.

In 1829, a freeborn African American from North Carolina, David Walker, published his *Appeal to the Colored Citizens of the World*, in which he advised African Americans: "If you commence, make sure work – do not trifle, for they will not trifle with you – they want us for their slaves, and think nothing of murdering us in order to subject us to that wretched condition – therefore, if there is an *attempt* made by us, kill or be killed." Two years later, in 1831, abolitionist editor William Lloyd Garrison produced, in January, the first edition of his journal *The Liberator*, which argued for immediate emancipation. "I am in earnest," Garrison declared, "I will not equivocate – I will not excuse – I will not retreat a single inch – and I will be heard." He may have been. In August, in Southampton County, Virginia, a slave named Nat Turner led an uprising that, although unsuccessful, unnerved large swathes of the South.

The reaction from southerners comprised a combination of counterattack and downright denial, a passive-aggressive position that sought to promote slavery as, in Calhoun's famous phrase, "a positive good" while simultaneously preventing anyone from talking about it at all (Figure 5.6). Naturally, such a response made slavery the one subject that people did want to talk about, and write about, and comment on, and criticize. Calhoun's defense of slavery emerged in the context of an 1837 congressional debate on abolitionist petitions. Congress was flooded with these, and in an attempt to minimize their impact, pro-slavery politicians had, the previous year, passed the "Gag Rule," – the tabling, unread, of such petitions. As might have been anticipated, although clearly not by southern slaveholders and apparently not by Calhoun, this only served to position slavery center stage. By the 1830s, the South had already gained a reputation as a section in which free speech was stifled and cruelty condoned, one in which the ideals of the Declaration of Independence, American ideals, were not just denied, but derided.

The 1830s was, in many respects, the decade of debate over slavery. Prompted by the appearance of *The Liberator* in 1831, chastened by Turner's rebellion, and provoked by Garrison's establishment the following year of the New England Anti-Slavery Society and, the year after that, the American Anti-Slavery Society by Arthur and Lewis Tappan in New York, northerners were forced at least to consider the subject from a moral perspective, although most preferred a practical one. There were not a few northerners who concurred with Calhoun that abolitionists threatened the Union, and that if their agitation were left unchecked, Americans

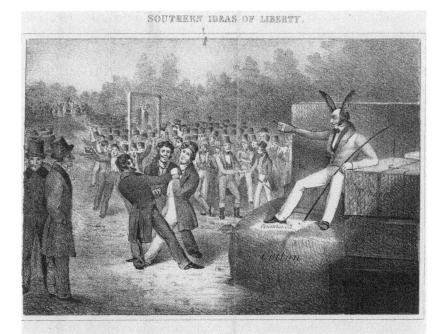

FIGURE 5.6. "Southern Ideas of Liberty" (Boston, 1835). This is an abolitionist representation of the southern treatment of slavery's opponents in the South in the mid-1830s. There were instances of the hanging and tarring and feathering of anti-slavery activists in Georgia, Louisiana, and Mississippi at this time. In 1835, resolutions were passed in the southern states calling for the suppression of abolitionist organizations, before the Congressional debate on the Gag Rule (the Twenty-First Rule). In the image, a judge with ass's ears and a whip is seated on bales of cotton and tobacco with the Constitution underfoot, condemning an abolitionist to hang. The text below the image reads: "Sentence passed upon one for supporting that clause of our Declaration viz. All men are born free & equal. Strip him to the skin! give him a coat of Tar & Feathers!! Hang him by the neck, between the Heavens and the Earth!!! as a beacon to warn the Northern Fanatics of their danger!!!!" Print courtesy of the Library of Congress Prints and Photographs Division (LC-USZ62–92284).

would "become, finally, two people."²⁵ Yet neither northern hostility toward nor support for the South in the antebellum period was driven by abolitionists alone. Slavery was the root cause of the South's problems, as northerners understood these. It hampered the South's material development, limited its educational opportunities, and made it unattractive to immigrants. It was, therefore, a drain on white society and, by extra-polation, on the nation.

The following decades saw less talk and rather more action, a shift that had nothing to do with the Gag Rule and everything to do with the nation's demographic growth and the technological and market devel-opments that accompanied and facilitated its concomitant geographic expansion. And the 1840s was the decade of westward expansion on a large scale. It was a decade that first heard the phrase "Manifest Destiny" applied to America's cross-continental drift, and the decade when this brought Americans into armed conflict with Mexico. As a consequence of both, it was, too, the decade that saw the beginning of the end for the short-lived Second Party System. With the appearance of the Liberty Party in 1840, anti-slavery announced itself as a potential political force. The 1848 election further raised the stakes of anti-slavery politics with the appearance of the Free Soil Party.

The Free Soil Party revealed the extent to which politicians and their constituents were beginning to realign along the fault lines in the Union created by slavery. Sectional division proved strong enough, in the end, to result in the disintegration of the Whig party and eventual emergence of a new, sectional political party, the Republicans, who first stood for national election in 1856 on the platform of preventing slavery's further extension westward. Driving this political realignment of the 1840s and 1850s was the concomitant construction of the idea of southern political influence, or the "Slave Power," as a threat to American liberties. All of these developments fed off and reinforced each other, and all expressed and exacerbated the growing sectional strain that the Union was under. From being essentially an extremist, minority perspective, opposition to slavery gradually moved mainstream.

Yet for some, abolition alone was not the answer. From motives that ranged from blind racism to blinkered benevolence, some believed that black and white could never coexist peacefully on the basis of equality in the United States. The American Colonization Society, founded in 1816, advocated the removal of free African Americans from the nation and their resettlement in African nations, an experiment that resulted in the establishment of Liberia in 1821 but that satisfied too few – not least African Americans themselves – to be successful. Yet what the Amer-ican Colonization Society highlighted was not just the disquiet that even well-meaning Americans felt regarding the likely success of a color-blind republic, but an underlying uncertainty about that republic's Manifest Destiny.

The concept of Manifest Destiny was, from the outset, both evocative and problematic in equal parts. The phrase had been coined in 1845 by John O'Sullivan, editor of the *Democratic Review*. He had used it in the context of the acquisition of Oregon and California, both territories that Britain had a claim to. His complaint was that the former colonial power was attempting to impede "the fulfillment of our manifest destiny to overspread the continent allotted by Providence for the free development of our yearly multiplying millions." As far as O'Sullivan meant it, it seemed straightforward. It harked back to the precolonial concept of America as a "virgin land" ripe for European exploitation, and certainly rode roughshod over the rights of the native populations who had themselves been forced ever further westward in the face of white settlement. None of this was new, and indeed the associations that the phrase conjured up would have resonated in a nation still not so far from its colonial past that it had forgotten it entirely.

Nor was there anything especially new in the idea of America's having a destiny to be made manifest. Thomas Paine had, after all, advised the Revolutionary generation that theirs was "the cause of all mankind." The problem for antebellum Americans, faced with a considerable percentage of mankind streaming across the new territories, was that the exact nature of this destiny, its moral and practical imperatives, was not quite as the Founding Fathers had anticipated. Given that white Americans had managed to construct a material distinction between the native nations and their own, tribal rights did not really enter into the equation at this point. The rights of white settlers did, however, in particular the kind of societies they would be able to construct in the West, and the impact these would have on the nation.

From a purely practical perspective, the problem came down to the balance of power in Congress and the maintenance of that balance in the Senate between free and slave states as established via the Missouri Compromise. Although O'Sullivan had asserted that as far as America's expansion went, slavery "had nothing to do with it," an increasing number of northerners believed that it had everything to do with it. They believed that the South was aggressively seeking to extend its "peculiar institution" to gain more political power, and in the process to compromise the integrity and curb the opportunities offered by the nonslaveholding states. Nor was this the paranoid ramblings of a minority of radical abolitionists. The idea that there might be a Slave Power conspiracy to control the nation had some substance at least as far as the power part was concerned. There was little that was conspiratorial about men like Calhoun's outspoken defense of slavery. If slavery was a subject white southerners did not wish discussed, it was hardly one they could keep secret.

The fact was, from the nation's inception, the South had wielded more power than the North. With the exception of John Adams's presidency, the executive office was held by Virginians between 1789 and 1824, when John Quincy Adams provided a brief northern interlude before Jackson took office in 1828. The three-fifths clause certainly afforded the South greater representation at the national level than its white population alone could have secured it, and parity between states in the Senate meant that, until the admittance of California in 1850, it took only one northern senator to vote with the South for any vote to swing the South's way. There was, in short, sufficient grist for the mill of northern opponents of the South to construct a plausible specter of southern domination, but no real reason for such opposition except slavery.

Slavery was, however, the moral conundrum at the heart of America's manifest destiny. Not everyone saw it that way; indeed, most did not. Yet the power politics that accompanied the nation's expansion produced a great many political abolitionists out of those whose moral compass was not aligned with the misery of enslaved African Americans but who nevertheless wanted a nation constructed on the basis of, as the new Republican party slogan put it, "Free soil, Free labor, Free men." At the same time, most did still want a single nation. Hindsight frequently presents the major political events between the Missouri Compromise of 1820 and the secession of the southern states in 1860–61 as a series of dominos falling decisively toward disunion. From the perspective of the period, however, disunion was a recognized danger, certainly, but not the inevitable outcome of sectional disagreement. In 1850, as this contemporary image reveals (Figure 5.7), Americans felt secure enough about their Union that they could mock those individuals and forces apparently ranged against it.

By that stage, northerners were long used to southern bombast in Congress and perhaps disinclined to take it seriously. Southerners, for their part, felt safe enough in a Union that the South had done so much to create, and one so reliant, they believed, on their agricultural output that, in the words of pro-slavery spokesman and former governor of South Carolina, James Henry Hammond, it "dare not make war on cotton. No power on earth dares to make war upon it. Cotton is king."[26] Hammond was not wrong. The North would neither make war on cotton nor on the section that produced it. Yet American attitudes in 1850 were not the result either of concern or complacency over cotton, but stemmed from

FIGURE 5.7. "The hurly-burly pot" (New York, James Baillie, 1850). This satirical political cartoon from 1850 represents abolitionist, Free Soil, and sectional interests as dangers to the Union. The figures represented comprise, from left: the Free Soil politician David Wilmot who, in 1846 proposed that slavery be prohibited in any territory resulting from the Mexican War. Although the "Wilmot Proviso" passed the House twice, each time it was defeated in the Senate. Nevertheless, it polarized opinion on the subject of slavery in the territories; the abolitionist editor William Lloyd Garrison; John C. Calhoun; and Horace Greeley, the radical editor of the *New York Tribune*. The man in the fire is the infamous Revolutionary traitor, Benedict Arnold. Apart from Arnold, all are attired in jesters', or fools' caps, and the three main figures (Garrison, Wilmot, and Greeley), represented like the witches in *Macbeth*, are in the process of adding various social and political ills to the cauldron: "Free Soil," "Abolition," and "Fourierism" (Greeley was a noted supporter of the utopian socialist, Charles Fourier) join "Treason," "Anti-Rent," and "Blue Laws" (the restriction of certain activities, usually commercial, on the Sabbath; frequently associated with the Puritans) already in the pot. The speech bubble for Wilmot declares: "Bubble, bubble, toil and trouble!/Boil, Free Soil,/The Union spoil;/Come grief and moan,/Peace be none./Til we divided be." For Garrison: "Bubble, bubble, toil and trouble/**Abolition**/ Our condition/Shall be altered by/Niggars strong as goats/Cut your master's throats/ **Abolition** boil!/We divide the spoil." For Greeley: "Bubble, buble [*sic*], toil and trouble!/Fourierism/War and schism/Till disunion come!" The diminutive Calhoun declares "For success to the whole mixture, we invoke our great patron Saint Benedict Arnold." Arnold adds: "Well done, good and faithful servants!" Print courtesy of the Library of Congress Prints and Photographs Division (LC-USZ62–11138).

the belief that compromise would cement the Union in the future as it had done in the past. In that regard, the Compromise of 1850, the political settlement that defused the growing tension between the free and slave states over the status of the land acquired in the Mexican War (1846–48), seemed to be simply the latest in a series of compromise measures between a North that wanted to extend "free soil" and a South that sought to expand slavery. In fact, it was the last.

As part of the Compromise of 1850, it was agreed that the status – whether slave or free – of new territories would be decided by their inhabitants. Known as popular sovereignty, this decision was ideally democratic in principle but proved less so in practice. Rather than stemming the rising tide of sectionalism, popular sovereignty simply highlighted the growing divergence between North and South over the issue of slavery's further expansion westward. When, in 1854, the doctrine was incorporated into the Kansas-Nebraska Act, the legislation governing the creation of two new states in the West, violence erupted between pro- and anti-slavery supporters in Kansas. And before the bill was even debated in Congress, across the North opposition to what was regarded by some as "an atrocious plot to exclude from a vast unoccupied region immigrants from the Old World and free laborers from our own States, and convert it into a dreary region of despotism, inhabited by masters and slaves" was widespread.[27]

The suspicion on the part of many northerners that slavery was gaining legislative ground was confirmed a few years later when the Supreme Court effectively endorsed popular sovereignty in slavery's favor in a landmark ruling. *Dred Scott v. Sandford* was a case brought by a slave from Missouri who, because he had spent most of his life in the "free states," claimed his freedom. In 1857, the then-Chief Justice Roger B. Taney denied Scott's application on the grounds that first, as a slave, he could not be a citizen, and second, that under the Fifth Amendment to the Constitution, no citizen could be deprived of property without due process. Any legislative attempt to deny the right of slave owners to take their property where they wished, such as the Missouri Compromise, was unconstitutional. Taney turned the prevarication of the Founding Fathers against America's black population by arguing that, at the time of the nation's founding, African Americans had long "been regarded as beings of an inferior order, and altogether unfit to associate with the white race, either in social or political relations; and so far inferior, that they had no rights which the white man was bound to respect."[28]

If slaves were property, not people, then there could be no state from which slavery was excluded, in theory at least. The main exponent of popular sovereignty in the Compromise of 1850 and the Kansas-Nebraska Act, Stephen A. Douglas, did not believe that the theory would necessarily result in universal practice, and intended the doctrine as one that might heal sectional division. Yet by the time he debated the issue with his political rival, Abraham Lincoln, in 1858, sectionalism was the engine driving America's political machine. The Kansas-Nebraska Act, perhaps more than any other single piece of legislation, destroyed Democratic Party unity and gave a crucial boost to the fledgling Republican Party whose victory in 1860 prompted the secession of the southern states. In the following year, in Lincoln's words, "the war came." Toward the end of the Civil War, Lincoln summed up the balance of blame between North and South. "Both parties deprecated war," he observed, "but one of them would *make* war rather than let the nation survive, and the other would *accept* war rather than let it perish."[29]

Ultimately, the conflict between North and South that began in 1861 revealed that neither the Revolutionary War nor the ratification of the Constitution represented the final act in the drama of America's emergence as a nation. The story of America was not a two-act play, and it had a cast of thousands, but too many of them were slaves. By the mid-nineteenth century, slavery was far more than a labor system for the South. It defined the white southern way of life; in Hammond's words, it was the basis of the "harmony of her political and social institutions." Increasingly, and despite any number of legal safeguards to slavery, southern slaveholders came to believe that such harmony was threatened by nation in which abolitionist sentiment criticized and political developments threatened to constrain – even though, in fact, they did not – slavery's expansion. The publication of what became perhaps the most famous abolitionist polemic, *Uncle Tom's Cabin* by Harriet Beecher Stowe, in 1852 contributed to a culture that slaveholders found increasingly less conducive to the retention of chattel slavery. By the time that radical abolitionist John Brown led his abortive and frankly ill-conceived raid on the federal arsenal at Harpers Ferry in Virginia in 1859 – and was hanged for the act – many southerners had reached the conclusion, despite all evidence to the contrary, that their "peculiar institution" was in real danger.

In some ways they were not wrong. Slavery was also more than a labor system for the North. It was, for the abolitionists, a moral affront. For others, it was an anachronistic feudal system that had no place in a new Republic and one that hampered the growth and development of that Republic. For still others, it represented a barrier to the economic development of free white society in the territories. Slavery was, according to Ralph Waldo Emerson, "no scholar, no improver; it does not love the whistle of the railroad; it does not love the newspaper, the mail bag, a college, a book or a preacher," all elements that Americans, since the Revolution, had considered crucial for individual development, for economic expansion, for national stability. In a slave society, Emerson concluded, "everything goes to decay."[30]

By the time Abraham Lincoln and the Republican Party won the election of 1860, North and South had developed not just contradictory but almost mutually exclusive understandings of their revolutionary inheritance. That inheritance had been spelled out in plain manuscript, or rather in two separate manuscripts: the Declaration of Independence and the Constitution. It would be an oversimplification to state that the North aligned itself with the former and the South with the latter, but certainly the Constitutional safeguards accorded both slavery and states' rights became more significant to the South as the ideals of equality set down in the Declaration of Independence became more important to the North.

Lincoln himself saw the Declaration of Independence as an active document that pointed the way toward an inclusive American nationalism. "We are now a mighty nation," he declared in 1858, but he was conscious that national ties were far from obvious in a nation of immigrants. Many Americans, he knew, could not trace their connections to America's past "by blood." They could, however, establish American nationality through the Declaration of Independence because, Lincoln averred, they had "a right to claim it as though they were blood of the blood, and flesh of the flesh" of those who wrote it. The moral sentiment of the Declaration of Independence, as Lincoln interpreted it, constituted the "electric cord" that linked the nation together.[31] Yet white southerners also claimed the Declaration of Independence, specifically that part of it that asserted that "whenever any form of government becomes destructive" of the rights of the governed, "it is the right of the people to alter or to abolish it."

For the North, the Declaration offered the basis for Union, for the South, it established the right of secession. When Lincoln took office, and the Union disintegrated, he had one main task before him. He had to deny the right of secession, to prove that the Revolution of the eighteenth century had established a single nation, and that the Declaration of Independence was not, in fact, a set of guidelines for the future establishment of any number of nations. As the war went on, however, he realized that to do so he would have to finish a task that the Founding Fathers had started but abandoned. He had to tackle the root cause of secession and the resultant Civil War; he had to abolish slavery. That alone would secure the Union in the long term, assuming, of course, that military success secured it in the first place. Only by abolishing slavery, as Lincoln knew, could Americans hope to achieve their manifest destiny as "the last, best hope of earth."

6

Westward the Course of Empire

From Union to Nation

Westward the Course of Empire takes its Way,
The four first Acts already past,
A fifth shall close the Drama of the Day;
Time's noblest Offspring is the last.
(George Berkeley, "Verses on the Prospect
of Planting Arts and Learning
in America," 1752)

Alexander Stephens's audience in Savannah, Georgia was clearly excited
as the newly inaugurated vice-president of the newly-formed Confederate
government rose to address it in March 1861. "I cannot speak so long
as there is noise and confusion," a slightly peeved Stephens observed,
threatening to remain there all night, if necessary. Not, he added, that
"I have anything very entertaining to present." It was a bumpy start to
one of the most famous speeches delivered in the context of America's
Civil War. Then again, pulling several states out of the Union to form a
separate republic was never going to be a smooth operation.

If Abraham Lincoln regarded the Declaration of Independence as a
promissory note for America's future, southerners such as Stephens preferred to ground their opposition to the nation in the Constitution. The
document allowed for that, certainly. A very large part of what being
American meant was encapsulated in the Constitution and the Bill of
Rights but, equally, the compromises and silences of both on matters
such as race were part of that meaning too. More problematic, however,
even than that was the final amendment of the Bill of Rights, Article X,
which stipulated that the "powers not delegated to the United States by

the Constitution, nor prohibited by it to the States, are reserved to the States respectively or to the people."

This, the final clause of what was, in essence, the Anti-Federalists' swan song, their legacy to the new nation, protected individual states' rights, long a concern of those fearful of federal power. Yet it also provided the path to the secession of the southern states in 1860 and 1861, and the possible dismantling of all that had been achieved in Philadelphia in 1787. That was the path Stephens found himself on in March 1861. Its signposts, provided by both the Constitution and the Declaration of Independence, were contradictory. All pointed to freedom, but freedom for whom, from whom, from what, and to do what rather depended on the individual traveler's orientation. For Stephens, freedom for the Confederacy resided in the freedom to own slaves, free from federal interference (albeit imagined interference). Secession was, from a southern perspective, a fundamental revolutionary right in a nation founded in and formed by revolution, one that fought for its freedom from colonial control. That was the nation's problem, and the Confederacy's opportunity.

The Revolution, clearly, had not transformed America into a unified nation, but it had established new rules by which the emerging nation, and nationalism, of the United States could orientate itself. Armed with both the Declaration of Independence and the Bill of Rights, and protected by the Constitution, the new nation had furnished itself with a complex combination of privileges and protections that may, in the years that followed, have been honored as much in the breach as in the observance but which, nevertheless, provided a standard to be aimed at, if not always achieved. Yet there was one thing that neither the Constitution nor the Bill of Rights had resolved. By 1791, Americans had fixed, if not fully defined, the freedoms and protections that accrued to "the people," but what they had not settled was who, precisely, "the people" were. They would not get around to doing so until after the Civil War. They might, indeed, never have gotten around to doing so without the Confederate challenge to the Union, and specifically the Confederate construction of citizenship.

This was the subject of Stephens's Savannah speech; citizenship and the Constitution. Not the one drafted in Philadelphia in 1787, but the Confederate variant, adopted by the several seceding states just ten days before Stephens spoke. If imitation is the sincerest form of flattery, then southerners clearly found little to quibble with in the American Constitution. They virtually duplicated it. An alternative cliché, of course, along the lines of time being of the essence may also have applied. Seceding from the Union, establishing an alternative government, and drawing up a new Constitution in the space of a few months did not allow for an entirely *ab initio* construction of a nation.

Nevertheless, the Confederate Constitution was not a carbon copy of the original. There were crucial differences between the two, and it was those differences, or rather, those "improvements," that Stephens wished to delineate, as soon as his audience allowed. Having got their attention, he assured them that the new constitution "amply secures all our ancient rights, franchises, and liberties." It incorporated the "great principles of Magna Charta," it preserved religious liberty, and it protected life, liberty, and property. Changes, however, had been made. Not all met with his approval, Stephens confided, but overall he felt confident enough to assert that the new Confederate Constitution was "decidedly better than the old." Above all, he assured his listeners, it "has put at rest, forever, all the agitating questions relating to our peculiar institution." He admitted that this, as Jefferson had predicted, "was the immediate cause of the late rupture and present revolution." America's founding ideas, Stephens pointed out, "rested upon the assumption of the equality of the races. This," he concluded, "was an error." By contrast, he declared:

Our new government is founded upon exactly the opposite idea; its foundations are laid, its corner-stone rests, upon the great truth that the negro is not equal to the white man; that slavery subordination to the superior race is his natural and normal condition. This, our new government, is the first, in the history of the world, based upon this great physical, philosophical, and moral truth.

Certainly the Confederate Constitution went to some lengths to ensure that "the right of property" in slaves should not be impaired. The irony of all this, however, was that whatever the American nation's founding ideals, not the least of the causes of the war between North and South had been the *Dred Scott* decision of 1857 that codified the very point that Stephens argued was unique to the Confederacy (Figure 6.1). With this ruling, slavery – supposedly the future Confederate cornerstone – became a national institution, at least potentially, and certainly safer in the Union than it would prove to be out of it.

The Confederate vice-president may have unashamedly named slavery as the Confederacy's cornerstone, but the individual seceding states did not see their labor system as the foundation for a new, unified national structure. Stephens's speech had anticipated the development of a "separate nationality" for the South, but the various declarations issued by the states detailing the causes of secession made it clear that each state saw

ARMS of yᵉ CONFEDERACIE.

FIGURE 6.1. "Arms of ye Confederacie" (G.H. Heap Inv., 1862). This cartoon commentary on the Confederacy hardly portrays it in a way that Confederates would have wholly disagreed with. Its critique, and its northern perspective, is implied rather than overtly stated. It presents a shield flanked by a planter and a manacled slave respectively. The shield incorporates much of the "standard" (by that point) imagery associated with the South: a mint julep, a bottle of whiskey, a pistol and a dagger, a whip and a manacle, cotton, tobacco, and sugar plants, and an image of slaves cultivating the soil. The Palmetto Tree symbolizes South Carolina specifically. Three planters are portrayed playing cards (left), while behind them two men are pictured in the act of dueling. A slave auction is portrayed (right) in front of a slave cabin. Above the shield, the Confederate flag is entwined with a skull and crossbones and between them a banner with the motto "servitudo esto perpetua" (servitude is perpetual); all clichéd images that represented the northern idea of the South as a hard-drinking, gambling, and immoral section. In the context of the *Dred Scott* ruling, however, the idea of perpetual servitude could no longer be safely assumed to be contained in the South. In the context of the Civil War that was ongoing when this image was produced, it is doubtless unintended, but certainly apposite as things turned out, that the manacled slave has a slightly more optimistic expression on his face than the apparently sulky planter manages. Image courtesy of the Library of Congress Prints and Photographs Division (LC-USZ62–305).

itself, as South Carolina did, as "separate and equal . . . among nations." The fact was that no such entity as the Confederacy seceded from the Union, far less any larger construct that could be termed "The South." Those states that seceded did so individually, and anticipated remaining independent in most crucial respects. South Carolina led the way in December 1861, followed by Mississippi, Florida, Alabama, Georgia, and Louisiana in January 1861, Texas in February, and Arkansas and North Carolina in May. Both Virginia, that seceded in April, and Tennessee, that finally seceded in June, remained very much divided throughout the war, the former so much so that it eventually enacted a mini-secession of its own, but from the Confederacy, and split into two states, Virginia (Confederate) and West Virginia (Union).

Slavery was what the Confederate states had in common, but southerners preferred to articulate states' rights as their common cause. No more did slavery's absence unify northerners. It was the preservation of the Union, not the abolition of slavery, that focused northern minds in 1861. New York Senator and later Secretary of State William H. Seward proposed in 1858 that the clash between slavery and freedom was an "irrepressible conflict between opposing and enduring forces," one that would inevitably result in the victory of one side over the other. Seward regarded any attempt at compromise as futile, but just because he saw political conflict as irrepressible did not mean that he saw its armed variant as inevitable. He regarded his country as a "theatre, which exhibits, in full operation, two radically different political systems," one predicated on slavery, the other on freedom.[1] When that country became a theater of war, most northerners focused on solving the symptom, disunion, not curing the cause, slavery. They concurred with Andrew Jackson that their federal Union must be preserved. They were not necessarily persuaded by the abolitionist argument that slavery must, concomitantly, be abolished.

This was perhaps unsurprising. Antebellum Americans revered the Union, saw it as fragile, and struggled to hold it together via the many political compromises from the Constitutional Convention onward. Secession represented the failure of those compromises, of that struggle, the failure, as many saw it, of republican government itself. "What hath God wrought?" ran Samuel F.B. Morse's first telegraph message, sent from Washington to Baltimore in 1844. For Morse, it was a rhetorical question. More so even than the newspapers distributed by the post office, the communication revolution promised by the telegraph made "one *neighborhood* of the whole country," as its inventor had anticipated. God had wrought a new republic, one legally connected by the

Constitution and, by the mid-1840s, drawn more closely together via the new technology that was the telegraph. By 1861, when the telegraph covered the continent, the first message to celebrate the fact expressed the then-perilous position of the nation God had wrought: "May the Union Be Perpetuated," it ran, more in hope than expectation. Secession was already a fact.[2] Soon, the wires would carry mainly news from the war.

So far from being a constitutional right, for many northerners secession was, as Lincoln described it, the "essence of anarchy."[3] The Confederacy was, as one contemporary cartoon (Figure 6.2) portrayed it, in league with Satan himself to remove democratic government from the earth. Such a government was, Americans knew, an "experiment." Further, it was an experiment that involved "not merely the future fate and welfare of this Western continent, but the hopes and prospects of the whole human race," as the *New York Tribune* put it. Such sentiments both echoed Thomas Paine and foreshadowed Lincoln's invocation of America as "the last, best hope of earth," a description the president would later distil most potently into his famous speech at Gettysburg in 1863. Although they undoubtedly boosted northern morale in 1861, the full implications of fighting a war to establish "the democratic principle of equal rights, general suffrage, and government by a majority" only emerged in the course of the war itself.[4]

Although both sides in the Civil War made preparations for a sustained confrontation, public opinion anticipated a short, sharp conflict. One big battle, northerners assumed, would be all it took to make southerners see the error of secession, dissolve the Confederacy, and reenter the Union. The same big battle, southerners assumed, would convince northerners that the Confederacy was serious, could defend itself militarily, and should be allowed, as *Tribune* editor Horace Greeley (among others) had initially suggested, to "go in peace." That first big battle, however, proved to be a wake-up call for both sides. First Bull Run/Manassas was fought on July 21, 1861. This was one battle, but in common with most Civil War engagements, it still has two names. Even today, the use of one over the other usually reveals the speaker's, or writer's perspective. The Union tended to locate its engagements proximate to the nearest water source (so, Bull Run Creek); the Confederacy, by the nearest town or transport hub (so, Manassas Junction). Even on this, Union and Confederate could not agree.

As both sides moved closer to that first engagement, some southern papers expressed a cautious optimism in the Confederacy's position at the start of what one termed the South's "War for Independence." If

FIGURE 6.2. "The Southern Confederacy a Fact!!! Acknowledged by a Mighty Prince and Faithful Ally" (Philadelphia 1861). In contrast to the previous cartoon, this is an indisputably critical, indeed damning portrayal of the Confederacy as being in league with Satan. The figures, from left, represent: "Mr Mob Law Chief Justice," armed with a pot of tar (referencing the tarring and feathering of pro-Union supporters in the South); the Confederate Secretary of States, Robert Toombs holding a "Letter of Marque" (a government certificate authorizing the seizure of foreign property, in this case a reference to the Confederate seizure of Fort Pulaski in Georgia in January 1861); the Confederate President Jefferson Davis; and vice-president Alexander Stephens holding "The Fundamental Principles of our Government," which include treason, rebellion, murder, robbery, incendiarism, and theft. The figure on horseback behind them is General Pierre Gustave Toutant (PGT) Beauregard, who effected the surrender of Fort Sumter in Charleston Harbor to the Confederacy in April 1861. Satan and his minions, seated under the South Carolina Palmetto flag, declare the Confederates "Truly! Fit Representatives of our Realm." Image courtesy of the Library of Congress Prints and Photographs Division (LC-USZ62–89624).

"we are victorious the enemy will be driven across the Potomac, and Washington will be at our mercy," the New Orleans *Daily Picayune* observed. "If we are defeated, we have safe lines to fall back upon." Reassuringly, the paper's correspondent reported, "each and every man

I meet looks forward with perfect confidence to the result," indeed, "the possibility of a defeat is hardly thought of."[5] Northern newspapers were even more robust in their expectation that theirs would not be the losing side when the armies met in Virginia. Sightseers, armed with provisions and parasols, streamed out of Washington on that hot July day, eager for a ringside seat at this, the first and, they anticipated, last battle between Union and Confederate troops.

Their confidence was misplaced. First Bull Run, although not the victory hoped for by the Confederates, was definitely a defeat for the Union. With the arrival of Confederate reinforcements in the afternoon, the Union line could not hold. What began as a tactical withdrawal soon became a rapid and unruly retreat back toward Washington on the part of Union troops and onlookers alike. The city was, as the Confederate papers had hoped, now at the Confederates' mercy, but they failed to exploit it. Reporting from his vantage point in the capital, British journalist William Howard Russell of the London *Times* was amazed, as much by the Union's defeat as by the Confederates' failure to seize the initiative. "The news seemed incredible," Russell reported. "But there, before my eyes, were the jaded, dispirited, broken remnants of regiments passing onwards. . . . Why Beauregard does not come I know not," Russell wrote, "I have been expecting every hour since noon to hear his cannon. Here is a golden opportunity. If the Confederates do not grasp that which will never come again on such terms, it stamps them with mediocrity."[6]

The road to Washington, briefly open to Confederate forces following First Manassas, was, however, not taken in July 1861. For southern commander Joseph E. Johnston, part of the problem lay in Confederate complacency, and in confusion. The "Confederate army was more disorganized by victory than that of the United States by defeat," he recalled, and "believed that the objects of the war had been accomplished by their victory, and that they had achieved all that their country required of them." As a result, many "left their regiments without ceremony to attend to wounded friends, frequently accompanying them to hospitals in distant towns," or simply returned home, proudly bearing "the trophies picked up on the field."[7] Their departure was premature, to say the least. Four years of fighting lay ahead.

If First Bull Run was something of an anticlimax, it certainly exploded northern assumptions that the seceded states could be brought back into the Union with a single show of strength, and dashed Confederate hopes that the seceded states might be permitted to depart the Union in peace. For both, it became apparent that theirs would be a protracted struggle, and that not just men but materiél and, crucially, morale would prove decisive to the final outcome. In a conflict fought mainly by volunteer troops on both sides, morale was no minor matter. Although the Union and the Confederacy were forced to turn to conscription to bolster their depleted ranks, for the most part both relied on voluntary enlistment to maintain their armies in the field. Once the initial enthusiasm for war had dissipated, such voluntarism needed a spur, for the North, perhaps, more than for the South.

For the Confederacy, fighting what was, politically and practically, a defensive campaign swiftly produced its own justification. As Union soldiers invaded "southern" soil and threatened both safety and slavery, so opposition to the Union grew, rather than diminished (Figure 6.3). For the Union it was not so straightforward. Washington had not found his countrymen rushing into the ranks of the revolutionary armies brandishing copies of *Common Sense* or citing the Declaration of Independence. Indeed, to his dismay, they frequently felt no compunction to enter the ranks at all. No more did the rhetoric of defending the Union necessarily persuade northern volunteers, almost a century later, that Union was a cause worth fighting for, worth dying for. Predisposed, as many young men are, to the call of conflict, initial enthusiasm among volunteers was high. The first few battles, however, a great many of which were Confederate victories, soon put paid to any romantic notions of chivalric engagement. "The excitement of battle comes in the day of it," wrote one Union soldier in the aftermath of the battle of Antietam, the war's single bloodiest day, in 1862, "but the horrors of it two or three days after." Such horrors were considerable. "No tongue can tell," observed another, "no mind conceive, no pen portray the horrible sights I witnessed."[8]

Sustaining support for the fight in the face of war's realities was not something the Union could take for granted. William H. Seward had, in criticizing slavery during his maiden speech in the Senate in 1850, argued that there was a "higher law than the Constitution."[9] In the midst of the Civil War, Union leaders, most notably Lincoln himself, had to direct northern minds to a cause higher than conflict in defense of that Constitution. In a very real sense, indeed, the modern American nation did not fully come into being until an alternative nation emerged within it.

As New York lawyer George Templeton Strong observed in the opening year of the war, the "political entity known as the United States of America is found at last." Prior to secession, Strong believed, America had "never been a nation" but only "an aggregate of communities, ready

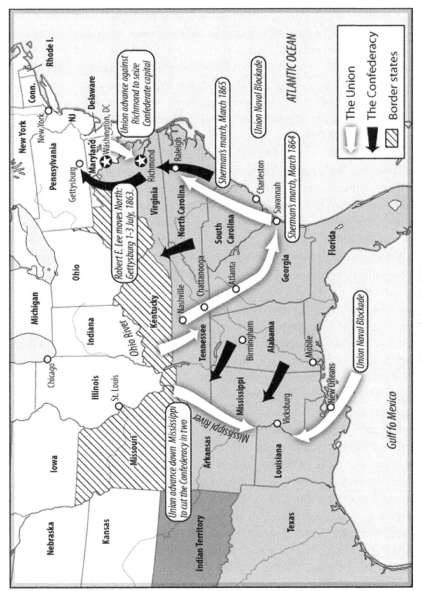

FIGURE 6.3. Map of the Civil War.

to fall apart at the first serious shock and without a centre of vigorous national life to keep us together."[10] The Civil War provided that center, in the long term for northerners and southerners alike. In the shorter term, fighting for the preservation of the Union prompted northerners to merge the ideals of the Declaration of Independence with the Constitution's promise to create "a more perfect Union." They could not, they understood, reconstruct the antebellum Union as it had been; they had to try to remake it as it ought to have been – without slavery.

Indeed, in fighting for independence, some white southerners eventually reached the same conclusion. They realized that their cause would be lost if they did not abandon slavery and arm the African-American population of the South. For others, the very idea of doing so signaled defeat. As Howell Cobb, secessionist spokesman and major-general in the Confederate army, argued, the Confederacy could "not make soldiers of slaves, nor slaves of soldiers." Appropriating slave labor in support of the war effort was one thing, but arming slaves quite another. "The day you make soldiers" out of slaves, Cobb warned the Confederate Secretary of War, James Seddon "is the beginning of the end of the revolution. If slaves will make good soldiers our whole theory of slavery is wrong," he admitted. Yet by this stage the Confederacy was on its last legs, and even Cobb was fully prepared to abolish slavery, if only to gain the foreign aid that had eluded the Confederacy throughout the four years of its existence. Grasp that straw, he advised Seddon, before you "resort to the suicidal policy of arming our slaves."[11]

Cobb's cynicism regarding the military capacities of slaves was neither unique to him nor to the Confederacy. At the war's outset, the Union had also rejected the idea of arming African Americans, a policy it could neither justify nor sustain for long. Several black Union regiments had been unofficially active since 1862, and when Lincoln announced his intention that year of emancipating the slaves of the seceded states, it paved the way for the official involvement of America's black population in the war for the Union. With the Emancipation Proclamation of January 1, 1863, America had turned a corner as far as race relations were concerned. Modern sensibilities frequently recoil from the paternalist implications of Lincoln's "*giving* freedom to the slave" to "*assure* freedom to the *free*," but in the context of a conflict that had begun, for many northerners, as a war simply to save the Union, its gradual transformation into a war for emancipation was no easy one.

As Lincoln well knew, not everyone concurred with his decision to issue the Emancipation Proclamation at all. Some did appreciate the exigencies of the situation. They understood the reason for Lincoln's justifying emancipation as a military necessity rather than a moral one. Boston businessman John Murray Forbes fully grasped that adopting the "higher law" invoked by Seward risked alienating not just the Border States but the "constitutional scruples" evinced by the conservative elements in the Union as a whole and, in particular, by Lincoln's Democratic opponents. "I buy and eat my bread made from the flour raised by the hard-working farmer," Forbes argued, and while "it is certainly satisfactory that in so doing I am helping the farmer . . . my motive is self-preservation, not philanthropy. Let the president free the slaves upon the same principle," Forbes advised, "and so state it that the masses of our people can easily understand it."[12]

Lincoln did indeed so state it, but that did not mean that the masses of the people then, or since, fully understood it. Many thought that by leaving slavery untouched in the loyal slaveholding Border States of Kentucky, Delaware, Maryland, Missouri, and West Virginia (after 1863), he had not gone far enough, whereas others believed he had gone too far altogether in challenging what was, after all, still a Constitutionally protected right to hold slaves. The Confederate states may have been seeking to remove themselves from the Union, but the whole point of the war was that the Union denied that they could, denied, indeed, that they had. If, as Lincoln himself believed, the war represented a rebellion in the South rather than a rebellion of the South, then the Constitution still applied; and if it applied, then slavery was safe.

Of course slavery was not safe, and Lincoln came to realize that a strict constitutional line on the issue was unsustainable, prompted in part by his own moral perspective but also by the direct action of the slaves themselves. As Union troops penetrated further into the seceded states, slaves flocked to their lines seeking protection, and freedom. The racial attitudes of the era meant that they did not always find it, but this in no way dampened the general hope that the Union army would prove to be the agent of emancipation for the Confederacy's chattel labor force. And the African-American exodus from the southern slave system established a momentum of its own, one the Union was forced to respond to, one the Confederacy could not stem.

To their dismay, many white southerners watched the comforting myth of the loyal slave disappear before their eyes, along with many of their belongings as their human "property" removed themselves from their authority taking the silverware with them. By the war's end, some southerners, such as Eva Jones of Georgia, still struggled to comprehend fully what had been lost. She was stunned when a former slave stole money from her. She was resentful that this "filthy lucre" had gone toward the "extravagancies and petty fineries" of the freedwoman's wedding, a legal ceremony forbidden under slavery's rules. Like so many other white southerners, Eva clearly failed to understand that slavery's demise meant the loss of more than wealth; it was the death of a way of life.[13]

On to Richmond and through the Rockies

Although the fate of the Union hung in the balance between 1861 and 1865, the fact is that large swathes of the United States remained untouched by the Civil War raging in Virginia and down the Mississippi in those years. As Lincoln struggled to persuade his countrymen and women that the achievement of America's manifest destiny required not just the nation's territorial but its moral integrity, based on equality between black and white, many of that country's inhabitants were manifesting their own destinies far from the fields of battle. As the Union armies were encouraged "On to Richmond," the site of the Confederate capital, to unite the nation by force, on the other side of the country, equally strenuous efforts were underway to bring it together by rail. America was, in this period, quite literally being forged through blood and iron.

The outbreak of the Civil War, indeed, facilitated this particular aspect of what historians term the "market revolution" in the nineteenth-century United States; the transformation of the nation in this period from an essentially local, rural, and mainly agrarian society to a centralized, urban, and mainly industrial one. This market revolution also entailed a shift in focus, away from the eastern seaports and the wider world beyond and toward the interior opportunities offered by the western frontier and, of course, California's gold fields. Developments in an area long held important by Americans both reflected and reinforced this shift: communication, first in the form of the kind of "imagined community" effected via the post office and the newspapers it carried, second via the telegraph, as its inventor had hoped, and third via the transport links that carried the post and, in time, the people themselves.

The appearance of a plethora of industrial journals in this period revealed both the growing importance of the new industries and the communication revolution that conveyed this commercial expansion to its audience. Journals such as the *Age of Steel*, first published in St. Louis in 1857, the *Chicago Journal of Commerce*, which became *Iron and Steel* in

1863, or the *Hardware Man's Newspaper and American Manufacturer's Circular*, begun in New York in 1855 and which became, in 1860, the *Iron Age*, in their titles alone invoked the dawn of a new age of iron and industry that coincided with, and in some ways was exemplified by, the Civil War. If newspapers – and we can include these commercial journals – represent, as playwright Arthur Miller once suggested, a nation talking to itself, then railways put that dialogue in motion. Both diminished distance and reinforced a common sense of a distinctive American nationality, one held together as much by iron as by ideology, by steel as by sentiment. That, at least, was the theory.

The development of the railways in the United States started in 1827, when the citizens of Baltimore, eager to compete with the economic might of New York and provide an alternative form of transport to the Erie Canal, instigated the construction of the Baltimore & Ohio Railroad. The event was attended by all the pomp and ceremony Baltimore could muster. The last living signatory to the Declaration of Independence, Charles Carroll, broke the ground for this new venture on, of course, July 4 of that year. After that, the Baltimore & Ohio's progress could best be described as slow but steady. By 1853, it had reached Wheeling, Virginia (later West Virginia) on the Ohio River, some 380 miles west. By that point, however, other states had followed suit. In 1835, *Niles' Weekly Register*, a general and commercial publication out of Baltimore, reported general enthusiasm for the opportunities offered by rail transport, the possibility of conveying passengers between the Cumberland and Ohio rivers "during the day-light of a single day," and from Baltimore itself to the Ohio in only twenty-four hours.[14]

That there would be a growing market for such speedy movement was without doubt. The same issue of *Niles'* that reported on the fledgling state of the railways noted, too, the interest in westward expansion and the arrival, in St. Louis (Missouri), of steamboat passengers bound for the West, "a scene of bustle and life, truly animating." Among the arrivals were "several families with their wagons, horses, household furniture, negroes etc, doubtless bound for the interior," it was observed, "while many reshipped to wend their way up the Mississippi, and toward the setting of the sun." In the following decades, many more private railway companies emerged to follow, or in some cases compete with, the Baltimore & Ohio, and increasingly these usurped the role of the steamboat in conveying Americans westward. Railroads, indeed, became one of the dominant symbols not just of American ambition and expansion, but of equality and opportunity in the new republic.

Railways were, according to contemporary accounts, all things to all people, and capable of transforming all people into one. The railway was "the poor man's road," it was announced at the Internal Improvements convention in New York in 1836, the means whereby the wealth of the minority was invested in the future of rich and poor alike.[15] Both steamboats and locomotives were, according to Ralph Waldo Emerson in 1844, "like enormous shuttles" that "shoot every day across the thousand various threads of national descent and employment and bind them fast in one web." Yet the railroad was special in "the increased acquaintance it has given the American people with the boundless resources of their own soil." By bringing Americans together, he argued, the railroad "has given a new celerity to *time*, or anticipated by fifty years the planting of tracts of land, the choice of water privileges, the working of mines. . . . Railroad iron," he concluded, "is a magician's rod, in its power to evoke the sleeping energies of land and water."

For Emerson, the railways were the route to the land, and the land was, as Madison and Jefferson had suggested, the source both of America's sustenance and social stability. "The land is the appointed remedy for whatever is false and fantastic in our culture," Emerson argued. "The continent we inhabit is to be physic and food for our mind as well as our body. The land, with its tranquilizing, sanative influences, is to repair the errors of a scholastic and traditional education, and bring us into just relations with men and things."[16] Emerson's idealistic invocation of the power of the interior to right America's wrongs, to provide both a home for and a haven from the surging population of the eastern seaboard cities, fed into the growing myth of the west, one of the nation's most potent and enduring symbols.

The myth of the west, of course, was neither specific to Emerson nor originated in America. Since medieval times, belief in the mystical lands of the west had resonated in European culture. For Europeans, the discoveries of their particular "Age of Exploration" offered tangible physical proof that a bountiful land lay to the west, and by the eighteenth century the idea of civilization's inevitable westward progress was already linked with America. These associations were as popular with poets as with the earliest pioneers. Both identified in the New World the possibility of a personal and political utopia. In "America: A Prophecy" (1793), radical English poet William Blake famously represented the American Revolution as an apocalyptic "wind" that "swept through America," overturning the power of "Albions Angels" to reveal a new "Angelic land."

Yet this land had, over half a century earlier, already been identified by Bishop (George) Berkeley as a place where "Nature guides and Virtue rules," the location of "another golden Age,/The rise of Empire and of Arts... Not such as *Europe* breeds in her decay;/Such as she bred when fresh and young,/When heav'nly Flame did animate her Clay,/By future Poets shall be sung."[17] The symbolism that emerged from the War of Independence, specifically the Great Seal, had already revealed how receptive Americans were to the idea of their republican experiment as ushering in a new "golden age."

By the nineteenth century, therefore, America's Anglo-Saxon population was already fully primed to regard the west as the natural home and outlet for the pioneer spirit that had brought Europeans to the New World in the first place, a spirit that was their birthright. Like the first adventurers, the nineteenth-century pioneers portrayed the continent they sought to conquer as a virgin land. The American West was a land ripe for exploitation, an uncharted and uninhabited wilderness that it was America's Manifest Destiny to dominate. In this context, Berkeley's eighteenth-century literary commentary on America's possibilities was reinterpreted afresh in periodicals and prints, by politicians and by painters alike. Together, they presented America as not so much exceptional as expected.

"Westward the Course of Empire takes its Way," Berkeley had declared. "The four first Acts already past,/A fifth shall close the Drama of the Day;/Time's noblest Offspring is the last." The idea that America was civilization's foreordained conclusion found visual expression in several paintings of the Civil War era. The most famous, by Emanuel Leutze, *Westward the Course of Empire Takes its Way* (1861), forms part of a mural in the United States Capitol. Another, by John Gast, *American Progress* (1872), dramatizes America's westward movement, the vigor of the immigrant spirit, and the technological advances that the pioneers brought with them – Gast portrayed the telegraph wire running alongside a giant figure of Columbia – as they struck out west in the mid-nineteenth century. Yet one of the most informative images of the nation's expansion in the nineteenth century was produced by the lesser-known artist Fanny Palmer (Figure 6.4). Palmer also invoked Berkeley's famous verse to accompany her less allegorical, much more modern representation of the railway forging a path toward the as-yet untamed wilderness and creating, in the process, a clear dividing line between European society and that of aboriginal America.

FIGURE 6.4. "Across the Continent (Westward the Course of Empire Takes its Way)," by Fanny F. Palmer (New York: Currier & Ives, 1868). This lithograph clearly juxtaposes the elements of white civilization as it proceeds westward on the left hand side of the steam train with Native American life on the right. On the left, the settlers are in the process of cutting down the forests to construct their schools, churches, and log cabins as well as the covered wagons that are seen, top left of the settlement, and heading off into the far distance. Telegraph poles run parallel to the railroad. The reception of this image today, of course, may differ considerably from its popular appeal in the nineteenth century. Even so, the viewer is invited to share the perspective of the two native figures not simply by virtue of the fact that all the "action" is located on the white settlers' side of the tracks, but because, by the time this print appeared, American audiences would have been familiar with the dramatic landscape paintings of the Hudson River School and with the work of artists such as Thomas Cole, Frederic Edwin Church, or Albert Bierstadt. They would certainly have been familiar with the nationalist message these artists conveyed. Toward the end of the Civil War, art critic James Jackson Jarvis's *The Art-Idea* (1864) was published, in which Jarvis noted that the "thoroughly American branch of painting, based upon the facts and tastes of the people, is...landscape." A national identity that was informed by and responded to images of the great American wilderness, however, was of necessity compromised by the destruction of that wilderness in the name of progress. In short, even such an apparently straightforward lithograph as Palmer's would not have been wholly unproblematic for contemporary audiences. Image courtesy of the Library of Congress Prints and Photographs Division (LC- DIG-ppmsca-03213).

Yet time's noblest offspring found their progress somewhat hampered by the very real practical and political difficulties attendant on their heliotropic impulses and ambitions. Emerson's optimism regarding the railways' unifying potential notwithstanding, mid-nineteenth-century Americans could not traverse their country as readily as they would have wished. In a north-south direction, a combination of differing track gauges and early antipollution legislation in cities such as Baltimore frequently necessitated a change of train midway through the journey. In an east-west direction, the problem was political rather than practical. Not until the Civil War had removed southern opposition from Congress was the first Pacific Railroad Act (1862) passed, with a second following two years later. Southerners were not opposed to the concept of a transcontinental railroad, of course; far from it. It was simply that they wished any such railroad, and the economic benefits it would bring, to detour through the South.

Indeed, the temporary removal of the political voice of the South from the U.S. Congress between 1861 and 1865 opened the way for a raft of legislation designed to facilitate both the nation's westward movement and the North's development. The Transcontinental Railroad, first mooted in the 1830s, only began to be built in 1863 (it was completed in 1869). Construction was intended to commence simultaneously from Iowa, under the auspices of the Union Pacific, and from California, by the Central Pacific, with the idea that the tracks would meet in the middle. Work on the Pacific Coast end did begin as planned, but in the east, the Civil War delayed progress until the conflict ended in 1865. The venture provided employment for a great many Civil War veterans, many of whom were fairly recent immigrants to America and had become familiar with the engineering requirements of the railways during the war. Labor, however, was more of a problem on the west coast, and the solution – the employment of an imported Chinese workforce – posed its own challenge to the ideal of republican equality in America in the longer term.

Physical distance, in the case of the United States, proved far easier to circumvent than physical difference. In the process of bringing both sides of the American continent together while simultaneously conducting a civil conflict in the eastern part of it, Americans found that they could not avoid the issue of race. As the Union and Confederate armies battled the problem out militarily, the railways served only to open up a whole new vista of racial conflict as they inched across the continent.

The South's slaves, it transpired, were not the only people in America to see the Civil War as an opportunity to undermine white hegemony.

Another challenge came from the indigenous population, who lived on the land that the railways were seeking to cross. At the time of the Civil War, about 1,500 miles separated America's eastern and western frontiers, divided into three main areas: the Great Plains, the Rockies, and the Sierras. The earliest white presence there mainly consisted of miners, missionaries, and Mormon settlements in Utah, as well as a transient population of hunters, prospectors, and traders. Prior to the completion of the transcontinental railroad, many migrants headed into the interior along the Oregon Trail, which ran from Missouri through the territories that would, in the course of the Civil War era and later nineteenth century, become the states of Oregon (1859), Kansas (1861), Nebraska (1867), Idaho, and Wyoming (1890).

North of the Oregon Trail, territories such as Minnesota, where the slave Dred Scott had spent a large part of his life, were growing fast. From about 6,000 in 1850, the number of white residents there had increased to approximately 170,000 in 1860. Two years later, the passage of the Homestead Act, which allocated 160 acres of land to any applicant willing to improve it, encouraged further white inroads into the territories. Until prospectors found gold in the Black Hills of North Dakota, a Sioux Reservation, in 1874, drawing, literally within months, 15,000 white settlers there, the bulk of the population remained indigenous.

The Great Plains, too, sustained some quarter of a million native inhabitants at the time of the Civil War, whose economy was structured around the buffalo herds that at that point numbered about 13 million. The population itself was divided between tribes such as the Cheyenne, Arapaho, and Sioux, all of them politically and culturally diverse. The Sioux Nation, for example, comprised seven tribal groups, broadly divided into three western ones, the Lakota Sioux, and four eastern ones, the Dakota Sioux. Together they occupied a vast area of territory between what became the state of Minnesota and the Rocky Mountains, and, inevitably, the relationship both with white settlers and with each other was a complex one.

For many of the indigenous tribes, white settlers were little more than an irritant. For others, they were not even that; they barely registered. For still others, they represented potential allies in the ongoing battles – not necessarily physical, but political – between the various interest groups within the Indian nations. Yet contact produced cliché, and in time it forced both indigenes and incomers into a box: white or "Indian." White settlers may have reinforced their idea of self, of civilization, against the "heathen" native, but in the process they produced a simultaneous reaction from the native peoples. By the later nineteenth century, tribal boundaries were strained by the need to cut across difference to define a separate "Indianness." In time, in the twentieth century, this would grow into a conceptual, and sometimes physical, resistance to Anglo imperialism. As had been the case since the colonial era, and in the course of the Civil War, in conflict identities were constructed.

Such conflict could be and frequently was destructive. When warfare broke out in Minnesota between white settlers and natives in 1862, sometimes termed the Great Sioux Uprising or the Dakota War, the immediate cause was not the railways directly but the difficulties arising out of the land treaties that, inevitably, grew out of the expansion of white settlement. Designed to transfer legal ownership of the territories to the federal government and relocate the native population to an ever-decreasing amount of "reservation" land on the frontier, these treaties provided financial compensation for the loss of land and livelihood. The distribution of the money itself, however, not only undermined traditional tribal relationships, but was often delayed. When a bad harvest in 1862 coincided with late payment of the now essential funds, some of the southernmost Dakota faced starvation. It was under these trying circumstances that a conflict costing hundreds of lives first broke out, but this was only the start of what would become a decades-long confrontation between natives and newcomers in the West.

Minnesota's first Episcopal Bishop, Henry Benjamin Whipple, had long feared that history, in America's case, would repeat itself, and violence would come to define the relationship between white settlers and the tribes. "Again and again," he recollected in his memoirs, "I had said publicly that as certain as any fact of human history, a nation which sowed robbery would reap a harvest of blood."[18] He was hardly the first to reach that conclusion. In a slightly different context, radical abolitionist John Brown, the leader of the failed attack on Harpers Ferry, Virginia, in 1859, which he had hoped might instigate a slave uprising across the South, had also professed his certainty that "the crimes of this guilty land will never be purged away, but with blood." Although Brown had long been a man of violence, and Whipple a noted man of peace, their respective perspectives were not as much at variance as might have been supposed. Their personal views may have been worlds apart, but the racialized landscape each looked out on was depressingly similar.

Whipple was not naïve about the causes of these "days of sorrow" in Minnesota. He saw past the sometimes overt racial hostility to the root of the problem. The native tribes occupied an unstable middle ground as far as both nation and nationality were concerned. Although treated as a separate nation, at the same time the federal government held that "a nation cannot exist within a nation," which left the tribes in a legal no man's land located on actual land that, as it turned out, a great many white men and women wanted very much indeed. Consequently, as Whipple recognized, the tribes enjoyed no sovereignty and, even if they had, it was extremely unlikely that white society would have "permitted them to exercise it in the duties necessary to a nation's self-existence."[19] National existence was, as Whipple understood, the main issue, on the battlefields of the Civil War as on those of the West; national existence and citizenship. Those had been the questions facing America since its inception, and the conclusion of the Civil War did not answer them. It only added further fuel to what had long been, and would long continue to be, a heated debate.

"The nation," Whipple had asserted, "cannot afford to be unjust." By the end of the Civil War, with the victory of the Union, that thought was uppermost in many minds, not least Lincoln's. With his sights set firmly on the cause of the Civil War and on its most likely termination, the newly reelected president interpreted the internecine conflict as the inevitable price of slavery. "Fondly do we hope – fervently do we pray – that this mighty scourge of war may speedily pass away," Lincoln declared. "Yet if God wills that it continue . . . until every drop of blood drawn with the lash, shall be paid by another drawn with the sword," then, he stressed, the nation should be prepared to pay that price. At the same time, Lincoln emphasized the need for "malice toward none; with charity for all," in bringing the Union together again.[20]

When Lincoln spoke, one nation, the Confederacy, was facing extinction, its cause so far lost that some of its political spokesmen and military leaders were willing to destroy the very cornerstone, slavery, on which it had been constructed. Another, the almost re-United States, was faced with the challenge of reconstructing a wholly new America, an America in which slavery would be finally and forever abolished by one Constitutional amendment and citizenship defined and protected by another (Figure 6.5). This was a nation, as Lincoln had described it on the occasion of his dedication of the cemetery to the Union dead at Gettysburg, Pennsylvania in 1863, "conceived in liberty, and dedicated to the proposition that 'all men are created equal.'" The Civil War was being fought, Lincoln reminded his audience, so that America could "have a new birth of freedom; and that this government of the people, by the people, for the people, shall not perish from the earth."[21] When he signed the Thirteenth

FIGURE 6.5. "Emancipation," by Thomas Nast (Philadelphia: King and Beard, c. 1865). Thomas Nast was a well-known political cartoonist who contributed regularly to the popular northern journal *Harper's Weekly* during the Civil War and Reconstruction eras and into the late nineteenth century. His cartoons also appeared in the *New York Illustrated News* and *The Illustrated London News*. He became most famous for his campaign against political corruption in New York in the late 1860s and 1870s. A great many of his cartoons took as their subject the injustices facing Native Americans, Chinese laborers, and African Americas suffering segregation in the South. This image, celebrating the emancipation of the slaves, offers an optimistic representation of the future after slavery. The central panel portrays an African American family secure in their comfortable domestic surroundings in a way that they could never have been under slavery, with Lincoln suitably acknowledged as the author of the Emancipation Proclamation of 1863 hanging in portraiture on the wall as well as in the panel insert below. The horrors of slavery as a system (a slave auction, whipping, and branding) are represented on the left, juxtaposed with the benefits of freedom (a freedman's home, children going to school, and the payment of wages) on the right. Image courtesy of the Library of Congress Prints and Photographs Division (LC-DIG-ppmsca-19253).

Amendment into law on February 1, 1865, the amendment that stated that "[n]either slavery nor involuntary servitude . . . shall exist within the United States, or any place subject to their jurisdiction," he made clear that for him, as for many Americans, emancipation was far more than a wartime measure, a martial necessity; it was the fulfillment of the nation's moral manifest destiny.

Lincoln himself, of course, did not live to see this aspect of his nation's destiny fulfilled. Shot by Confederate sympathizer John Wilkes Booth, the president who had held the Union together through four years of war died on Good Friday, 1865. The task of bringing the Union together again, frequently defined as the period of Reconstruction (1865–1877) fell to others. Yet the reconstruction of the nation that Lincoln had envisaged involved far more than the political reentry of the Confederate states into the federal union; it involved, indeed, far more than the stabilization of the relationship between North and South or the eradication of slavery. Race relations in America had always been more complicated than that.

The 1790 Naturalization Act had stipulated that only "free white persons" could be considered for naturalization. This was modified over the years. In particular, and following the passage of the Fourteenth Amendment in 1868, in 1870, the act was amended to allow African Americans to be naturalized. "All persons born or naturalized in the United States, and subject to the jurisdiction thereof, are citizens of the United States and of the State wherein they reside," the Fourteenth Amendment finally made clear. "No State shall make or enforce any law which shall abridge the privileges or immunities of citizens of the United States," it further asserted, "nor shall any State deprive any person of life, liberty, or property, without due process of law; nor deny to any person within its jurisdiction the equal protection of the laws." In this one amendment to its Constitution, America had both defined citizenship and denied the legality of the 1857 *Dred Scott* decision. In principle, nothing could have been clearer. In practice, nothing turned out to be more obtuse.

The Stride of a Century

Victory for the Union in the Civil War can too readily create a false sense of division in the moral as in the material landscape of America between the antebellum era and the decades following the "War Between the States." The very idea of victory, indeed, becomes elusive the closer one approaches it. The North "won" the Civil War, but the price of that victory is too frequently downplayed while the cost of defeat for the South continues to absorb historians and the public alike. The nation, apparently, "won" the West in the years after the war. Yet both the lineaments and the limitations of that victory became simplified via the twentieth-century fascination with film, particularly the "Westerns."

Their rendition of western history did not easily make the shift to glorious "Technicolor" from black-and-white. No more did the West itself. And it was there, in the dramatic and evocative landscape of the West, rather than on the battlefields of the Civil War, that modern America's racial landscape was defined and debated. The emphasis was very much on the latter activity. It was hardly a straightforward matter.

Not that the Civil War was necessarily as straightforward as it can seem. Moving from the center of the action, as it were, from the battles between Union general Ulysses S. Grant and Confederate Robert E. Lee, and from the political conflict between radicals and conservatives over race, reveals a more complex picture of the issues at stake between 1861 and 1865 and in the years following. For recent immigrants to the United States, the bulk of whom arrived and remained in the North, the war provided an opportunity to assert, or prove, loyalty to their adopted nation, to align with its ideals of equality of opportunity if not always agree with its newfound emphasis on equality of race. Yet ethnic regiments in the Union army frequently served multiple agendas, whether the ethnicity in question was Irish, "Indian," or African American.

Even African-American motivation, so central to America's Civil War story, should not be assumed. Frequently leading African-American spokesman Frederick Douglass's advocacy of arming his people is positioned as a universal perspective. "Once let the black man get upon his person the brass letters U.S., let him get an eagle on his button, and a musket on his shoulder and bullets in his pocket," Douglass asserted, "and there is no power on earth which can deny that he has earned the right to citizenship in the United States." Yet others argued against this, suggesting that African Americans had "nothing to gain, and everything to lose, by entering the lists as combatants," and should not feel compelled "to fight under the flag which gives us no protection."

Fighting for inclusion in the nation, however, was only ever part of the story. Some fought in the hope that by so doing they might be kept out of it. The Green Bay Tribes of Wisconsin, the Menominee, Oneida and Stockbridge-Munsee nations, did not have citizenship in mind when they volunteered to fight for the Union. They simply wished to protect their land from further white encroachment, and hoped that service in the war might force the federal government to recognize their rights. As was the case for African Americans, however, the services of the Green Bay Tribes were initially rejected. Wisconsin's Adjutant-General, Augustus Gaylord, remained unconvinced of "the *propriety* of using *Indians* in the present contest with our brothers, so long as there are so many volunteers from civilization." For Gaylord, the enemy, the Confederates, were "brothers," whereas the prospective ally constituted an uncivilized alien. This perspective was racist, certainly, but not necessarily wholly at odds with the separatist ambitions of the native volunteers themselves.

Further west, the multiplicity of agendas that revolved around inclusion and exclusion, assimilation of and self-assertion, for native peoples and immigrants was highlighted in the experience of California. As Congress, on the east coast, struggled to ratify and then implement the Fourteenth Amendment, the crucial contractual statement of American citizenship, on the other side of the country, the people were struggling with the implications of national expansion and immigration. Tensions arose from the simple fact that there were two paths to citizenship, two routes to nationality. One could be born American. Simply being born in the land called America would not suffice, however, as an 1884 court ruling made clear in the case of Native Americans, and revisited to reach the opposite conclusion in 1898 regarding the children of Chinese parents. One could become American. To achieve this, however, one sometimes had to run a gauntlet of racial and religious opposition frequently, but not exclusively, focused on the immigrant. In California, the immigrant in question was Chinese.

Welcomed – indeed whisked with all precipitate speed – into the Union in 1849 thanks to the discovery of gold there the previous year, California's original constitution was nothing unexpected for an American state. It began with the assertion that all "men are by nature free and independent," entitled to all the usual "unalienable rights" of life, liberty, and property, said rights protected by the political power that resided in the people and that were expressed via a government "instituted for the protection, security and benefit of the people." No distinctions either of ethnicity or race were stipulated. Yet three decades later, California revised its constitution, and its 1879 variant offered a rather different proposition. By 1879, whereas "[f]oreigners of the white race or of African descent" were accorded equal rights with "native-born citizens," said rights did not extend to all. No "native of China, no idiot, insane person, or person convicted of any infamous crime" was entitled to "exercise the privileges of an elector in this State," it asserted. Further, no business in California was permitted to employ "any Chinese or Mongolian." If that were not enough, it stipulated that "all laws of the State of California" should be "conducted, preserved, and published in no other than the English language."

The most surprising aspect of this was not, perhaps, that such exclusions should have been codified at all, but that they should have been codified in California. At its point of entry into the Union, California had already attracted a considerable number of immigrants eager for its promised riches. It also had an indigenous population of Spanish-speaking former Mexicans, whose territory *Alta California* had been. They had gained American citizenship under the 1848 Treaty of Guadalupe Hidalgo that had ended the Mexican-American War and ceded both *Alta California* and *Santa Fe de Nuevo México* to the United States. Consequently the debate over the state constitution in California was more complex than for many states, but also, in the end, productive of an inclusive conceptualization of citizenship.

Not only did California come in as a free state, without slavery, but in the course of the constitutional debates, the equality between those who had recently been "Mexican" and the American people was emphasized. As one of the delegates to the convention, Kimball H. Dimmick, originally from New York and in 1849 *alcalde* (Spanish magistrate) for San Jose, stressed, no "line of distinction" could be "drawn between native Californians and Americans." His constituents, recently Mexicans, now "all claimed to be Americans. They would not consent to be placed in a minority," he explained, and "classed themselves with Americans." They were, therefore, "entitled to be considered in the majority. No matter from what nation they came," Kimball concluded, "he trusted that hereafter they would be classed with the American people."[22] The final constitution largely reflected this position and was, further, disseminated in both English and Spanish to reflect the bilingual nature of the state's population. It was not a position the state could maintain.

California's shift from ethnic and linguistic inclusion in 1849 to its frankly bizarre anti-Chinese position in 1879, however, was in many ways in line with national trends. These trends predated the Civil War. In many respects, indeed, the growing sectional hostility between North and South in the antebellum period served to distract from the anti-immigrant and, especially, anti-Catholic sentiment that had its roots in the colonial era and remained an intrinsic part of the North's political, religious, and social landscape. The brief emergence, in the 1850s, of the nativist American Party, or Know-Nothings, revealed both the persistence and the limitations of this trend. Certainly the high profile accorded many of the ethnic Union regiments, particularly the Irish, sought to counter such anti-Catholic biases. It did so less effectively in a state such as California in part because of the west coast's distance from the battlefields of the east, but also because anti-Catholicism was potentially that much more poisonous in a state where an indigenous Catholic population merged with both Catholic and Protestant immigrants, to the consternation of the mainly Protestant elites.

As had so often been the case in America's history, the identification of an external threat served to unify a disparate population. In California's case, that threat was deemed to be the Chinese. Brought into America to provide the labor force necessary for unifying that country by rail, they ended up by unifying parts of it, at least, by race, trumping the religious divisions that threatened stability in California and across the nation. In a single decade, the numbers of Chinese migrants grew from less than a hundred in 1870 to well more than 100,000 by 1880. After that, numbers declined, mainly because Congress, in 1882, codified anti-Chinese sentiment via the Chinese Exclusion Act, forbidding further immigration of Chinese labor into America.

The Civil War had slowed, if not entirely stopped, immigration to America and simultaneously had slowed, but not entirely silenced, nativist sentiment. In the years following the war, both gathered momentum. Hostility toward the immigrant may seem paradoxical in the land that Thomas Paine described as an "asylum for mankind," especially in a period that quite literally elevated Paine's blueprint for utopia into the physical form of the Statue of Liberty, dedicated in 1886. Yet those who advocated equal rights for all Americans found that neither the Civil War nor the subsequent Constitutional amendments – the three "Reconstruction Amendments" – had established, beyond argument, the ground on which a new and inclusive American national identity could be constructed. Slavery had been abolished via the Thirteenth Amendment; citizenship had been defined by the Fourteenth; and the Fifteenth Amendment had, in theory, secured voting rights for all, regardless of race, although not, notably, of gender. In theory, armed with these amendments, America could look forward to a more positive future. In practice, it proved difficult, if not impossible, to escape the backward momentum of the past.

The new Golden Age anticipated for America by Bishop Berkeley in the eighteenth century had become, at least according to one of that nation's foremost authors and satirists, Mark Twain, no more than a "Gilded Age" by the later nineteenth century. Following Twain's novel of that name, *The Gilded Age: A Tale of Today* (1873), coauthored with his friend the editor Charles Dudley Warner, the designation "Gilded Age" is frequently applied to the period between the conclusion of the Civil

War and the turn of the twentieth century. Although a pithy indictment of the political corruption and elite excesses of the period, it is perhaps misleading in terms of how that half-century is understood.

The post–Civil War era constituted a period of rapid growth for the United States, one driven as much by the sheer scale of immigration as by the technological developments, particularly the transport revolution, after 1865. Yet the scholarly triumvirate of urbanization, industrialization, and immigration is perhaps too readily invoked as the driver of those forces, positive and negative, pushing America toward the twentieth century, toward the "American Century" of global impact and influence. From the perspective of the time, this was a less decisive process than hindsight makes it seem. Certainly Americans understood this to be a transitional period for their nation; but it was a transition influenced as much by the legacy of the past as the lure of the future.

For the defeated white South, economically devastated by the Civil War, the past became a Golden Age of plantation legend. Myopic and mythical in equal measure, this legend posited a prewar past of contented slaves and beautiful belles, of gentlemen and gracious living. Neither the sad and steady tramp of the slave coffles heading south nor the agonies of the auction block echoed in this "New South" version of what became known as the "Old South." In their memories of and memorials to the Confederate dead, (Figure 6.6), the white South constructed a separate civic tradition, one predicated on defeat and on difference from the rest of the nation. Under the terms of the Reconstruction Acts (1866, 1867), the former Confederate states remained under military occupation, some until 1877, when federal troops finally left the South. Required to swear individual loyalty oaths to the nation, and for their state legislatures to ratify the Fourteenth Amendment, many former Confederates sought solace in the cultural construction of the "Lost Cause" that developed after Reconstruction and persisted well into the twentieth century. The irony, of course, was that the Confederacy's main cause, a fixed racial divide between the white and black South, proved to be very far from lost; if anything, it had only just been discovered.

Slavery had been many things. It was a system of cruelty and fear, of physical exploitation and economic deprivation, but the one thing it was not was a system of segregation. Black and white had lived proximate to each other in the antebellum South. In the postwar decades, they began to move apart. What followed, in the form of the "Black Codes" implemented by many of the former Confederate states, sought to return African Americans in the South to a position close to slavery in all but its

FIGURE 6.6. "The Conquered Banner" (New Orleans: A.E. Blackmar, 1866). Cover of sheet music mourning the defeat of the Confederacy. The image represents a Confederate flag draped over a cannon, the whole surrounded by weeds. The title invokes a poem by the "poet laureate of the Confederacy," Father Abram Joseph Ryan, published that same year. Ryan's poem, "The Conquered Banner,"

legal form. In the absence of the rules that had governed both contact and conduct under slavery, new rules based on race emerged. Slavery's rules had been devised to sustain the South's "peculiar institution," but the racial rules that followed slavery were not specific to the South, and there was little that was peculiarly southern about them, as the experiences of natives and immigrants, on the eastern seaboard and across the West, made clear.

The process of Reconstruction was drawing to a close in America by 1876, and in that year it was not just the white South that was contemplating the past. The year of the nation's centennial found poet Bayard Taylor, the composer of the "National Ode" for July 4, 1876, musing on the implications of America's first hundred years (Figure 6.7). For Taylor, the centennial celebrations constituted an "infallible test . . . an absolute gauge of the strength of our concrete enthusiasm. . . . Our after ages can see no anniversary so solemn as this. Our struggle into life is near enough for us to remember it with emotion; living memories link us to it still: it is distant enough to have become traditional, venerable." The centennial offered Americans the refuge of the Revolution, a conflict far enough in the past to have acquired the mystique necessary for national consolidation, and close enough to the present to mute the memories of the more recent, internecine conflict that the nation had endured.[23]

Yet the nation that was preparing to celebrate its centennial in 1876 was an unsettled one, suffering economic depression, political corruption, and racial unrest, on the streets of South Carolina as on those of California and most points in between. By 1876, Americans could feel justifiably confident in their country's sovereignty, but there was little room for complacency as far as cultural unity was concerned. America was, by 1876, a successful, politically unified, and vibrant nation, but its national identity continued to be contested. Visitors to the two-acre International Exhibition of Arts, Manufactures and Products of the Soil and Mine exhibition – or World's Fair for short – in Philadelphia in 1876 were not invited to contemplate that issue. Instead, they were presented with the overwhelming proof of their nation's natural abundance and

---

FIGURE 6.6 (*Continued*) reads in part: "Furl that Banner, for 't is weary;/Round its staff 't is drooping dreary:/Furl it, fold it, – it is best;/For there's not a man to wave it,/And there's not a sword to save it . . . Furl that Banner, softly, slowly!/Treat it gently – it is holy,/For it droops above the dead./Touch it not – unfold it never;/Let it droop there, furled forever, –/For its people's hopes are fled." Image courtesy of the Library of Congress Prints and Photographs Division (LC-USZ62–91833).

THE STRIDE OF A CENTURY.

FIGURE 6.7. "The Stride of a Century" (New York: Currier and Ives, c. 1876). This centennial image is of "Brother Jonathan," a younger precursor to the later "Uncle Sam" image of the United States. He is pictured astride the American continent, a continent crossed, as the picture makes clear, by the railroad. The main building at the Philadelphia World's Fair of 1876 is directly under him, at the center of the image. Image courtesy of the Library of Congress Prints and Photographs Division (LC-USZ62–106472).

technological progress since 1776 as it was displayed to them alongside that of other nations.

Elevators, engines and electric lights, minerals, meteorites and marble, the telephone, the typewriter, and Heinz tomato ketchup were just some of the new wonders on display in Philadelphia that year. Stuffed animal specimens, including an elk, a walrus, and a polar bear, represented the indigenous fauna that, at the time of the exhibition, was already facing a degree of threat from the incoming human population to the continent. Less than a decade after the exhibition in Philadelphia, the 13 million buffalo that had roamed the Great Plains had all but wiped out by hunting. Fewer than 1,000 remained by 1883. Such was the price of America's progress and productivity.

America was not just about productivity, of course, or even product; it was about people. On this subject, the World's Fair was a little less celebratory and a great deal more circumspect. As for the indigenous populations, some of whom had relied on the fast-diminishing herds of the Plains, their fate was hardly so uplifting, their future not so promising as it seemed from the Fair. Their existence was acknowledged as a colorful aboriginal presence in the United States, but one expressed mutely in the form of manikins rather than living, breathing men and women in Philadelphia in 1876. Yet although they may have been rendered as static as the stuffed animals on display, America's natives were very much alive. That fact was forcibly brought home in the midst of the centennial celebrations when news of Colonel George Custer's defeat at the hands of the Sioux under Sitting Bull and Crazy Horse at the Little Bighorn River in Montana Territory reached Philadelphia.

In their centennial year, therefore, Americans had cause to contemplate not just how far their country had come, but also the distance it still had to travel. The whole question of who the people were, what an American citizen was and what rights pertained to citizenship, remained a perennial predicament for a nation of immigrants. The rhetoric, if not the rules, that accompanied the birth of this particular nation was certainly inclusive. The reality was rather more limited.

There were, over the years, a great many variants on Crèvecoeur's theme of "the American, this new man," from nineteenth-century physician and author Oliver Wendell Holmes's description of Americans as "the Romans of the modern world – the great assimilating people" to the "melting pot" metaphor of American society as popularized in Israel Zangwill's 1908 play of that name.[24] America had furnished itself with the means of making this ideal real; what was sometimes absent was the motivation. Madison's fears for the flimsiness of paper promises proved well founded indeed at various points in America's history. The Bill of Rights did little to protect African Americans from the extremes of white supremacy, and nothing to defend the Constitutional rights of those Japanese Americans forced into internment camps during World War II.

Arguably, this tendency to ignore the ground rules reached its fullest and most poisonous potential in the anticommunist scares of the twentieth century and in the behavior of the House of Representatives' investigative committee, the House Committee on Un-American Activities (HUAC), in the 1950s. Here, the clue to the fears motivating what was, in essence, a modern-day witch hunt was most definitely in the title. Yet such fears had been present at the creation, at that point when the new nation was working out just what America, what being American, meant. They persisted through the antebellum period and the Civil War years. And they really came to the fore on the frontier.

In seeking to manage the land, the federal government had, since the Northwest Ordinance of 1787, established that the territories were, in a legal and practical sense, transitional states that would in time become actual states of the Union. In seeking to manage the population, there was also a transitional element to the equation, but one hedged about by a plethora of prejudices and preconceptions that permanently positioned a great percentage of that population beyond the boundary lines of belonging to the nation. With the Union victory in 1865, and with the passage of the Thirteenth Amendment closely followed by the Fourteenth, African Americans were fully accepted as a constituent part of "the people," legally at least. Slavery was finally abolished, but the racial mindset that had supported it proved more resilient. In the century that followed, racial distinctions and divisions proved, too often, to be the cornerstone of the nation's development. And it was not just African Americans who had to face up to that disturbing reality.

7

A Promised Land

Gateway to the American Century

With a tear for the dark past, turn we then to the dazzling future, and, veiling our eyes, press forward. The long and weary winter of the race is ended. Its summer has begun. Humanity has burst the chrysalis. The heavens are before it.

(Edward Bellamy, *Looking Backward*, 1888)

Ida B. Wells was just five months old when Confederate forces under Earl Van Dorn raided her home town of Holly Springs, Mississippi, in December 1862, their target the supply depot established there as support for the Union general Ulysses S. Grant's assault on Vicksburg, Tennessee. She was a teenager when, in 1878, a yellow fever epidemic devastated her community, killing both her parents and one of her brothers. And in 1884, at the age of twenty-one, she was forcibly ejected from a ladies' coach while traveling on the Chesapeake, Ohio and Southwestern Railroad on the grounds that it was for whites only. In some ways Wells's experiences were all too typical of the dangers and difficulties facing many Americans in the latter part of the nineteenth century, especially in the South where "yellow jack" posed a persistent, if not perennial, threat to life. Yellow fever, however, takes little account of race. The same could not be said of the railways in this period. Ida B. Wells was as susceptible as any other American to the threat of viral infection; she was particularly susceptible to the virulence of racial vindictiveness, however, for the simple reason that she was black.

Ida had taken on the burden of supporting her family when her parents died, and she was not likely to accept meekly the reactionary opinions of a railroad conductor. She successfully sued the railroad. When the

Tennessee Supreme Court overruled the agreed settlement – she had been awarded compensation – it was a wake-up call for a young woman who had, technically, been born a slave but who had believed, as had so many others, that the "America of the past is gone forever" and that the "new nation," the America of the future, "is to be wholly free. Liberty, equality before the law, is to be its great corner stone," as Illinois congressman Isaac N. Arnold had asserted in 1864.[1] Too often, however, that freedom had to be enforced in the face of frequently violent opposition, especially on the part of some extremists in the former Confederate states. In time, the most destructive aspects of that violence would become the focus of Ida Wells's life and would define her legacy.

While Ida was still an infant, the emergence, in Pulaski, Tennessee, in 1866 of the notorious Ku Klux Klan, a vigilante group of white suprem-acists, revealed the determination of at least part of the white South to undermine the efforts of those, like Arnold, who had long advocated abolition and, when that was achieved, the protection of equal rights for all in the nation. Linked to the Democratic Party, and comprising mainly, but not exclusively, former Confederates, the Klan was devoted to intimidating Union sympathizers and Republicans generally but partic-ularly African Americans and preventing them from asserting their legal rights to liberty and property and, in extreme cases, life itself. Visitors to the South such as businessman John Murray Forbes quickly recognized the deadly message spelled out via the "death's heads and cross bones" and "daggers dripping blood" symbols that "decorated" so many south-ern cities in the late 1860s.[2] Yet whereas the symbolism may have been peculiarly southern, the attitude was not confined to the former Confed-erate states, but was an intrinsic element in the Democratic Party's racist rhetoric at that time (Figure 7.1).

In 1868, however, the nation was not prepared either to turn its back on the achievements of the Civil War or align itself with such overt racial divisiveness as the Democratic Party then represented. It made this clear in its choice of a former Union general, Ulysses S. Grant, as president. During Grant's first term, the federal government passed three separate enforcement acts (1870, 1871) designed to curb the violence of the Klan and backed these up by sending federal marshals into the South to ensure compliance. In particular, Grant authorized Hiram C. Whitley, chief of the Secret Service Division of the Treasury, to gather evidence against individual Klan members. Whitley was proud to recollect in his mem-oirs that he had helped secure "over two thousand indictments" against "this infamous organization," but as he well knew, the cost involved for those who testified to achieve these indictments was high.[3] Merciless beatings, but also sometimes lynchings, were the most common form of intimidation directed at blacks and whites alike in the attempt to silence opposition to the Klan.

The worlds of Hiram Whitley and Ida B. Wells, wholly and utterly separate in all other senses, collided on this single subject; except, of course, it was not just a single subject. It was not just about white aggression clashing with black assertiveness, white entrenchment in the face of emancipation. It was far more complicated than that. Had it not been, then an individual like Hiram Whitley, a man who had worked as a slave catcher, a man opposed to abolition, and later to extending the franchise to African Americans, a man who had, briefly, entertained the idea of fighting for the Confederacy before he threw his lot in with the Union, would not have been so active in protecting the civil rights of people with whom, clearly, he had little sympathy and nothing in common. In the figure of Whitley, a multiplicity of practical and personal agendas met and merged, as they did in the nation itself in the later nineteenth century. It was a world of contradictions. It was the world in which Ida B. Wells grew up.

Late-nineteenth-century America was a postwar world. This fact can frequently become obscured by the rapid rise of the cities, the technological and transport advances, and the westward expansion of America at this time. Yet all this took place in the context of a nation still suffering from the aftereffects of conflict, physically, practically, and psychologically. The Civil War ended in 1865, but it had left more than 600,000 Americans dead, almost as many wounded or disabled for life, and the national economy in a precarious position. The dead could be mourned. The often struggling survivors had to be maintained. This was the problem facing both the North and the South. It was not just the cities of the South that required rebuilding, not just the economy that needed stabilizing. Many of the living veterans of the violence that had been the Civil War had to be supported for the remainder of their lives, lives that would stretch, in some cases, well into the twentieth century.

In addition, because the war had been a civil conflict, naturally, the greater economic devastation and physical destruction experienced by the South was not a problem that the nation could walk away from; neither was it the one likely to be solved in the space of a few short years. The value of southern real estate had halved over the course of the war, and the value of its agricultural output in 1860 was not matched until the turn of the century, and lagged far behind the nation as a whole

"THIS IS A WHITE MAN'S GOVERNMENT!"

"We regard the Reconstruction Acts (so called) of Congress as usurpations, and unconstitutional, revolutionary, and void."—*Democratic Platform.*

until after World War II. Both black and white farmers in the postwar South swiftly found themselves trapped in a system of, effectively, debt peonage, or sharecropping, as it was known. Working on land owned by others in return for a share of the crop, most found themselves growing cotton rather than crops to service loans that they had no choice but to secure yet could never hope to pay off. At the national level, matters were exacerbated by the fact that Grant, while a great military commander, proved a less effective peacetime president. The political and financial corruption that marred his two terms of office, and that prompted Mark Twain's derogatory designation of the period as a Gilded Age, resulted in a vacillating federal policy toward the South generally and African Americans in particular.

Although the federally funded Freedmen's Bureau was established in 1865 to smooth the transition from slavery to freedom by, among other things, setting up schools and hospitals and providing general aid and advice, it lasted only five years and never enjoyed the resources necessary to achieve its ambitious ends. It never received the resources, indeed, necessary to maintain the basic health of the freedmen and women, already compromised by slavery and exacerbated by conditions in the

←——————————————————————————————————

FIGURE 7.1. "This is a white man's government" (Thomas Nast). This cartoon, which appeared in *Harper's Weekly* on September 5, 1868, mocked the Democratic Party's platform in the 1868 election, the slogan of which the cartoon's title invoked. The three white figures represented comprise (from left) a caricatured image of an Irish immigrant, Nathan Bedford Forrest, the leader of the Ku Klux Klan (whose belt buckle, "CSA," and knife engraved "The Lost Cause" made it clear that he represented the Confederate States of America), and Horatio Seymour, the Democratic presidential nominee who opposed the "Reconstruction Acts." They are portrayed as standing both on an African-American soldier and on the American flag that he was carrying. The soldier reaches in vain for a ballot box, just out of his reach (bottom right). The legend at the foot of the image reads: "We regard the Reconstruction Acts (so called) of Congress as usurpations, and unconstitutional, revolutionary, and void." Under these acts, passed in the context of the resounding Republican victory in the Congressional elections of 1866, the South was divided into five military districts, each former Confederate state was required to implement universal manhood suffrage, and each had to draft a new state constitution as well as ratify the Fourteenth Amendment. The background imagery here is even more disturbing, consisting as it does of a school or asylum in flames and a lynching (a clear reference to the violent opposition to the Civil War that broke out in the New York City Draft Riots of July 1863, during which the Colored Orphan Asylum on Fifth Avenue was attacked and several individuals were lynched). Image courtesy of the Library of Congress Prints and Photographs Division (LC-USZ62–121735).

"contraband camps" in which many had ended up – breeding grounds for cholera and other life-threatening ailments.

The problems facing the Medical Division of the Freedmen's Bureau were in several senses symptomatic of the broader issues involved in the shift from slavery to freedom. Beleaguered doctors battled a federal bureaucracy more concerned with protocol and procedure than practical help, with curbing chaos rather than managing medical, never mind social, imperatives. The presence of Union troops in the South could, too, only do so much to help implement this early and internal version of regime change in a region where grassroots opposition to federal interference generally and equality specifically frequently stymied any attempt to secure lasting political, economic, and social stability there.

In legislative terms, certainly, progress was made. The Enforcement Acts of the early 1870s, which allowed for the prosecution of racial crimes in a federal rather than a state court, were followed by the passage of the 1875 Civil Rights Act. This sought to equalize the social and cultural landscape of the South by promising "the full and equal enjoyment of the accommodations, advantages, facilities, and privileges of inns, public conveyances on land or water, theaters, and other places of public amusement" to "citizens of every race and color, regardless of any previous condition of servitude." Nevertheless, a massive gulf remained between the assertion of equal rights in principle and the assurance of the same in practice. Some, like Whitley, sought to narrow the gap; others worked to widen it.

Critiques of the political power of African Americans, and Republican rule generally, in the Reconstruction South sometimes emerged from the most unexpected sources. Whitley's prewar racial perspective may have proved no hindrance to his fighting white extremism in the postwar South, but for others their apparent shift in perspective went in the other direction. One example was the journalist James Shepherd Pike, whose antebellum abolitionist credentials lent contemporary credence to his vituperative attack on Reconstruction in South Carolina. South Carolina was an unusual state, because the majority of its Reconstruction legislature was African American, which is perhaps why Pike pounced on it. Nevertheless, his attack was extreme. Promulgated at first via newspaper editorials that were later published as *The Prostrate State* (1873), Pike painted a damning picture indeed of post-emancipation politics in one southern state, a perspective that may have surprised his audience.

Pike had been the Washington correspondent for the radical *New York Tribune* in the 1850s and in that capacity had frequently argued against slavery, which he termed "this detestable institution." By the 1870s, however, his views had shifted. Then, he expressed his dismay that the slaveholding "aristocracy" of which he had previously been so scathing lay "prostrate in the dust," governed by a "strange conglomerate" of African-American political leaders, "the dregs of the population habilitated in the robes of their intelligent predecessors," as he described them. This state of affairs, the postwar Pike argued, was nothing less than "the rule of ignorance and corruption, through the inexorable machinery of a majority of numbers. It is barbarism overwhelming civilization by physical force," he asserted, it "is the slave rioting in the halls of his master, and putting that master under his feet."[4]

Pike's change of heart on the matter of slavery, as indeed Whitley's, may seem incomprehensible were it not for the fact that for them as for many others, the issues at stake in nineteenth-century America had only ever been tangentially related to the morality of slavery. Both men inhabited a world in which the threat of "barbarism" seemed very real and was a cause of consistent concern. Broadly defined in contemporary minds as the absence both of religious and republican principles, barbarism, according to Horace Bushnell, one of America's leading theologians, was the nation's "first danger." Bushnell issued his warning in 1847, at which time slavery and westward expansion – or a combination of the two – seemed to pose the greatest threat, but he placed both in the context of the broader continuum of America's national development, harking back to its colonial past and looking forward to its future struggles. For Bushnell, America's battle against barbarism was "continually repeating itself under new modifications," and his warning constituted "a double argument of fear and hope" for his nation.[5]

Highlighted by the press and the pulpit alike in the antebellum era, reinterpreted during the Civil War as a crucial component in both the moral and practical arguments for Union, the threat of barbarism, as Bushnell predicted, never went away. Fears for the future of the nation, indeed, seemed much more real in the age of "machine politics," and the corruption attendant on it, that followed the Civil War. Slavery had gone, but slavery had been both symptom and cause of the social and spiritual decline Bushnell had railed against; in any case, it could not, even then, be firmly quarantined in the South but was already spreading westward. In the later-nineteenth century, Bushnell's fears were confirmed as the disease of social decline appeared to present itself in a new, more vigorous national form.

The racial insecurities inculcated by Pike in relation to politics in South Carolina in the 1870s had their echo in the northern states, and especially in New York City, where the Democratic political machine's gears remained firmly stuck in reverse as far as racial equality was concerned. Yet even when shorn of its racial dimension, the political picture hardly improved. In the late 1860s and early 1870s, New York Democrat congressman William M. Tweed and his associates – the infamous "Tweed Ring" – operated an elaborate system of bribes, backhanders, and electoral and financial fraud from their headquarters on East 14th Street – Tammany Hall – accruing millions of dollars in the process (Figure 7.2). There was undoubtedly a certain "Robin Hood" element to "Boss" Tweed's financial activities. Some of his ill-gotten gains did find their way to his mainly Irish immigrant constituency in the form of educational and practical aid (via grossly inflated salaries in some cases), and part of the rest of it was spent on civic improvements, albeit fantastically expensive ones, most notably the New York County Courthouse, begun at the outbreak of the Civil War and finally completed in 1880.

Such blatant mishandling of public funds in the service of private gain may not strike the modern observer as particularly unusual. In the context of the financial corruption, exacerbated by the worldwide financial panic of 1873, which was slowly sinking the Grant administration, Tweed's activities did not strike the contemporary observer as especially out of step with the times either. Despite its trickle-down economic benefits, the "Tweed Ring" was certainly no Arthurian Round Table, and was widely perceived as symptomatic of an age defined, as Hiram Whitley put it, by "fraud and wrong-doing." The fuel for the fraud that Whitley perceived was the immigrant. "Persons of almost every nationality are *continually* landing upon our shores," he complained, many of whom were "felons of the Continent to-day and citizens of the United States tomorrow. Each year brings its accession of anarchists, counterfeiters, forgers, and thieves," many of them drawn from the ranks of "the ambitious poor who enter upon a style of living far beyond their humble means."

For Whitley, "[p]overty and disease has its localities, but crime creeps in everywhere."[6] Mainly, as he chose to recollect it in his memoirs, it crept in from abroad, but as he must have known, the homegrown variety was equally pervasive and much more potent. In many respects, Whitley's memoirs were revealingly selective in what they chose to highlight and what to hide as far as his career in law enforcement was concerned. Choosing to focus on the bootleggers, the forgers, and the crime syndicates of the northern cities, Whitley had little to say about his agency's

"STONE WALLS DO NOT A PRISON MAKE."—*Old Song.*

"No Prison is big enough to hold the Boss." In on one side, and out at the other.

FIGURE 7.2. "Stone Walls Do Not a Prison Make" (Thomas Nast). Although his cartons on subjects such as emancipation and white supremacy in the South were widely distributed in the mid-nineteenth century, Thomas Nast's reputation was really made via his strenuous efforts to highlight the political and financial corruption perpetrated by the "Tweed Ring." This cartoon, which appeared in *Frank Leslie's Illustrated Newspaper* on January 6, 1872, shows "Boss" Tweed half in and half out of prison. It suggests that "no prison is big enough to hold the Boss." In fact, Tweed did end up in prison and died there in 1878. Image courtesy of the Library of Congress Prints and Photographs Division (LC-USZ6–951).

activities in the Reconstruction South. In this respect, he followed, or at least recognized, a national trend that grew out of both frustration and fatigue as far as the South was concerned.

Reconstruction had never just been about bringing the South back into the Union. At a fundamental level it had been about transforming the

South into the image of the North, or at least into how the North preferred to see itself. In the decades following the Civil War, the realization that this was impossible began to dawn. As the former Confederate states came back into the Union, the power of the Democratic Party in those states increased as that of the radical Reconstruction Republicans declined. And with Democratic resurgence came racial retrenchment (Figure 7.3). Across the South, but especially in Louisiana, Mississippi, and South Carolina, black voters were forced away from the polls as their states reestablished white rule and inaugurated a process of slowly but surely unpicking the legislation designed to ensure racial equality.

By 1875, as the nation prepared both to celebrate its centennial year and conduct a presidential election, both incumbent president and public alike had grown, if not disenchanted with, then certainly despairing of the whole subject of the South. As President Grant dispatched his former army colleague, Union general Phillip H. Sheridan to New Orleans to curb the violence of the White League there, in South Carolina, the supporters of former Confederate general Wade Hampton were gearing up for the gubernatorial (state governor) elections that would see Hampton elected and the state "redeemed" from Republican rule in 1876. It was, therefore, a somewhat weary Grant who, at the start of 1875, confronted the Senate with a litany of extralegal abuses that had occurred in the southern states, and especially in Louisiana. In particular, he drew the Senate's attention to events in Colfax on Easter Sunday, 1873, when the white militia had attacked a group of armed blacks at the courthouse, killing most of them, even after they had surrendered.

Grant, who knew whereof he spoke, described what became known as the "Colfax Massacre" as an event "which in blood-thirstiness and barbarity is hardly surpassed by any acts of savage warfare." He did not spare his colleagues the gruesome details of what had occurred, nor the clear evidence of the summary executions by gunshot of fifty-nine of the prisoners, "the great majority in the head, and most of them in the back of the head," that had taken place. "To hold the people of Louisiana generally responsible for these atrocities would not be just," Grant conceded, but he nevertheless described it as "a lamentable fact that insuperable obstructions were thrown in the way of punishing these murderers, and the so-called conservative papers of the State not only justified the massacre, but denounced as federal tyranny and despotism the attempt of the United States officers to bring them to justice." Grant had good reason to fear that "no way can be found in this boasted land of

FIGURE 7.3. "The Union as it was/The Lost Cause worse than slavery." This cartoon by Thomas Nast appeared in *Harper's Weekly* on October 24, 1874, the year before the Civil Rights Act was passed. It forcibly highlighted the fact that, despite the passage of the 1870 and 1871 Enforcement Acts, specifically the 1871 Ku Klux Klan Act (the third Enforcement Act), and the establishment in June 1870 of the Department of Justice, a variety of white supremacist groups, such as the "White League" (named here by the badge on the figure on the left) and the "Red Shirts" in Mississippi and, later, in South Carolina, continued to suppress the civil rights of African Americans in the South. Image courtesy of the Library of Congress Prints and Photographs Division (LC-USZ62–128619).

civilization and Christianity to punish the perpetrators of this bloody and monstrous crime," and every reason to believe that the American "public are tired out with these annual, autumnal outbreaks in the South."[7] In that year, *United States vs. Cruikshank* (1875), the Supreme Court overturned some of the convictions that had, via the 1870 Enforcement Act, been achieved in the aftermath of the Colfax Massacre.

United States vs. Cruikshank was a case with repercussions. It restricted the legal reach of the federal government in civil rights cases by invoking a states' rights interpretation of both the First and Second Amendments to the Constitution. "Sovereignty," it asserted, "for the protection of the rights of life and personal liberty within the respective States, rests alone with the States." The court further asserted that the charge that the white defendants had sought to compromise the "rights and privileges" of their victims on the grounds of race was "too vague" to be proved. "We may suspect," it admitted, "that race was the cause of the hostility," but beyond that it would not go.[8] *United States vs. Cruikshank* effectively constituted a "get out of jail free" card for white supremacists, one that proved valid for almost a hundred years. In parts of the South, Grant had concluded, "the spirit of hatred and violence is stronger than the law." That spirit would prove to be even stronger, and certainly had more scope with the law on its side.

Neither the Fifteenth Amendment nor the 1875 Civil Rights Act proved able to stem the gradual but growing racial divide in the South, nor the concomitant removal of African-American voting rights. Via a range of restrictive legislation, the southern states established a system of segregation designed not so much to separate the races as to assert white supremacy and ensure that the black vote would not work to undermine this. Some of the legislation was frankly ludicrous and susceptible to challenge. The so-called grandfather clause, for example, disenfranchised the descendants of slaves. This was a little too obviously in breach of the Fifteenth Amendment, and was overturned in 1915. Poll taxes and literacy tests (Figure 7.4), even though they also disenfranchised many poor or illiterate whites, were the preferred legislative means of reestablishing white elite rule in the post–Civil War South; through them, the "Lost Cause" of the Confederacy turned out to have been only temporarily misplaced. By the start of World War II, only some 3 percent of black southerners eligible to vote were registered to do so.

The effective removal of African Americans from the polity, together with the 1883 *Civil Rights Cases* that made discrimination a matter of private conscience rather than Congressional concern, paved the way for a raft of state laws, known as the "Jim Crow" laws, that established separate and supposedly equal accommodations for black and white Americans. In 1896, the "separate but equal" doctrine was codified in one of America's most famous legal cases, *Plessy vs. Ferguson*. In this ruling, the

Supreme Court confirmed the legality of segregation, so long as the separate facilities in question were in fact equal. Of course, most were not. On the railroads as in restaurants, in schools and streetcars, from hotels to housing, an increasingly strict "color line" was drawn in the aftermath of the *Plessy* ruling. Even death, the great equalizer, was forced to toe the color line; the cemeteries, too, were segregated.

It was in the year after the *Civil Rights Cases* that Ida B. Wells clashed with the railroad. By that point, she was fully aware that being forcibly ejected from a "white" ladies railway carriage was not the worst fate that could befall anyone who challenged the southern segregation system. The system may have enjoyed national sanction, or at the very least national complicity, but that alone could not ensure its long-term survival, nor protect it from continuous attack in the courts. The one thing that could mute opposition to segregation was to make the consequences of challenging it too grim to contemplate. The threat of violence always had been part, overt or otherwise, of slavery and it served the same purpose in the system of segregation that, in many senses, simply replaced chattel servitude. The tragedy of America in the later nineteenth century was that what underpinned segregation's always dubious legality was the most extreme violence of all: lynching.

Lynching, the illegal execution and sometimes brutal torture of the victim concerned was not unique to the South or to the later nineteenth and twentieth centuries. Nor did lynch mobs confine their attentions to African-American men. The Chinese, Native Americans, and Mexicans were also susceptible to the worst extremes of white mob violence, as were African-American women and white men themselves. The reasons why lynching became associated with the southern execution of African Americans, however, are not too complex. Although accurate figures for what was, after all, a vigilante action are necessarily elusive, the majority of lynchings – some 5,000 in total – took place between the 1880s and the mid-twentieth century, peaked in the 1890s, and occurred mainly – although certainly not exclusively – in the South, and especially in Mississippi, Georgia, Texas, Louisiana, and Alabama. All 5 states witnessed in excess of 300 lynchings in that period. There is also little doubt that, although whites were victims of lynch mobs, lynching was predominantly a race crime. In the case of Mississippi and Georgia, fewer than 10 percent of the victims were white. In Louisiana and Alabama, slightly more than 10 percent were white. Only Texas spread lynching more equitably, but only in relative terms; some 25 percent of Texan lynch victims were white.

THE COLOR LINE STILL EXISTS—IN THIS CASE.

Whatever else lynching was, it was not just about implementing a dubious extralegal "justice" in criminal cases or even as simple a matter as a "lynch mob" taking the law into its own hands. As far as the lynching of African Americans was concerned, it is hardly sufficient to describe it as an expression, albeit the most extreme expression, of the white impulse to control the black population, to assert white supremacy in the face of any challenge to this. The extremes of cruelty meted out to some victims, and the fact that lynching was frequently a public spectacle (Figure 7.5) that drew crowds of, at times, in excess of 10,000, defy simple analysis. The fact that some onlookers proudly distributed photographs of a lynching to friends and relatives is perhaps more unsettling and even less susceptible to explanation.

Justifying "Judge Lynch" was hardly credible, yet justifications were sought, and frequently found in the fabricated myth of the black rapist. This was the case in 1899 in Georgia, when African-American laborer Sam Hose was accused of raping his employer's wife and was physically mutilated, dismembered, and burned alive before an approving crowd of some 2,000 white witnesses. Hose's case was just one of many that Ida Wells highlighted in her study of *Lynch Law in Georgia* (1899). She noted that Hose's death "gave to the United States the distinction of

←——

FIGURE 7.4. "The color line still exists – in this case" (1879). This cartoon, mocking the literacy tests, and indeed southern white literacy rates, imposed to disenfranchise African Americans, appeared in *Harper's Weekly* on January 18, 1879. It shows the figure of "Uncle Sam" writing "Eddikashun qualifukashun. The Black man orter be eddikated afore he kin vote with US Wites, signed Mr. Solid South." The cartoon was in some senses ahead of its time; the 1880s and 1890s were the decades that witnessed the most determined "retreat from reconstruction" in terms of discriminatory legislation, beginning with – and facilitated by – the 1883 *Civil Rights Cases* that overturned the Civil Rights Act of 1875. It was the 1883 ruling that allowed a segregated society to develop. The idea of the "color line," too, became more prominent in the twentieth century, especially after African-American leader W.E.B. Du Bois asserted, in *The Souls of Black Folk* (1903), that the "problem of the Twentieth Century is the problem of the color-line," by which he did not mean in America alone. In the American case, however, both the phrase and the idea were common in the nineteenth-century. "Mr Solid South" refers to the Democratic Party's total electoral dominance in the region following the South's "redemption" from Republican Reconstruction. The South stayed reasonably "solid" in this regard until well into the twentieth century. In many respects, therefore, this cartoon really did recognize the writing on the wall. Image courtesy of the Library of Congress Prints and Photographs Division (LC-USZ62–83004).

JOHN HEITH, lynched on Feb. 22, 1884, by infuriated citizens in Arizona.

FIGURE 7.5. The body of John Heith (sometimes designated Heath), lynched in February 1884 in Tombstone, Arizona. Photographer Noah Hamilton Rose. Despite Tombstone's later reputation – secured via Western "dime novels" and, later, film – as perhaps the epitome of the "Wild West," lynching was far more common in the states of the former Confederacy than in frontier towns, and was frequently a racially motivated crime. Nevertheless, the idea of maintaining social order – whether that was defined racially or otherwise – lay behind many lynchings. John Heith had been convicted, in a court of law, for murder and sentenced to life imprisonment in Yuma Penitentiary, a sentence that some clearly deemed unacceptably lenient. In this case, the *New York Times* reported that a placard (not visible here) was attached to the telegraph pole asserting that "John Heith was hanged to this pole by citizens of Cochise County for participation in the

having burned alive seven human beings during the past ten years," and detailed for her readers the full extent of the "sickening sights of the day," sights that included the removal of "souvenirs" in the form of the victim's bones by members of the white crowd.[9]

Only a few years earlier, when Wells, along with many other African-American advocates and activists, explored and published *The Reason Why the Colored American Is Not in the World's Columbian Exposition* (Chicago World's Fair) in 1893, Frederick Douglass's introduction highlighted the fact that the "crime to which the Negro is now said to be so generally and specially addicted, is one of which he has been heretofore, seldom accused or supposed to be guilty." Although, as Douglass recalled, the African-American male had frequently been accused of "petty thefts," he had never been "accused of the atrocious crime of feloniously assaulting white women. If we may believe his accusers," Douglass observed, "this is a new development," but Douglass well knew that it was white behavior, not black, that had altered, and that what had caused the change was "the pretended and baseless fear" of black political supremacy in the South.

For Ida Wells, understanding the white lynching mindset was less important than exploding at least some of the myths that sustained it. In particular she attacked the myth that had, as Douglass noted, grown in parallel with and as the pretext for many of the lynchings that took place. In *Southern Horrors* (1892), she charged the South for "shielding itself behind the plausible screen of defending the honor of its women," a screen that had "closed the heart, stifled the conscience, warped the judgment and hushed the voice of press and pulpit on the subject of lynch law throughout this 'land of liberty'."[10] Here, as in her contribution to *The Reason Why* and *Lynch Law in Georgia*, she graphically detailed the horrific nature of lynching, provided the hard numerical, along with disturbing descriptive and visual, evidence of its spread and growing

---

FIGURE 7.5 (*continued*) Bisbee massacre as a proved accessory at 8.20 A.M., Feb 22, 1884 (Washington's Birthday,) to advance Arizona."[11] The invocation of Washington and the premise that a lynching might "advance Arizona" offer some clues to the bizarre mental processes at work in this case, to a mindset that linked the "Father of his Country" to the idea of preserving stability on the (then) frontier of that country. Heith's was, however, a straightforward lynching, if such a relative term can have any meaning in such cases, compared to many of the excessively brutal extralegal murders that occurred in the late-nineteenth-and twentieth-century United States. Image courtesy of the Library of Congress Prints and Photographs Division (LC-USZ62-109782).

barbarity, and reminded her readers that despite the emphasis on rape that frequently underpinned it, in fact this was a crime that spared neither women nor children.

Slavery was already on the road to extinction when Ida Wells was born in 1862, but its repercussions overshadowed her entire life and, in many respects, that of her nation. The kinds of "southern horrors" detailed by her and others had a national resonance and invoked a natural revulsion that did not, unfortunately, result in much in the way of decisive action. When she died in 1931, segregation was still firmly entrenched in the South and inequality – racial and economic – entrenched nationally. Writing to John Murray Forbes in 1891, the noted poet John Greenleaf Whittier commented that he was "thankful that we have outlived chattel slavery," but expressed his dismay that "the rights of the colored citizen are denied. . . . Will the time ever come," he asked, "when the Sermon on the Mount and the Declaration of Independence will practically influence our boasted civilization and Christianity?"[12] It was a good question, and one that preoccupied many minds as the nineteenth century drew to its close and the twentieth beckoned.

Looking Backward

For many Americans, lynching seemed but a baleful part of the broader rise of "barbarity" across the land, proof of the social and national decline that ministers such as Bushnell had warned against and law enforcement operatives such as Whitley had identified as imported by the immigrant. Evincing not so much xenophobia as a practical, if cynical, recognition that the borders were perhaps easier to police than the South, the American response to the perceived corruption and cruelties of the Gilded Age was to side with Whitley and start to close the nation's hitherto relatively open doors. This was an era in which the Statue of Liberty was erected as both the symbol and simultaneously the safeguard of all that the United States stood for, but with a growing emphasis on the latter. Liberty's upraised arm was too often understood to be the guardian against, rather than the welcoming beacon for, the dispossessed of the world.

Six months prior to the statue's unveiling, labor unrest in Chicago revealed just some of the divisions within American society, this time between labor and capital, divisions that appeared to be deepening in the context of immigration. Such concerns found confirmation in the explosion of a bomb and resultant riot in which eight policemen and an indeterminate number of civilians died during a labor rally in Haymarket

TABLE 7.1. *American Foreign-Born Population, 1850–1920*

Year	U.S. Population (total)	Number of Foreign-Born	Percentage of Foreign-Born
1850	23,191,876	2,244,602	9.7
1860	31,443,321	4,138,697	13.2
1870	38,558,371	5,567,229	14.4
1880	50,155,783	6,679,943	13.3
1890	62,622,250	9,249,547	14.8
1900	75,994,575	10,341,276	13.6
1910	91,972,266	13,515,886	14.7
1920	105,710,620	13,920,692	13.2

Source: U.S. Bureau of the Census, *Statistical Abstract of the United States, 1999* (Washington, DC: Government Printing Office 2000).

Square, the center of the manufacturing district in Chicago, on May 4, 1886. Supposedly the work of anarchists (six of whom were identified as immigrants), the tragedy only reinforced such anti-immigrant sentiment as did exist at that time. More crucially, it established a link between anarchist and incomer in the public mind, an exaggerated fear that socialist subversives were working to undermine American republicanism. This first "Red Scare" in America's history has been tracked back to the "Haymarket Riot," but at best this was only the catalyst. More diffuse social, political, and economic forces were at play in this period, forces that impacted on immigrant and indigene alike.

Anti-immigration sentiment was, of course, nothing new. In 1855, Abraham Lincoln, critiquing the nativist "Know-Nothing" party of the period, had observed that as "a nation we began by declaring that '*all men are created equal.*' We now practically read it 'all men are created equal *except Negroes.*' When the Know-Nothings get control, it will read 'all men are created equal except Negroes, *and foreigners, and Catholics.*'"[13] Yet immigrants were a necessary element, perhaps the crucial contribution, to the nation's development, both before and in the decades following the Civil War. Between 1870 and 1900, the period of the so-called New Immigration, some 12 million immigrants arrived, and many – although by no means all – remained, the very necessary human resources that enabled the rise of America as an economic and industrial power.

Although significant for the nation's growth, purely in percentage terms, immigration was not the sudden overwhelming force that the language used to describe it frequently implies (Table 7.1). Comprising around 13 percent (in 1880) to almost 15 percent (in 1890) of the

American population as a whole (roughly the same percentage as for the African-American population), the percentage of foreign-born remained fairly constant from 1860 through 1920. Although the falling birthrate of the period may have heightened concerns, in fact the nation was in little danger of being overrun by outsiders in the later nineteenth and early twentieth centuries, any more than the white South was in peril of political dominance by the black South. Nevertheless, what historian Roger Daniels has critiqued as the "hydraulic metaphors," frequently used to describe the "waves" of migrants surging onto America's shores in this period, was increasingly the contemporary perspective, both within America and abroad.[14]

This perspective had less to do with numbers than with nature. Nineteenth-century British historian and political commentator Lord Bryce had, in his survey of *The American Commonwealth* (1888), differentiated between the "earlier immigrants" and those of the Gilded Age. The former, he proposed, may have been "uneducated" but were nevertheless "intelligent peasants of strong stocks, industrious, energetic, and capable of quickly accommodating themselves to the conditions of their new land and blending with its people." The latter, by contrast, were, according to Bryce, "on a lower grade of civilization" and "in every way more alien to American habits and standards."[15] Bryce's was a conclusion with which many Americans concurred. Quite why the new nation, then as in the eighteenth century, revealed such a marked tendency to accept the opinions not just of outsiders but of aristocratic outsiders may be something of a mystery. Bryce's opinions in 1888, as Crèvecoeur's in 1782, were hardly rules to raise a republic on. Yet these foreign opinions clearly resonated with a nation informed from its inception by the desire to create a "city on a hill" and constrained by the fact that cities, and their populations, were complex conglomerations of people, pressures, and political perspectives.

Nevertheless, the rise of the city was one of the defining aspects of America's expansion between 1870 and 1900. In those three decades, the number of urban communities, as defined by the census, along with their populations, had tripled overall, with some cities experiencing phenomenal population increases. In 1870, for example, New York's population was just under a million, Philadelphia's just over half a million, and Chicago's just over a quarter of a million. By 1900, these three cities alone had seen their populations increase to, in New York's case, almost 3.5 million, in Philadelphia's to 1.3 million, and Chicago – by then the second largest city in the nation – sustained 1.7 million inhabitants.

Although few Americans in the 1880s and 1890s still adhered to Jefferson's vision of an agrarian republic, many did perceive in the growth of urban America, and in particular the emergence of what were effectively immigrant ghettoes in many of the cities, a potential threat to the stability and safety of the nation. Literature in this period frequently explored the changing landscape of both city and society, seeking to position the individual within the new industrial and urban world that was emerging. This was the world of Stephen Crane's Maggie Johnson, as described in his novel *Maggie: A Girl of the Streets* (1893), a novel set in New York's Bowery district within which the eponymous heroine struggles and, perhaps inevitably, succumbs as poverty drives her into prostitution.

Crane's novel, among others, was perceived, at the time and since, as inaugurating the birth of a new realism, or naturalism, in literature. In fact, Maggie Johnson was the direct descendent of any number of unfortunate heroines who came to grief in the urban environment, whether the city in question was William Hogarth's London of the eighteenth century, Boston in the 1830s, or New York in the 1890s. Men fared little better in the literary and social critique of the city, although the details of their downfall were frequently more varied than the single sexual fate that most writers envisaged for women. William Dean Howell's *The Rise of Silas Lapham* (1885) tracked the rise and fall of a hero whose literary progeny would wind up contemplating the view from the Brooklyn Bridge, or possibly leaping off it when writers such as Eugene O'Neill and Arthur Miller got around to the subject of the crushing, impersonal social forces that constrained American idealism in the mid-twentieth century.

The problem in the late nineteenth century was that social critics tended to place a personal face on the essentially impersonal forces with which the hapless Maggie Johnson and Silas Lapham were contending, and that was the face of the immigrant. This was the period that saw the emergence of the Social Gospel movement, whose founder, Protestant minister Josiah Strong, promulgated his thoughts on the social and economic evils of the day in *Our Country: Its Possible Future and its Present Crisis* in 1885. The crises in question comprised, as Strong saw it, a combination of seven deadly sins: Romanism (Catholicism), Mormonism, Intemperance, Wealth, Socialism, Urbanization, and of course, Immigration. This last, according to Strong, "furnishes the soil which feeds the life of several of the most noxious growths in our civilization." Although Strong acknowledged that many immigrants "come to us in full sympathy with our free institutions," the "typical" immigrant,

GOTHAM COURT.

FIGURE 7.6. "Gotham Court." This illustration appeared in Jacob Riis's 1889 article that preceded his book, "How the Other Half Lives: Studies among the Tenements," *Scribner's Magazine*, Vol. VI, No. 6 (December 1889). In this, as in the subsequent book, Riis highlighted the fact that New York – and by implication the nation as a whole – had "lost opportunities for healthy growth that have passed not to return." His was in part a class criticism of New York's gradual expansion up Manhattan Island, a process that took the individual away he believed, was "a European peasant, whose horizon has been narrow, whose moral and religious training has been meager or false, and whose ideas of life are low."[16]

Immigration, Strong warned, increased crime and depleted the "morals of the native population," in equal measure; it was "the mother and nurse of American socialism," and its effects were especially acute in the "rabble-ruled cities" where voting blocs of Irish and German already compromised the democratic process. Social studies such as Jacob Riis's *How the Other Half Lives: Studies among the Tenements of New York* (1890), a photojournalistic exploration of the slums and immigrant ghettoes within which the less fortunate "other half" were living, tended only to reinforce such anti-immigrant sentiments. *How the Other Half Lives* was not anti-immigrant as such, but nor did it present an especially uplifting vision of the state of the city or its inhabitants. Their lives, as Riis described and depicted them (Figure 7.6), were hard enough, but it was their deaths that really revealed the extent of their poverty and its social repercussions. For "five years past," Riis reported, "one person in every ten who died in this city was buried in the Potter's Field," a damning indictment indeed against a society that prided itself on the opportunities it had to offer.

Riis, himself an immigrant, was driven by a strong moral purpose to expose the harsh living conditions of New York's Lower East Side, but the evidence he presented, combined with his own impulse to distinguish between the deserving and undeserving poor/immigrant, rather blurred the distinction, one that all nations struggle with to this day, between economic cause and social effect. When, a decade later, the journalist Lincoln Steffens presented his take on *The Shame of the Cities* (1904), it was less social deprivation than political corruption that concerned him. Steffens, like Riis one of a new breed of so-called muckraking social commentators and journalists devoted to uncovering crime and corruption

---

FIGURE 7.6 (*continued*) from her original landing point and from her original status as impoverished immigrant, drawing her inexorably further up the island and toward wealth and success. As a metaphor for becoming American, this constant urban renewal and upward mobility was hard to beat; as Riis stressed, however, it was, for too many, impossible to achieve. "It was in the old historic homes downtown," he proposed, "that the tenement was born of ignorance and nursed in greed.... Turn but a dozen steps from the rush and roar of the Elevated Railroad where it dives under the Brooklyn Bridge at Franklin Square, and with its din echoing in your ears you have turned the corner from prosperity to poverty" (p. 643).

at all levels of society, attacked what he identified as America's "moral weakness; a weakness right where we think we are strongest." If political corruption existed, he proposed, it was nevertheless a democratic dishonesty. The political boss, Steffens argued, "is not a political, he is an American institution, the product of a free people that have not the spirit to be free."

Steffens held the American people complicit in the corruption that he investigated. He identified "the lady at the custom-house, the lyncher with his rope, and the captain of industry with his bribe and his rebate" as little more than component elements in a national moral laxness. "The spirit of graft and of lawlessness," he famously charged, "is the American spirit." Ultimately, however, Steffens's apparently damning indictment of a nation that had lost its moral compass was not without hope. Steffens was certain that Americans were guilty of tolerating bad government, but he was equally certain that they were more than capable of demanding good government. There "is pride in the character of American citizenship," he argued, and "this pride may be a power in the land."[17]

The arguments of both Riis and Steffens were hardly unique to the United States; there was more than a whiff of Charles Dickens about both. Yet their concerns had a unique New World resonance when couched, as Steffens's was explicitly and Riis's rather more implicitly in the belief that these conditions, this corruption should not exist in the "land of the free." It was the hope that America might yet approximate the utopia that its first colonists had sought that drove some of this social criticism, and in particular informed the work of one of the most influential best sellers of the era, Edward Bellamy's *Looking Backward* (1888). Bellamy's hero, notably named Julian West, is projected into the future and finds, in the year 2000, that the United States has been transformed into a socialist utopia in which inequality has been abolished. West's visit to the future causes him to reappraise the present: the "scales had fallen from my eyes since that vision of another century," he reports. On his return to a dinner party in 1897, he berates his fellow guests with the benefit of his new understanding of the world they inhabit. "I have been in Golgotha," he announces. "I have seen Humanity hanging on a cross! Do none of you know what sights the sun and stars look down on in this city, that you can think and talk of anything else? Do you not know that close to your doors a great multitude of men and women, flesh of your flesh, live lives that are one agony from birth to death?"

The reality of 1897, as in 1887, when Bellamy wrote his novel, was that many Americans would not have considered the inhabitants of the urban slums as flesh of their flesh. Because they did not have the luxury of seeing into the future, all they had to go on was the past, and that seemed all too familiar in some respects. Neither the political corruption exemplified by "Boss Tweed" and Tammany Hall in New York nor the bootleggers and criminals that Whitley waged war on had gone away; if anything, the problem had become more acute. This seemed to suggest to some that Bryce's perspective – and Bryce's vision of America's future, of course, appeared in the same year as Bellamy was looking backward – on the immigrant as politically naïve and prone to corruption was not far off the mark. Bryce did not believe that most immigrants arrived in the United States bearing either anarchist or socialist tendencies, nor did they come with criminal intent. Nevertheless, if Crèvecoeur had flattered Americans in his description of the "American, this new man," a utopian union of the best that the Old World had to offer, Bryce delineated the limitations of this ideal by reminding Americans that transforming the immigrant into the "new man" was neither an easy process nor one guaranteed to succeed.

Immigrants, indeed, hardly regarded themselves as just so much moldable Old World clay primed for New World reshaping; far from it. One Romanian migrant, writer and Rabbi Marcus Eli Ravage, recalled his "initial shock" on arriving in America, a reaction that he partly ascribed to his own cultural baggage. As Ravage explained it:

The alien who comes here from Europe is not the raw material that Americans suppose him to be. He is not a blank sheet to be written on as you see fit. He has not sprung out of nowhere. Quite the contrary. He brings with him a deep-rooted tradition, a system of culture and tastes and habits – a point of view which is as ancient as his national experience and which has been engendered in him by his race and his environment. And it is this thing – this entire Old World soul of his – that comes into conflict with America as soon as he has landed.[18]

Ravage's "Old World soul" took a while to acclimatize itself to its new environment and its inhabitants, many of whom viewed the immigrant as, at best, "something rather comical" or, at worst, as "the scum of Europe." By the time that Ravage arrived, American immigration law and practice was tightening up. The year 1882 saw the introduction of the first federal immigration law. This excluded convicts, lunatics, paupers, and those likely to become a public charge from the nation. In the same year, the Chinese Exclusion Act of 1882 was passed. Although initially designed to block the importation of cheap Chinese labor in the West, this proved to be the template not just for immigration control but for racial attitudes more broadly as America expanded its sphere of influence – or operations, at least – beyond its own shores. Closer to home, of course, America already had tried and tested, if hitherto regionally specific, procedures to follow. Barely a decade after the Statue of Liberty was dedicated, it was proposed (in 1897) by the Immigration Restriction League that new immigrants, in common with African Americans seeking to vote in the South, be subjected to literacy tests.

The Immigration Restriction League, established by a group of Harvard Graduates in 1894, was a powerful, not to say privileged, pressure group, but it was hardly the sole opinion maker on immigration in the nation. Its views, indeed, met with strong opposition, and its literacy bill was vetoed in Congress by several presidents of the period; Grover Cleveland (1893–97), William Howard Taft (1908–12) and Woodrow Wilson (1912–20) all sought to block its passage.

Cleveland, in particular, denounced the very idea "as illiberal, narrow, and un-American," and the proposal itself as "unnecessarily harsh and oppressive." It represented, Cleveland asserted, a "radical departure from our national policy relating to immigration," a policy that "had encouraged those coming from foreign countries to cast their lot with us and join in the development of our vast domain, securing in return a share in the blessings of American citizenship." He reminded Congress that the "century's stupendous growth, largely due to the assimilation and thrift of millions of sturdy and patriotic adopted citizens, attests the success of this generous and free-handed policy," and attacked the kind of scaremongering that linked the immigrant to unemployment, crime, and social and economic decline. "The time is quite within recent memory," Cleveland pointed out, "when the same thing was said of immigrants who, with their descendants, are now numbered among our best citizens."[19]

Cleveland's last argument touched a nerve. Some of America's best citizens did not necessarily relish reminders of their European origins. And immigrants were very powerful reminders indeed both of the world and, in many cases, of the individual that had been left behind (Figure 7.7). They were perhaps also a reminder of rather more than that. "It is the free American," Ravage had argued, "who needs to be instructed by the benighted races in the uplifting word that America speaks to all the world. Only from the humble immigrant, it appears to me, can he learn just what America stands for in the family of nations." The immigrant, in short, was a challenge to complacency, a wake-up call to a nation that seemed to have forgotten its origins and its founding ideals, that sought to deny "the patent fact that Americanism is a compromise ... that the adoptive American has always been and will always remain a composite American."[20]

FIGURE 7.7. "Looking Backward" (Joseph Keppler). This cartoon appeared in *Puck Magazine*, January 11, 1893. It represents a powerful visual depiction of the point later made by Grover Cleveland that Americans were reluctant to admit to their "Old World" origins by showing the shadow, or specter, of these origins behind the successful businessmen of the nation, who are portrayed as seeking to bar the immigrant's entry into America. The depiction of the immigrant was echoed in Rabbi Ravage's sharp observation that the "alien himself, in his incredible garb, as he walks off the gang-plank, appears like some sort of an odd, moving bundle. And always he carries more bundles.... He is, for certain, a character fit for a farce." Image in public domain.

Many Americans fully accepted that Americanism was a compromise; exactly what kind of compromise it was, as far as citizenship was concerned, was less certain. Earlier in the nineteenth century, the debate over Americanism had mainly revolved around internal challenges to the white Anglo-Saxon "norm" offered by African Americans, Mexicans, Chinese migrant labor, and indigenous native inhabitants in the West. The mass influx of Irish immigration following the potato famine of the 1840s and early 1850s had produced a flurry of anti-Catholic fury in some parts of the northeast, but the sectional tensions and resultant Civil War of the 1850s and 1860s had both distracted from anti-Catholicism and made anti-immigrant sentiment appear, at best, churlish when so many immigrants had fought and died to defend the Union.

As the nation recovered from that conflict, industrial and urban development, both fed by the influx of immigrants after 1870, changed the face of the nation economically as the immigrants changed it physically, prompting renewed attacks on the foreign-born. Yet the opposition to the immigrant expressed by men such as Strong and organizations such as the Immigration Restriction League, together with the defense of an open-door policy advocated by Cleveland, were simply the latest installments in the debate over American identity, ideology, and immigration that had, arguably, been ongoing since colonial times. This debate had juxtaposed colonial and native, loyalist and revolutionary, North and South, and black and white perspectives. The Gilded Age, in its turn, highlighted the clash between "American" and "immigrant," but this was simply an additional permutation in the perennial struggle between those who believed they held the line of American national identity and those who sought to cross it.

Holding the line was not just a direct confrontational position; sometimes it was a more subtle cultural one. Edward Bellamy was not the only American looking backward in this period. The later nineteenth century witnessed an upsurge of interest in genealogy as some of the America's more established white families sought to confirm their validity in the face of the new incomers. They tried to establish a tradition that denied any taint of recent immigration but, instead, harked back to the colonial or Revolutionary past. The cult of the Confederate dead that was the Lost Cause in the South in the 1890s found its echo in the North and nationally, in new associations such as the Sons of the American Revolution (SAR) and the Daughters of the American Revolution (DAR), but these were simply the most prominent organizations; there were dozens more, across the Northeast and in the Midwest alike.

These patriotic bodies held meetings and erected historical markers across America's landscape that asserted both the historical significance to the American national story of the people and places commemorated and firmly established those engaged in the act of commemoration as a vital and ongoing part of that story. This was not so much a case of "America first" as one of "we were here first." Yet there was more to all this than establishing the longevity of one's national and cultural credentials. There was a distinctly Anglo-Saxon strain to this impulse, and a martial strain at that.

In the South, the dead Confederate warrior was aligned with a romanticized European past. This is most graphically illustrated in the J.E.B. Stuart Memorial Window in St. James's Episcopal Church in Richmond that portrays the ultimate Confederate cavalryman, Stuart, as a chivalric medieval knight. At the same time in the West, writers such as Owen Wister created a new kind of literary hero, the cowboy, investing him with a similar aristocratic Anglo-Saxon ancestry that nevertheless found its fullest and best expression on America's frontier. "Directly the English nobleman smelt Texas," Wister observed in one of his short stories, "the slumbering untamed Saxon awoke in him," and drawing on genes honed by centuries of jousting and hunting, proved himself to be "a born horseman, a perfect athlete, and spite of the peerage and gules and argent, fundamentally kin with the drifting vagabonds who swore and galloped by his side." If the cowboy was "kin" to "drifting vagabonds," however, he was entirely unrelated to the "hordes of encroaching alien vermin" that, as Wister saw it, were turning America's "cities to Babels and our citizenship to a hybrid farce, who degrade our commonwealth from a nation into something half pawn-shop, half brokers office."

The frontier symbolized freedom. For Wister it symbolized freedom from the city and from the "Poles, Huns or Russian Jews" that contaminated the urban spaces of the nation. The frontier remained "untainted," the last bastion of the "spirit of adventure, courage, and self-sufficiency" that defined America. Most importantly, on the frontier, Wister noted, "one speaks English."[21] This really was a triumph of fantasy over fact; unfortunately, it was also an early inkling of the future direction that the debate over American citizenship and nationalism would take, a debate that continues to this day.

Americanism, American nationalism, had always been both an optimistic, open proposition and an oppositional, closed construct: a constant tension between theory and practice, between the ideal and the reality and, in large part, between those who spoke English, and those who did not. For many Americans such as Wister, the city was, and indeed had long been, a focus for their fears, islands of unsettling heterogeneity in a nation that had long viewed itself as homogeneous. Yet the city was only one element in, one location for, the transition processes that America was experiencing in this period. Far beyond the Bowery, the argument over Americanism continued, with different players, different permutations, far more, indeed, than Wister's fictional frontier cared to admit to.

A Progressive Nation

Unease about immigration in the later nineteenth century was compounded by a series of financial panics, the worst of which lasted from 1893 to 1897. In this context, the nation's new industrial magnates attracted almost as much criticism as did immigrants. Men such as John D. Rockefeller, Andrew Carnegie, Andrew W. Mellon, J. P. Morgan, and

Cornelius Vanderbilt, men whose money came from transport (shipping and the railroads), factories, and finance, and oil, iron, and steel, drove the nation's material development but also raised questions about its moral direction. In their critiques of the imbalance of wealth that increasingly defined American society, journalists such as Riis and Steffens, and writers such as Bellamy, were in effect lifting the rock on which America's growing economic power was constructed, and what they uncovered was unsettling. Literary disapproval found its echo in the antitrust movement of the later 1880s and 1890s, disseminated to a general audience by, among others, the popular cartoonist Thomas Nast, codified in 1888 in the Sherman Antitrust Act, and almost immediately rendered nugatory in the so-called "Sugar Trust Case," *United States vs. E.C. Knight Co.,* in 1895.

The establishment of antitrust legislation, and the first significant challenge to this, crossed a virtual historical divide; the transition from the Gilded Age to the "progressive era." Of course such divisions are for the convenience of historians; they meant nothing at the time. Although the Panic of 1893 is usually the designated "starting point" for the progressive era, the financial and social forces impacting on America after 1893 were not in themselves new; the form they took, however, was. What underpinned the nation's industrial growth in this period was not just the personal ambitions of individuals such as Rockefeller, Morgan, or Carnegie, nor indeed the largely immigrant workforces they employed; it was their business methods. Men such as Rockefeller made their money by, in essence, imposing order on a hitherto relatively unrestrained market or, to put it another way, by absorbing or obliterating the competition.

Rockefeller's Standard Oil Company of Ohio, founded in 1872, became the Standard Oil Trust ten years later. It was one of the most powerful examples of American "Big Business," the first and most successful of the trusts, as popular with conservative social commentators as it was condemned by concerned social critics. Rockefeller's rigorous rationalization of each phase in the production process – he constructed his own pipelines, built his own warehouses, and negotiated competitive transport contracts – certainly improved efficiency.

A similar approach was adopted by J. P. Morgan, who pulled the nation's railroads back from the brink of bankruptcy before turning his attention to the subject of steel and founding, in 1901, United States Steel. In business terms, both Standard Oil and the "Morganized" railroads really were a case of strength being achieved through unity. This might not seem an especially challenging idea in a nation only a few decades distant from a civil war fought, at least in part, to make that very point. Yet where finance is concerned, faith was and remains the free radical in any system; and not everyone was sold on the laissez-faire religion that became known as the gospel of wealth.

Those who were, however, perceived in businessmen such as Rockefeller and Morgan an approximation, if not the epitome, of the self-made masculine ideal, an individual forging ahead on the financial frontier and opening up whole new vistas of opportunity for the nation in the process. As with Wister's cowboys, however, there was a slightly exclusionary element in the equation of wealth with national health and vigor. The language used to debate the subject frequently revealed the biases that informed it. As Rockefeller himself put it, the "growth of a large business is merely the survival of the fittest." It was no more than "the working-out of a law of nature and a law of God."[22] Again, there was nothing obviously un-American about such sentiments, which echoed the seventeenth-century Puritan perspective in large part. At the same time, not everyone was convinced that either nature or God enjoyed a free rein in a free market from which many African Americans and other immigrant groups were excluded or included only on white Anglo-Saxon terms.

Despite the fact that the gospel of wealth as preached by Rockefeller, Carnegie, and others included a substantial element of public philanthropy, and in the face of falling prices that rather contradicted the criticism that "Big Business" was bad for business, opposition forces rallied around the idea that this "Social Darwinist" mindset was both immoral and restrictive. The Sherman Antitrust Act attempted to curb the power of the trusts, restrain the growth of commercial combinations in any form, and provide a federally assured level of protection for competition. Previous state attempts at regulation had proved ineffective because all any company had to do to avoid restriction was move to a state less inclined to impose it. Yet the Sherman Act was hardly more effective. When challenged, and effectively defeated, in the Supreme Court, as it was in the Sugar Trust Case of 1895, the legal ground was clear for increased consolidation, for the unfettered growth of Big Business into the twentieth century.

What did not grow in the United States was any coherent labor organization in parallel with the consolidation of companies. This in itself served only to fuel anti-immigrant sentiment, because it was essentially the employment of a largely immigrant workforce in a nation already riven by racial antagonisms that prevented the development of the type of trade union organizations common in Europe at that time. As strangers in a strange land, the workers of the world found it hard to unite in America, which is not to say the attempt was not made. The Knights of Labor, founded in Philadelphia in 1869, preached an earlier variant of the gospel of wealth, one previously espoused by presidents such as Andrew Jackson and Abraham Lincoln.

In essence, the Knights, too, looked backward, to an age when the idea of every man becoming his own master seemed viable. Their ideal world was one in which, as Lincoln put it in 1861, labor was not only "prior to and independent of capital" but was fundamentally "superior to capital." This was a world in which there was not "of necessity, any such thing as the free hired laborer being fixed to that condition for life." Lincoln's expectation that the "prudent, penniless beginner in the world, labors for wages awhile" and later "labors on his own account" was a fundamental tenet of faith for many even toward the end of the nineteenth century. This was the dream that, as Lincoln asserted, "opens the way to all – gives hope to all, and consequent energy, and progress, and improvement of condition to all."[23] It was Lincoln's hope and this dream that drew so many immigrants to America in the first place, of course, but for many it was Rockefeller's reality that they encountered.

Not everyone accepted this version of the brave New World that the nation had become, and some tried to meet it head on. In time, the Knights of Labor ceded the field to the rather more pragmatic American Federation of Labor (AFL), founded in 1881, but the last decades of the nineteenth century witnessed persistent, almost perennial outbreaks of industrial conflict; beginning with the Railroad Strike of 1877, through the Haymarket Riot and a strike at Carnegie's Homestead steel plant in 1892, to the more famous Pullman strike in 1894, the clash between man and the machine that was the new industrial nation intensified. And at the center of it all was the immigrant. The political arena even sustained, for a brief time, a political party – the Populist or People's Party – that challenged the rise of Big Business and at the same time called for immigration restriction. The solution to the nation's ills, it seemed, lay in business and on the border. Regulate both, some argued, and all would be well.

For some, the conflicts of the late nineteenth century, whether over industrial relations or immigration restriction, were an inevitable stage in America's development. The sociologist Simon Nelson Patten, for one, believed that a large part of the problem lay in the fact that the nation's "civic instincts" were still in their "infancy." This applied across the

nation and cut across race and class, city and frontier, to create opposi-
tions formed from the ongoing debate over Americanism. Each "class or
section of the nation is becoming conscious of an opposition between its
standards and the activities and tendencies of some less developed class,"
he observed:

> The South has its negro, the city has its slums, organized labor has its "scab"
> workman, and the temperance movement has its drunkard and saloon-keeper.
> The friends of American institutions fear the ignorant immigrant, and the work-
> ingman dislikes the Chinese. Everyone is beginning to differentiate those with
> proper qualifications for citizenship from some class or classes which he wishes
> to restrain or to exclude from society.[24]

Patten was optimistic that America's "civic instincts" would develop in
time, and that the end result would be "a social integration through which
a truly American society can be formed." Social integration, however,
was a loaded concept in the late nineteenth century. For some, informed
integration was what mattered; integration informed by the white Anglo-
Saxon norm.

"No man," Josiah Strong had asserted, "is held upright simply by the
strength of his own roots; his branches interlock with those of other men,
and thus society is formed." Yet Strong was not anticipating that through
immigration a new national hybrid, the composite American that Ravage
described, would be produced; quite the opposite. Immigration was, for
Strong, not only "demoralizing," but immigrants themselves represented
a disease within the body politic and it was disease, he emphasized, "and
not health which is contagious."[25] The cure for this contagion, as he
perceived it, lay in Americanization, a catch-all cure for the nation's ills
and, as some would interpret it in the future, for the ills of the world.

The newly constructed immigration station on Ellis Island, opened in
1892, could be relied on to keep out the obviously physically ill, but the
kind of disease that concerned Strong and others was not a medical but
a cultural complaint, and stopping it at the borders was not an option.
"Many American citizens are not Americanized," Strong had observed
in dismay, a situation as "unfortunate" as it was "natural." Although
Strong would later develop his argument about the need to Americanize
the urban hordes in a subsequent study of the city, in the 1890s, his
particular locus of concern was the West. He was not alone. A great many
reformers viewed with a degree of alarm the part of the nation already
designated, with some justification, as "wild," whether their concern was
for the native inhabitants or the more recent immigrants.

Writers such as Wister – and later Hollywood – may have elevated the story of fighting on the western frontier into something approximating a national rite of passage, but there was little real romance in the "Wild West." The "Indian Wars" of the 1870s and 1880s certainly dwarfed the nation's Civil War in the extent of their brutality and their cost in lives. The later description of many of these as massacres conveys the general levels of violence well enough. At the same time, highlighting individual clashes between white settlers and natives – the Sand Creek Massacre, Little Big Horn, or even Wounded Knee – rather positions them as isolated incidents of conflict rather than what they actually were; a fundamental part of the (re)construction of the nation after the civil conflict of the mid-nineteenth century. And as with all America's wars, it was never just about the combat; it was about hearts and minds.

The battle over hearts and minds in the last decades of the nineteenth century, however, cannot be divorced from another juxtaposition: that of accommodation and dispossession, whether that was framed in the context of bringing the states of the former Confederacy back into the Union, facing up to white extremist violence, dealing with the implications of increased immigration, or acclimatizing to the changing economic and employment landscape inculcated by "Big Business" and the industrial unrest that ensued. At stake was the question of what the American was, what America represented, a question that became pressing in the face of the great industrial, urban, and immigrant challenges to the national ideal. It is sometimes difficult to unpick the multiplicity of concerns that exercised American reformers in relation to the urban environment, so interwoven were they in regard to the triumvirate of industrialization, urbanization, and immigration.

On the frontier, the motivations of reformers may have been no less complex, but the actions they took were straightforward enough. The open warfare between native and newcomer had, at some point, to cease. Withstanding the combined forces of industrialization and immigration was not a long-term option for the native nations west of the Mississippi. The inevitable ingress of the railroad and the telegraph, accompanied by settlers and soldiers, miners and missionaries, those looking to stay or those simply passing through en route to the west coast, spelled the end of a way of life, an end effected in large part by the eradication of the buffalo herds on those plains.

Yet it was not simply the loss of either land or livelihood that undermined the native nations; it was a rather more insidious cultural attack – some today go so far as to term it ethnocide – whereby their very culture was removed. That was the cost of entry into the American polity. It was, in fact, a cost extracted from almost all immigrants in the end, but in the West the process was fast-forwarded by a deliberate policy of encouraged or at times enforced regime change.

Merging the native with the nation, however, was particularly problematic, and certainly had not been achieved by the late nineteenth century. In 1816, Congress had passed the Indian Civilization Act, which encouraged assimilation as a means of facilitating white settler expansion into aboriginal territories. Native Americans then had the option, assuming they rejected their tribal affiliation, of naturalization as citizens of the nation growing up around them, but only up to a point. Voting rights were not automatically accorded (Figure 7.8), and many natives inhabited a legal halfway house, sustaining a dual nationality that compromised their tribal position but did not allocate them equal status either with established Americans or naturalized immigrants. As Minnesota Bishop Henry Benjamin Whipple observed in his introduction to one of the most damning indictments of America's treatment of the native, Helen Hunt Jackson's *A Century of Dishonor* (1881), the "Indian is the only human being within our territory who has no individual right in the soil . . . his title is merged in the tribe – the man has no standing before the law."[26]

By the later nineteenth century, the impulse to assimilate the "Indian" in the United States paralleled the approach adopted elsewhere by societies whose origins were British white settler–dominated, notably Australia and Canada. In America, former abolitionists such as William Lloyd Garrison and Wendell Phillips became very active in the Indian reform movement, which operated through such bodies as the Indian Rights Association and the National Indian Defense Association. These operated a residential school system that removed native children from their familial and social environments in an attempt to inculcate them with the religious, educational, and linguistic values of white society. Such blatant attempts to assert white nationalist values over native ones were reinforced by a tranche of supporting measures, the most notable of which was the General Allotment (Dawes) Act of 1887. This offered citizenship to natives willing to relinquish tribal affiliations and subdivided reservation lands into individual family holdings, the better to approximate the Jeffersonian agrarian ideal in the West.

However idealistic it was in theory, perhaps inevitably all the Dawes Act did in practice was to facilitate the acquisition of the land by whites. Between the passage of the act in 1887 and 1934, the time of the so-called Indian New Deal, 86 million acres – more than 60 percent of the

"MOVE ON!"
HAS THE NATIVE AMERICAN NO RIGHTS THAT THE NATURALIZED AMERICAN IS BOUND TO RESPECT?—(See Page 255.)

FIGURE 7.8. "'Move on!' Has the Native American no rights that the natural-ized American is bound to respect?" (Thomas Nast) This cartoon appeared in *Harper's Weekly* in April 1871. It shows an African-American policeman moving a Native man way from a polling booth, which is surrounded by some of Nast's rather typically stereotyped "naturalized" Americans. Nast may have been a firm supporter of African-American and Native-American rights, but his caricatur-ing of immigrants was not, perhaps, quite as high-minded either in intention or execution. Nevertheless, there are multiple layers of irony in this image, starting with its title. The direct invocation of the famous *Dred Scott* ruling of 1857, when Chief Justice Roger B. Tanney concluded that legally the African American had "no rights which the white man was bound to respect," was an apposite reminder that the nineteenth-century nation was not so much moving on as mov-ing in ever decreasing circles as far as the debate over citizenship rights was concerned. Image courtesy of the Library of Congress Prints and Photographs Division (LC-USZ62–77909).

remaining Indian Land base – had passed into the control of non-natives. Naturally, there was a backlash against this enforced acculturation and land redistribution, and one of the forms this took was the emergence, in 1889, of the Ghost Dance religion. An obvious but by no means univer-sally adopted ritual response to, and rejection of, white cultural intrusion and domination, it did play some part in fomenting the final, and per-haps most infamous, armed confrontation between the Sioux and the American government in the nineteenth century. Although its fame alone ensured the survival of the issues at stake well into the twentieth century, the battle at Wounded Knee, South Dakota, in 1890 marked a point of closure, for all practical purposes, for control of the West.

The year 1890, of course, was also a point of closure in another significant way. It was the year in which the Superintendent of the Census declared that "at present the unsettled area has been so broken into isolated bodies of settlement that there can hardly be said to be a frontier line." In that regard, at least, America's Manifest Destiny to cover the continent had been achieved. In other respects, the racial, religious, and social implications of the very idea of the nation's Manifest Destiny had only begun to be explored.

By the last decade of the nineteenth century, America had two narratives in place, both of which spun out into the century to come; both looked forward, both backward. One was a story of suppression, segregation, and suffering; the other of persistence in the face of these all-too human realities, an alternative vision of hope and expectation that through effort the promised land could be achieved. It was the vision of Ida Wells and Grover Cleveland versus that of Owen Wister and the Immigration Restriction League, the real battle for hearts and minds that would come to define the "American Century."

8

The Soldier's Faith

Conflict and Conformity

The day of our country's life has but broadened into morning. Do not put uniforms by. Put the harness of the present on. Lift your eyes to the great tracts of life yet to be conquered in the interest of righteous peace, of that prosperity which lies in a people's hearts and outlasts all wars and errors of men.

(Woodrow Wilson, Address at Gettysburg, July 4, 1913)

The shooting in New York, on September 6, 1901, of President William McKinley by the anarchist Leon Czolgosz marked the end of an era in the most tragic way possible. McKinley died on September 14, 1901, almost twenty years exactly since another president, James A. Garfield, had succumbed, on September 16, 1881, also as a result of an assassin's bullet. Beginning with the murder of Abraham Lincoln in 1865, McKinley became the third American president to be assassinated, and the last of a generation of American leaders whose lives had been shaped – and in Lincoln's case, abruptly terminated – by the Civil War. Garfield and McKinley were both Union veterans of the Civil War, as indeed every elected president had been since 1868. Garfield's Civil War record had been a distinguished one. He was promoted to major general before taking up political office at the end of 1863. McKinley, by contrast, was the only Republican president since Lincoln not to have been a general in the Civil War, but his public life had begun with that conflict. He had joined the Ohio Volunteer Infantry at just eighteen years of age, and ended the war as a brevet major.

McKinley's Civil War career played a significant role in his presidential campaign and victory in 1896 when he had first stood against the

Populist/Democrat William Jennings Bryan. At thirty-six, Bryan was the youngest presidential candidate ever proposed by one of the main American parties, but his youth worked against him. When it came to the main issues of the day – and in 1896 these mainly revolved around tariffs and the stability of the currency – Americans were not yet prepared to place their faith in the younger generation. In the course of the campaign, one famous cartoon portrayal of McKinley in his Civil War uniform was juxtaposed with the image of Bryan in his cradle (Figure 8.1). The message was clear. The nation would be safer in the hands of a man forged in the furnace of war rather than one simply fired by his own youthful ambition.

The 1896 election indeed evoked the Civil War on many levels. Some of the biggest guns of the former Union army, including Dan Sickles, who had fought at Gettysburg, and Oliver Otis Howard, who later headed the Freedmen's Bureau, supported McKinley. As disabled veterans (Sickles had lost a leg at Gettysburg in 1863 and Howard had lost an arm in the Peninsula campaign the previous year), both men served as potent visual reminders of some of the issues at stake. The McKinley camp invoked the hardships of the nation's civil conflict in the context of the financial downturn that had begun in 1893 to reinforce its point that America's economic and by extrapolation that social stability depended on "sound money." This, they argued, was only achievable if the nation retained the business-orientated gold standard. The Bryan camp, by contrast, advocated basing the dollar on silver. The nation had silver and to spare since the discovery of the "Comstock Lode" silver mine in Nevada in 1859. Using silver as security, its proponents argued, would increase the money supply and alleviate the financial distress of, among others, Civil War widows and veterans – both Union and Confederate – the subjects of many of the cartoons that appeared in the course of the campaign.

In many respects, the currency debate, although obviously a genuine issue in its own right given that the nation was suffering a severe economic crisis, served as shorthand for a more fundamental disagreement over America's moral as much as its monetary stability. This was, in addition, by no means a straightforward party-political divide between Republican and Democrat. There were "gold bugs" among the Democrats and there was, too, a third potential party in the equation; the Populists. The Populists' origins lay in the Farmers' Alliance of 1876 and their core constituency comprised rural America, hard-hit by falling farm prices and feeling both excluded from the industrial and urban nation that was fast emerging and threatened by the rise in immigration since

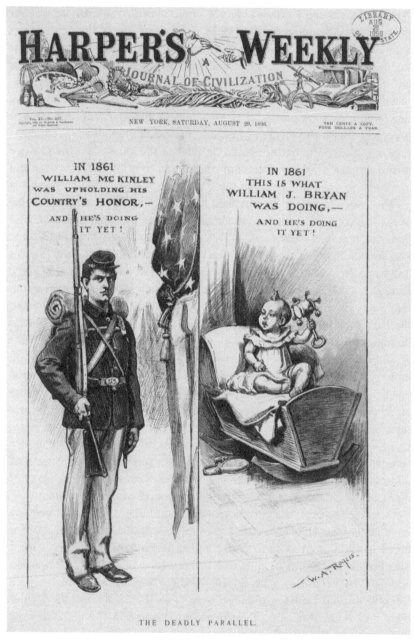

FIGURE 8.1. "The Deadly Parallel" (Artist: W. A. Rogers). This cartoon appeared as the cover of *Harper's Weekly* on August 29, 1896. McKinley stood against and defeated Bryan twice, in fact, in 1896 and again in 1900, with his margin of victory even greater in 1900 than it had been in 1896. Image courtesy of the Library of Congress Prints and Photographs Division (LC-USZ62–97504).

1870. The standards at stake in the 1896 election, therefore, involved far more than the financial variety and the precedents it established resonated far beyond the political sphere, or rather enabled the political sphere to resonate more broadly across the nation.

The rhetoric of the 1896 campaign was both emotive and martial in its stridency and in its imagery, particularly in the Democratic camp, divided as it was over the extent to which to absorb the Populist agenda, nominate Bryan as their candidate, and thereby retain a two-party political system. The Populists themselves split over this question. The so-called fusionists advocated joining the Democrats, whereas the more radical Populists preferred to seek political power in their own right. During the Democratic nominating convention in Chicago, it swiftly became clear that the fusionist option was the more likely outcome. This in itself represented something of a sectional shift in the American political system. The economic rise of the West and the political recovery of the South – together they comprised the "Chicago platform" at the Democratic nominating convention – represented a clear challenge to the traditional power structures and national influence of the eastern cities. And Bryan's was quite clearly the voice of the West. It was in the name of "those hardy pioneers who braved all the dangers of the wilderness, who have made the desert to blossom as the rose" that he spoke.[1]

Yet not all Democrats were happy at the implications of adding a Populist plank to their platform. Both Bryan as an individual and the ideals he espoused were too radical for some (Figure 8.2). Former Democratic Senator for Missouri, J. B. Henderson, a coauthor of the Thirteenth Amendment, denounced the Chicago platform as a revival of "the old doctrine of State resistance to Federal authority." If the twinned specters of states' rights and secession proved to have any substance, Henderson declared, Democrats should "do as men did in 1861. We asked simply then that the constitution which Washington and others framed should be preserved and we are going to defend it now...as we did in 1861–1865."[2]

This military and political veteran's perspective did not, however, carry the day for those Democrats opposed to Bryan. When it came to invoking the past to persuade the present, the Founding Fathers trumped the Civil War generation. And this was essentially what Bryan was offering. He held up Jefferson's vision of the agrarian, if not exactly Arcadian, American dream and stressed the importance of supporting the nation's farmers. Critiquing the detrimental impact of the gold standard on "the plain people of this country," Bryan argued that "this is not a contest among persons" but "the cause of humanity." He acknowledged the

FIGURE 8.2. "History repeats itself" (Louis Dalrymple, 1896). This cartoon appeared in *Puck* on October 28, 1896. It shows a cartoon image of William Jennings Bryan holding a paper that states: "We denounce arbitrary interference by federal authorities, in local affairs, as a violation of the Constitution, etc" over a group of figures including Ben Tillman, John P. Altgeld, and Eugene Debs who between them are raising a flag to "dis-order" and "mis-rule." "Pitchfork" Ben Tillman was the former governor of South Carolina (1890–94) whose "redshirts" had "redeemed" the state from Republican rule in 1876 and helped establish white political supremacy there. John Peter Altgeld was the governor of Illinois and a left-wing Democrat, widely regarded as the power behind the Chicago Platform at the Democratic convention that nominated Bryan. Eugene Debs was America's foremost socialist and union leader. A founder-member of the Industrial Workers of the World and the International Labor Union, he stood for election in his own right in 1900 and in most elections up to 1920. To the right of the image, emphasizing the point that Bryan threatened disruption if not quite disunion, Confederate president Jefferson Davis holds an identical paper in front of Abraham Lincoln and the Union Army. Image courtesy of the Library of Congress Prints and Photographs Division (LC-USZC4-4361).

shadow of the Civil War in his description of the battle of the standards as one in which "brother has been arrayed against brother, and father against son," in which the "warmest ties of love and acquaintance and association have been disregarded." Yet this was no rerun of the "War Between the States." Rather, Bryan declared, it was a war between "the idle holders of idle capital" and "the struggling masses." Via an invocation of Edward Bellamy's *Looking Backward* that would certainly have resonated with contemporary audiences, Bryan famously defied the gold bugs: "[Y]ou shall not press down upon the brow of labor this crown of thorns," he declaimed. "You shall not crucify mankind upon a cross of gold."

Bryan's impassioned "Cross of Gold" speech gained him the Democratic nomination but ultimately failed to secure victory for the party in 1896. His defeat also spelled the end for the Populists as a potential political force and inaugurated sixteen years of Republican rule. Yet although unsuccessful, Bryan's candidacy, together with McKinley's campaign, marked a new departure in American politics, in political campaigning generally and in public perceptions of the political process.

It was the scale of deployment of the media that set the 1896 McKinley campaign apart from the electioneering efforts of previous decades and the agenda for the future. Bryan's impact depended on his personal engagement with his audience, but McKinley's relied on his audience's mainly impersonal engagement with him. As the outsider in the 1896 race, Bryan had no choice but to take his message directly to the people, and campaigned in person the length and breadth of the nation. The McKinley campaign, by contrast, funded and organized by Ohioan entrepreneur and political enthusiast Mark Hanna, enabled the candidate himself to remain aloof from the frantic fundraising and propaganda efforts being undertaken on his behalf. And such efforts were considerable. What Hanna constructed was, in effect, a McKinley machine that promoted the Republican candidate, in Theodore Roosevelt's famous phrase, "as if he were a patent medicine."[3] What gave this particular medicine its potency was its use of the media, in the form of the press, periodicals, and, crucially, a new medium – film.

First shown in New York in October 1896, *McKinley at Home*, a short (less than a minute) recording of the future president reading a telegram on his front lawn, was silent, of course, but spoke volumes in a way that today's electorate, almost too sophisticated for television now, more used to Tweets and Facebook, the Web and the smartphone, can hardly imagine. One New York paper observed that so "perfectly natural" was the recording "that only the preinformed will know that they are looking upon shadow and not upon substance."[4] The interplay between shadow and substance sums it up. At its most basic, as the first presidential campaign to employ film, McKinley's image – and his ultimate victory – could be disseminated across a broader demographic in a much more direct way.[5] Combined with a tighter control of the press, to which selected candidate statements were released, the 1896 campaign truly was the beginning of a new era of sound (bite) and vision. Although not yet connected, their combined impact should not be underestimated.

Yet the films of McKinley, at home or at his inauguration ceremony in 1897, were not the first to be shown. As early as 1894, American urban audiences had the opportunity to marvel at this glimpse into the future of what would become a multimillion-dollar business. Not that the earliest products of this new communication medium were necessarily directed at Americans specifically. The commercial and cost implications of film steered it toward a world market even at this tentative, early stage of development. In contrast to Europe, America's domestic market was large enough to support the nation's nascent film industry, but ethnically and linguistically so diverse as to encourage – indeed necessitate – an international approach. Early American cinema, therefore, with its roots in vaudeville and theater, presented images – acrobats, dancers, and boxers – and individuals – William Frederick "Buffalo Bill" Cody, sharpshooter and show-woman Annie Oakley, and Native American Last Horse – that were both culturally specific to the United States, particularly to the West, and had international appeal.

One of the earliest cinematic experiences that American audiences could enjoy, however, did have a decisive nationalist resonance. Only a few months before Americans had the opportunity to observe *McKinley at Home*, the Vitascope Company produced a film that proved remarkably prescient as far as McKinley's presidency was concerned. The subject of *The Monroe Doctrine*, first shown in April of 1896, was America's invocation of its hemispheric authority against the threat of intrusion by Great Britain in a dispute between Venezuela and British Guiana.

This border skirmish provided a rare opportunity for America to invoke a doctrine long in danger of gathering dust. As a nation, the United States had been fortunate in both the timing and location of its founding. European conflicts, combined with America's relative geographic isolation, meant that, with the exception of the War of 1812, the new republic was little troubled by European designs on or challenges to its sovereignty. Nevertheless, in 1823, the then-President, James Monroe (1817–1825) sought to remove any lingering doubt on the subject and asserted "as a principle . . . that the American continents, by the free and independent condition which they have assumed, are henceforth not to be considered as subjects for future colonization by any European Power."[6]

The film invoking Monroe's famous, if somewhat nugatory, doctrine portrayed the American national stereotype of "Uncle Sam" in the act of preventing the encroachment of the British "John Bull" into America's self-appointed sphere of influence, to the audience's great amusement. Their approval signified not just Anglophobia – although there was a healthy dose of that involved, no doubt – but also a growing sense among many Americans that new horizons were coming into focus along with the new century. Selling the nation on the silver screen, or early flickering versions of it, offered a glimmer of a global future, the promise of an international impact that might merge power with profit – in short, a moral marketplace beckoned, one in which to sell, metaphorically but also materially the colonial vision of the "city on a hill."

The American Revolution had, as Monroe's assertion made clear, ushered in a period during which Americans had been less concerned to promote the "city on a hill" as to protect it. Washington's warning to his nation to avoid European entanglements, issued in his Farewell Address of 1796, had, in the century since, become something of an article of faith. Yet as a faith that was never really tested, it soon faded, replaced by an expansionist, some might say aggressive, determination, in part fueled by the financial crisis the nation was enduring, to expand America's influence and her markets abroad. In this respect, what is sometimes termed the "new" imperialism of the last decade of the nineteenth century was no more than a return to first principles for a nation whose origins had been as ambitious and as contradictory as America's, settled as it had been by pioneers driven by both piety and profit.

The very notion of a nation of immigrants somehow remaining aloof from international affairs was, of course, vaguely absurd. Given that the world was determined to come to America, it was inevitable that America would be forced to engage not just with the broader Atlantic and Pacific worlds in which it was geographically positioned, but with the European and African worlds beyond: preexisting ties of trade as much as the influx of immigrants made isolationism in practice impossible, even if the idea was promulgated in principle. Indeed, immigration informed, in a very real sense, such imperialistic impulses as America expressed at the end of the nineteenth century. It was never a straightforward case of the nation, having achieved its Manifest Destiny to conquer a continent – as the "closing" of the frontier in 1890 suggested – suddenly turning its attention offshore.

Nevertheless, such a tidy argument was proposed by, among others, Alfred T. Mahan, the prominent naval officer and author of *The Influence of Sea Power upon History* (1890). As Mahan saw it, Americans had established authority over the land and now it was time to turn their attention toward the sea, for reasons of profit and protection as much as of power. For too long, he argued, American industries had concentrated on the home market, a practice that had "assumed the force of a tradition" and was "clothed in the mail of conservatism." As a result, these industries now resembled "the activities of a modern ironclad that has heavy armor, but an inferior engine and no guns; mighty for defence, weak for offense." Yet the "temperament of the American people," he suggested, was "alien to such a sluggish attitude," and he predicted that "when the opportunities for gain abroad are understood, the course of American enterprise will cleave a channel by which to reach them."

Mahan was, perhaps inevitably, keen on his naval metaphors. He was even more enthused by the idea that American enterprise might result in an American empire, one to rival – or at the very least keep pace with – those of the European nations. His view enjoyed widespread currency at a time when said nations were embroiled in the "scramble for Africa," and whereas few in America considered that particular scrum worth diving into, the general point about the opportunities of expansion was not lost on them. In comparison to some, too, Mahan's was a relatively uncluttered proposition. In both career and inclination he tended toward the belief in an aggrandizement of American sea power because he detected "restlessness in the world at large" that he feared might prove problematic for his nation in the long term. America's security, he observed, such at it was, was due to "natural advantages" rather than to "intelligent preparations," and as a consequence, the nation was, he warned, "wofully [sic] unready . . . to assert in the Caribbean and Central America a weight of influence proportioned to the extent of her interests."[7]

For others such as clergyman Josiah Strong, the impulse toward empire was of a piece with their fears for the impact of immigration on the nation. The desire to secure a political and cultural Anglo-Saxon dominance within America – "the moral conquest of this land" – led them to the somewhat ambitious conclusion that this might best be achieved by inculcating it outside America as well. In effect, just as individual presidents – indeed world leaders in general – frequently seek to distract from domestic disarray by focusing on foreign affairs, some of America's reformers in this period mooted a modern and more expansive Manifest Destiny for their nation. In part they simply sought vindication for their reform agenda and hoped that other nations, other peoples, might be more receptive to its precepts than indigenous natives in the West and recent immigrants in the expanding cities had so far proved to be. In larger part they were crusaders for a cause, and that cause was America.

Their evangelism was exercised by the idea of conflict. "Our national salvation," asserted Congregationalist clergyman Austin Phelps in his introduction to Strong's *Our Country*, "demands in supreme exercise certain military virtues." And the military virtues Phelps had in mind were those of the nation's Civil War. "What the campaign in Pennsylvania was to the Civil War," he proposed, "what the battle of Gettysburg was to that campaign, what the fight for Cemetery Hill was to that battle, such is the present opportunity to the Christian civilization of this country." The battle that Strong's work concentrated on, of course, was nationalism. Americans, he emphasized, were in the process of "making a nation," and an Anglo-Saxon (by which he meant English-speaking, rather than a distinct *ethnie*) nation at that. America, as Strong saw it, already lay "in the pathway of nations" and was thereby destined to be the great home of the Anglo-Saxon, the principal seat of his power, the center of his life and influence." From America, the influence of this Anglo-Saxon nationalism would spread outward, to the undoubted benefit of the world's "inferior peoples." His argument, he concluded, in an echo of his seventeenth-century ancestors, was therefore "not America for America's sake; but America for the world's sake."[8]

This merging of the martial with the moral perspective in the name of the nation – and, indeed, the world – became more than a theoretical meeting of minds between men such as Strong and Mahan in 1898, when America intervened in the independence struggle then underway in Cuba. Cuba, an exception to the Monroe Doctrine, was just one of several Spanish colonies to change hands, in effect, after 1898. Guam, the Philippines, and Puerto Rico were also all under Spanish jurisdiction, but it was Cuba that served as the catalyst for a conflict that dominated, to a great extent, McKinley's first term in office. The idealism that informed intervention notwithstanding, the war to free Cuba launched America into the stormy international waters of *Realpolitik*.

Fueled by reports of Spanish atrocities carried by several of the newspapers of the day, in particular Joseph Pulitzer's *New York World* and William Randolph Hearst's *New York Journal*, American indignation at the oppression of a colonial people so close to their shores had reached a peak by the year of McKinley's election. Yet the president was initially disinclined to commit the country to a conflict the popular support for which was in large part driven by the so-called yellow press and informed by the circulation wars of two rival media giants (Figure 8.3). At the start of 1898, however, a minor diplomatic faux pas – the publication of a letter written by the Spanish minister to Washington that

FIGURE 8.3. "The big type war of the yellow kids" (Leon Barritt). This cartoon, dated June 29, 1898, depicts Joseph Pulitzer and William Randolph Hearst each dressed as the "yellow kid." The "yellow kid" was a cartoon character in a popular comic strip, "Hogan's Alley," that appeared in the *New York World*, but the character himself also appeared in the *New York Journal* when its creator, Richard Outcault, moved from the former to the latter in 1896. The kid himself was depicted as a child from the slums, attired in a nightshirt on which was inscribed his speech. The derogatory description of the *World* and the *Journal* as examples of the "yellow press" or "yellow journalism" derived from this cartoon strip and suggested – accurately – that both papers rarely let the facts stand in the way of a good story. Their popularity was largely predicated on the winning combination of sensationalist stories that fueled its readerships' fears of crime, corruption, and general societal decline – especially in the nation's cities – and a rather gung-ho, almost jingoistic patriotism; such an approach to "news" coverage would hardly raise an eyebrow today in many European countries, but it was a new departure for American print capitalism at the time. In the particular case of Cuba, the perspective in both papers was strongly anti-Spanish and pro-U.S. intervention, as this cartoon makes clear. Ironically, it appeared at a time when the circulation war between Pulitzer and Hearst was dying down, but the martial fervor both had helped inculcate had already flared into open conflict. Image courtesy of the Library of Congress Prints and Photographs Division (LC-USZC4–3800).

criticized McKinley – was followed by a major catastrophe. An explosion on the American battleship *Maine* while at anchor in Havana destroyed the ship and killed more than 260 of its crew. The assumption was widespread, if ill-founded, that the destruction of the *Maine* had been an act of deliberate sabotage by the Spanish. The cry "Remember the Maine! To hell with Spain!" summed up America's response. By the late spring of that year, the United States was at war.

The call to "Remember the Maine," and a prominent monument in Columbus Circle, New York, erected in its memory notwithstanding, possibly few Americans today would position the Spanish-American war as central to the nation's history, to its nationalism. Even fewer might identify the subsequent war with the Philippines (1899–1903) as a major turning point for America. Both were, however, critical conflicts on several levels. What had begun as a limited attempt simply to liberate Cuba ultimately became the means by which America assumed control of the former Spanish colonies in the Philippines, Guam, and Puerto Rico and, in addition, Hawaii, which had nothing to do with Spain. America had already brokered a deal with Hawaii to secure Pearl Harbor for a naval base, and formally annexed the islands in 1898 because they were crucial as far as American trade with China and Japan was concerned. Indeed, in the package deal that was America's acquisition of what was, in effect, a ready-made empire, what dominated was the desire for trade, not territory. Commerce, not colonialism, was what most Americans had in mind when the decision to challenge Spain was taken.

As a consequence, America was rather unprepared for the war that she found herself in, but fortunately for her, not as unprepared as the Spanish. The four-month Spanish-American War was from the outset an uneven contest, which in no way diminished the media's representation of American victories as a vindication of the nation's martial, but especially naval, superiority. American theater audiences could soon thrill to the sight of naval battles, as the projection of their nation's power into the Caribbean and the Pacific was replicated on the big screen (Figure 8.4). Uncertainty over the merits of expansion, any lingering desire to retreat behind the Monroe Doctrine, gave way to widespread, although certainly not universal, support for the nation's new imperial ambitions.

Initially, such enthusiasm was echoed in the Philippines, Cuba, and Puerto Rico, whose inhabitants perceived new opportunities in the overthrow of old colonial regimes. However, as it became clear, in the Philippines in particular, that any such opportunities were not intended for the local population, armed resistance to American involvement increased. The resultant conflict, which did not end until 1903, was not only destructive in terms of lives lost – more than 100,000 Filipino and slightly more than 4,000 American – but, some argued, in terms of American values. Warning voices sought to return the nation to its original

FIGURE 8.4. "Lyman H. Howe's new marvels in moving pictures" (Courier Lithograph Company, New York, c. 1898). This poster advertising a theater show of a naval battle during the Spanish-American War was not, of course, actual film footage of the engagement being portrayed, but a reenactment, more accurately a simulation, of events constructed in a film studio using models. Given that late-nineteenth-century audiences would have been familiar with the idea, and the reality of "staged" historical events – already a popular form of entertainment – this

mission statement, to prevent what the Anti-Imperialist League (established in 1899) described as a betrayal of "American liberty in pursuit of un-American ends." The "proper influence of the United States," it argued, was "moral, commercial and social," but this influence was threatened by America's determination to assert control over the Philippines.[9]

Worse still was the attempt on the part of the McKinley administration, as the League perceived it, "to extinguish the spirit of 1776 in those islands" (the Philippines had adopted a constitution modeled on America's) and to extend "American sovereignty by Spanish methods." America, the League emphasized, had a moral duty not to impose on others the kind of colonial rule that she herself had overthrown. Imperialism, the League warned, was both "hostile to liberty and tends toward militarism, an evil from which it has been our glory to be free." On this last point the League was expressing a view somewhat at odds with American reality at the start of the twentieth century, as any Native American might have reminded it. The "spirit of 1776" had been, after all, been expressed in martial form, whatever moral imperatives became associated with it in the years that followed. And the spirit that informed so much of American politics and society in the last decades of the nineteenth century had, similarly, merged the martial with the moral. By the end of the century, although the Civil War armies had long since melted away, their influence had not.

For a generation who had either fought in the Civil War or who had been raised on reminiscences of that conflict, the war with Spain may have seemed, as the then Secretary of State and former private secretary to Abraham Lincoln, John Hay described it, a "splendid little war," even if some regarded its repercussions as far from diminutive, and not, in certain respects, entirely splendid. The Spanish-American War was a conflict that saw former foes fight alongside rather than against each other for the first time. Class conflict had too, in 1896, functioned as a divisive force, for the Democrats especially, and the shadow of the Civil

←——————————————————————————————

FIGURE 8.4 (*continued*) was not unusual, nor would it have been regarded as in any sense duplicitous. The message that the audience sought and received from such entertainment was essentially one of validation, not verisimilitude; these productions were patriotic in intent and in effect, a precursor of the plethora of war films from an American perspective with which the twentieth and twenty-first centuries are familiar. Image courtesy of the Library of Congress Prints and Photographs Division (LC-DIG-ppmsca-05942).

War served only to remind Americans of old wounds. Yet within only a few years, these wounds achieved a closure of sorts in the context of a very different conflict that unified former adversaries under the banner of a more ambitious American nationalism.

This nationalism looked inward as much as it did outward, however, and the acquisition of an overseas empire, at least of sorts, was not its sole driving force. The Civil War generation had bequeathed a complex legacy to its nation. It was not simply that the executive had been dominated by veterans since 1868. The cultural and ritualistic impact of the conflict, encouraged by the various veterans' organizations North and South, but especially the Union's Grand Army of the Republic (GAR), was not confined to Memorial Day celebrations. It resonated in classrooms across the country as a new generation of Americans learned to recite daily the Pledge of Allegiance and salute a flag that had come to demarcate more than national boundaries. In short, it symbolized a national mission and a military legacy.

Speaking to that new generation in 1895, former Union soldier and future Associate Justice of the Supreme Court Oliver Wendell Holmes, Jr. invoked what he termed the "soldier's faith." War, Holmes observed, was "out of fashion" by the end of the nineteenth century; the "aspirations of the world," he noted, were now "those of commerce." Yet Holmes himself had little respect for a world in which "philanthropists, labor reformers, and men of fashion" might feel "comfortable and may shine without much trouble or any danger," one in which "love of country" was no more than "an old wife's tale." It was with more than a degree of scorn that Holmes critiqued the modern "revolt against pain in all its forms" and soberly advised his listeners to "pray, not for comfort, but for combat; to keep the soldier's faith against the doubts of civil life."[10] Before the new century had dawned, Holmes's particular prayer in this regard had been answered. Yet in the years that followed, not a few of his audience, along with their nation, would have cause to contemplate the full ramifications of the soldier's faith, and the uneasy path between commerce and combat that led into the twentieth century.

The New Nationalism

"Out of heroism grows faith in the worth of heroism," Holmes had asserted, and for one individual these words had a particular resonance. Theodore Roosevelt found presidential power suddenly thrust on him when McKinley was assassinated, but authority was not something that

Roosevelt had ever lacked; he had prepared for it all his life. By 1901, America's youngest president, at forty-two, had already established a reputation as a man of action. In his particular case, the action in question was the successful seizure of San Juan Hill near Santiago in Cuba in 1898. Yet Roosevelt and his "Rough Riders," the volunteer cavalry unit he had raised, were not the only troops to gain renown in that particular engagement. African-American regiments had been decisive in securing American victory that day, a fact highlighted by future commander of American forces in Europe in World War I, then Lieutenant John J. Pershing. "White regiments, black regiments, regulars and Rough Riders, representing the young manhood of the North and South, fought shoulder to shoulder," Pershing enthused, "unmindful of race or color, unmindful of whether commanded by an ex-Confederate or not, and mindful only of their common duty as Americans."[11]

Pershing's pride in the ability of the troops he commanded to set aside racial differences did not mean that he could, in the long run; and no more could Roosevelt. Both struggled with the racial ramifications of the inclusive civic nationalism they desired in theory yet too often denied in practice. The dominant narrative that came down from the top of San Juan Hill was not one of a new, racially inclusive nation, but of individual heroism, and that heroism was Roosevelt's. In Roosevelt, indeed, a great many of the contradictory aspects of American nationalism and mythmaking met and merged. He was an individual who seemed to encapsulate the American Dream; not the rags-to-riches strand – he had been born into wealth – but the ideal of forging of one's fate on the frontier.

Roosevelt recounted his own ranching experiences in what was then still Dakota Territory in, among other publications, *Ranch Life and the Hunting Trail* (1888). Illustrated by his friend and fellow Western enthusiast, the noted artist Frederic Remington, the emotional thrust of the work was summed up by its author's choice of epigraph: some lines from Robert Browning's "Saul" that dwelled on "manhood's prime vigour" in which "No spirit feels waste./Not a muscle is stopped in its playing nor sinew unbraced."[12] This reflected not only Roosevelt's approach to his own life and to the opportunities afforded by the West, but was the essence of his vision for the nation that, in 1901, he found himself leading.

Roosevelt advocated what he termed "the strenuous life," a phrase forever associated with him after he gave a speech of that title in Chicago in 1899. He argued, rather like Holmes, that Americans should uphold "not the doctrine of ignoble ease, but the doctrine of the strenuous life, the life of toil and effort, of labor and strife. . . . A life of slothful ease," he stressed, "is as little worthy of a nation as of an individual." A "healthy state," in Roosevelt's opinion, depended on its citizens leading "clean, vigorous, healthy lives" and raising their children "not to shirk difficulties, but to overcome them; not to seek ease, but to know how to wrest triumph from toil and risk."[13] What is, in essence, a middle-class, martial morality has, of course, been expressed in many other nations, and by many other people, but rarely as exhaustively as in America at the start of the twentieth century. In advocating the "strenuous life," Roosevelt both reflected and reinforced a reform impulse already well entrenched in American culture, society, and, increasingly, politics.

Given that Roosevelt's own career had begun in the navy (and his first publication had been on the War of 1812), it is perhaps unsurprising that echoes of Mahan's perspective on America's naval and national power could be heard in Roosevelt's speeches, or that Strong's advocacy of the Anglo-Saxon ideal might also provide another element in the president's philosophy. Indeed, Roosevelt brought Strong and Mahan onto the same page, quite literally, when he introduced them to each other in 1900. Mahan's contribution to the composition of one of Strong's later works, *Expansion: Under New World-Conditions* (1900), was fulsomely acknowledged by the author, but it was not Mahan's influence alone that informed Strong's prescription for America's domestic agenda and new global imperative; it was the spirit of the age, and many assumed, with some justification, that it would be an American age.

Expansion was intended as a wake-up call for the United States at the turn of the century. In its argument that the Spanish-American War had provided America with "a new temper, a new national consciousness, a new apprehension of destiny," it bridged both generations and agendas. It appealed to many of those who had fought in the nation's Civil War and those, like Roosevelt, born too late for that particular conflict and, perhaps, seeking to prove that they nevertheless did not lack the martial spirit. More crucially, in positing what was essentially a "war without end" paradigm for the United States, it appealed to the social reformer and the soldier alike. Both could identify with the proposition that "on God's great anvil of war are struck the mighty blows which shape the nation to higher uses," and position it within their own frame of reference.[14] Both could perceive, in the new world conditions that Strong spelled out for them, the opportunity to fight – literally and metaphorically – for the nation, to defend it from both internal and external threats.

FIGURE 8.5. "School Begins" (Louis Dalrymple, 1899). This cartoon, which appeared in *Puck* Magazine in January (25), 1899, encapsulated some of the concerns surrounding America's new imperial venture and the prospect of inculcating nonwhites with the Anglo-Saxon American ethos. It shows the figure of "Uncle Sam" as a schoolteacher facing, in the front row, four children representing the Philippines, Hawaii, Puerto (Porto) Rico, and Cuba. The back row shows rather more studious pupils each holding books named for different states. Sitting by the door, a Native American figure is portrayed as holding a book upside down, and a Chinese child hesitates on the threshold. Behind Uncle Sam, an African American cleans the windows. Image courtesy of the Library of Congress Prints and Photographs Division (LC-USZC2–1025).

On the subject of potentially hostile foreign bodies, indeed, American reformers such as Strong proved expansive in their thinking. By the turn of the century, it was not just men but microbes that concerned them. The danger of contagion from abroad, as Strong perceived it in 1900, was now more than metaphorical. Fear of disease, as fear of dilution of democratic values by immigrants, was a fundamental part of the defensive mindset that dominated America in the early twentieth century, at home and abroad. The threat posed by what Strong perceived as the "unsanitary . . . savage and partially civilized races," one that encompassed both illness and ignorance, must, he argued, "be controlled by enlightened nations both for their own sake and for the sake of the world" (Figure 8.5). Yet Strong's advocacy of what one historian has described as "missionary diplomacy" was not unique to the United States in this period.[15] America was hardly the only nation to position itself as especially enlightened, but it was perhaps slower than others to follow the idea to its logical conclusion. A nudge was needed, and was soon forthcoming.

English poet Rudyard Kipling well knew that he was addressing a transatlantic audience when he advised the United States to "take up the White Man's burden/Have done with childish days," and reminded it that "Comes now, to search your manhood/Through all the thankless years/Cold, edged with dear-bought wisdom,/The judgment of your peers!" Kipling's perspective may have been informed by Britain's own imperial frontier, but as the poem's subtitle, "The United States and the Philippine Islands," made clear, he recognized its likely resonance in a nation struggling with its own disruptive racial dynamic even as it sought to explore the possibilities of foreign influence and sent its still segregated armed forces abroad in pursuit of that ever-elusive end. Others were rather more cynical about America's fitness for empire, or influence of any kind. One satirical response to Kipling's poem, composed by his fellow countryman, the politician Henry Labouchère, entitled "The Brown Man's Burden," ended with the lines: "Pile on the brown man's burden,/And through the world proclaim/That ye are Freedom's agent/ There's no more paying game!/And, should your own past history/Straight in your teeth be thrown,/Retort that independence/Is good for whites alone."[16]

Roosevelt's reaction to Labouchère's critique is unrecorded. As far as Kipling was concerned, however, he regarded "The White Man's Burden" as bad poetry but good advice. America under Roosevelt's leadership certainly sought new opportunities both beyond its shores and at home. The long-desired acquisition of the Panama Canal site in 1903 (construction began the following year), for example, offered increased strategic and trade opportunities for the United States. The negotiations themselves, involving as they did a degree of intervention on America's part in the conflict between Colombia and Panama – America sent the USS *Nashville* to Panama's aid – introduced a new phrase, a new concept into the debate over American foreign policy: gunboat diplomacy. At first glance, this seemed a somewhat different proposition from missionary diplomacy. On closer inspection, the martial and the moral reinforced each other in this case, too, as they had done from the colonial era onward, as they did, to powerful effect, in Roosevelt himself.

As the first of three so-called Progressive presidents (the others being William Howard Taft and Woodrow Wilson), Roosevelt's program for his nation was both innovative and reactionary. His particular pet projects, whether the Panama Canal, environmentalism and conservation, or America's international influence, all revolved, to varying degrees, around the idea of "Americanism." This was another concept often associated with Roosevelt following his discussion of "true Americanism" in 1894, but it was a perennial theme to which many politicians and spokesmen returned. At the start of the twentieth century, the idea of "true Americanism" was invoked most frequently, as it was by Roosevelt, in the context of immigration and that of a nation struggling to marry up the dreams of economic, racial, and political equality with the harsh reality of widespread industrial and urban poverty, global responsibilities with domestic unrest. It meant far more than simply the need to inculcate immigrants with an identifiably American patriotism; it meant pinning down that patriotism in the first place.

For Roosevelt, Americanism was simultaneously a communal and a confrontational proposition incorporating several strands. Only one of these involved "the Americanizing of the newcomers to our shores" and the assurance that "English, and no other language, is that in which all the school exercises should be conducted." At its most basic, Americanism was, as Roosevelt, echoing Lincoln, declared: "a question of spirit, conviction, and purpose, not of creed or birthplace." He had little time for those who adhered to their European origins, who "with incredible and contemptible folly, wander back to bow down before the alien gods whom our forefathers forsook." Imitation, in Roosevelt's view, was far from the sincerest form of flattery, but was instead a sign of weakness. When Americans had "striven hardest to mold themselves in conventional European forms," he proposed, "they have succeeded least." In contrast to an "over-civilized, over-sensitive, over-refined" European culture, Americanism resided in "the hardihood and manly courage" that Roosevelt was so keen on, and tried so hard to embody; above all, it consisted of "waging relentless war on rank-growing evils of all kinds."[17]

The progressive perspective, as Roosevelt and others expressed it, was resolutely optimistic in outlook but essentially pessimistic in its premise that there existed a multitude of evils to wage war on in the first place. It divided, roughly, into two main camps: social and conservative. The former focused on improving the lives of America's poorest classes and was mostly aimed at what were perceived as the evils of the urban environment: the inequalities of housing and health, child labor laws, crime – organized or otherwise – prostitution, and temperance were just some of the issues that exercised the social progressive. The latter took a broader approach to the need for balance between the excesses of the industrial age and the imperatives of an organic society, between the consumer and the capitalist, and between the nation and its natural resources. Focused more at federal level, it engaged in "trust-busting" in expanding the power of the central state in relation to, for example, railroad rates and tax, and on pushing for legislation, such as the eight-hour working day. Its successes included the creation of both the Department of Labor and a Federal Children's Bureau along with a raft of legislation aimed at protecting employees and consumers. What social and conservative progressives had in common, however, was that both functioned through a combination of faith and fear.

Although grounded in an evangelical Protestant tradition that reached as far back as the nation itself, the progressive mindset was too frequently exercised by fear. America's reformers and politicians saw evils everywhere, and the efforts of muckraking journalists and the "yellow press" ensured that the American public never lost sight of the danger it was in. That danger lurked in the twinned threat offered by anarchism and socialism, it resided in the city and its slums and saloons, in immigration and industrialization, in the imbalance between labor and capital, in crime and its corollary, punishment, and in the class, race, health, and gender disparities that blighted the republican ideal. Social deprivation was bad enough, but the challenge it posed to "true Americanism" demanded action.

One solution was to combine moral uplift with its material variant. The experiment was attempted, with a degree of success, by, among others, Jane Addams and Ellen Gates Starr in Hull House in Chicago. Taking its inspiration from Toynbee Hall in London, Hull House – the first (it was founded in 1889) and most famous example of what were known as "settlement houses" – was designed to alleviate some of the practical difficulties facing mainly immigrant families in Chicago's West Side. With its combination of practical, social, and educational programs – a nursery and a library, lectures, workshops, and concerts were provided – Hull House was particularly valuable for women struggling to straddle the demands of employment with childcare. Hull House was not a hothouse for Americanization as such. Although it did, among other educational provisions, offer English-language classes, the learning of a new language was not perceived as the catalyst toward the total abandonment of a previous culture. Hull House anticipated informing, not indoctrinating, immigrants.

Working on the traditional assumption that it was the woman who functioned as the moral mainstay of the family, middle-class white women like Addams and Starr, some of whom had no families of their own, turned their energies toward directing the lives of others to secure, it was hoped, a more stable – but not necessarily homogenous – national family. Yet many of the issues that Addams and Starr sought to address were certainly not specific to immigrants struggling to cope in a new world, but were intrinsic to the exigencies of the capitalist/consumer nation that America had become. Political corruption, so comprehensively condemned by Lincoln Steffens in *The Shame of the Cities* (1904), was, in later publications – notably Upton Sinclair's *The Jungle* (1906) – charged with compromising not just the moral well-being of the nation, but the physical health of its inhabitants. A damning indictment of the working and hygiene conditions in Chicago's meat-packing industry, *The Jungle* was, largely thanks to its detailing of those things "that were quite unspeakable" (notably the possibility of human body parts in the beef lard), an instant best seller.

In fact, the horrors of the slaughterhouses – something of a perennial fascination for Americans, as the success of Eric Schlosser' *Fast Food Nation* (2001) revealed – paled in comparison with the stunted lives of their mainly immigrant workforces that Sinclair described. Here was a world that contained disturbing echoes of the nineteenth-century plantation South, one inhabited by "a population, low-class and mostly foreign, hanging always on the verge of starvation, and dependent for its opportunities of life upon the whim of men every bit as brutal and unscrupulous as the old-time slave-traders." Such comparisons were not immediately obvious, Sinclair averred, because in the stockyards, unlike the antebellum South, "there was no difference in colour between master and slave."[18]

Yet the evocation of an uncomfortable past had, perhaps, less impact than the thought that contaminated food was making its way onto American dinner plates. The passage of both the Meat Inspection Act and the Pure Food and Drug Act in the same year that *The Jungle* appeared showed just how fast the fledgling fast-food nation could move when it wanted to. Exactly how far it should move in the direction of federally legislated solutions to social and economic problems, however, was a moot point. In a nation predicated on the idea of individualism, the prospect of an interventionist state was anathema. Squaring the strenuous life with the idea of, in essence, social welfare programming was never likely to prove an easy task.

Adding an offshore burden – white man's or otherwise – to the equation hardly helped matters, but in marketing terms, at least, America rose to the challenge. Everything was deemed to be new in the new century. Roosevelt promised a "New Nationalism" that emphasized a stronger central state as the means to achieve social and economic equality – what he termed the "square deal" – as the central tenet of his 1912 bid for the presidency. Woodrow Wilson offered the contrary concept of the "New Freedom" that emphasized a more laissez-faire approach to the vexed issue of balancing private power and profit with public and political parity. Everything, in short, was exciting and new. All that was missing was the word "improved."

Improvement was, of course, the nub of both the nationalist and reform impulses at work in America in this period, as in those preceding it. The American ideal, if not its reality, had always held out the hope, indeed the imperative, of improvement for the individual and the collective alike, within certain racial, religious, and gender parameters, of course. These parameters remained pretty firmly in place even after 1900. In that sense, there was little that was new about the "New Nationalism" or indeed the "New Freedom" of the early twentieth century except, perhaps, the ambitions of the nation that the phrases invoked.

Roosevelt had vacated the presidential office in 1908. As might have been anticipated, he went out in style. One of his last acts as president was to orchestrate the circumnavigation of the globe by sixteen battleships from the Atlantic Fleet – this came to be known as the Great White Fleet – in a fourteen-month voyage that began in December 1907 and concluded in February 1909. The world was suitably impressed, and the American crowds that flocked to see these ships confirmed that the home market was equally appreciative of this overt display of their nation's naval might (Figure 8.6). Yet away from the high seas lurked the fear that the United States was developing power without responsibility, capitalism without conscience, and that patriotic displays of the nation's international reach simply obfuscated the internal inequalities that blighted so many American lives.

Despite the popularity of *The Jungle*, literary musings on the matter certainly did not limit the impact of impersonal capitalist forces to the immigrant workers of the meat-packing industry. The upper echelons of society seemed equally vulnerable to the vagaries of both the market and modern manners. Upton Sinclair had at least posited a shared misery among the downtrodden, but equally popular authors such as Edith Wharton delineated a "new" world of wealth within which individualism

FIGURE 8.6. "Welcome home!" (William Allen Rogers, 1909). This powerfully patriotic cartoon appeared in the New York *Herald* on February 22, 1909 (the date is on Washington's hat). It portrays (from left) the figures of "Uncle Sam," George Washington, and Theodore Roosevelt welcoming the Great White Fleet back to the naval yard at Hampton Roads after its round-the-world voyage. Image courtesy of the Library of Congress Prints and Photographs Division (LC-USZ62–136026).

could too swiftly become isolation. This world was both inherently unstable economically and practically bankrupt spiritually. Wharton's heroines, unlike Stephen Crane's, were not likely to fall into prostitution, but slide down the social scale they did in novels such as *The House of Mirth* (1905). The clue to Wharton's social critique, of course, was in the title: "the heart of the wise is in the house of mourning," according to Ecclesiastes (7:4), "but the heart of fools is in the house of mirth."

By the second decade of the twentieth century, however, American sentiment had every reason to tend more toward mirth than mourning, but that did not make Americans fools. Roosevelt was concerned, however, that prosperity had perhaps made them forgetful, if not complacent, and he was sufficiently confident in his own abilities to try and steer them back on course. Founding a new party – the Progressive Party – he sought reelection as president in 1912. Given that Roosevelt first adumbrated his notion of the new nationalism in 1910 in Kansas, with its historic connection to the radical abolitionist John Brown, and that his audience included members of the GAR, it was perhaps inevitable that he would highlight the "heroic struggle" that had been the Civil War. He emphasized "the men of the past partly," as he put it, "that they may be honored by our praise of them, but more that they may serve as examples for the future."[19] By that point, however, the nation had already moved on. Roosevelt's harking back to the nation's Civil War in support of a supposedly "new" nationalism seemed already outdated to a citizenry many of whom had no direct link back to the mid-nineteenth century and whose ancestors had been elsewhere when America was tearing itself apart.

Three years later, the man who defeated Roosevelt's bid for reelection, Woodrow Wilson, also found himself facing an audience of war veterans when he spoke at a reunion commemorating the fiftieth anniversary of Gettysburg, the three-day (July 1–3, 1863) battle that, with hindsight, was deemed to be the turning point of the Civil War and, consequently, of the nation. In fact, Wilson had not been anticipating attending the event, and although persuaded to do so, a degree of reluctance to dwell too much on the past crept in to his speech that day. Wilson, like Roosevelt, acknowledged the "manly devotion" of the "venerable men" he was addressing, but was perhaps rather keener to emphasize that "their task is done," that their "day is turned into evening." America's day, by contrast, Wilson stressed, "is not over; it is upon us in full tide." And while he accepted the baton of responsibility handed down from the Civil War generation, Wilson nevertheless anticipated that the future would be one of "quiet counsel, where the blare of trumpets is neither heard nor heeded."[20]

Unfortunately for Wilson, as for the nation over which he had just assumed leadership, this really was the triumph of optimism over reality. America, in 1913, had every reason to assume that both Roosevelt and Wilson were right: the former in his assertion that on America's success rested "the sake of mankind," the latter in his assurance that America's international influence would ensure a future in which "things are done which make blessed the nations of the world in peace and righteousness and love." The two were not necessarily compatible, and in any case, after 1914, the world had different ideas.

The outbreak of war in European was a shock for America, but not an immediate cause for concern. As Roosevelt kept telling them, Americans enjoyed the security of "a continent on which to work out our destiny," a continent on which to fight for justice, for a "square deal" for all. Roosevelt's martial rhetoric, as that of the progressives generally, remained largely metaphorical. In selecting to couch his campaign in the language of battle, however, Roosevelt was aware of the unifying power of conflict in a nation as heterogeneous as the United States. Political divisions, progressive reforms, public dissension could all find common cause in the call to arms in the name of the nation. In this respect, the soldier's faith proved persistent in theory and in the end prescient in practice. Although the voyage of the Great White Fleet had emphasized how small, in real terms, the world was, the battlefields of Europe still seemed safely far away when Roosevelt rallied America to his, ultimately doomed, political cause. "We fight in honorable fashion for the good of mankind; fearless of the future; unheeding of our individual fates; with unflinching hearts and undimmed eyes; we stand at Armageddon," he declared, "and we battle for the Lord."[21]

The New Freedom

Having secured victory over Roosevelt, and despite being faced with European turmoil, Woodrow Wilson had no intention of transforming the military metaphors of America's political battleground into actual conflict. "We are at peace with the world," he declared. The European war, he stressed, was one "with which we have nothing to do, whose causes cannot touch us."[22] Impartiality was what he advocated; yet how impartial could a nation of immigrants hope to be? That question remained to be answered, but not quite yet. In the short term, the progressive imperative continued as the only game in town, keeping the nation's attention fixed on a complex domestic agenda with its own battles to fight and win. One of these was the battle over female suffrage. With his emphasis on the strenuous life, Roosevelt may have provided a high-testosterone introduction to the twentieth century for America, but in the same year as the European nations launched themselves into the "war to end all wars," some Americans at least were debating whether or not women might, in the twentieth century, finally be enfranchised.

America's civic nationalist creed had long been racially compromised, but the gender implications of citizenship had frequently been subsumed by the broader reform impulses that exercised America, from abolitionism in the antebellum period to the ongoing debates over immigration and true Americanism in the early twentieth century. The first major women's rights convention had taken place at Seneca Falls, New York, in 1848, but the noted journalist Margaret Fuller had published *Woman in the Nineteenth Century* (1845) three years before that. Although fully aware that, as she put it, "there exists in the minds of men a tone of feeling towards women as towards slaves," Fuller had nevertheless regarded it as "inevitable that an external freedom, an independence of the encroachments of other men, such as has been achieved for the nation, should be so for every member of it."[23]

The Seneca Falls Convention had reinforced Fuller's message by adopting a "Declaration of Sentiments" that deliberately evoked the Declaration of Independence to make its point. "We hold these truths to be self-evident," it announced, "that all men and women are created equal," before going on to detail a list of grievances perpetrated against women. These included denying her "inalienable right to the elective franchise," a right, the Declaration noted, accorded "the most ignorant and degraded men – both natives and foreigners." In light of "this entire disfranchisement of one-half the people of this country," it concluded, "and because women do feel themselves aggrieved, oppressed, and fraudulently deprived of their most sacred rights, we insist that they have immediate admission to all the rights and privileges which belong to them as citizens of the United States."[24]

In the American case, the idea of inalienable rights lent weight to the demand for equality between the sexes. The rhetoric of the republican experiment, in theory at least, made it that much harder to exclude women from the polity; in practice, of course, it was a different matter. Individual state legislation had secured, for example, property rights for women, and in several (all western) states, women did have the vote, but the main goal of full representation continued to elude them. By the time Wilson assumed office, women were still agitating for a national suffrage. Part of the problem was the positioning of women's rights within the broader reform nexus. The Seneca Falls Convention had come about in part as a result of the efforts of Elizabeth Cady Stanton and Lucretia Mott, whose connection was initially forged in the context of anti-slavery. More than six decades later, women's rights and racial equality were still largely conjoined issues, embedded within the larger question over American citizenship and nationality that the Fourteenth Amendment had only partly resolved and World War I would resurrect.

"It is difficult to believe," observed African-American activist Mary Church Terrell, "that any individual in the United States with one drop of African blood in his veins can oppose woman suffrage." Male black opposition struck Terrell as more bizarre than female. Writing in *The Crisis*, the paper of the National Association for the Advancement of Colored People (NAACP), she described it as "queer and curious enough" for a woman to oppose suffrage for her sex, but male opposition seemed to her "the most preposterous and ridiculous thing in the world. What could be more absurd," she asked, "than to see one group of human beings who are denied rights which they are trying to secure for themselves working to prevent another group from obtaining the same rights?" Terrell may have found it absurd but, in global terms, let alone American ones, it was hardy atypical.

Yet in an American context, the argument for female suffrage was both influenced by and itself informed class and ethnic issues that persisted from the Declaration of Sentiments onward. Terrell's argument, indeed, differed little from that of 1848. Invoking the founders' establishment of "government of the people, for the people, and by the people," Terrell revealed that she, in common with antebellum reformers, drew a distinction between the "intelligent, virtuous and cultured" who were denied the vote and the "illiterate, degraded and vicious" to whom it was automatically granted.[25] This argument for what was effectively a moral requirement for membership in the nation was not unique to suffragist activists, of course, but merged with Roosevelt's notion of the strenuous life, it contributed to rather an exclusive concept of citizenship and a somewhat narrow nationalism that became known as "100 percent Americanism."

The idea of 100 percent Americanism emerged with America's entry into World War I in 1917, although the war was not the cause, simply the catalyst. Wilson had hoped that America might broker a peace between the belligerents, and that by its example alone the nation might show "what liberty and the inspirations of an emancipated spirit may do for men and societies, for individuals, for states, and for mankind." Neither side in the European conflict, however, welcomed Wilson's attempt at moral arbitration. Because Wilson's reelection in 1916 appeared to confirm America's hands-off approach, neither Germany nor the allies felt the need to meet around an American table. Yet Wilson's assurance, offered in 1914, that the causes of Europe's conflict could not touch America was ultimately compromised by the fact that its effects most certainly could.

Germany, in particular, was prepared to risk America's material involvement by conducting a U-boat campaign that it knew might draw the United States into the war. The infamous sinking of the Cunard liner *Lusitania* in 1915, with the loss of 128 American lives, did not single-handedly drag America out of neutrality, but the U-boat campaign eventually had its effect. On April 2, 1917, Wilson announced to Congress

FIGURE 8.7. "That liberty shall not perish from the earth" (Joseph Pennell, 1918). To raise funds for the war effort, the federal government issued Liberty Bonds, which were marketed as both patriotically and economically sound investments. This poster highlighted the way in which American support for the Allies during World War I tied in with the nation's historical sense of mission, which had

that America was at war with Germany. "We are accepting this challenge of hostile purpose," he advised the American people, because in the face of Germany's "organized power, always lying in wait to accomplish we know not what purpose, there can be no assured security for the democratic Governments of the world." Ultimately, Wilson asserted, the "world must be made safe for democracy. Its peace must be planted upon the tested foundations of political liberty" (Figure 8.7). He also assured that world that in abandoning neutrality, America had "no selfish ends to serve. We desire no conquest, no dominion. We seek no indemnities for ourselves, no material compensation for the sacrifices we shall freely make," he promised. "We are but one of the champions of the rights of mankind."[26]

Warfare, of course, has a tendency to suspend, even if only temporarily, some of the rights of mankind, and America found that in this it was no exception. Following his reluctant assumption of the burden of belligerent on April 2, Wilson's formal declaration of war came four days later. By then, the practicalities of America's position, not its moral or political purpose, took priority. The need for the identification and possible containment or removal of "alien enemies" occupied the bulk of Wilson's April 6 message; but a necessary wartime measure could too easily offer the opportunity for the passage of legislation that, in peacetime, might have faced greater opposition and the public expression of sentiments that, in peacetime, would not readily be tolerated. German Americans, naturally, swiftly came under suspicion, and their language and culture under attack.

If it seems vaguely ludicrous with hindsight that the playing of Beethoven was banned in, of all places, Boston, or that sauerkraut was renamed "liberty cabbage," it was no minor matter at the time. The enthusiasm with which, for example, some Americans signed up for the American Protective League (APL), an essentially quasi-vigilante body formed to

---

FIGURE 8.7 (*continued*) expanded, as Wilson put it, to make the world "safe for democracy." This poster advertising Liberty Bonds offers an imaginative rendition of the carnage that might ensue if the world is not rendered secure – the image of Liberty is in ruins – and suggests that America would not be immune from the effects of global conflict. In light of subsequent events almost a century later in the United States, this image is a particularly emotive one, but it was so at the time as well, although for rather different reasons. The irony, of course, was that liberty, while not necessarily in ruins, was compromised to a very great extent by the aggressive patriotism that prevailed in America after 1917. Image courtesy of the Library of Congress Prints and Photographs Division (LC-DIG-ppmsca-18343).

help root out radicals, revealed the darker side of democracy and an unhealthy determination to suppress domestic opposition. This was the Puritan village writ large, Puritanism in the service of patriotism, which was not the most salubrious combination at the best of times, and it set an ominous precedent for the future.

More serious were the effects of the Espionage Act (1917) and the Sedition Act (1918), and the ways in which they were used to enforce a conformity that, in most cases, had never been compromised, a patriotism that was only perceived to have been misplaced. Socialist leader Eugene V. Debs was relatively fortunate in only being jailed for ten years in 1918 for daring to question the American war effort (he was released by Wilson's successor, Warren Harding, in 1921). IWW (Industrial Workers of the World) leader Frank Little was not so lucky and was lynched by a mob in Montana. These were extreme examples, but only the tip of an iceberg that had been gathering both size and momentum for decades: the urge to define Americanism, and to define it in such a way as to exclude those deemed unworthy of the rights of American citizenship or force them into a more homogeneous American norm. In 1917, for example, in the face of opposition from the president, the literacy bill, long the bee in the bonnet of the Immigration Restriction League, was finally forced onto the statute books.

Exclusion was not, of course, the only response to conflict. More positive progressive programs found themselves fast-tracked into law by the war, most notably female suffrage. The Nineteenth Amendment granting women the vote was passed by the House of Representatives at the start of 1918. Southern intransigence slowed it down some in the Senate, but in 1919, it was ratified and came into effect the following year. However, the U.S. Senate was not the only opportunity for opposition to this particular measure. In many southern states, segregation, and the dubious poll tax and literacy legislation supporting it, still held. So although in theory African-American women in the South could vote after 1920, in practice many were still denied that right.

For African-American men, by contrast, America's entry into World War I seemed – as all previous wars had – to offer the opportunity, yet again, to prove their patriotism and thereby advance the cause of equality. If twentieth-century suffrage activists sounded a lot like their antebellum counterparts, so too did black spokesmen who addressed themselves to the question of what the war meant for African Americans. Both believed, or at least hoped, that service for the nation at this time of crisis would result in acceptance by the nation, a permutation of the soldier's faith that neither Holmes nor Roosevelt had fully anticipated. "Out of this war will rise," opined one writer in *The Crisis*, "an American Negro, with the right to vote and the right to work and the right to live without insult."[27] Yet African Americans still fought in a segregated army, and not at all in a navy that – in stark contrast to the navy of America's Civil War – debarred them entirely. Their white commanders certainly evinced a degree of concern for the impact of the conflict on black troops, but not quite in the way that black leaders had envisaged.

John J. Pershing, now a general, had clearly moved on from his apparent approval of the implications of black and white troops fighting together on San Juan Hill in 1898. Twenty years later, he issued a directive to inform America's French allies "of the position occupied by Negroes in the United States" so that said position might not be compromised by any liberal European leanings. "*American opinion is unanimous on the 'color question' and does not admit of any discussion,*" Pershing asserted, somewhat disingenuously given the demographics. What the French may have failed to realize, Pershing suggested, was that African Americans posed for the "white race in the Republic a menace of degeneracy were it not that an impassable gulf has been made between them." He therefore cautioned against any "*familiarity and indulgence*" on the part of the French toward African-American troops. Any such familiarity would, he emphasized, be an "affront" to American "national policy" and, worse, might well "inspire in black Americans aspirations which to them (the whites) appear intolerable."

This was a depressingly familiar – although presumably news to the French – story, and one that black activists such as Frederick Douglass and Ida B. Wells had countered all their lives. "Although a citizen of the United States," Pershing explained, "the black man is regarded by the white American as an inferior being with whom relations of business or service only are possible. The black is constantly being censured for his want of intelligence and discretion," he averred, "his lack of civic and professional conscience, and for his tendency toward undue familiarity." If that were not enough, Pershing fell back on the "attempted rape" charge as further "proof" that African Americans were "a constant menace to the American who has to repress them sternly."[28] Whether Pershing was expressing his own views or simply acknowledging the widespread racism in the American armed forces and in Washington, this was fighting talk, and African-American leaders were not slow to respond.

Leading African-American intellectual and spokesman, co-founder with, among others, Ida B. Wells of the NAACP in 1909, and founder, the following year, of *The Crisis*, W.E.B. Du Bois drew the battle lines clearly in 1919. African-American soldiers had, he stressed, "fought gladly and to the last drop of blood" in the name of a "shameful" nation that still lynched, disenfranchised, and persecuted them. "This is the country," Du Bois observed, with a degree of irony, "to which we Soldiers of Democracy return. This is the Fatherland for which we fought! But," he reminded his readers, "it is our fatherland. It was right for us to fight." Now that the war in Europe was over, however, Du Bois asserted, a new war in America had only just begun, "a sterner, longer, more unbending battle against the forces of hell in our own land." In an echo of Wilson, of progressive rhetoric more generally, but from a perspective almost diametrically opposed to theirs, Du Bois declared: "Make way for Democracy! We saved it in France, and by the Great Jehovah we will save it in the United States of America, or know the reason why."[29]

Woodrow Wilson, and possibly Pershing, may have been appalled at such rhetoric, but one could hardly blame the French for inculcating African-American anger on this subject as on others. The outbreak of race riots in East St. Louis, Illinois, in 1917 and in Chicago in 1919 – one of the latter followed the murder of a black youth who had crossed the "color line" on a Lake Michigan beach – suggested a future of at least sporadic violence between black and white in America. This was not at all what Wilson had hoped for, neither for his nation nor the world. He had believed that America might, by example alone, point the way to a more peaceful future, within and between nations. With this in mind, he composed his idealistic "Fourteen Points" for postwar settlement and future international cooperation – including a League of Nations – which he placed before the peace negotiations in Paris at the start of 1919.

Neither Wilson's own nation nor the Allied leadership fully supported his vision for a new world order. The Allies did at least accept the idea of a cooperative League, and this was established under the Treaty of Versailles (1919) that officially ended World War I. Wilson himself received the Nobel Peace Prize for his work on the League but, ironically, the one nation he sought above all to influence rejected his efforts. The United States never joined the League of Nations. In the end, the peace proposed by Wilson proved elusive; peace in general, indeed, proved elusive. World War I was not, as it turned out, the "war to end all wars," but the precursor of a century of conflict. In material terms, the United States was in better shape to meet this. She had not been devastated to the degree experienced by the European nations. Her losses – slightly more than 100,000 – in the war were high, however, especially given how brief a time she had been involved. They were light in comparison with European casualties, of course, but high enough for a nation that had never wanted to be involved in the first place.

The impact of World War I on America was not, therefore, physical but psychological and, in some respects, practical. The war could be said to have effected a merger of sorts between Roosevelt's new nationalism and Wilson's new freedom. The American central state had never – at least not since the Civil War – been more powerful and, with some 5 million men in uniform, outwardly so united. The need to support the war effort resulted in federal legislation impacting on most areas of industry and business, all under the remit of the War Industries Board. This was commerce controlled in the name of conflict. Many progressives regarded this as a positive by-product of war, and few would have made any cynical connection between industrial standardization in the name of national efficiency and its social equivalent in the name of nationalism, although both, clearly, derived from similar impulses.

In World War I, too, it was the state that sought to inculcate the kind of patriotism so necessary for morale in wartime. Where private bodies, religious and secular, had interpreted the Civil War for nineteenth-century Americans, in World War I it was the Committee on Public Information (CPI) that disseminated wartime propaganda and defined, for the America Public, the causes at stake. This represented, as one of its members, future public relations expert Edward Bernays, would later describe as the "engineering of consent" – a concept that he perceived as "the very essence of the democratic process, the freedom to persuade and suggest."[30]

The fact that consent was not, at times, so much engineered as enforced in America after 1917 in no sense undermined the nationalist message promulgated by the CPI. Its very existence, indeed, represented something of a culmination of, or at least the next step in, a communications revolution that had begun with early colonial broadsheets, speeded up when Samuel Morse enabled Americans to telegraph each other, gathered momentum when the railways crossed the Plains, and finally made it onto the big screen in the output of the early motion picture industry. The CPI was simply the federal face of a not-so-new nationalism, predicated on the idea of freedom, of faith in American democracy, of faith in the future. This was not, however, the faith founded on freedom from conflict that Wilson had envisaged. It was Theodore Roosevelt's version, and Oliver Wendell Holmes's, and W.E. B. Du Bois's. It was a soldier's faith that defined American democracy after 1917, and all too soon the nation would have need of it again.

9

Beyond the Last Frontier

A New Deal for America

U.S.A. is the slice of a continent. U.S.A. is a group of holding companies, some aggregations of trade unions, a set of laws bound in calf, a radio network, a chain of moving picture theatres . . . U.S.A. is a lot of men buried in their uniforms in Arlington Cemetery. U.S.A. is the letters at the end of an address when you are away from home. But mostly U.S.A. is the speech of the people.

(John Dos Passos, *U.S.A.*, 1938)

Persistent rain and gray skies made it difficult to see the USS *Olympia* as she sailed up the Potomac River on Wednesday, November 9, 1921. Formerly the flagship of Commodore George Dewey, and made famous by her action in Manila Bay during the Spanish-American War, one of her last acts before being decommissioned was to bring home the body of an unknown American soldier from the Great War. Even if they could not quite make out the ship in the general gloom, onlookers could nevertheless track the *Olympia* by the sound of the guns that saluted her progress toward Washington that day. The body she carried was brought to lie in state in the Rotunda of the Capitol in Washington, DC, where it remained with an honor guard for the night. The solemn ceremony accompanying the arrival of the remains had been, as the press reported, brief, involving only the president, Warren Harding, his wife, General Pershing, and a few other military dignitaries. The next day, however, the clouds cleared and, after the formal laying of official wreaths, the crowds arrived to pay their respects. This was, the *New York Times* reported, a veritable "river of humanity, American men, women and children, Americans by heritage, Americans by election," that "flowed as the life blood of the

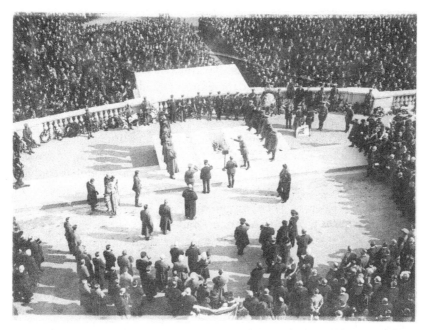

FIGURE 9.1. Crowds at the burial ceremony of the Unknown Soldier in Arlington (1921). Image courtesy of the Library of Congress Prints and Photographs Division (LC-USZ6–1754).

nation itself – a slow but overwhelming torrent of humanity, gathered to attest the valor of America's dead in France."

The following day – Armistice Day – the Unknown Soldier was interred in Arlington Cemetery, where his burial, as the president reminded the audience, was "rather more than a sign of the Government's favour, it is a suggestion of a tomb in the heart of the nation" (Figure 9.1). Arlington represented nothing less than the final resting place for the "armed exponents of the nation's conscience," whose task it had most recently been to fight a new kind of war, one that was "no longer a conflict in chivalry, no more a test of militant manhood," but simple "cruel, deliberate, scientific destruction."[1]

At the center of the solemn ceremonials, therefore, lay the even more sobering idea that at the heart of the nation lay a tomb. It should be remembered that such rhetoric, one that modern audiences are all-too used to, was not yet, in 1921, familiar to Americans. On the one hand, the notion of the "heroic dead" was hardly alien to a nation barely five years beyond its Civil War semicentennial; on the other hand, the extreme destruction of World War I lent more contemporary credence than hindsight affords us to the belief that, like America's Civil War, the Great War was somehow an aberration, a madness from which mankind had emerged wounded but wiser. To Americans who witnessed it, the burial of the Unknown Soldier therefore marked an end rather than a beginning. They believed, as Harding promised, that "no such sacrifice shall be asked again."

Of course that was not to be. The ceremonies attending this most famous symbol of America's sacrifice certainly represented an end and a beginning, but not the end of American involvement in global conflict, rather the beginning of what would become a far greater engagement with the world and its wars. There was no rush, however – quite the opposite. Shocked by World War I, America famously retreated, if not exactly into isolation, then certainly into a reluctance to acknowledge, let alone shoulder, its new world role. This reluctance was partly born of distaste at having been, as some Americans saw it, dragged into a war in which the nation's actions, although decisive to the war's outcome, had nevertheless not been dominant. At the same time, the burial of the Unknown Soldier held special resonance in a nation many of whose war dead had not come home. The American war cemeteries of Europe offered evidence enough that the nation had left at least a part of itself behind; the internment of French soil with the unknown warrior himself – specially brought from Suresnes Cemetery – reaffirmed a link between the Old World and the New that World War I had not forged but had, in the most tragic way, reinforced.

The fact that American losses in World War I amounted to some 1 percent of the total casualties from that conflict did not mean that the postwar period in the United States was necessarily any easier for Americans than for Europeans. Progressive-era America had been about the establishment of order above all things, an order that had been threatened by the war. Post-Revolutionary America, indeed, had arguably always been about the establishment of order in the face of potential chaos, the construction of a nation out of individual states, the military defeat of sectional forces, the making of an American out of an immigrant, and, above all, the forging of a unified nationalism out of many conflicting class, state, and racial loyalties. This last continued to exercise imaginations and inspire concern. The crowds that flocked to Arlington in November 1921 to listen to their president talk of a "world awakened" by the selfless sacrifice of the Unknown Soldier had just lived through one of the worst periods of domestic unrest and racial violence that the nation had yet seen.

Beginning in the summer of 1919 – "Red Summer" – in cities across the nation, including Washington itself, hysteria mounted and American turned on American in a frenzy of fear-inspired fury, driven in part by the "Red Scare" that followed the Russian Revolution and the formation of the Third International in March 1919. The belief that the forces of socialism, if not anarchy, had been unleashed on a vulnerable postwar world, further fueled by industrial unrest within America itself, translated the wartime rhetoric of freedom onto a new language of legislation as the sole means through which that freedom could be secured. In effect, the war-induced upsurge of intensive patriotism, coupled with the fear of radical forces operating within America, produced an intolerant atmosphere that transformed fear of extremists into a form of extremism itself. Much of this was relatively short-lived and, as the case of jailed socialist leader Eugene Debs showed, did not long outlast the war. Some of it was a touch bizarre, most notably the court case *United States vs. The Spirit of '76* that indicted a film producer for attempting to release an anti-British film – entitled *The Spirit of '76* (1917) – but equally brief. Indeed, the film in question, which was certainly overtly anti-British, fell back into favor after the war when American audiences proved more receptive to its sentiments.

Other Supreme Court decisions, notably *Schenck vs. United States* (1919), upheld the legality of the Espionage Act from First Amendment (free speech) challenge. The defendant, Charles Schenck, Secretary of the Socialist Party, was charged with distributing antidraft leaflets. The then-Associate Chief Justice Oliver Wendell Holmes, Jr. argued that the right to free speech may not hold in times of conflict. "The question," he argued, was "whether the words used are used in such circumstances and are of such a nature as to create a clear and present danger.... When a nation is at war," Holmes ruled, "many things that might be said in time of peace are such a hindrance to its effort that their utterance will not be endured so long as men fight."[2] The real danger here was the legal weight this case lent to the idea that an internal challenge of any kind might in itself constitute "clear and present danger" to the United States. American reaction to domestic dissent could at times function as a form of low-level, undeclared warfare in its own right; and in any case, the twentieth century hardly provided the United States with many years when it did not field men and women in uniform.

The most notorious case to emerge from the "Red Scare" syndrome was that of anarchists Nicola Sacco and Bartolomeo Vanzetti. Sacco and Vanzetti, both Italian immigrants, were charged with armed robbery and murder in Massachusetts in May 1920. Their subsequent trial split the nation, and their execution by electric chair in 1927 attracted worldwide condemnation. Although later ballistic evidence – not available until the 1960s – suggested that the fatal shots had, in fact, resulted from Sacco's gun, contemporary opinion believed the evidence too flimsy to secure a safe conviction and the judge too biased against immigrants and radicals to provide one. Sacco and Vanzetti were readily positioned as victims of a class war, symbols of a divided nation. The novelist John Dos Passos expressed the sentiments of many when he drew the distinction he did, in *The Big Money* (1936), between the "old judges the small men with reputations" and the crowds whom they "clubbed... off the streets," between "the beaten crowd" and the "oppressors" of America. "America our nation has been beaten by strangers who have turned our language inside out who have taken the clean words our fathers spoke and made them slimy and foul," Dos Passos charged, before concluding "all right we are two nations."[3]

The "two nations" notion did not, of course, originate with Dos Passos, nor indeed with British prime minister Benjamin Disraeli whose novel *Sybil, or the Two Nations* (1845) popularized the term for the nineteenth and early twentieth centuries. The origin of the idea of permanent division between the two nations of the rich and poor respectively can be traced back to Plato's *The Republic*, but the power of Dos Passos's assertion lay in the fact that, in the American republic, no such divisions had been anticipated. America was supposed to be a new kind of republic, a republic of equality, of opportunity for all, exclusion for none, a civic nation that recognized no distinctions of race, religion, or class. Yet after World War I, America experienced a wave of labor strikes in cities from Seattle to Boston, and in industries from shipbuilding to steel. This caused many to equate labor with radicalism and to confuse the justifiable opposition to what were, in many cases, quite appallingly exploitative working conditions with an insidious socialist class consciousness that threatened the nation's stability.

In the case of Seattle, the 1919 strike spilled out from the shipyard where it had originated to bring the entire city to a standstill for a week. In Boston, law and order itself was threatened when nineteen policemen were fired for the crime of belonging to a union and the resultant walkout by their colleagues led, perhaps, unsurprisingly, to widespread looting and violence. A series of bomb threats beginning in the spring of that year against opponents of organized labor simply exacerbated an already tense situation. Attorney-General A. Mitchell Palmer responded by implementing what became known as "Palmer raids" against the unions and their supporters that continued into early 1920. Coordinated by the then-director of the Radical Division of the Justice Department, J. Edgar Hoover, the Palmer raids proved to be a step too far. By the end of 1920, Americans had had enough. The "Red Scare" specter appeared less terrifying in the cold light of the dawn of a new decade and the possibility of a new presidency. The explosion of a bomb in the heart of Wall Street in September of 1920 shocked Americans, certainly, but it no longer sent them rushing to check for Reds under their beds.

Although fear is frequently a powerful political and fiscal weapon, and one America's leaders would wield again, no population can remain in a heightened state of tension indefinitely. No more can any population sustain a continuous demand for reform. With its multitude of programs, progressivism was, in many senses, quite exhausting, and Wilson's campaign for the League of Nations seemed to promise even greater global responsibilities on top of those at home. It was therefore with some relief that Americans listened to Ohioan Senator Warren Harding argue that their nation's "present need is not heroics but healing, not nostrums but normalcy, not surgery but serenity," and promise them "not experiment but equipoise, not submergence in internationality but sustainment in triumphant nationality."[4]

Harding frequently spoke like this. Although it sounded impressive, what it meant in practice once he became president was rather less than the sum of the statement itself. Normalcy in action translated into a toned-down progressive program that dismantled, to a great extent, many of the restrictions of the wartime state, supported enterprise, introduced tax cuts to stimulate business, and sought to improve working conditions by, for example, pushing for an eight-hour workday, long the demand of the labor unions and their members. Harding's sudden death in 1923 brought Calvin Coolidge to the helm, but as far as Coolidge's policies went, it was business as usual. Coolidge, indeed, famously remarked that "the chief business of the American people is business." And in the 1920s, it certainly was.

The 1920s was a decade of unparalleled expansion and innovation for the United States. Measured purely in terms of the gross national product (GNP), which rose from $72.4 billion in 1919 to $104 billion in 1929, the American market was booming. Some of that growth was architectural; for many businesses, skyscrapers catered both to egos and economics, and they soon became one of the defining features of the American cityscape and a symbol of a nation quite literally going up in the world

FIGURE 9.2. Empire State Building, New York City. View of Chrysler Building and Queensboro Bridge, low viewpoint. This 1932 photograph was taken from the top of the Empire State Building, New York City, which had been completed the previous year. It was the tallest building in the world at that time. From it Americans could look out on a modernist cityscape that reflected the engineering expertise and economic might of New York, which then, as now, often symbolized the nation as a whole. The Art Deco building in the center of the photograph is the Chrysler Building; completed in 1930, it held the title of world's tallest building for less than a year (but remains the most stunning building in New York). Photo created by Samuel H. Gottscho, January 19, 1932. Image courtesy of the Library of Congress Prints and Photographs Division (LC-G612-T01–17578).

(Figure 9.2). "There is an epic implication in man's defiance of the laws of gravity," enthused the architectural critic Sheldon Cheney, author of *The New World Architecture* (1930). "Perhaps," he mused, "commercialism is a new God, only too powerful and too appealing, to whom men are now building their highest and most laudatory structures."[5] America's metropolitan vision of 1925 was resolutely optimistic, driven by an architectural enthusiasm that predated World War I and appeared to take little account of that conflict. This was the America of the Panama-Pacific International Exposition of a decade previously, held in San Francisco to celebrate the completion of the canal. It was an exposition structured around "ideas of victory, achievement, progress and aspiration," and designed to showcase "the perfect co-operation of American architects, sculptors and painters."[6]

The construction boom was just the most obvious expression of this optimism and of the nation's new conspicuous industrial and domestic consumption. The 1920s introduced many of the trappings of the modern world that we now take for granted. Electric refrigerators, cookers, and irons were not yet the mass-produced commodities they are today, but they swiftly became so. Some 16 percent of Americans in 1912 had electricity in their homes, but by 1927, 63 percent of households could actually plug in their new appliances. Americans could, in theory, store their food in their new fridges, hygienically packed in newly invented plastic boxes. In practice, they were increasingly likely to eat tinned food, the use of which doubled between 1914 and 1929. They could use Bakelite ware for cooking (although its main use was in radio and telephone casings); and they could dress in a new man-made fabric, rayon (although this rather made the clothing iron redundant). They could quite literally tune in to their nation on the radio, because as radio sales soared, so radio stations came on air to inform and entertain this new market.

Outside the home, new highways were being built at a cost of more than $1 billion annually, along which Americans could drive in their increasingly affordable automobiles. The cost of a Ford Model-T had fallen from $805 in 1908 to $290 in 1925, which equates to about $3,500 in purchasing-power terms today. The speed of its manufacture had also increased. Ford's new assembly lines had reduced the time it took to construct a Model-T from some fourteen hours to just ninety-three minutes. And there were more than enough Americans waiting for these cars to roll off the factory floor. From approximately 9 million cars at the start of the decade, by its end there were some 27 million. At this level of growth, the car industry really did drive the American economy in the 1920s, not just in terms of private sales, but in the numbers of workers it employed both directly and indirectly in supporting industries such as steel, rubber, and oil. Other forms of transport also required these commodities, of course, but not yet to the same degree. Air transport remained the preserve of the wealthy, but it took off after Charles Lindbergh flew *The Spirit of St. Louis* from New York to Paris in 1927. By the end of the decade, approximately half a million Americans annually traveled by air.

If the ground beneath their feet – or tires – as well as the airspace above them was changing rapidly, nevertheless there were some depressing consistencies about Americans' lives in the 1920s. Most of the nation's leading industrialists, backed by government, battled the unions at every turn and sought to undo progressive legislation relating to child labor or women's wages. Some businessmen went to extreme lengths to protect their particular employment practices. Car manufacturer Henry Ford, for one, kept his plant union-free via violence and intimidation, tactics distinctly at odds with the progressive vision of a workers' paradise that he promulgated for public consumption. Paid company spies ensured that Ford's workers adhered to a strict lifestyle line that Ford had drawn: no smoking or drinking, no sitting down for a rest break, houses had to be painted, lawns planted, children educated, all according to Ford's own, frequently contradictory notions of the ideal society. Ford, who had famously advised customers that they might have any color of car that they wanted "so long as it is black," by the 1920s insisted that his workers could also buy any car they wanted, so long as it was a Ford.

Yet Ford's fear of what his workforce might get up to if left to its own devices was little more than an extreme version of the progressive impulse toward control. Ford was, after all, operating in a nation that did not trust its population to drink responsibly, that had, in 1918, passed the Eighteenth Amendment, or National Prohibition Act (commonly known as the Volstead Act), which came into effect at the start of 1920 and remained in force until 1933 (Figure 9.3). Temperance, of course, had a long tradition in the United States, stretching back to the 1840s at least, and in the twentieth century, even before the Volstead Act was passed, several states had already banned the sale of intoxicating liquor. The decision to implement such a policy nationally derived from a combination of factors: by bringing into disrepute the product of German-American breweries, namely beer, World War I played its part, as did pressure from businessmen like Ford who wanted more disciplined – or rather wanted to discipline their – workforces. Yet the argument for prohibition mainly derived from social, religious, and political reformers whose fears of the city environment increasingly focused on saloons as ungodly sites of social decay and political machination.

One need not be an inveterate inebriate, however, to want a drink on occasion. Many Americans resented prohibition and sought to bypass the legislation any way they could. In this respect one of the achievements of the Volstead Act was the effective criminalization of a hitherto law-abiding component of the population. Furthermore, if the suppression of the social and political evils of the saloon was what temperance reformers had intended, prohibition proved a singularly unsuccessful means of securing this. Illicit stills, breweries, and bootlegging (the illegal

FIGURE 9.3. New York City Deputy Police Commissioner John A. Leach (right) overseeing agents pour liquor into a sewer following a police raid during Prohibition (c. 1921). Prohibition lasted in the United States until 1933, by which time the "wet" (as opposed to the "dry") lobby could plausibly argue that the brewing industry was an important element in the attempt at economic recovery following the Wall Street Crash of 1929 and subsequent Great Depression. The Twenty-First Amendment, passed in December 1933, repealed the Eighteenth Amendment and finally abolished prohibition. Image courtesy of the Library of Congress Prints and Photographs Division (LC-USZ62–123257).

distribution of, in this case, alcohol) became widespread. Cities such as New York and San Francisco saw a proliferation of "speakeasies," saloons that supposedly sold alcohol secretly, although in reality both their locations and activities were very much an open secret. The period of prohibition saw a doubling of saloons in New York alone; by 1929, there were some 32,000 of them.

The decade that perhaps its foremost author, F. Scott Fitzgerald, designated the "Jazz Age" thus became famous for an excess of drinking rather than widespread sobriety. Of course that was not all it became famous for. Certainly drinking and drink-related disease did decline in the 1920s, and there were fewer arrests for drunkenness, but overall crime increased rather than diminished in the absence of drink. Organized crime was not quite the kind of consumer control that temperance reformers had had in mind, of course, but even they could hardly deny that, in the 1920s, it became very well organized indeed.

The distribution of illegal liquor was the catalyst for an expanded network of tangential illegal activities, including gambling, drug manufacture and consumption, and prostitution, that focused on the speakeasies and exploited the fact that, having crossed the legal line as far as liquor was concerned, many customers could be induced to venture just that bit further beyond it. With the opportunity for profit that prohibition provided, city and government officials, law-enforcement agents, and judges were readily corrupted into complicity with the criminal gangs who had assumed control of the trade in alcohol, or intimidated into ignoring them altogether. This was a period that saw the rise of one of the most notorious gangsters of all, Al "Scarface" Capone, who established a brutally effective criminal empire in Chicago that, at its height, was turning over some $60 million annually. The extent of Capone's power was such that he felt it unnecessary, or perhaps unwise, to act discretely, and traveled around in an armor-plated Cadillac – naturally he had several – complete with outriders. For a decade he evaded the law and was eventually indicted in 1931 for, of all things, tax evasion.

Ultimately, both the contemporary and current fascination with Capone was that his seemed to be a very American story, the moral of which was that crime certainly does not pay, but only when the criminal in question neglects to pay his taxes. As an individual, Capone appeared to embody both the conformity and the rebellion that characterized the 1920s, and he certainly was in step with the nation's new business agenda. Indeed, the crime syndicates – and Capone's was only the best known – in some ways hardly deviated from legitimate business in the managerial and marketing side of their operations; the enforcement side of the equation was another matter entirely, of course. Ford may have deployed men with connections to the Detroit Mafia to ensure conformity with company policy, but the cost of noncompliance meant, at worst, temporary loss of livelihood, not permanent loss of life. The media glamor of the American gangster persists to this day, but in reality he represented yet one more source and symbol of fear at a time when Americans really had nothing to fear but fear itself; and yet, they were afraid.

Indeed, the designation of the 1920s as the Jazz Age or the Roaring Twenties disguises the strain that America was under in this decade, a strain that the exuberance of the period in part denied and in part was a natural reaction against. In many respects, Dos Passos's charge that America was "two nations" was a succinct summation of the situation, but the juxtaposition was not just between rich and poor, but between native and immigrant, black and white, male and female, criminal and law-abiding citizen, the city and the country, and to a great extent it focused on World War I.

Contemporary literature both responded to and informed these divisions. Writers such as Dos Passos, in *Three Soldiers* (1921), e. e. cummings, in *The Enormous Room* (1922), Ernest Hemingway, in *A Farewell to Arms* (1929), and T. S. Elliot in *The Waste Land* (1922) explored the disillusionment following the war directly. Others such as Sinclair Lewis, in *Main Street* (1920) and *Babbitt* (1922), F. Scott Fitzgerald in *This Side of Paradise* (1920) and *The Great Gatsby* (1926), and Thomas Wolfe in *Look Homeward, Angel* (1922) acknowledged the war indirectly in their focus on the alienation of the individual American in the brave new material world of the 1920s. Many of these writers were part of the loose collective known as the "Lost Generation," who found themselves in Paris in the aftermath of World War I. Viewing their nation from a distance, it was the personal struggle with essentially impersonal forces that they identified as the central motif of the age.

This was an age that had no use for such concepts as "glory, honor, courage," Hemingway observed, in an echo of Harding at Arlington. Such words, Hemingway proposed, had been rendered "obscene beside the concrete names of villages, the number of roads, the names of rivers, the numbers of regiments and the dates." Yet this loss of individuality was not something that could be ascribed to World War I alone. Industrialization was an increasingly impersonal force, and not simply in a literary or metaphorical way; it eroded the individualism of ability. The automobile industry in Detroit, for example, moved from employing a 75 percent skilled workforce in 1910 to a 10 percent skilled one ten years later. The burial of the Unknown Soldier in 1921 had positioned his anonymity as an emotive symbol of the nation, but for too many Americans, it was not war, but work, not armed conflict, but the advent of the assembly line that rendered them anonymous. They, too, were in a sense lost, but in the crowd, not in Paris. Such was the price of progress and, some feared, part of its meaning for America.

Blues Scale

Both Hemmingway and Harding posited a clear division between perceived traditional values and modernism that has come to define the cultural and social shift that World War I produced in Europe. At first glance, this seems hardly applicable to America, as buoyant as its economy and as vibrant as its culture was after 1921. Yet that culture was still driven, to a great extent, by America's disturbing dialectic of class and race. The latter, moreover, could no longer be consigned to "The South," however that was defined, mentally, morally, or on a map. It was a national debate. It always was, but before the twentieth century it had almost been possible to pretend otherwise. Not so after 1910. The "Great Migration" of African Americans out of the rural South between 1910 and the 1930s (well more than a million moved in the 1920s alone) and the subsequent growth of black communities in, among others, Detroit, Chicago, and New York merged with a new influx of immigrants from the West Indies and diversified an already eclectic social and cultural mix in the northern cities.

The new arrivals were sharply surprised by the extent of racism in the United States at that time. Southern migrants perhaps found it less surprising, but both groups encountered a bifurcated urban environment that was, for them, as it still was for many European migrants, economically exclusionary and sometimes overtly hostile. The reemergence of the Ku Klux Klan at this time (which purported to stand for American patriotism) was just one extreme example of the ways in which the economic buoyancy of the 1920s simultaneously brought America new opportunities and exacerbated old problems (Figure 9.4). In the context of the rise of "100 percent Americanism" and thanks to an aggressive and very modern marketing drive, the Klan expanded from some 5,000 members in 1920 to several million by the middle of the decade.

The Klan had also expanded its remit since its first incarnation in the post–Civil War period. In reaction to the tensions produced by immigration, progressivism, and World War I, it almost reached a point where it seemed inaccurate to accuse it of prejudice because it appeared to be opposed to everything and everyone and on any and all grounds, from racial to religious and all points in between. It also became a more urban-focused organization, partly in response to the migration of southerners, black and white, to the northern cities, especially those such as Detroit where there were employment opportunities in the burgeoning automobile industry. Yet the heartland of the Klan's influence was the

FIGURE 9.4. Ku Klux Klan parade, Washington, DC (Pennsylvania Avenue), September 13, 1926. Much of the symbolism associated with the KKK came from its second iteration in the early twentieth century, and through the kind of overt public displays such as the one pictured, positioning the KKK, visually at least, at the heart of the nation. By the time this demonstration of its "power" took place, however, the Klan was no longer the potent political force it had been at the start of the 1920s, although, clearly, not an entirely spent one either. Image courtesy of the Library of Congress Prints and Photographs Division (LC-USZ62–59666).

Midwest, and especially Indiana where it effectively controlled the Republican Party in that state. When Klan leader David C. Stephenson was convicted of the assault and second-degree murder of a young woman, Madge Oberholtzer, in 1925, however, and subsequently made public a list of prominent politicians and judges in the pay of the Klan in Indiana, its influence began to wane, at least politically.

Culturally it was a different story. The Klan had tapped into at least a portion of the *zeitgeist* of the 1920s in its opposition to immorality – broadly defined, but alcohol usually came into it – and to immigration. Largely it had exploited the inevitable tensions between the modern, business-driven, heterogeneous, and secular nation that America was becoming and the supposed traditional, family-oriented, homogeneous, and God-fearing one that it was popularly supposed to have been prior to World War I. The fact that America had never even approximated such a restricted and constricted nation was beside the point. Just as postwar Britain wallowed in a prewar fantasy built around the supposed stability and security of Edwardian England, so America invented for itself – not for the first time – a mythical history that bore absolutely no relation to the reality of its past but certainly influenced its future, which also involved a degree of invention – that of the ideal American.

The urge to define an American, and by extrapolation Americanism, could at least genuinely be described as an American tradition, stretching all the way back to Crèvecoeur's famous question in 1783: "What, then, is the American, this new man?" What the twentieth century brought to the debate, however, was a scientific and pseudoscientific perspective on what had hitherto been deemed a social and cultural process. As far as immigration was concerned, the 1920s saw new restrictions, based increasingly on the vague conception of race, come into force. The ideals of civic nationalism, the new nationalism first expounded by Crèvecoeur and refined by Roosevelt, were predicated on the rejection of what Crèvecoeur termed "ancient prejudices and manners" in favor of a "new mode of life."

In the 1920s, however, this became inflected – or perhaps infected – by something perilously close to a biological determinist interpretation of nationalism that rejected the notion of the ideal American as a "strange mixture of blood" and instead emphasized ethnic exclusiveness. This idea was most famously promulgated in a popular publication of the period, Madison Grant's *The Passing of the Great Race: The Racial Basis of European History* (1916). Grant, the president of the New York Zoological Society and a noted eugenicist, posited a "Nordic" superiority thesis that resonated with those already inclined toward an Anglo-Saxon perspective. In comparison to the reception of his ideas in interwar Europe, indeed, it is all the more remarkable that America proved relatively immune to the extremes of his argument, especially given that many of the nation's leaders were not.

There is a certain irony in the fact that Calvin Coolidge, while he was still vice-president, published what was in effect an anti-immigration diatribe in, of all places, *Good Housekeeping* magazine. Much of what he had to say here almost echoed Roosevelt's analysis of Americanization, but ultimately revealed Grant's pernicious influence. Immigrants must, Coolidge asserted, show "a capacity for assimilation" if they expected to be allowed "through the gates of liberty." Yet Coolidge did not believe that all peoples had this capacity. "There are racial considerations too grave to be brushed aside for any sentimental reasons," he argued. "Biological laws tell us that certain divergent people will not mix or blend. The Nordics propagate themselves successfully. With other races, the outcome shows deterioration on both sides. Quality of mind and body," he concluded, "suggests that observance of ethnic law is as great a necessity to a nation as immigration law." Exactly what spurious "biological laws" Coolidge had in mind was a mystery, but then he did seem to have confused the "gates of liberty" with those of heaven, so adamant was he that the "only acceptable immigrant is the one who can justify our faith in man by a constant revelation of the divine purpose of the Creator."[7]

Coolidge's secretary of labor, James J. Davis, held equally strong views on the subject of biological laws and immigration. Based on his belief in the tenacity – and superiority – of his Welsh heritage (he had migrated to the United States when he was eight), he concluded "that racial characteristics do not change. In letting immigrants into this country we must remember this." Dividing mankind into two animal types – beavers and rats – he moralized a message straight out of a children's storybook: that beavers build homes and store food, and rats move into the attic and steal it. "A civilisation rises," he sermonized, "when the beaver-men outnumber the rat-men.... Beware," he warned, "of breeding rats in America."[8]

Davis's views, however unusual they seem today, were simply a metaphorical mutation of the fear expressed by many of America's legislators at that time, whose great and growing terror was that the nation was on the verge of being swamped by undesirable aliens. Absent the optimistic assumption that any new arrivals might be Americanized, and in the context of the concerns induced by the crime statistics, many concurred with Indiana Congressman Fred S. Purnell that there was "'little or no similarity between the clear-thinking, self-governing stocks that sired the American people and this stream of irresponsible and broken wreckage that is pouring into the lifeblood of America the social and political diseases of the Old World."⁹ In 1921, Congress had passed emergency legislation to restrict the number of migrants from Southern and Eastern Europe and subsequently engaged in debating the desirability of permanent restriction.

The debate was heavily informed by eugenicist assumptions. It called as its expert witness Harry H. Laughlin, director of the Eugenics Record Office and a vocal advocate of what was termed "eugenical sterilization," an extreme variant of the progressive impulse toward improvement of America's population. "The matter of segregating, sterilizing, or otherwise rendering non-reproductive the degenerate human strains in America is," Laughlin argued, "in accordance with the spirit of our institutions." If "the human breeding stock in our population is to be purged of its defective parenthood," he proposed, then the federal government must be prepared "to enforce laws which take on the appearance of racial discrimination but which," he stressed, "would not be such." Ultimately, the "immigration policy of the eugenicist, who has at heart the preservation, upbuilding and specialization of our better family stocks," Laughlin advised, "is to base the criterion for admission of would-be immigrants primarily upon the possession of sterling natural qualities, regardless of race, language, or present social or economic condition."¹⁰

With this new emphasis on breeding and on biological laws, the message that was coming from the top in the 1920s was that the ideal American was born, not made. Coolidge and Davis both emphasized the importance of education in building the nation, but simultaneously argued that some ethnicities could never be educated into the American way. Exclusion, then, was the only safe solution, and the 1924 Immigration Act secured it. Extending the Emergency Quota Act of 1921, it set a lower quota on the number of immigrants permitted to enter the United States based on their national origins; in theory, this was 2 percent of the population from each nation resident prior to 1890 – in other words, before Eastern European immigration increased – although there were no limits on those emigrating from Latin America and a complete ban on those from the Asian nations. From an asylum for the oppressed, America, with this single act, transformed itself into a glorified gated community; the city on a hill now had very high walls indeed, as befitted a sanctuary of Anglo-Saxon values. That, at least, was the theory.

In practice, this closing of the "Golden Door" came too late. For some, this seemed to presage the nation's destruction, but it was, in the end, its salvation. Without a doubt, the Klan marching through the heart of the capital hardly offered an edifying example of a nation supposedly predicated on the belief that all men are created equal; but nor was it an American variant of the Nuremberg Rallies. It is crucial to remember that in the same year that America finally slammed shut its hitherto open-door policy, it also passed the Indian Citizenship Act (1924) that finally recognized Native-American voting rights. This was no panacea as far as settler-Native relations were concerned, because as a right devolved to individual states, it was not fully implemented until 1948. Nevertheless, it did highlight the rising interest in the distinctiveness of "minority" cultures, which was beginning to supplant the melting-pot ideal of a nationalism predicated on assimilation.

By the mid-1920s, America was already too diverse ethnically and culturally, too grounded in a democratic civic ideal that emphasized equality for all, and too wedded to republicanism as the means through which to achieve this to be wholly susceptible to the arguments of men such as Grant or Laughlin, or to follow, to its logical conclusion, their eugenicist agenda. This is not to say that some states did not head off down that road; they did.

Several states already had laws on their statute books that allowed for the involuntary sterilization of the insane (but insanity was hardly an unproblematic diagnosis even then, and in the case of women was too often synonymous with simply being sexually active outside of marriage). In 1927, the Supreme Court validated the constitutionality of this legislation in *Buck vs. Bell*, a case brought to test Virginia's Eugenical Sterilisation Act (1924). Supreme Court Justice Oliver Wendell Holmes, Jr. observed that it would be "better for all the world, if instead of waiting to execute degenerate offspring for crime, or to let them starve for their imbecility, society can prevent those who are manifestly unfit from continuing their kind," before upholding the act and concluding: "Three generations of imbeciles are enough."[11]

Involuntary sterilization – in the end, more than 60,000 Americans were sterilized under this program – was in many respects yet one more facet of the political predisposition toward enforced conformity, moral, medical, and mental, in this period. Prohibition and the forcible prevention of pregnancy were just the extremes of a spectrum of racial, religious, and cultural conservatism that ran from restrictions on gambling, on birth-control advice and contraception, to literature, textbook, theater, and film censorship. Ultimately it was about control and it was about free-dom, in both a positive and negative sense. The perspective of the contro-versial birth-control advocate Margaret Sanger, founder of the American Birth Control League (ABCL) in 1921, provides a case in point here. On the one hand, her drive to free women from the burden of perpetual pregnancies, and the horrific deaths that frequently followed backstreet abortions, was intended to relieve suffering. On the other, the eugeni-cist arguments that she proposed, arguments that chimed with those of Justice Holmes, sometimes shifted the emphasis from the positive freedom to choose for oneself to the negative freedom to impose one's own beliefs on others. An extreme example of where this logic could lead occurred in Dayton, Tennessee, in 1925. Here religious fundamentalists took, in effect, the eugenicist lobby's argument that Americans were born and not made and applied it to evolution.

The "Scopes Trial" (sometimes termed the "Monkey Trial") focused on a Tennessee high-school biology instructor, John T. Scopes, and on his right to teach his pupils about Charles Darwin's *On the Origin of Species*. As with *Buck vs. Bell*, this was a test case, brought by the American Civil Liberties Union (ACLU) to challenge the state's "Butler Act," which stipulated only the Biblical version of the creation of man (the Butler Act did not apply either to animals or plants) be taught in the public schools. The trial was a national sensation – it could even be followed via the radio – in part because William Jennings Bryan was called as the expert witness for the antievolutionists. Yet it was not because of Bryan's presence but in spite of it that the constitutionality of the Butler Act was upheld (and not repealed until 1967). Scopes was found guilty, but Bryan's less than convincing performance in the courtroom, and his death only a few days after the trial ended, rather deflated antievolutionist enthusiasm. Scopes's conviction was overturned the following year on a technicality (the fine imposed – $100 – was too high) but the main point, that the Butler Act did not contravene the First Amendment's separation of Church and State, was upheld.

Both contemporary and subsequent representations of the Scopes Trial (a film loosely based on it, *Inherit the Wind*, appeared in 1960, starring Spencer Tracy and Gene Kelly) tended to portray it as a comical circus sideshow that did little more than entertain, if not thoroughly embarrass, large swathes of the nation. The court itself, indeed, in the subsequent appeal, *Stokes vs. State* (1926), even referred to it as "this bizarre case." Yet given that the antievolution impulse remains a potent force in parts of America to this day, it was perhaps rather more than that. Certainly the Scopes Trial was a product of its period, one in which the forces of tradition clashed with those of the modern secular state. It was in some respects a clash of faiths, between God and science, but it was also a product of fear: fear of crime, of immigrants, of the city, of excess of any kind, and, above all, of challenge and change. That a small town in Tennessee might feel itself to be not just out of step with but threatened by mainstream culture revealed just some of the pressures the nation was under, as well as the persistence of the urban/rural divide in America.

When not tuning in to events in Dayton, Tennessee, American city dwellers, especially New Yorkers, had plenty of entertainment to distract them from the trials of smalltown life, and from their own. Indeed, the image of the Roaring Twenties was, and remains, a coastal one. Popular representations of the Jazz Age tend to locate it in New York, in a slightly different variant, California, and – with the exception of Chicago – nowhere in between. It is perhaps true that no city exemplified the optimistic side of the 1920s more than New York, which seemed to offer, as it always had, both a haven from and an entry into a broader world. New York's Harlem, for example, had housed immigrant families for decades. It had gone from being predominantly Irish to mainly Jewish, but in the 1920s it became the locus of the African-American community and the cultural surge that was known as the "Harlem Renaissance." African-American culture did not, of course, originate in New York in the 1920s, but the city served as a prism through which its many rays, musical, literary, and political, could be burned into mainstream and hitherto mainly white culture. From Harlem, many of the leading black scholars and writers of the day, including jazz poet and author of *The Weary Blues* (1926) Langston Hughes and anthropologist and author Zora Neale Hurston, found their way to a national audience.

The musical accompaniment to all this activity, whether in the clubs of New York or nationally, in clubs, speakeasies, and via the increasingly ubiquitous radio, was, of course, jazz, in all its many permutations. Popularly identified as the sound of the South in the northern city, jazz was the ultimate metaphor for America in this period, in its individual sound and in its improvisational structure, in its energy as dance music, and its influence, most notably via George Gershwin's *Rhapsody in Blue* (1924), on what was perceived to be mainstream "classical" compositions. Jazz may have begun as African American, but it evolved into a uniquely American form of musical expression. Yet jazz was just one element in the Jazz Age. It provided the soundtrack to the new modernity, but the era's popular image was recorded for posterity by Hollywood. From silent films such as *The Plastic Age* (1925), starring Clara Bow, the first and most famous "flapper," to the first full-length "talky," *The Jazz Singer* (1927), starring Al Jolson, America's by now established and expanding film industry both entertained contemporary audiences and informed – although not necessarily with any degree of accuracy – future ones about the '*The Mad Whirl*' (another film, from 1924) that was America in the 1920s.

With approximately 50 million Americans (about half the population) regularly attending the movies in the early 1920s, and more than 80 million by the decade's end, print capitalism had been transformed into popular entertainment. The nation's "imagined community" had come of age, but what kind of imaginings Hollywood induced was a moot point. Because the film industry then, as now, preferred to portray the young and the beautiful, the popular message America sent itself, and by extrapolation the world, was one of youth and vigor, energy and economic excess. Yet not a few Americans concurred with Scott Fitzgerald's description of the Jazz Age generation as *The Beautiful and Damned* (1922). And they were especially concerned about Hollywood.

When it came to selling sex and celebrity culture, Hollywood started as it meant to go on, but the adverse publicity resulting from several high-profile scandals prompted it into self-censorship before the government could get to it. The Hays Code (named for former Postmaster General Will H. Hays), introduced in 1922, was intended to prevent films from portraying anything likely to offend the moral sensibilities of the audience. It recommended that, among other potentially reprehensible acts, representations of homosexuality, interracial relationships, nudity, excessive kissing, and adultery should not appear on the silver screen.

The Hays Code notwithstanding, Hollywood, inevitably, presented no more than a mask of American modernity, particularly as far as women were concerned. American audiences soon became used to a steady diet of beautiful young women, frequently challenging convention – within proscribed limits – from Greta Garbo in *Love* (1927) and *Anna Karenina* (1935) to Bette Davis in *Jezebel* (1938). Such escapism became more than ever popular during the Depression of the 1930s, but it was escapism, especially for women whose lives did not resemble those they saw on screen, nor ever were likely to (possibly something of a relief, given the themes of many early films). The continuing emphasis on the woman as the moral heart of the home had hardly changed from the start of the century (Figure 9.5), and rather contradicted the flapper stereotype of the fast-living, hard-drinking, and chain-smoking young woman of the 1920s who, despite the drinking and smoking, nevertheless managed to dance the night away in a manner quite likely to break the bounds of the Hays Code.

It was not, of course, just the reality of women's lives that bore little resemblance to the on-screen or popular media representations of the Jazz Age. It may have been the case that some 40 percent of American families owned a radio by 1930, but that left 60 percent without one. America's wealth was hardly evenly distributed, and more than 70 percent of the population earned less than what at that time was considered the minimum liveable wage – $2,500 per year. The gulf between the "two nations" of urban and rural, rich and poor, was widening even as options were reducing. Car manufacturing was a case in point. Roads, the leisure time to drive down them, and the wages needed to buy cars were all on the increase. Car manufacturing, however, was almost wholly restricted to only three companies, Ford, General Motors, and Chrysler. Yet no one was concerned. Although both his employment practices and his vituperative anti-Semitism had somewhat tarnished his public image, Ford remained a national – indeed an international – hero, a symbol of the successful application of the American assembly line. Management-speak had a new concept, *Fordism*, shorthand for standardization and its resultant productive efficiency. *Fordism*, indeed, became synonymous with *Americanism* as the economic model of the future, a future of consumer confidence and ever-growing economic power.

When, in 1929, Ford organized a celebration of another kind of power, that of the light bulb – and the opening of his own Edison Institute of Technology – it was an occasion for optimism. The newly elected president, Herbert Hoover, attended, and delivered a rousing speech (streamed live to the nation by radio). Scientific research, Hoover declared, "is one of the most potent impulses to progress. It provided "better standards of living, more stability of employment, lessened toil, lengthened human life, and decreased suffering. In the end," he asserted, "our leisure expands, our interest in life enlarges, our vision stretches. There is more joy in life." Above all, Hoover enthused, Thomas Edison had "converted the pure physics of electricity into a taxable product."[12] Just three days after this confident prediction of the economic benefits of scientific and social rationality, America's stock market crashed, plunging the nation – and with it the rest of the world – into the economic meltdown of the Great Depression.

THE above cut represents a beautiful little girl at seven—as pure as a sunbeam—she comes from a fine Christian family. Going to the left you see her at thirteen reading "Sapho," a vile novel that was suppressed several years ago in New York—it had a bad effect on our model little girl; at nineteen *Flirting and Coquetry;* third stage, a step lower; at twenty-six, *Fast Life and Dissipation*—this tells the sad story; at forty she is *an outcast*—the miserable result of *Social Impurity.*

To the right we have a brighter picture—at thirteen, *Study and Obedience;* next a young lady in church—*Virtue and Devotion;* at twenty-six—*A Loving Mother* – a most inspiring and lovely scene; at sixty—*An Honored Grandmother.*

FIGURE 9.5. This illustration appeared in Prof. And Mrs John W. Gibson, *Social Purity: or, The Life of the Home and Nation* (New York: J L Nichols, 1903). It showed the two possible paths on offer to the seven-year-old sunbeam, pictured top-center. On the left, a combination of inappropriate (French) literature has set her on the slippery slope to social exclusion; on the right, more uplifting reading matter and regular church attendance has secured her stable future. Given that

Brave New World

In 1925, New Yorkers could contemplate the possible future of both commercialism and construction in an exhibition, "The Titan City: A Pictorial Prophesy of New York, 1926–2006." Here the city was imagined as a futuristic metropolis, but not the dystopian version envisaged by German filmmaker Fritz Lang only two years later (in *Metropolis*, 1927). America's metropolis was a streamlined, high-rise world, an ordered world, made to order for the New World peoples. For a nation so consistently at odds with the very idea of the city, one still haunted by Thomas Jefferson's Arcadian vision, this represented a substantial shift in perspective on the city, on the nation, and on American values.

This vision of physical upward mobility was also a symbol of a fundamental social and demographic shift. Whereas the 1920s celebrated conspicuous consumption in the cities, in the rural areas, farmers still struggled, quite literally left behind as the nation rushed toward urban living with its canned foods and household conveniences, its cinemas, saloons, and skyscrapers. At the start of the twentieth century, more than half of America's population lived in rural communities of less than 2,500; by 1930, a little more than 40 percent did. That did, of course, still leave a fair number in the rural environment, but it was indicative of a trend, expressed most obviously architecturally, that privileged centralization over decentralization, the city over the small town, the urban/industrial economy over the agrarian one.

In the face of the stock market crash, cinema audiences were directed to this vision once again in a now almost forgotten comedy, *Just Imagine* (1930), set in a 1980s skyscraper cityscape. Despite its deliberate levity,

←――

FIGURE 9.5 *(continued)* the girl in question would have been in her early twenties when the "Roaring Twenties" took off, the left-hand side of the equation was a real risk; at least that was popularly supposed to be the persistent fear of parents across America. In reality, the sunbeam stood a higher chance of getting divorced than her mother had, and was likely to produce fewer children of her own (birthrates fell from just below 30 percent in 1920 to just above 20 percent by 1930). She would also have a far broader range of potential jobs open to her, and although most of these were in either offices or hospitals, not all were. This was the period, after all, when Amelia Earhart first took to the skies, crossing the Atlantic (accompanied) the year after Lindbergh (1928) and repeating the feat solo in 1932. Although the cost of a plane was beyond most women, nevertheless, by the end of the 1920s, more than 10 million of them went out to work. Image courtesy of the Library of Congress Prints and Photographs Division (LC-DIG-ppmsca-02925).

the film hinted at the downside to a utopia where people had become numbers and life was controlled by committee. This dystopian specter of mankind's future, which had been raised before, in novels dating all the way back to Voltaire's *Candide* (1759), emerged most graphically in 1932, in Aldous Huxley's *Brave New World*.

Huxley's novel was set in a futuristic London, not New York, but a London that dated from 1908, when the first Model-T was produced. In this A.F. (After Ford) era, the "principle of mass production" had been "applied to biology," and the resultant population, scientifically separated into Alphas and Betas, Gammas and Epsilons, amused themselves by attending the "feelies" (rather than the "talkies") and looking back with a faint indulgence at the foolishness of their founder's own lifetime when people were allowed to play games that did "nothing whatever to increase consumption." That was about as far as their interest in the past went, because the motto of this brave new world was Ford's famous charge that "History is bunk." This was a civilization that had no need for the past and "absolutely no need of nobility or heroism," not because World War I had rendered such concepts either obsolete or obscene, but because they were deemed "symptoms of political inefficiency."

Despite its overt critique of Fordism (and indeed of Ford), Huxley's novel worked on several levels as far as utopian ideals went, and was no simplistic attack on the United States as such. Nevertheless, the immediate context both of its composition and its reception was the explosion, or implosion, of the republican experiment's economic dream. On "Black Tuesday" (October 29, 1929), America's markets lost some $14 billion in a single day, $30 billion by the week's end. These figures are staggering enough in themselves, but in the context of today, the equivalent would be (and as it turned out in 2008, pretty much was) around $170 billion and $360 billion, respectively.

The markets remained in freefall for the next three years. In that time, prices fell (by some 40 percent) as unemployment rose (to around 14 million), and the value of shares continued their seemingly relentless downward spiral. Shares in U.S. Steel, for example, fell from $262 in 1929 to $22 in 1932, the company's workforce from some 225,000 to precisely zero. Banks across the world collapsed as their customers rushed to withdraw their savings, fearful that the gold standard would not (as indeed it could not) sustain this sudden surge. As William Jennings Bryan had warned, mankind was, metaphorically, being crucified on a cross of gold. This was a global disaster, but in America it seemed that much worse because of the consumer, construction and commercial confidence that had characterized the 1920s. It was precisely this, however, that had, in part at least, prompted the crash. The optimistic assumption that the nation was, in economic as in social terms, moving ever onward and upward produced an overenthusiasm for production that outran the nation's capacity for consumption.

Yet the problem was only partly America's inequalities of wealth. The main issue was equality of expectation. With a population – indeed, an international market – that believed it could buy or borrow its way into the American dream, and too many banks prepared to service that sentiment via a combination of low-interest rates and unsecured lending, to other nations as well as to domestic customers, America fast reached a point where the stock market itself, and not the industries whose stocks were being traded, became the economic driver of the nation. America was, in effect, trading only on faith. So when the bubble burst, it was not just money that was lost – it was morale. It was not just finance that failed, but faith in America as a nation whose population had, as Hoover told them when elected in 1928, "reached a higher degree of comfort and security than ever existed before in the history of the world." "Through liberation from widespread poverty," he asserted, "we have reached a higher degree of individual freedom than ever before," and on the back of this freedom "are steadily building a new race – a new civilization great in its own attainments."[13]

Hoover's response to the monetary crisis that made a mockery of his confidence in American credit – material and moral – was to stand firm on the principles he had espoused during his election campaign. He turned to private charities and state authorities to alleviate the worst effects of job losses, seeking voluntary cooperation between employers and the workforces that they could no longer afford to employ. He continued to adhere to the Republican Party creed that America's strength lay in what he termed the "rugged individualism" of its citizens. Americans, Hoover believed, were "in an extraordinary degree self-sustaining," and would soon "lead the march of prosperity" once again. He dismissed Democratic calls for greater federal intervention with the argument that economic "depression cannot be cured by legislative action or executive pronouncement. Economic wounds must be healed by the action of the cells of the economic body – the producers and consumers themselves." Federal intervention was, Hoover concluded, not just wrong but fundamentally at odds with the American way.[14]

Given that America had clearly lost its way, such a response was inadequate at best, and interpreted by some as insensitive at worst. Federal relief to corporations was, eventually, forthcoming, under the auspices of the Reconstruction Finance Corporation (RFC), but the assumption remained that individual Americans would benefit indirectly from this aid. Direct federal support for the people, it was still believed, was a dangerous step toward socialism. And yet as the depression dragged on, it was clear that more than the traditional invocation of American individualism was needed. When more than 20,000 veterans marched on Washington in early 1932, demanding the payment of a bonus promised them for service in World War I, the disproportionate response on the part of the government revealed how wide the fissure between the leaders and the American people had become. General Douglas MacArthur dispersed the veterans with guns, tanks, and tear gas; not a move designed to bring an already desperate nation on side and, for the Republicans, hardly the best course of action in an election year.

Even putting this outburst of violence against veterans aside, the election of a Democrat in 1932 was, given the circumstances, perhaps inevitable. The Democrat in question, Franklin Delano Roosevelt (FDR), in a phrase that would come to define not just his presidency but a new political and social direction for America, promised a "new deal for the American people." This was not, of course, the first deal that they had been offered by a Roosevelt. The previous President Roosevelt (in fact, a distant cousin of the new president) had promised the nation a "square deal," in the sense that it would square the circle between labor and capital, natural resources and industrial requirements, corporation and consumer. It fell now to the new Roosevelt to try and recapture that idealism of an earlier age, to furnish a "New Deal," one informed, as it now had to be, by some unwelcome economic and social developments since Theodore Roosevelt's time.

Roosevelt could, at times, sound pessimistic in his appraisal of the problems America faced in the 1930s. "A glance at the situation today," he suggested in an early campaign speech, "only too clearly indicates that equality of opportunity as we have known it no longer exists.... Our last frontier has long since been reached, and there is practically no more free land." And land, as Roosevelt understood, had long been both a practical and a psychological "safety valve" for the American people; the West, in particular, he proposed, sounding rather like the first Roosevelt, had represented a sanctuary "to which those thrown out of work by the Eastern economic machines can go for a new start." All that had gone. "We are not able to invite the immigration from Europe to share our endless plenty," he observed, and worse, all America could offer was "a drab living" for its own population. The time had come, Roosevelt asserted, for "a re-appraisal of values."

In fact, what Roosevelt was offering was not a reappraisal of values as such, but more a reassertion of first principles. The president who would do so much to shape the future of the nation was especially adroit at using the past to pull his proposals, and the population, together. To calm fears that some kind of socialist state was on the Democratic agenda, Roosevelt invoked the Revolution as a time when the threat from government prompted change; now, he argued, it was "economic units" that posed the threat. These simply needed to be overhauled, he suggested, not overthrown entirely. Government had now to "assist the development of an economic declaration of rights, an economic constitutional order" designed "not to hamper individualism but to protect it." In that sense, what Roosevelt summed up as "the new terms of the old social contract" simply required a reassertion of faith: "Faith in America, faith in our institutions, faith in ourselves demands" he stressed, the belief that Americans could create "the apparent Utopia which Jefferson imagined for us in 1776."[15] Ultimately, what Roosevelt did was to throw down the Revolutionary gauntlet; a traditional way of making any point stick in American politics. Faith was what he invoked; the faith of the nation's Founding Fathers.

Yet beyond the belief that, with some help, the American ship of state might right itself, the new president had no blueprint for Utopia in mind. Consequently the New Deal was more evolutionary than revolutionary. It comprised a combination of sometimes contradictory legislation and widespread public-works programs – often divided by historians into the New Deal and, after 1935, the Second New Deal – whose intentions were twofold: short-term economic recovery and longer-term economic and social reform. It also witnessed the emergence of what came to be called the New Deal "coalition," the combination of organized labor with voting groups that, until the advent of the New Deal, were more usually at odds: southern white with northern black, rural Protestant with urban Catholic and Jewish, minorities with intellectuals. This coalition changed the face of American party politics; perhaps most notably it switched African Americans away from the Republican Party – the party of Lincoln, of emancipation – and toward the Democrats, where they would by and large remain.

In a larger sense, the New Deal represented the second of three major transformative shifts in American social and political development, shifts effected by the expanded power of the federal state. The first occurred as a result of Union victory in the Civil War in the nineteenth century, not just in the growth of central state authority during and after that conflict, but specifically in regard to the so-called Reconstruction amendments, the Thirteenth, Fourteenth, and Fifteenth amendments to the Constitution that eradicated slavery, defined citizenship, and established voting rights, together providing a powerful judicial reinterpretation of freedom. The third consisted in the equal rights legislation enacted during the "Second Reconstruction" in the 1960s. The bridge between them was the New Deal that sought to extend the power of the central state to secure a further extension of the idea of freedom: freedom from poverty, economic security, equal opportunity for all.

Although it began with the Emergency Banking Act, at the heart of the "first" New Deal's economic program lay the National Industrial Recovery Act (1933) that created a National Recovery Administration (NRA) under which commerce, rather as it had been under the remit of the War Industries Board established during World War I, could be organized and controlled (membership was voluntary, although strongly encouraged), but this time in the name of a war on poverty. Additional agencies, each with its own specific remit, soon followed.

The Agricultural Adjustment Act (AAA) addressed the problem of falling farm prices by restricting production, offering farmers compensation if they limited their output. This did have the desired effect of raising farm prices, but also the undesirable one of the eviction of many sharecroppers and poorer tenant farmers from land that was no longer cost-effective to farm; they were left relying on state relief or joined the mass exodus of unemployed on the highways of the nation (Figure 9.6). The Civilian Conservation Corps (CCC) sought to provide employment via a series of projects aimed at conservation of the natural environment. The Public Works Administration (PWA) attempted the same thing in the cities via a program of road, bridge, and building construction, and in the rural South, the Tennessee Valley Authority (TVA) instigated a program of flood prevention and dam construction on the Tennessee River that finally enabled thousands of homes to install electricity. Indeed, some of the most visible and long-term effects of the New Deal were the massive construction projects along America's rivers, of which the largest was the Grand Coulee Dam on the Colorado that, in time, produced almost half of the nation's hydroelectric power.

Taken together, these various programs – and there were a lot of them – represented an ambitious attempt to effect economic recovery, but they

FIGURE 9.6. Depression refugees from Iowa (Dorothea Lange, 1936). This photograph depicts three members of a family (of nine) in New Mexico, refugees from Iowa, at the height of the Depression. It was taken by the noted photojournalist Dorothea Lange as part of her work on the Photography Project that was organized on behalf of the Resettlement Administration (1935), one of the reform agencies established under the auspices of the Second New Deal (it was later merged into the Farm Security Administration [also 1935]).Lange later recorded another unwelcome example of resettlement, that of Japanese-American citizens forcibly removed by the War Relocation Authority (WRA) and detained in camps during World War II. Image courtesy of the Library of Congress Prints and Photographs Division (LC-USZ62–130926).

did attract criticism. Labeled the "Alphabet Agencies" by their opponents (who developed the point to dub the New Deal programs "Alphabet Soup," after the children's pasta dish), their success in achieving economic and social stability was certainly mixed. This was not entirely the fault of the agencies themselves. Nature was not on the New Deal's side. A sustained drought (it lasted the best part of the decade in some regions) produced violent dust storms that turned the Great Plains into the "Dust Bowl" that, perhaps more than anything else, came to define the devastation of the Great Depression in America. The worst effects were felt in the Texas and Oklahoma panhandles (best described as internal peninsulas; in Europe, the common term is the salient) and spread as far as New Mexico, Kansas, and Colorado. The populations of these regions, left without support, became, in effect, migrant workers in their own land; captured on camera by photographers such as Dorothea Lange and in literature by writers such as John Steinbeck (whose novel, *The Grapes of Wrath* [1939], about a dispossessed family from Oklahoma, is the most famous literary depiction of the Depression), their plight became symbolic of the widespread suffering of the nation in the 1930s.

The post-1935 phase, the so-called Second New Deal, was constructed around the Social Security Act (1935) that implemented a program of social welfare including unemployment insurance and pensions. It also took job creation a stage further, via the Works Progress Administration (WPA). This ultimately employed almost 9 million people across America, many of them writers, musicians, and artists, commissioned to produce work ranging from murals on post office buildings to state guidebooks, to put on concerts and theater productions, and to create folklore archives. Indeed, as far as the writing of America's history was concerned, one of the WPA initiatives, the Federal Writers Project, by voluminous indexing of newspapers, historical records, and archives or by interviewing and recording the voices of those African Americans who still remembered slavery, organized much of the raw materials for a narrative of the nation's past that historians still pore over and reinterpret for the present.

Yet even such apparently innocuous activities as putting on a play could, and did, attract suspicion and fomented the fear that behind the New Deal lay a socialist or, worse, a fascist agenda, designed to replicate in the United States what one critic, the journalist Raymond Gram Swing, described as "the pattern of Germany and Italy, the coalition between the radicals and the conservatives in the name of national unity." This was but the first step, Swing warned, toward the brave new world of American fascism, a world in which individualism would be eradicated and Americans "told that it is un-American to oppose and to criticize."[16] Swing's voice, long familiar to American radio audiences but increasingly so as events in Europe prompted greater coverage of international news, was not that of a lone prophet in an isolationist wilderness untouched by or uninterested in the rise of Fascism in Italy or National Socialism in Germany. Sinclair Lewis's *It Can't Happen Here* (1935), the premise of which was, of course, that "it" easily could, was one of the most popular books of the decade. Sponsored by the Federal Theater Project, the play based on it enjoyed national coverage; both English and Yiddish versions opened to New York audiences in 1936, a Yiddish version in Los Angeles, a Spanish version in Tampa, and a black version in Seattle.

In fact, the chances of America becoming a New World version of the National Socialist state in the 1930s were slim. Taken as a whole, the interwar period in the United States was one in which the meaning of both liberty and democracy was, once again, up for debate but not in real danger of being destroyed. Herbert Hoover may have attacked the New Deal as "the most stupendous invasion of the whole spirit of Liberty that the nation has witnessed since the days of Colonial America," but Roosevelt countered that by stressing (rather as Lincoln had done during the Civil War) the need for a "broader definition of liberty," one that would provide both "greater freedom" and "greater security for the average man than he has ever known before in the history of America."[17]

Whether this was true was a moot point, and much depended on how one defined the "average" man. The suffering of the Great Depression was unevenly distributed, and some New Deal programs, while intending to alleviate the problem, only exacerbated it. The so-called Indian New Deal was a case in point. The Indian Reorganization Act (IRA) of 1934 attempted to effect a reversal of previous assimilation policies. It sought to recover what the newly appointed Commissioner of the Bureau for Indian Affairs, John Collier, believed had been lost not just to the Native nations but to the American nation as a whole by the destruction of Native culture and the division of tribal lands into individual holdings under the Dawes Act. In what may be seen as a microeconomic (and cultural) version of the New Deal itself, Collier sought a reconsolidation of native lands, an enforced pooling of resources toward the common good. Of course, not all Native Americans were willing to see their carefully husbanded land disappear into common ownership. They were perhaps even more suspicious of, and resistant to, this sudden enthusiasm on the part of Washington bureaucrats for a return to traditions that some of them had long since left behind. Many of the Native nations wanted progress and the promise of a future rather than an enforced return to some white idealistic version of a far-from-ideal past.

Other groups in American society found themselves not so much directed toward the past as unable to escape it. African Americans, more dependent overall on the cotton crop, found the New Deal's attempts at agricultural adjustment of little benefit. It was also the case that most New Deal initiatives were segregated, be these the CCC or the new model towns established by the Resettlement Administration. Segregation, of course, did not originate with the New Deal. Throughout the 1920s and 1930s, America remained a nation in which free did not mean equal, one still driven, to some extent, by an Anglo-Saxon supremacist perspective that was revealed, and to an extent reinforced, by the popular culture of the time. Both the literature and the films of the era revealed the tensions between the new, civic nationalist common culture that Roosevelt championed and the persistence of the "rugged individualism" paradigm that his opponents preferred. In both cases, however, the American ideal was racially coded, its civic nationalism ethnically exclusive, and the successful individualism rarely that of the immigrant.

The most enduring best-selling novel – and later film – to come out of the 1930s was, of course, Margaret Mitchell's Civil War epic, *Gone With the Wind* (1936). This offered a retreat from the dilemmas of the Depression in its historical setting, but also an affirmation of the idea that out of adversity triumph would emerge if the individual in question proved up to it. There was little of the sisterly or indeed social solidarity about its central character, Scarlett O'Hara, who, apart from the fact that she was a woman, represented a cultural conflation of the screen heroes of the day. Pretty much all of these were male, but they divided between the noble common man as in, for example, *Mr Smith Goes to Washington* (1939) and the ignoble criminal one, as in *Public Enemy* (1931) or *Scarface* (1932).

Indeed, the fascination with the gangster that began with Al Capone in the 1920s became something of a fixation for American fiction and film audiences in the 1930s. The message here, however, was mixed, not in the moral perspective of the films in question, but in the immigrant origins of the criminal antihero and his ultimate destruction within the organization that defined and eventually destroyed him. For Scarlett O'Hara as for Scarface, the American Dream was a precarious proposition, especially for those on the margins of social respectability. The underlying uncertainty in the portrayal of American life on the silver screen was more consistently resolved in the increasingly popular "hard boiled" or "pulp" detective fiction of the period. This, too, offered a combination of escapism and confirmation, and frequently posited a central common-man character, be it Dashiell Hammett's Sam Spade or Raymond Chandler's Philip Marlowe, triumphing, up to a point, over whatever plot adversity their creators had invented for them.

The representation of American urban life in such fiction was resolutely downbeat, as befitted the Depression era in which much of it was set, but that was the point. The essence of detective fiction in the 1930s was what might be described as the triumph of informed idealism over the adversity of reality. At its heart was the cynical optimism of the Anglo-Saxon detective upholding "American" values while recognizing the corruption and compromise that lay beneath the dream. "Down these mean streets a man must go," Chandler observed, "who is not himself mean, who is neither tarnished nor afraid." And increasingly Americans came to identify with, or to hope that they might identify with, that "common" and yet "unusual man" that Chandler later described.[18] Even if the "crime" in question was the threat of Nazism, or perhaps especially if the crime in question was the threat of Nazism, American popular culture toward the end of the 1930s seized the opportunity to define the individual American, and by extrapolation the nation and its ideals, against that threat. In the trial scene that concluded *Confessions of a Nazi Spy* (1939), the first overtly anti-Nazi propaganda film released in the United States, the prosecutor proclaims: "America is not simply one of the remaining democracies. America *is* democracy. A democracy that has a God-given inspiration of free men determined to defend forever the liberty which we have inherited."

By the time American audiences saw this film, of course, Europe was on the brink of war. Germany would invade Poland just five months after its release. The New Deal had too, by this point, mostly lost momentum, undermined by persistent industrial unrest and further economic collapse beginning in the summer of 1937. A flurry of new legislation attempted to stabilize the economy, protect farmers, and establish a minimum wage, but Roosevelt had to battle to get this implemented and, in his Annual Message to Congress in January 1939, acknowledged that the main priority for Americans might no longer be national recovery, but national defense. Not that the United States faced any immediate threat. When World War II began, Roosevelt, as Wilson had done, issued a proclamation of neutrality with the addendum that arms and supplies could be sold to the Allies; democracy could thereby be defended, Roosevelt hoped, but at a distance.

The Nazi war machine, unfortunately, could cover distance at considerable speed, and not for nothing was it termed *Blitzkrieg* (lightning war). Within a matter of weeks, starting in the spring of 1940, Germany had occupied Denmark and Norway, the Netherlands, Belgium, and Luxembourg, beaten the British back from France at Dunkirk, and forced France to surrender. That left only Britain standing between Germany and complete control of Western Europe and, crucially, the eastern Atlantic. In the United States, Roosevelt ramped up support for the Allies along with the nation's defenses. He increased military spending, created the National Defense Research Committee, and pushed the Selective Service and Training Act, America's first peacetime conscription measure, through a reluctant Congress. Support for his actions came from the Committee to Defend America by Aiding the Allies and opposition from the America First Committee; together, these represented the mix of opinion in the United States regarding the feasibility, or indeed desirability, of becoming embroiled in a conflict that still seemed far enough away as to pose no threat to the American people.

The American people, however, and their nation's power, did pose a threat to others. The decision for war was, in the end, not America's to make. World War II was, in a sense, the violent confluence of three separate expansionist agendas: that of the Italian and German Fascists in Europe, and the Japanese in Southeast Asia. The danger it posed for the United States came, in the end, not from the European war crossing the Atlantic – although the nation was, by 1941, already embroiled in an uneasy and undeclared war with Germany over U-boat attacks on American shipping – but from Japanese ambitions in the Pacific.

For the Japanese, the presence of the U.S. Pacific Fleet at Pearl Harbor, Hawaii, represented a potential problem as far as their imperial ambitions were concerned – one they decided to remove. On the morning of December 7, 1941, Japanese aircraft launched a sudden and devastating attack on Pearl Harbor (Figure 9.7). In the end, after all the negotiations between politicians over the previous two years, the heated debates in Congress over supplying arms to the Allies and over the advisability of extending American involvement in a conflict that many continued to hope would not touch the United States, it only took about an hour and a half to destroy much of America's Pacific Fleet, kill more than 2,000 Americans in the process, and bring the nation into World War II.

Two decades before Pearl Harbor, Harding had promised that the sacrifice of American lives in war would never be asked for again. It always had been an unrealistic assertion, one that no modern nation can

FIGURE 9.7. Pearl Harbor, December 1941 (Official U.S. Navy Photograph). A rescue boat heads toward the USS *West Virginia* (foreground), a *Colorado*-class battleship, in flames; inboard is the USS *Tennessee*. The *West Virginia* eventually sank, taking more than sixty of her crew with her. She was eventually rebuilt and returned to Hawaii in September 1944 as part of the invasion of the Philippines, and later took part in the Battle of Iwo Jima. Image courtesy of the Library of Congress Prints and Photographs Division and the Office of War Information (LC-USW33–018433-C).

really make. Yet many Americans throughout the 1920s and 1930s had hoped, along with the central character in Dos Passos's *Three Soldiers* (1921), that they would "never put a uniform on again."[19] By the war's end, some 16 million Americans had done so and some half a million had died in them. By, in effect, clothing the growing ranks of the unemployed in military uniform, of course, World War II accomplished what the New Deal ultimately could not: the economic recovery of the nation. Yet it did a great deal more than that.

In 1776, the path to becoming America, to becoming American, had lain through warfare, and many of the nation's leaders had, in the decades since, held that up as a reminder of what America stood for, of what being an American meant. Former president Herbert Hoover, who had opposed

America's entry into World War II, nevertheless linked American sacrifice in war to the concept of freedom: "at Plymouth Rock, at Lexington, at Valley Forge, at Yorktown, at New Orleans, at every step of the Western frontier, at Appomattox, at San Juan Hill, in the Argonne," he reminded the nation, "are the graves of Americans who died for this purpose."[20] The extent to which they had achieved it, of course, remained debatable. As America prepared to send her still segregated armed forces into the field, the meaning of American freedom would find itself challenged and reformed, yet again, in the crucible of a conflict that many hoped might finally forge the fully inclusive civic nationalism that the New Deal had struggled toward but failed to reach.

10

A Land in Transition

America in the Atomic Age

"The things they carried were largely determined by necessity."
(Tim O'Brien, *The Things They Carried*, 1990)

"In the first place," the irate letter began, "a U.S. Army uniform to a colored man makes him about as free as a man in the Georgia chain gang and you know that's hell." Over the course of a two-day "troop movement from Camp Lee, Virginia, during the long run which would carry us deeper into the black-hearted South," it continued, "we had one (1) meal to last us." Writing from his hospital ward in Mississippi, Private Norman Brittingham was having an equally miserable time of it. "The doctors treat us as if we were dogs," he complained, and "the whites beat and curse the colored soldiers [and] at times they have put them in the Camp Stockade for no reason at all." "We have come out Like Men," another soldier wrote, "& we Expected to be Treeated as men but we have bin Treeated more like Dogs then men." "We feel as though our Country spurned us," observed James Henry Gooding, "now that we are sworn to serve her. Please," he pleaded with the president, "give this a moment's attention."[1]

Four different letters, but essentially one complaint: that the African American soldier was not accorded equal treatment with his white comrades. That drew the writers together. What separated them was the best part of a century. The first two letters were composed by soldiers during World War II, the second two by troops serving in the Union Army during the Civil War. Norman Brittingham's war was a generation and more beyond that of James Henry Gooding. Their nation, however, seemed to be stuck in a time warp as far as the experiences of its black soldiers were concerned. As one officer observed in 1943, segregation in the military was an unwelcome echo of the past, one that forced his men to endure "sectional customs and traditions that were defeated in a war seventy-five years ago." The Army, he argued, "is not only to build soldiers but useful citizens in the post war regardless of race. However," he concluded, "if these injustices continue to exist I am fearful that the United States shall see one tenth of her Army indifferent and somewhat disappointed in their belief of our creed, 'Liberty and justice for All'."[2]

The idea that it was the armed forces, rather than the nation's schools and communities, that were responsible for constructing useful citizens was revealing in itself about American attitudes regarding the relationship between the military and the nation by the mid-twentieth century. This relationship was reinforced by the fact that Americans were, unsurprisingly, bombarded with some serious military marketing after 1941. Yet war propaganda took various forms, and in America's case went far beyond simple inducements to shoulder a rifle, build a tank, or nurse the wounded – although there was a lot of that – to address, once again, the question of what an American was and what American nationalism meant. For an immigrant nation, and one that had so recently come through a conflict that had prompted some introspection on the matter of Americanism as that related to German immigrants, this was perhaps inevitable.

In this context, the argument that so long as the nation remained segregated the national creed would continue to be compromised was especially apposite. Roosevelt had, after all, urged that the nation at war "must be particularly vigilant against racial discrimination in any of its ugly forms. Hitler will try again to breed mistrust and suspicion between one individual and another," he warned; but the distrust between black and white Americans could hardly be blamed on the German dictator.[3] What made the entire situation particularly galling for African Americans was the clash between the public image of their nation at war and the private persecutions they experienced. Directed by one of the most famous and enduring propaganda posters produced during World War II (Figure 10.1) to the assertion that "Americans will always fight for liberty," not a few black soldiers wondered whose liberty, exactly, they might be fighting for.

The twin pillars that constituted the official line on the subject of what America was fighting for were informed by two of Roosevelt's most famous declarations, both made before the United States had joined the Allied forces but was supporting them. The first was his description of America

FIGURE 10.1. "Americans will always fight for liberty," poster produced by the U.S. Office of War Information. It remains widely reproduced even today (perhaps especially today); copies can be purchased on Amazon. It juxtaposed the World War II soldier with his Revolutionary counterpart to create an emotive appeal to patriotism, one grounded in the acknowledgment and reinforcement of the military origins of the American nation. Image courtesy of the Library of Congress Prints and Photographs Division (LC-USZC4-9540).

as the "Arsenal of Democracy." The second derived from the president's delineation of what a world devoted to democratic values would hold most dear, or what came to be known as the "Four Freedoms": freedom of speech, freedom of worship, freedom from want, and freedom from fear. Both pillars were supported by a nationalist imperative that placed on American shoulders the full weight of tradition and positioned the American people within an historical continuum that had begun with the Revolution.

"In Washington's day the task of the people was to create and weld together a Nation," Roosevelt declared. "In Lincoln's day the task of the people was to preserve that Nation from disruption from within. In this day the task of the people is to save that Nation and its institutions from disruption from without." Roosevelt urged Americans to consider what their "place in history has been" and reminded them that the "spirit" of the nation, its very "vitality was written into our own Mayflower Compact, into the Declaration of Independence, into the Constitution of the United States, into the Gettysburg Address."4 Roosevelt's message was reinforced by traveling exhibitions and patriotic publications alike, all designed to draw to the forefront of American minds the pivotal position their nation held as a democratic exemplar in a world that had already descended into dictator-driven destruction. A giant poster display representing the Four Freedoms and the nation as the Arsenal of Democracy was unveiled in Defense Square, Washington, DC, in November 1941 before going on tour to cities across the country.

The most famous visual conceptualization of the Four Freedoms, however, was created by artist Norman Rockwell, who composed a series of four (one for each Freedom) homely images representing small-town life: a town meeting; a mix of religious groups praying together; a Thanksgiving dinner; and parents standing by the bed of their two sleeping children (Figure 10.2). These, too, became disseminated in the form of an Office of War Information poster, but one whose message was more mixed than perhaps seemed obvious at first glance. In essence, with its emphasis on the private as opposed to the public sphere, Rockwell's Four Freedoms was a fairly conservative and inward-looking idealized representation of the American way of life. Despite its enormous popularity, it was oddly out of step with a nation gradually coming to terms with its expanding influence in what Roosevelt described as "the narrowing circle of the world." Yet that, of course, was the root of its appeal. What Rockwell offered was not simply an idealized image of a world on the other side of war, but one neither challenged nor changed by conflict. His portrayal of

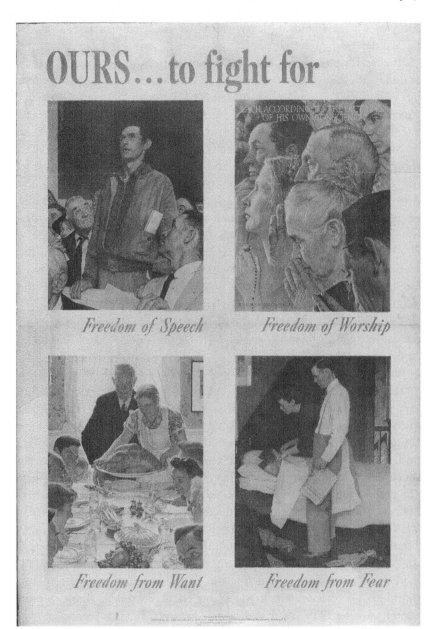

FIGURE 10.2. "Ours to fight for ... " (Norman Rockwell, 1943). These four images were published initially in the *Saturday Evening Post* in 1943, together with essays that highlighted the essential "American-ness" of the freedoms portrayed. The images themselves were immediately and immensely popular, and also formed the centerpiece of a traveling exhibition – the Four Freedoms Show – that was designed to encourage investment in war bonds. Image courtesy of the Norman Rockwell Family Agency, Inc.

America was as a land of plenty, certainly, but hardly an arsenal, never mind a defender of democracy.

Rockwell's peaceful, gentle, and mainly white America was not only at odds with the reality of the period in which the image was composed, but in no sense reflected the aspirations of the many disgruntled African Americans serving in the military. Ultimately, it was the more overt and aggressive "fighting for liberty" message that proved of most use to those in American society seeking to establish – and to force the nation to recognize – their claim to the full and equal rights of citizens, and who recognized World War II as an opportunity to make their variant of the American dream real at home as well as abroad. In 1938, the writer and poet Langston Hughes had published a clarion call for action in this direction in his emotive "Let America Be America Again." In this poem, Hughes juxtaposed the call "Let America be America Again" with the repeated refrain "(America never was America to me.)" not merely to highlight the exclusionary nature of segregation but to emphasize the nation's potential for change. "We, the people, must redeem," he concluded, "The land, the mines, the plants, the rivers,/The mountains and the endless plain/All, all the stretch of these great green states/And make America again!"

Hughes's poem made its way into *The Pocket Book of America*, a 1942 publication that sought to encapsulate, between its covers, the very essence of the nation. Comprising an eclectic mix of short stories, plays, historical documents, poems, songs, and facts and figures about the United States, it concluded with a detailed description of how to display, fold, and salute the American flag. The book's overtly patriotic purpose was undisguised; this was a collection composed in the context of conflict, and designed not simply to inculcate nationalist sentiment but to direct it. "In times of great crisis," its Introduction began, "nations, like individuals, have to rediscover what it is they live by." America, it continued, was a nation founded on "a social faith"; this was "the miracle of America." An American, it asserted, was identifiable "by the way he thinks, and by the behavior based upon that thought. And without the ties of common tradition and commonly held ideas, this country would collapse into an anarchy greater than any that threatens Europe."[5]

Edited as it was by Philip Van Doren Stern, a Civil War historian, the Revolution got a look in, but it was the Civil War short story by Edward Everett Hale, *The Man Without a Country* (1863), that opened the volume and set the tone for what followed. This mid-nineteenth-century morality tale detailed the dreadful fate that befell one man,

Philip Nolan, who in the heat of the moment, and inadvisably, as it transpired, declared: "Damn the United States! I wish I may never hear of the United States again." The price of such disloyalty to the nation was to be banished onto the high seas for the remainder of his life, on a ship with a captain and crew detailed never to utter, in Nolan's presence, the name of the United States. "For a half century and more," Everett intoned, "he was a man without a country." The point of the story was not the excessive punishment meted out for one unpatriotic outburst as such, but the psychological effect that being "a man without a country" had on the central character who, by its end, finds both God and a renewed love of country just in time to meet his maker.[6]

It was in no way the fault of Van Doren Stern that this particular story was, with hindsight, an unfortunate example to select, given that one group of Americans discovered, very soon after the attack on Pearl Harbor, what it was to be without a country, and through no unpatriotic behavior on their part. There were a great many things that the United States could be proud of as far as World War II was concerned, but her treatment of West Coast Japanese Americans was not one of them (Figure 10.3). Executive Order 9066, signed by Roosevelt in February 1942, was perhaps the most shameful and blatant attack on civil liberties that America had yet perpetrated on her citizens. What was worse was that no other minority action group – not the NAACP, not even the American Jewish Committee – stepped up to the plate to defend Japanese Americans. Banished to concentration camps (the official terminology was "Relocation Center"), their property seized, the very identity of the Japanese American was placed, temporarily at least, in state-enforced suspension.

The irony attendant on the expectation that African Americans would fight for liberty in segregated forces was bad enough. For Japanese Americans, many of whom also enlisted, the situation was beyond bizarre, because the question of their loyalty proved to be to be location-sensitive. Japanese Americans not living on the West Coast, and notably those in Hawaii – which was a greater potential invasion target than California – were not deemed potential enemies of the state, and not removed to relocation camps. It may seem all the more remarkable that more than 30,000 Japanese Americans selected to serve a country that compromised, and in so contradictory a fashion, their claim to citizenship. Of course not all did, and after the war, some 5,000 renounced their citizenship and left the United States. Yet for most Japanese Americans, as for African-American and Native-American troops, fighting a war abroad in the name of a

FIGURE 10.3. First-grade children at the Weill public school in San Francisco pledging allegiance to the flag (Photo by Dorothea Lange, April 1942). Many of them would end up in concentration camps located in states such as Arizona, Colorado, Wyoming, and Arkansas, some of them on Indian Reservation land. In the aftermath of World War II, of course, the phrase "concentration camp" took on a rather different resonance, but that was what Roosevelt called the "relocation" centers at the time. Dorothea Lange created this image on behalf of the War Relocation Authority, but the WRA, disturbed by the message it sent out, impounded it and the others she had made of the Japanese-American experience in California in 1942. Image courtesy of the Library of Congress Prints and Photographs Division (LC-USZ62–42810).

nation that denied many of them equality at home offered the opportunity not just to prove their loyalty to that nation, but to secure that nation's loyalty to them.

Operating within the culture of conflict necessarily invoked as a spur to morale during World War II, Americans hitherto relegated to the margins of the nation were able, as they been had during the Revolution, the Civil War and World War I, to position themselves more squarely near its center. In this respect they, too, were following a national tradition informed by conflict. Americans had, as the propaganda proposed, always fought for liberty; from what came to be perceived as imperial domination in the eighteenth century, from slavery and the sundering of the nation itself in the nineteenth, and from inequality throughout. Americans, black and white, Langston Hughes emphasized in his 1942 song "Freedom Road," were "marching down freedom's road" together: "United we stand, divided we fall/Let's make this land safe for one and all," it proclaimed; "I've got a message, and you know it's right/Black and white together unite and fight." For Hughes, as for others, America was "a land in transition," one in which, despite segregation, despite inequality, it was still possible to make the journey "from a log cabin to wealth and fame," even in the face of opposition. It was a land where "a finer and better democracy than any citizen has known before" remained an option.[7]

In the twentieth century, however, the idea of democracy itself underwent a transition of its own – from a national ideal to an imperialist precept, largely because of World War II. For America, this war differed from previous conflicts in two main ways: first, the new global imperative it imposed on American idealism, and second, the sheer weight of matériel that the mid-twentieth-century United States could bring to bear in the service of its moral message. This distinction was succinctly expressed in General George C. Marshall's promise "that before the sun sets on this terrible struggle our flag will be recognized throughout the world as a symbol of freedom on the one hand and of overwhelming force on the other."[8]

By the spring of 1945, Marshall's prediction appeared fulfilled. American military might had proved decisive to Allied victory over Germany, and American flags, symbolic both of the nation's patriotism and power, had been firmly planted atop Mount Suribachi on Iwo Jima, unfurled from balconies across Europe as towns were liberated from German occupation and, on VE (Victory in Europe) Day, waved over and by enthusiastic crowds of every nationality in New York, Paris, London, and all points in between. The cover of *Life* magazine for May 14, 1945 did not carry a flag, but it did present a Robert Capa photograph of an American GI posing in front of a giant swastika at Nuremberg Stadium. Entitled "Victorious Yank," it offered a more personal expression of the combination of relief and pride with which Americans greeted the end of the war in Europe. It served as a counterbalance to the propagandist flag-waving images that were as ubiquitous as the flag itself seemed to be, and that hid so much of the war's realities behind that patriotic bunting.

As Europe celebrated liberation, however, hundreds of thousands of American troops were still slogging their way through Japanese defenses, from Iwo Jima, a small volcanic island lying to the right of the Ryukyu

FIGURE 10.4. "Raising the Flag on Iwo Jima" (February 23, 1945). This image is possibly the single most iconic symbol of America at war. Taken by Associated Press photographer Joe Rosenthal, it won the Pulitzer Prize for Photography in 1945 and has been reproduced, and parodied, innumerable times since its first publication. It was most notably reproduced in the U.S. Marine Corps (USMC) Memorial just outside Arlington Cemetery in Washington, DC, dedicated by John F. Kennedy in 1961. Used with permission of Associated Press.

island chain leading up to the tip of Japan itself, to Okinawa, the largest island in the chain. These proved to be hard-fought victories, with American casualties exceeding 50,000 at Okinawa alone. The symbolic raising of the American flag on Iwo Jima in February of 1945 – an image captured for posterity by photographer Joe Rosenthal and since duplicated on posters and postage stamps, parodied by the peace movement, and revisited any number of times by artists and photographers seeking to make a serious point or a cynical one – was a powerful assertion of the kind of overwhelming force that Marshall had in mind (Figure 10.4). At the same time, the actual event represented no overwhelming victory, merely one success in an ongoing battle that would last another month in a war that would require the ultimate expression of American power, the atomic bomb, to end more than six months later. For America, the war had begun in the Pacific and it would end there, but not until August 1945.

For many Americans, consequently, the Pacific Theater was and remains the emotional locus of their nation at war, largely because it had been the attack on Pearl Harbor that had brought them to belligerent status in the first place. Conflict in the Pacific, in contrast to that in Europe, was also rather more clear-cut, conceptually, for a nation long suspicious of European entanglements and, in 1940, as bemused as it was horrified by the rise of Nazism. The initial reluctance, highlighted by English Literature professor and war veteran Paul Fussell, on the part of many young Americans to join what General Dwight D. Eisenhower described as a "Great Crusade" to liberate Europe revealed that it was not just African-American troops who may have questioned the wisdom of fighting for the freedom of others. Some saw little reason to engage with or in what one GI dismissed as this "goddamn Europe" at all, never mind Great Britain, the former imperial power they had, as Winston Churchill was forced to remind the British Commons, thrown off in 1776.[9]

Americans' understandable resentment at finding themselves overseas was matched by the resentment they encountered from a population who saw, unsurprisingly, what the Americans wished them to see in the way of the overwhelming force and overt optimism that was the public face of the United States. Of course, they also saw what the Americans were rather less keen to highlight: the segregated facilities that were imposed on the nation's armed forces, and on those cities and towns in which they were stationed. From any angle, American power, pride, and – as far as race relations were concerned – prejudice did not always endear the United States to her allies, but it was not their allies that America's military and political leaders had to persuade of the value of American involvement, the necessity of paying the price for it.

When, on the eve of the D-Day landings in Normandy on June 6, 1944, General George Patton of the 3rd U.S. Army declared that all "real Americans love the sting and clash of battle" and advised his troops that "Americans have never lost nor ever will lose a war," he did so not necessarily because he believed it to be true, of course, but to provide inspiration. He invoked a martial tradition, as much of the contemporary propaganda did, that originated with the American Revolution and with which few Americans would have demurred. Whether this tradition helped sustain the troops on D-Day in their assaults on Omaha and Utah Beaches, in the Battle of the Bulge that cost almost 20,000 American lives (the same number of civilians were killed in the process of liberating

Normandy), on Iwo Jima, at Okinawa, or when they reached Dachau and came face to face with the realities of the Nazi's "final solution" may be a moot point. What is certain is that overwhelming force turned out to have an overwhelming cost. Not simply, or not only, in terms of casualties and lives lost: the cost in the end was commitment, the commitment of the nation to almost continuous conflict after 1945 and, consequently, the realignment of its national identity with war.

In this respect, World War II was the ultimate transitive force, at a personal level for those Americans who fought in it and on a political level for America as a nation. It shifted it away from what was always an imperfect isolation (in effect, only isolation from Europe) toward what is frequently presented as a reluctant global involvement informed by a Wilsonian idealism. Every aspect of the economic, political, and ideological power that the postwar United States wielded in the Cold War world was driven by the destruction wreaked by World War II, a destruction that seemed, at least on the surface, not to have affected America; quite the opposite. In material terms, the United States emerged from the war the most powerful nation on earth. Between 1940 and 1945, it achieved unparalleled industrial growth and national consolidation as the entire country was pulled into the war effort.

Military expansion was, obviously, immediate and dramatic. Military employment rose from around 300,000 or so personnel in the 1930s to some 12 percent of the population (around 16 million) during the war, and never returned to prewar levels. It dipped only briefly to around 1.5 million before rising again in the context of the Cold War. Military spending overall rose from 1.7 percent of the GDP in 1940 to 37.8 percent in 1944. And military mobilization, directed via federal agencies such as the War Production Board (which became, in 1943, the Office of War Mobilization) and the War Manpower Commission, necessarily had an impact at all levels of commerce and community as civilian industries were subsumed into a federally directed military machine. Tanks, trucks, and the new four-wheel-drive "Jeeps" rolled off the assembly lines where there had been cars before; aircraft production, mainly of military planes, increased almost tenfold in five years; and speedier-built (because they were welded rather than riveted) cargo vessels, known as "Liberty" ships, were produced at the rate of more than one a day during the war.

Servicing all this activity took manpower and, importantly, womanpower too. Unemployment fell from some 9 million in 1940 to slightly more than 700,000 in 1943, and a general shortage of labor for the expanded wartime industries brought many more women – 50 percent more – into workplaces traditionally defined as male preserves. This sudden equality of opportunity was not, however, matched by equality of remuneration, and the increased presence (up to one-fifth of the total) of women in the labor unions did little to close the pay or prejudice gender gap. Indeed, income levels generally were an issue in the context of such sudden and significant federal spending. As union membership, now positively encouraged by the government, soared, overtime and wage increases became a fact of wartime life, leading to the risk of runaway inflation. The National War Labor Board responded with what was known as the "Little Steel" formula that restricted cost-of-living increases to 15 percent. Yet this line proved impossible to hold in the face of the inevitable work-pattern upheavals of wartime, and in 1943, a strike by the United Mine Workers produced wage settlements in excess of the Little Steel limit.

The 1943 strike was a sharp reminder that other pressures beyond those produced directly by the war influenced the United States between 1941 and 1945. Nor was the strike the only indication that beneath the surface of what became known as the "Good War" lay some traditionally bad ideas. Not the least of the upheavals that the war produced was the further movement of many African Americans – around 700,000 – out of the South to the northern cities, many more than the "Great Migration" of the early twentieth century had produced. The resultant tensions erupted in Harlem in the summer of 1943, when a riot broke out following the shooting of a black soldier by a white policeman. The riot, according to the *New York Times*, represented "a social explosion in a powder keg that has been years in the filling."[10] It was a powder keg being filled from both sides of the country. In that same summer, violent clashes between white sailors and Mexican Americans, the so-called zoot suit riots (after the clothing style adopted at the time by young Latino men), provided further evidence of the limits of wartime solidarity in a nation still divided, to a great extent, by racial discord.

If individual Americans' efforts in support of economic and military mobilization were informed by both personal and propagandist injunctions on the need to pull together, nevertheless the war could not, and did not, eradicate those forces – financial, social, religious, racial, or political – that had always pulled Americans apart. What the war did do was highlight the discrepancies between the rhetoric and the reality, especially with regard to race. The juxtaposition between American values and those of Nazi Germany – the mainstay of much of the propaganda to appear during the war – was the crucial catalyst that drew to the surface a more strident sense of the importance of civil rights, of making the American creed, popularly defined in the Four Freedoms, match the conditions under which individual Americans lived their lives. The surge in membership of the National Association for the Advancement of Colored People (NAACP) during the war – from some 50,000 to 400,000 – and the formation of the Congress of Racial Equality (CORE) was revealing in itself of this new stridency, a new optimism that equality could be achieved and the full democratization of America could be finally accomplished.

Clearly, an American nationalism constructed around an Anglo-Saxon ideal was no longer tenable in the face of the "final solution." As was pointed out in *The Nation* in 1943, American "cannot fight fascism abroad while turning a blind eye to fascism at home. We cannot inscribe our banners 'For democracy and a caste system.' We cannot liberate oppressed peoples while maintaining the right to oppress our own minorities."[11] In this climate, the idea of the "melting pot" gradually gave way to a more heterogeneous conception of the nation, although not without a struggle. At the same time, ensuring the Four Freedoms necessitated America's moving from a purely defensive to a more overtly offensive strategy as far as its democratic ideals were concerned. In this sense, just as World War II had been, for the United States, a war on two fronts, so the Cold War that followed was one fought at home and abroad. The result – an uneasy balancing act between domestic and foreign policy – would underpin, but also at times undermine, America's efforts to defend its national interests and define its national identity in the postwar era.

American Century

"We Americans," declared publisher Henry Luce in *The American Century* (1941), "are unhappy. We are not happy about America. We are not happy about ourselves in relation to America." And Americans, according to Luce, ought to be happy because, in material terms and in contrast to most of the world, the United States was "just plain rich . . . rich in food, rich in clothes, rich in entertainment and amusement, rich in leisure, rich." The problems of the American body politic, as Luce saw it, were all in the mind. Essentially, these boiled down to the fact that although "their nation became in the 20th century the most powerful and the most vital nation in the world, nevertheless Americans were unable to accommodate themselves spiritually and practically to that fact. Hence they have failed to play their part as a world power," Luce charged, "a failure which has had disastrous consequences for themselves and for all mankind."

As his nation sat on the fence between the free world and fascism, Luce attempted to invoke a new "vision of America as a world power which is authentically American and which can inspire us to live and work and fight with vigor and enthusiasm" toward the creation of an "American Century."[12]

To other nations, of course, the very idea of an "American Century" undoubtedly rankled, but not all Americans were entirely sold on the notion, either. They may have concluded, in the face of Nazi atrocities in Europe, that their war had been more of a crusade than they had originally believed, but that did not necessarily translate into the desire, as Luce urged, "to promote, encourage and incite so-called democratic principles throughout the world." Luce called for greater internationalism, but to some that sounded too much like imperialism. Others, such as Vice President Henry A. Wallace, promulgated a similar message but sought to downplay America's dominance in the freedom-loving democracies department. Instead, Wallace stressed international cooperation between nations – a New Deal for the world, in effect – that would result not in an "American Century" but in a "century of the common man" constructed out of a "people's peace." This, in the end, was the great crusade, not the war itself but its meaning, not the idea of victory as conclusion but rather as the start of a "people's revolution" devoted to freedom. This, according to Wallace, was "The Price of Free World Victory."[13]

In making his case for an American-inspired – but not yet imposed – process of universal democratization, Wallace cited his nation's own nineteenth-century battle between freedom and slavery. World War II, like the Civil War, was "a fight between a slave world and a free world," and just as "the United States in 1862 could not remain half slave and half free," so the mid-twentieth-century battle for freedom, this fight for a rebirth of democracy, had to have a decisive outcome. For America, however, the parallels between the two wars were more than moral. In 1945, for the second time in the nation's history at a crucial juncture in that history, America lost its leader. The sudden death of Franklin D. Roosevelt on April 12, 1945 precipitated widespread shock across the nation.

Few knew that the president's health had been declining; indeed, until his death, most Americans did not know that Roosevelt had been paralyzed since 1921 and had used a wheelchair since that time. Roosevelt had been as adroit at manipulating his own image as he had proved adept at managing America's self-image through the turmoil and financial crisis of the 1930s and then through the trauma and chaos of World War II. For more than a decade he had driven the nation toward a new economic and ideological vision of itself, one that would take it beyond the confines of its comfort zone, beyond the "city on a hill," and force it to contemplate not just a new relationship between state and citizen – in the form of the New Deal – but a new relationship between the United States and the world in the form of the United Nations. With the death of a president who still ranks, along with Lincoln, as one of the nation's greatest leaders, Americans were forced to negotiate the postwar landscape without the comforting voice of Roosevelt delivering his "Fireside Chats" on the radio to remind them that they were a crucial part of an international drive toward democracy, to praise the "magnificent ability and energy of the American people," and to assure them that, at home and abroad, they made a difference.[14]

As the United States, now led by Harry Truman, moved into the postwar world, not the least of the issues facing the nation was how big a difference it should, or could, continue to make. America had ended the war with a devastating show of strength, of course, in the deployment of the atomic bombs, developed in Los Alamos Laboratory, New Mexico, as part of what became known as the Manhattan Project. The dropping of these weapons of mass destruction on Hiroshima and Nagasaki in August, 1945 proved controversial, and not just because of the loss of life and widespread material devastation that followed: some 80,000 people died, and some 70 percent of the city was destroyed at Hiroshima alone. Atomic technology, and the state programs that developed it, posed challenging questions concerning the relationship between state, science, and society on many levels, not just in terms of future military deployment. In slightly more than a decade, scientific research had changed, in political and public perception, from Herbert Hoover's relatively unproblematic description of it as "one of the most potent impulses to progress" and a force designed to extend human life and decrease suffering to a deadly and dangerous threat not just to life but to national security.

America's atomic monopoly, although as devastating in deployment as it was decisive in ending hostilities, did not long outlast the war. Neither did the blueprint for future international cooperation and the establishment of democratic governments drawn up between Roosevelt, Churchill, and Stalin at Yalta in February (4–11), 1945. Less than a month after the Yalta Conference, the Soviet Union, by imposing a communist regime on Romania, made it clear that it was working on its own agenda, and not to that of any grand Allied alliance. When the now new lineup of Allied leaders, Truman, Clement Attlee (Great Britain), and Stalin, met at Potsdam in July 1945, it was clear that the rules of engagement had changed. Cooperation was already crumbling, and instead of acting in unity, the former allies acted unilaterally to effect the regime changes they wanted on the parts of Europe that they now controlled.

On America's part, the fear that war-torn Europe was in danger of a wholesale Communist takeover resulted in a more strident approach to what seemed to be a growing Soviet/communist threat; containment, or what became known as the Truman Doctrine. This attempt to restrict the spread of communism was America's line in the sand in the fast-developing Cold War, an economic and ideological conflict between the Western powers – but mainly America – and the Soviet Bloc, which overshadowed the remainder of the twentieth century. The choice the world faced, as Truman articulated it, was between America's "free institutions, representative government, free elections, guarantees of individual liberty, freedom of speech and religion, and freedom from political oppression" and Soviet-style "terror and oppression, a controlled press and radio, fixed elections, and the suppression of personal freedoms." It must, he insisted, "be the policy of the United States to support free peoples who are resisting attempted subjugation by armed minorities.... The free peoples of the world," he stressed, "look to us for support in maintaining their freedoms."[15]

Despite the hint of military intervention in Truman's declaration, America initially waged the Cold War on a financial front. Still following what was essentially a Rooseveltian road map for international cooperation, the United States implemented the Marshall Plan (named for the army general, by then Secretary of State). Although condemned by its critics as a covert "Martial Plan," it was an economic program designed to aid European recovery and, in the process, boost the American economy once a revivified Europe could once again afford American markets. "Prosperity," its propagandist slogan declared, "Makes You Free." Or at least free from communism, which was the whole point. The Marshall Plan was the ultimate capitalist response to communism. It was both very successful and itself symbolic of the nation's success; but only up to a point. America could certainly afford the Economic Cooperation Act (1948), which allocated more than $13 billion in overseas aid; but she could not afford thereafter to have its image clash with its ideals. Freedom was what America promised the peoples of the world, yet at home, for some, it remained elusive.

Nevertheless, behind the opening rhetorical salvos of the Cold War ran a patriotic spectacle the scale of which only America could have devised. The Freedom Train – seven red-white-and-blue cars pulled by a locomotive named "The Spirit of 1776" – carried a selection of significant Americana – including the Mayflower Compact, the Declaration of Independence, the Emancipation Proclamation, and the flag from Iwo Jima – through every state of the Union between 1947 and 1949. The train had its own song, composed by Irving Berlin and sung by Bing Crosby and the Andrews Sisters: "[T]here comes the Freedom Train/you better hurry down/just like a Paul Revere/it's comin' into your home town." It had its own comic (*Captain Marvel and the Freedom Train*) and virtually every popular comic-strip character of the day, from Mickey Mouse to L'il Abner, was portrayed visiting the Freedom Train as it rolled across the nation. Hugely popular, it received some 3.5 million visitors who were encouraged to take a Freedom Pledge and sign a Freedom Scroll that was later presented to President Truman. "Freedom," the exhibition announced, "is everybody's job."

Of course the idea behind the Freedom Train was not new. Sanitary Fairs held during the Civil War of the nineteenth century exhibited patriotic and symbolic documents, flags, and weaponry to remind the public of the issues at stake, and *The Pocket Book of America* served a similar purpose during World War II. The Freedom Train, no less, represented an impulse for consensus conceived in conflict, albeit that the war was a virtual one and its weaponry mainly words. Yet the train traversed an embattled landscape all the same, one that had recently undergone demobilization and endured yet more strikes in the steel, mining, and car industries and on the railroads. The year before it set off, indeed, a national rail strike prompted the president to suggest drafting the strikers into the army. And alongside industrial unrest lay the big questions that had exercised Luce and Wallace about America's new global responsibilities, questions that the Soviet detonation of an atomic bomb in September 1949 – rather earlier than the Americans had anticipated – made more pressing than ever (Figure 10.5). Less than a year after the Freedom Train pulled into Washington, DC in January, 1949, concluding its journey with Truman's inauguration, the future itself, never mind freedom, could hardly be taken for granted.

America's loss of the atomic monopoly in 1949 significantly raised the stakes in a Cold War complicated almost at the outset by communist victory in the Chinese civil war that same year. Internationally, the establishment of the North Atlantic Treaty Organization (NATO) by the United States, Canada, and Western Europe offered some sense of mutual protection, but for America external security was only one side of the Cold War equation. As far as domestic matters were concerned,

FIGURE 10.5. This image is of the atomic explosion over Nagasaki on August 9, 1945. Atomic testing continued in the Pacific after 1945, most notably at Bikini Atoll between 1946 and 1958. The extent to which the nuclear threat overshadowed the world in the decades following World War II cannot be overestimated; it had not yet become the low-level background concern that it is in the context of the twenty-first century's "war on terror." Contemporary cultural responses to the threat included Nevil Shute's post-apocalyptic novel *On the Beach* (1957), later made into a film (1959) starring Fred Astaire and Ava Gardner and, most famously, Stanley Kubrick's 1964 satirical film, *Dr. Strangelove*. Literary treatment of the subject originated with the discovery of radiation in the late nineteenth century, a subject dealt with in Robert Cromie's *The Crack of Doom* (1895) and in any number of novels and films since then in which nuclear destruction is either a threat in its own right or a metaphor for the angst of the modern world. There was little that was metaphorical about the fear in the 1950s and 1960s, however, that the world would end not, as T.S. Elliot proposed, with a whimper but with a very big bang indeed, and that imminently.

indeed, the nuclear threat appeared more capable of containment than communism itself, which was deemed to threaten the very foundations of American identity. As the nation moved toward a more inclusive civic nationalist creed after World War II, one predicated on the importance of inclusiveness, it was no longer outsiders that many Americans came to fear, but those who were already part, an established part, of the nation; in short, America became obsessed – and in some respects has remained so – with "the enemy within." The result in the 1950s was a new "Red Scare," more extreme but also more contradictory than that following World War I, with implications more destructive, in the long term, of those American freedoms that communism ostensibly threatened.

The roots of the second Red Scare lay, obviously enough, in its first incarnation, but by 1950, the context had changed beyond recognition. After World War II, no president could promise America, as Warren Harding had, that there might be a return to "normalcy," and Truman did not try. Indeed, Truman, having delivered his "containment" speech in March 1947, indicated which way the wind was blowing by establishing the Federal Employee Loyalty Program, barring Communist Party members and sympathizers from government employment. Whereas Freedom Pledges were intended as an entertaining (and educational) part of the Freedom Train experience, Loyalty Oaths became a very serious part of American life. They had been before, of course, but only in times of armed conflict. Their Cold War incarnation revealed the extent to which the United States really had embarked on a war without end. And as with all wars, there were casualties. Truman's executive order (9835) instituting "a loyalty investigation" of federal employees saw several hundred lose their jobs. This was not a staggering statistic given that more than 4 million were investigated, but it was the fallout that did the most damage.

The year 1938 had seen the establishment of the House Committee on Un-American Activities (that became the House Un-American Activities Committee [HUAC] in 1945) whose remit it had been to prevent Nazi infiltration of American society. Now, in the context of the Cold War, it turned its attention to the communist threat, ably supported by the FBI under J. Edgar Hoover and by newly created bodies, such as the Central Intelligence Agency (CIA), which took over the international side of American security, and the National Security Council. Charged with looking for danger, inevitably they found it, and in the process produced a nationwide anticommunist hysteria. This came to be dubbed "McCarthyism," after Republican Senator for Wisconsin, Joseph R. McCarthy, who, in early 1950, announced that he had a list of the names of some 200 communist sympathizers working for the State Department. The list never actually materialized, but the idea that it might fueled popular fears of subversion. This is not to suggest that there was no risk of subversion; there was, but possibly not concentrated either in university dormitories or the Hollywood film industry to the degree that the subsequent FBI investigations and HUAC hearings suggested.

Anticommunism as a cultural and political force in postwar America was pump-primed by the trial (or trials; there were two) in 1949–50 of prominent former State Department official Alger Hiss as a communist spy. Eventually indicted on the grounds of perjury, Hiss was imprisoned for five years, but it was the process of his prosecution that gripped America and the world. The Hiss case was symbolic, as noted journalist Alistair Cooke put it, of *A Generation on Trial* (1951), and proved as fascinating to follow as its outcome was ominous. Hiss's guilt or innocence became rather a moot point when a British scientist, Dr. Klaus Fuch, admitted passing atomic secrets to the Soviets. This resulted in perhaps the most notorious of the anticommunist convictions, that of Julius and Ethel Rosenberg, who were executed for the crime of leaking atomic secrets on the basis of evidence that was, at the time, considered controversial. In fact, the Venona project – a joint US-UK covert counterintelligence code-breaking operation designed to intercept and defend against the Soviet threat, which was initiated during World War II – revealed that Julius Rosenberg did engage in espionage and in the passing of atomic secrets to the Soviets.

The problem with covert intelligence, of course, is its tendency, as far as public consumption is concerned, to foment fear in the absence of facts, to encourage paranoia without providing proof, and America in the 1950s hardly needed any encouragement in that department. Without doubt, the Soviets did compromise American security as far as atomic research was concerned, but McCarthy, with the help of the FBI, was able to elevate the (perhaps inevitable) espionage threat posed by a foreign nation into a more diffuse fear of widespread subversion within America itself and, further, to associate this potential for subversion within the liberal Left. This process, which has been termed "Cold War alchemy" by Canadian political scientist Reg Whitaker, managed to muddy the distinction between spying and subversion and helped create the climate of fear that gripped America in the post–World War II period.

This was not, of course, the first time that the nation had experienced a "Red Scare," but in the 1950s, the color palette of the "paranoid style," a phenomenon identified as far back as the nineteenth century, expanded: the Red scare was accompanied by Pink, Lavender, and Black scares, invoking women's rights, homosexuality, and African-American civil rights, respectively. And the Cold War may have not been the sole catalyst in this respect, given that fears of subversion in the 1950s were accompanied by echoes of the critique against "Big Government" and the dangers of a socialist state that had been voiced by opponents of the New Deal. In 1950, the Electric Light and Power Companies ran an advertisement in *U.S. News and World Report* alerting readers to what it termed "this move toward a socialist government." The symbolism that accompanied this offered, in the hands of a young boy, a simplified version of the Four Freedoms through which Americans might counter the threat to their freedoms: a bible, a key, a pencil, and a ballot slip, although whether the key symbolized the ability to lock out or open up was a moot point.

Its marketing legacy aside – and that did prove persistent – McCarthyism had run its course by 1954. It had, in many respects, represented an insular nationalism in the construction of what was, in essence, no more than a self-serving specter of subversion produced when one man's demagogic ambitions fed into the Republican Party's bid for power in the 1952 election. The new president, Dwight D. Eisenhower, personally loathed McCarthy but found it politic to lend official credence to his charges. The American public's willingness to go along with this, however, pointed to the precariousness of American ideology and identity in a postwar world in which the United States was struggling to find its feet, but this precariousness had a positive aspect. The darker side of democracy as represented by McCarthyism was only one example of the American tendency, in moments of crisis, to turn on itself in a critical way. Although the fall-out from the "Red Scare" is generally located in a widespread conformity across an American society frozen by the fear of communist subversion, there was one area in which many Americans were no longer prepared to conform to traditional norms: racial inequality.

As Luce and Wallace were contemplating the possibilities and challenges posed by the American century of the common man, Swedish economist Gunnar Myrdal had been considering the perennial problem of American race relations. His exhaustive report, published as *An American Dilemma: The Negro Problem and Modern Democracy* (1944), was in many ways a damning and hugely influential indictment of inequality in America, especially in the South, which, Myrdal argued, remained at odds with the "American creed" of freedom and opportunity for all. Few southerners could have relished reading Myrdal's descriptions of the "dullness and insecurity" of the rural South, its domination by an "emotional puritanical religion" and its "unhealthy emphasis upon sex," all of which had, the economist concluded, a part to play in the violence and intimidation used to control the region's African-American population.[16]

Several contemporary southern authors, of course, from novelist William Faulkner to playwright Tennessee Williams, reached similar conclusions about the relationship between sex and violence in the South; but fictional portrayals had a certain romance for their audiences that an economist's report, one running to well more than 1,000 pages, rather lacked. From lynching to the legal system, Myrdal showed how black and white America, particularly in the South, were locked in a destructive relationship of fear and aggression, one that had its roots in slavery and was perpetuated by broader American attitudes toward poverty, crime, and social disengagement. Indeed, racial prejudice was not the sole dilemma that Myrdal identified but it was, in the context of the Cold War, the dominant one.

Three years after Myrdal's report appeared, the Commission on Civil Rights, established by Truman, published *To Secure These Rights* (1947). Less weighty than *An American Dilemma* but broader in its assessment of minority groups – including Native Americans, the citizens of American protectorates, Japanese and African Americans, and Mexican immigrants – it called for federal action against segregation. Discrimination, it argued, was not just antithetical to the "American creed" but posed a serious threat to the health and well-being of the population as a whole, not just those groups who suffered discrimination. The report picked apart the "separate but equal" doctrine of "racial segregation in both public and private institutions which cuts across the daily lives of southern citizens from the cradle to the grave." It condemned it as one of "the outstanding myths of American history for it is almost always true," it asserted, "that while indeed separate, these facilities are far from equal," and argued:

The separate but equal doctrine stands convicted on three grounds. It contravenes the equalitarian spirit of the American heritage. It has failed to operate, for history shows that inequality of service has been the omnipresent consequence of separation. It has institutionalized segregation and kept groups apart despite indisputable evidence that normal contacts among these groups tend to promote social harmony.

The report ended with a brief review of America's history. "Twice before," it noted, "the nation has found it necessary to review the state of its civil rights": in the period between declaring independence and adopting the Bill of Rights, and in the course of the Civil War. "It is our profound conviction," it stated, "that we have come to a time for a third re-examination of the situation" for reasons "of conscience, of self-interest, and of survival in a threatening world. Or to put it another way," it concluded, "we have a moral reason, an economic reason, and an international reason for believing that the time for action is now."[17]

Truman was convinced. Congress was not. Wars, however, even cold ones, have always been of value to American leaders seeking to enact unpopular legislation; in 1948, therefore, Truman formally desegregated the nation's armed forces. In fighting a Cold War, Truman realized that there could be no glaring discrepancies between the ideals America espoused and the practices it tolerated. It was not, unfortunately, the case that with this single act, segregation ended; very far from it. Yet when the United States sent its forces into the field again, as it did only two years later in Korea, it no longer sent a segregated army. The Korean War, a conflict frequently obscured by the impact of the two larger conflicts, World War II and the Vietnam War, that flanked it, was therefore symbolic on several levels (Figure 10.6). It was not just the first war in which the United States fielded desegregated forces, but the first armed confrontation of what had been, until the summer of 1950, an entirely Cold War. America's response to the invasion of South (anticommunist) by North (communist) Korea represented the first example of containment in action, as it were, with the United States in direct confrontation with both North Korea and China.

After 1950, the world witnessed a very different America, at least the version in uniform; the one kept for domestic consumption still had some way to go to achieve full equality. In terms of timing, indeed, the Korean War was something of a hiatus in the Cold War abroad and a turning point in how it played out in the United States. The death of Stalin in 1953, the same year as the armistice between the United States and North Korea, the year in which Julius and Ethel Rosenberg were executed and in which African-American author James Baldwin explored the interaction between racism and religion in his semi-autobiographical novel, *Go Tell It on the Mountain*, ushered in at least a temporary thaw in Soviet-American relations. Yet many Americans were still acutely aware that they were locked in an ideological battle with the Soviets, and that desegregation remained a priority if they hoped to win it. The following year witnessed a dramatic advance in this direction when the Supreme Court, under Chief Justice Earl Warren, ruled on five NAACP-sponsored cases that became summarized as *Brown vs. Board of Education* (1954).

FIGURE 10.6. The Korean War Memorial, Washington, DC (Photo by Peter Wilson). For many years, the Korean War was an almost forgotten conflict. This memorial to it, however, quite deliberately emphasizes the heterogeneous makeup of the American armed forces in this war. Comprising nineteen statues, all larger than life-size at 7 feet 3 inches tall, it represents American troops in an arrowhead formation as if on patrol, consisting of twelve Caucasian figures, three African-American, two Hispanic, one Oriental, and one Native-American. It also reflects the composition of the American military at that time, with fourteen Army personnel, three Marines, one Navy, and one Air Force figures. This kind of memorial was hardly conceivable in the 1950s. Its construction was not mooted for several decades; it was finally inaugurated in 1995.

These cases derived from Kansas, Washington, DC, Delaware, Virginia, and South Carolina, and challenged educational segregation, as established under *Plessy vs. Ferguson* (1896), as unconstitutional. Citing, among other evidence, Myrdal's *An American Dilemma* in support of its decision, the court finally ruled that "in the field of public education the doctrine of 'separate but equal' has no place. Separate educational facilities," it asserted, "are inherently unequal" and denied African-American children "the equal protection of the laws guaranteed by the Fourteenth Amendment."[18]

The *Brown* decision represented a significant first step toward complete desegregation, toward an inclusive, color-blind civic nationalism. Yet it hardly met with universal enthusiasm and was evaded more than it was enacted, especially in those parts of the South where conditions remained pretty much as Myrdal had found them and violence against African

Americans remained widespread. The year following *Brown* witnessed an appalling example of just how far some white southerners were prepared to go to protect white supremacy when a fourteen-year-old boy from Chicago, Emmett Till, was murdered – and before that, mutilated – when on a visit to relatives in Mississippi. Yet that year, too, showed that African Americans were not prepared to accept the status of second-class citizens that some whites accorded them with the start of the Montgomery (Alabama) Bus Boycott, the challenge to segregated transport facilities in the South. Only a little more than seventy years after Ida B. Wells had been ejected from a whites-only coach on the railroad, African-American activist Rosa Parks refused to give up her seat to a white passenger, and was arrested.

Opposition to the arrest of a woman who black minister Martin Luther King, Jr. described as "one of the finest citizens in Montgomery" (and who, in 2000, was designated one of the hundred most significant individuals of the twentieth century) was organized at once, establishing a tradition of black church leadership in the African-American civil rights movement that persisted into the 1960s. Martin Luther King, Jr., who would become the personification of nonviolent direct action against racism, formed the Southern Christian Leadership Conference (SCLC) in the wake of the boycott; a powerful pressure group dedicated to desegregation, it nevertheless faced an uphill struggle, because the boycott, which lasted a year, ended only with another federal ruling (*Browder vs. Gayle*, 1956) that determined segregation on public transport to be unconstitutional. Although this represented another milestone toward an inclusive definition of American citizenship, nevertheless the bus boycott itself was just one step in a process that continued to provoke a hostile response from some parts of white America determined to retain an Anglo-Saxon stranglehold on the nation.

Final Frontiers

The first violent clash between America's Cold War international ideological imperative and its insular Anglo-Saxon impulse came the year after the Montgomery Bus Boycott terminated; 1957, the year that the Soviets launched their *Sputnik* satellite and the year in which Central High School in Little Rock, Arkansas, took a stand against the *Brown* decision. Arkansas's governor, Orval Eugene Faubus, declared that blood would run in the streets were the school forced to desegregate; he was only slightly exaggerating. The image of white children protesting against the very idea of sitting in the same classroom as their black peers or hurling abuse at the black pupils as they tried to enter the school (they were eventually escorted in by the 101st Airborne) was not the kind of media coverage that the land of the free really needed; but then, as in the years to come, parts of the white South seemed utterly oblivious to how the media portrayal of racism in action might play out to the rest of the nation, let alone to a horrified yet fascinated world. And there was no doubt that in the late 1950s, with print media booming, a radio in almost every home, and television starting to ease its way toward total dominance of modern life, the world's biggest global player was playing to a global audience.

In the mid-1950s, however, the global audience's attention was focused more on events in Europe, Asia, and the Middle East than those in Montgomery or in Little Rock. Although the postcolonial world was, in America's view, inherently unstable and therefore at risk of communist control, Stalin's successor, Nikita Khrushchev, in condemning his predecessor's record, seemed to offer the potential for a more balanced relationship between the United States and the Soviet Union. Certainly the United States was not always prepared to wade in to oppose every move communism made; in the case of Hungary, in 1956, it stood well back from the Soviet suppression of the anticommunist uprising. In the Middle East, on the other hand, and in the context of the Suez Crisis (also 1956), the United States moved with greater alacrity to move France and Great Britain aside and assume greater responsibility for the stability of this oil-rich region.

In January 1957, Eisenhower laid out America's position relative to the Middle East and stressed his nation's commitment, in what became known as the Eisenhower Doctrine, "to assist to defend the territorial integrity and the political independence of any nation in the area against Communist armed aggression." He couched his argument in the context of the many "sacrifices," both physical and financial, that America had made "in the cause of freedom" since the end of World War II. "These sacrifices," he stressed, "must not be thrown away."[19] At the same time, assuming the burden of controlling the fallout from previous colonial regimes in defense not just of global stability but of America's self-image as defender of the free world was hardly an unproblematic proposition. As racial unrest in Little Rock and the expansion of the American-Soviet standoff into space with the launch of *Sputnik* revealed, America had more to worry about as the Eisenhower presidency drew to a close than the stability or otherwise of the Middle East.

The launch of *Sputnik* caused a media and a political storm in the United States. Comparisons with Pearl Harbor revealed how seriously some Americans took this simultaneous challenge to their scientific and social superiority and a threat to their national security. The Democrats, headed by Lyndon B. Johnson, attacked Eisenhower over what they perceived as his failure to secure American superiority both in space and on the planet. In a derogatory yet pithy phrase, the White House became known, in some circles, as "the tomb of the well-known soldier." "Failure to master space," Johnson argued, "means being second best in every aspect, in the crucial arena of our Cold War. In the eyes of the world first in space means first, period; second in space is second in everything." Johnson's perspective was echoed, possibly unsurprisingly, by the National Advisory Committee for Aeronautics (NACA), who expressed regret at America's failure to accomplish "a manned lunar landing in advance of the Soviets. Such an accomplishment," NACA argued, "would firmly establish Western technological supremacy and be of great psychological value. Due to the strategic location of the moon for space travel and warfare, an even greater and more permanent value would be derived from such a landing – that of claiming the moon for the United Nations of the Western World."

NACA wanted, in its own words, "to catch up with and ultimately surpass the Soviets in the race for leadership on this planet and for scientific and military supremacy in space." Eisenhower finally acknowledged this imperative. What "makes the Soviet threat unique in all history," he announced, "is its all-inclusiveness. Every human activity is pressed into service as a weapon of expansion. Trade, economic development, military power, arts, science, education, the whole world of ideas. . . . The Soviets are, in short, waging total cold war."[20] He agreed to a man-in-space program that became *Project Mercury*, and to the establishment of new federal bureaucracies designed to address the issues raised by *Sputnik*. The underfunded NACA became, in 1958, the National Aeronautics and Space Administration (NASA), together with two new standing committees in Congress: the Senate Committee on Aeronautical and Space Sciences and the House Committee on Science and Astronautics.

For future American presidents, as for the American people, the legacy of the Eisenhower Doctrine, along with the president's perceived failure in the face of the Soviet space program, proved far-reaching in their effects. And at first, the election of John F. (Jack) Kennedy in 1960, America's first Catholic president, was seen as a new beginning, the passing of the torch to a "new generation," as Kennedy himself described it, one "born in this century, tempered by war, disciplined by a hard and bitter peace." This youthful generation, however, certainly as Kennedy read it, was located firmly within the American revolutionary tradition, but one positioned in a Cold War context. Kennedy's famous inaugural address was that of a cold warrior, who promised that his nation would "pay any price, bear any burden, meet any hardship, support any friend, [and] oppose any foe to assure the survival and the success of liberty."[21] Yet Kennedy's Cold War idealism was a world away from that of another Jack, the "beat" novelist Jack Kerouac, whose famous autobiographical manifesto against middle-class conformity, *On the Road* (1957), suggested that far from fixing themselves in what Kennedy termed America's "ancient heritage," America's youth were rather less certain about the particular road that their nation was heading down.

The 1960s in America are often equated with the rise of youth culture – the fruits of the baby boom of the war years – but the impact of this culture can only be understood in context. Although the American population as a whole was on the increase, birthrates fell dramatically after World War II – by more than a third between 1955 and 1975. Death rates, however, were also on a decline and life expectancy at birth higher than in the prewar era; from 62.6 years in 1940 it had risen to 69.9 years in 1960. In short, America's population was already ageing, which had the effect of positioning younger Americans outside the mainstream statistically, quite aside from what they were up to culturally. And in broad cultural, certainly educational, terms, theirs was a privileged generation. Although the so-called "G.I. Bill of Rights" program that furnished college tuition and maintenance fees for veterans of World War II and Korean War was terminated in 1956, the momentum toward tertiary education for young Americans did not diminish. The number of colleges and universities almost doubled between 1940 and 1970, and their enrollment almost tripled, creating a campus culture with its own perspective on the nation, its nationalism, and its international role.

This perspective was heavily influenced by the "beat generation" of the 1950s, by writers such as Kerouac (b. 1922), Allen Ginsberg (b. 1926), and William S. Burroughs (b. 1914), who rebelled against both the materialism and the militarism that they saw as destructive of the American creed as they perceived this. The fact that many of them perceived it through a drug-induced haze may, of course, have influenced their responses. As Ginsberg famously declared in his poem *Howl* (1956): "I saw the best minds of my generation destroyed by/madness, starving hysterical naked/dragging themselves through the negro streets at dawn/looking for an angry fix." There were a lot of angry young men around in the mid-1950s, of course; it was hardly a phenomenon unique to America, but it had a particular resonance in a nation that seemed, to some of its citizens, to combine complacency with corruption, material wealth with moral poverty.

The contrary, possibly complacent view of America on the eve of Kennedy's election was most famously expressed in the extemporaneous "kitchen debate" between Khrushchev and the then-Vice President Richard Nixon at the American National Exhibition in Moscow in 1959, which highlighted the domestic comfort and general prosperity enjoyed by citizens of the United States. In the slightly surreal yet symbolic setting of a modernist kitchen display, Nixon took the opportunity to emphasize the superiority of the capitalist over the communist lifestyle, the power of economic abundance over ideological austerity. It was a power that Khrushchev, of course, dismissed with disdain. And one that America perhaps took too much for granted. Yet there was plenty to be positive about.

America's GNP doubled between the end of the war and 1960. Federal spending on defense did not, unsurprisingly, diminish during the Cold War, and consumer spending kept pace, facilitated by credit and its physical manifestation, the credit card, which soon became ubiquitous. Americans had always looked toward the future, of course; now they could put off paying for things until it arrived. In all, postwar America experienced a boom to rival that of the 1920s. And if jazz had been the soundtrack to that era, rock-and-roll provided the frequently provocative sound of the 1960s. The "King" of rock-and-roll, Elvis Presley, was on the nation's turntables and, after 1956, its television screens. At the end of World War II, only some 16,000 Americans enjoyed the luxury of television, but by 1953, two-thirds of America's increasingly suburban homes had one. Their suburban location also meant that most American families had a car, and their nation – especially in its cities – had the air pollution and inner-city decline that resulted from the car and the post-war flight to the suburbs, respectively. For America, mobility came at a price. And Americans in the 1950s and 1960s were, as they remain, a very mobile people, with more than a quarter of the population in 1960 living in a state other than the one in which they had been born. It was no surprise, therefore, that when Kerouac went looking for America, he headed for the highway.

When Kennedy went looking for America, he set his sights on the frontier, the "New Frontier" that he described as "not a set of promises" but "a set of challenges." The nation, Kennedy asserted, had experienced "a slippage" in its "intellectual and moral strength" and too readily confused "what is legal with what is right." He promised to set it back on track, to take it to the new frontier beyond which lay "the uncharted areas of science and space, unresolved problems of peace and war, unconquered pockets of ignorance and prejudice, unanswered questions of poverty and surplus." America, he declared, stood "at a turning-point in history. We must prove all over again whether this nation – or any nation so conceived – can long endure," he announced, in an invocation of Lincoln's Gettysburg Address, but the challenge came now from "the single-minded advance of the Communist system," not that of the Confederacy.

On this last point, however, Kennedy was only partly right. The year of his election opened with civil rights protests in the South, as African-American students in Greensboro, North Carolina, challenged the "whites only" tradition at a lunch counter in their local Woolworth's store by sitting in seats designated for white use, despite being asked to leave. Their persistence paid off. Although it took five months, the Woolworth's chain finally agreed to end discrimination at its lunch counters. This was another victory in the fight for equality, and its timing was significant.

In 1960, the South, the white South at least, was readying itself for the Civil War Centennial, the commemoration of that time in its history when it went to war with the rest of the nation in defense of Anglo-Saxon dominance, in defense of slavery, albeit slavery wrapped up in a convoluted Constitutional package that it termed states' rights. It had unwrapped that particular defense once more in Little Rock in opposition to the presence of federal troops, sent to enforce the Supreme Court ruling in *Brown*, and would continue to invoke it in the face of growing national opposition to segregation in the 1960s. The year following the lunch-counter sit-ins saw the first of the "Freedom Rides" to the South. Organized by CORE, these sent integrated groups of passengers on buses into the states of the Deep South to test the desegregation of public transport ruling. The Freedom Riders encountered widespread violence in states such as Alabama and Mississippi; in Alabama, one of their buses was firebombed in Anniston, and in Birmingham, the Freedom Riders were attacked by the Klan. The following year, when black student James Meredith attempted to enroll at the University of Mississippi, a mob blocked his way. Kennedy, as Eisenhower before him, was forced to send in the army.

It was especially poignant that this upsurge in African-American protest and the concomitant white backlash against equal rights in the early 1960s should take place against the backdrop of Civil War battle

FIGURE 10.7. Civil Rights March on Washington (Warren K. Leffler, August 28, 1963). Image courtesy of the Library of Congress Prints and Photographs Division (LC-DIG-ppmsca-03128).

reenactments and the celebration of a defeated Confederate cause. Civil Rights was not absent from the agenda, but with black delegates barred from the hotel in Charleston chosen for the start of the Centennial, the whole event got off to a bumpy start – and continued that way. Hopes that the president might, on January 1, 1963, endorse a second Emancipation Proclamation were dashed when Kennedy declined to attend the commemoration ceremony at the Lincoln Memorial. For the rest of that year, the demonstrations and the violence continued.

The violence reached a peak of sorts in Birmingham in May 1963, when images of the local police attacking African Americans – some of them children – with fire hoses, dogs, and truncheons, were broadcast on television to a shocked and sickened America. The following month, NAACP field secretary, Medgar Evers, a World War II veteran who had served in Europe, was shot dead in Jackson, Mississippi. On August 28, 1963, some quarter of a million Americans attended the March on Washington (Figure 10.7) organized to raise awareness not just of the violence being perpetrated on African Americans in the South, but the full range of inequalities in jobs, housing, and education that blacks experienced. It fell to Martin Luther King, Jr. and not, in the end, to

Kennedy to invoke Lincoln's Emancipation Proclamation of 1863 and to remind Americans that "one hundred years later, the Negro still is not free. One hundred years later, the life of the Negro is still sadly crippled by the manacles of segregation and the chains of discrimination." "I have a dream," King famously declared, "that one day this nation will rise up and live out the true meaning of its creed: 'We hold these truths to be self-evident, that all men are created equal.'"

How far Kennedy would have gone to effect the fulfillment of King's dream will forever be a moot point. Certainly the violence in Alabama and the March on Washington had begun to impinge on a consciousness hitherto too focused on the Cold War, too concerned with the "single-minded advance" of communism to address the single-mindedness of America's segregationists. And Kennedy's commitment to the containment of communism produced some unfortunate results, including the infamous "Bay of Pigs" failed invasion of Cuba in 1961, undertaken with the intention of overthrowing Fidel Castro's regime and, more worryingly for the world, the Cuban Missile Crisis of October 1962, when the United States and the Soviet Union engaged in a deadly standoff that could have resulted in nuclear war. By the summer of 1963, however, Kennedy had not only cooled on the Cold War, but had warmed to civil rights. In June, he gave public commitment to the federal enforcement of desegregation, but he did not live to see the 1964 Civil Rights Act passed. His assassination on November 22, 1963 ended a presidency that had expressed the hopes and encapsulated the fears of a generation now facing a frontier that seemed far from new, only as violent and as unpredictable as any in its nation's history.

Armies of the Night

Counterculture and Counterrevolution

America – the land where a new kind of man was born from the idea that
God was present in every man not only as compassion but as power, and
so the country belonged to the people.
(Norman Mailer, *The Armies of the Night*, 1968)

Lyndon B. Johnson, abruptly elevated into the Oval Office by the assassination of Kennedy at the end of 1963, had more than his predecessor's
popularity to contend with; he had the legacy of more than half a century of liberalism to live up to. Virtually every president before him since
Theodore Roosevelt had offered the nation a deal or the promise of a
new start; Square Deal, Fair Deal, New Deal, New Freedom, and, in
1960, a New Frontier, "a frontier of unknown opportunities and perils –
a frontier of unfulfilled hopes and threats," as Kennedy had described it.
There was, possibly, a limit to how many fresh starts any single nation
could hope to sustain, especially one as new as the United States was in
1963. Yet Johnson had his own plan, one that would both incorporate
and encapsulate all the promises that he had grown up with and through,
one not grounded in the alleviation of national poverty but in the potential for attacking individual poverty that the nation's postwar prosperity
provided, one that would finally fulfill the promise of the United States
of America: the "Great Society."

As yet unelected in his own right, however, Johnson initially confined
himself to fulfilling what he presented as the Kennedy legacy; the passage
of the Civil Rights Act (1964) that, in theory, ended public discrimination
across the board, in libraries, schools, restaurants, hotels, sports facilities,
and jobs, across the nation. In the face of southern opposition to the

act, the Equal Employment Opportunity Commission (EEOC) was also established to ensure equal pay not just for African Americans and other minority groups, but for women as well. Yet the spirit of the murdered Kennedy was not sufficient in itself to assuage the hostility of opponents of legislation that, in the context of the violence and hostility that civil rights provoked, was a controversial move in the direction of a fully civic nationalism for the United States. Faced with not just racist but Republican opposition, Johnson knew, as he advised the then-Democratic Whip in the Senate and his future vice president, Hubert Humphrey, that he had to make the Civil Rights Act "an American bill and not just a Democratic bill." Even as it passed, however, Johnson feared that in this he had failed. As he observed to his then aide, Bill Moyers, "I think we just delivered the South to the Republican party for a long time to come."[1]

The Civil Rights Act may have delivered the South to the Republicans. It certainly did not deliver it from violence. The summer of 1964 witnessed more violent clashes between civil rights activists and southern segregationists in Mississippi. The catalyst was the issue of voting rights, the one thing that the Civil Rights Act had not directly addressed. In June, the Mississippi Summer Project (or Freedom Summer) was launched in an attempt to increase the percentage of African Americans on the voting rolls. Civil rights groups, including CORE, the NAACP, and the Student Nonviolent Coordinating Committee (SNCC), organized voter-registration drives directed at the African-American population in Mississippi. The SNCC had done this before, in 1961, and then its efforts had been beaten back and one of its local organizers murdered. So the SNCC had no illusions about the implications of attempting to enforce the Fifteenth Amendment (the right to vote) in a state where opposition to the black ballot could take such extreme form. Nevertheless, the extent of open aggression the campaign faced could hardly have been imagined. The bombings and beatings were the least of it; some two dozen activists were murdered in the cause of civil rights in the South in the period between Kennedy's election and the passage of the Voting Rights Act in 1965.

White supremacists crossed more than just the color line, however, when they kidnapped and murdered three activists, Michael Schwerner, Andrew Goodman, and James Chaney, two of whom (Schwerner and Goodman) were white students from New York. Faced with the public outcry that followed, the government was finally persuaded to act. In what seemed like a depressing rerun of history, Johnson, like Ulysses S. Grant almost a century before him, sent federal forces, the FBI, into the South, but the discovery of the bodies of the three activists did not automatically result in a murder trial. Murder is (mainly) a state, not a federal crime; even the murder of an American president was not, until 1965, a federal offense. And in this case, the state declined to prosecute. So the federal government was forced, as it had previously done in the case of the Medgar Evers murder, to invoke legislation from the nineteenth century, from the period of the supposed Reconstruction of the South, to prosecute those accused of the murders – the Force Act of 1870.

If some of the parallels between the nineteenth- and twentieth-century United States were depressing as far as white-on-black violence and the legislative limits to preventing this were concerned, some were more promising; it was not for nothing that the 1960s became known as America's "Second Reconstruction." Head of the FBI, J. Edgar Hoover, like Grant's Secret Service chief Hiram B. Whitley, had his own pre-occupations that initially distracted him from prioritizing civil rights. Whitley had been obsessed with immigrants in the cities, Hoover with communism in the country as a whole, and neither evinced any especial empathy with the plight of African Americans, but both were color-blind when it came to crime fighting. Certainly Hoover authorized wiretaps on Martin Luther King, Jr., and the counterintelligence program he controlled, COINTELPRO, targeted "Black Hate" groups that, it was decided, included not just the Nation of Islam (an African-American religious activist organization), but also the SNCC and the SCLC. Yet in the aftermath of the murders in Mississippi, COINTELPRO turned its attention to "White Hate" organizations, including the Klan, with considerable success.

In the political arena, the fallout from the Civil Rights Act coalesced around the 1964 presidential campaign. The Democratic Convention in Atlantic City, New Jersey, faced a challenge from the Mississippi Freedom Democratic Party (MFDP). Formed in response to the disenfranchisement of African Americans in Mississippi, the MFDP had registered some 60,000 black voters and now demanded the state's seats at the convention. The media momentum was on the side of the MFDP, focused as this was on civil rights activist Fannie Lou Hamer's detailed description of the horrors of growing up in segregated Mississippi and the police brutality she had endured in the process of attempting to register black voters there. Despite this, some of the white delegates threatened to walk out of the convention. This had happened before, in 1948, in the wake of Truman's desegregation of the armed forces and, indeed, storming out seemed to be something of a white southern tradition, but not one Johnson could afford to indulge in 1964.

Johnson may have feared that he had lost the Deep South, but he did not want to alienate white voters there entirely. He did, after all, have his own priorities, the "War on Poverty," which would evolve into the "Great Society" program, to get through Congress after the election – assuming he won. And the white backlash against the Civil Rights Act, against federal imposition of desegregation on the South, was potentially a potent political force in 1964. In the primaries, the governor of Alabama, George Wallace, had done surprisingly well; not well enough to place Johnson's candidacy in question, but well enough to suggest that Wallace's segregationist message met a receptive audience, and not just in Alabama. Wallace had achieved national prominence, or notoriety, on his election as governor the previous year, when he had famously declared that he stood for "segregation now, segregation tomorrow, segregation forever," a statement he later repudiated, and one that may have owed more to political expediency than deep-seated sentiment.

In 1964, however, political expediency for the Democrats required some form of compromise between hard-line segregationists in their party and the MFDP. The one arrived at, the promise that the 1968 convention would be fully integrated, risked satisfying no one. As a result, the 1964 Democratic convention represented a crucial turning point for the civil rights movement, the moment when an unbridgeable gap began to open between those, like Martin Luther King, Jr., who saw the promise of future integration as one to work toward and those who believed that Democratic desegregation deferred was simply not good enough. Consequently, the period after 1964 witnessed the rise of a new militancy, the "Black Power" movement. The concept of Black Power had originated with the radical black nationalist, Malcolm X, who was assassinated in 1965, but was popularized by the SNCC leader Stokely Carmichael after Malcolm X's death. Black Power was more than just a political position; it was an entire cultural shift among those who, like Carmichael, increasingly regarded integration as "irrelevant" and who wanted not the promise of future change, but "Freedom Now!"

The Republicans also had freedom on the agenda in 1964: freedom from federal interference and freedom from communism. They put up Barry Goldwater, who advocated an essentially conservative agenda that revolved around a reduction in "Big Government" and included the "rollback" of communist forces in China and of social welfare programs at home. His conservative "states' rights" message, come the election itself, played well in the Deep South (Alabama, Georgia, Mississippi, Louisiana, and South Carolina) but almost nowhere else apart from his home state of Arizona. The Klan's support of Goldwater (Figure 11.1)

FIGURE 11.1. Ku Klux Klan members and opponents clash at a Klan demonstration in support of Barry Goldwater's campaign for nomination at the Republican National Convention in San Francisco in July 1964 (Photo by Warren K. Leffler). Image courtesy of the Library of Congress Prints and Photographs Division (LC-DIG-ppmsca-03195).

may have borne out Johnson's fear that the Civil Rights Act had delivered the South to the Republicans, but overall the election returns made it clear that the Deep South was out of touch with the rest of the nation, and the Klan just out of touch. The Democrats tried to imply that Goldwater himself was out of step, not with the nation, but with sanity. In response to the less-than-stimulating Republican slogan "in your heart you know he's right," Democrats countered with the rather snappier "in your guts you know he's nuts." Of course Goldwater was far from that; his political message failed to resonate with voters in 1964, but it established a marker for a future in which conservatism would, unlike the segregationist Deep South, rise again.

The 1964 campaign proved memorable in other ways too, not just in its sloganeering but in the screening – just once, officially, but on any number of news channels thereafter – of the controversial Democratic "Daisy" commercial, devised in response to Goldwater's refusal to rule out, categorically, the future use of nuclear weapons. This sixty-second ad showed a young girl counting to ten as she picked the petals from a flower; when the last petal had gone, a male voice began a countdown to detonation, as the camera focused in on the child, on her face turned up to the sky, on her eye, and on her pupil in which a nuclear explosion was reflected. "Vote for President Johnson on November 3," the sonorous voice-over intoned. "The stakes are too high for you to stay home."[2] Attacked for the suggestion that Goldwater might, if elected, instigate nuclear war, the "Daisy" ad was immediately pulled; but it tapped into the residual fear of nuclear Armageddon that hung over America, over the world, in the 1960s and, to a lesser degree ever since. The "Daisy" ad, indeed, has proved a persistent political weapon that has been reworked several times since its initial incarnation in 1964, most notably in the 1996 Republican campaign, by which point the threat to the child was deemed to be narcotics, not nuclear war.

A single commercial, however hard-hitting, cannot take the credit for Johnson's landslide victory in the 1964 election. Having won so decisively, with just over 61 percent of the popular vote, Johnson finally had the mandate for his own legislative program, and civil rights activists had his promise that future Democratic conventions, at least, would be integrated; but even Martin Luther King, Jr. did not want to wait that long. In the immediate aftermath of the election, he decided to seize the momentum provided by it to push for an expansion of voting rights in Alabama, to face head on Wallace's assertion that segregation would forever rule in that state. The Selma-to-Montgomery March that King organized in March 1965 to highlight the campaign offered yet another opportunity for the television cameras to capture southern law enforcement officers beating and tear-gassing civil rights activists as they attempted to cross the Edmund Pettus Bridge. For black activists such as Carmichael, this really was a bridge too far, but consensus among the various civil rights organizations as to how best to proceed was compromised by their increasingly clashing agendas.

When, the following year, James Meredith, having endured what for him was the rather trying experience of education at the University of Mississippi, mooted a "march against fear" to encourage African Americans in the South to capitalize on their recent enfranchisement by registering to vote in time for the midterm elections in November, few civil rights groups were interested. Undaunted, Meredith, with two companions, began the march anyway; barely ten miles into it he was shot (fortunately not fatally) by a white extremist. This at least raised the profile of his protest, which was taken up by CORE and SNCC to become the more militant "Meredith March," itself symbolic of a move away from passive resistance to white supremacy and toward the more aggressive and exclusionary position represented by Black Power. The irony was that as radical civil rights activists turned away from white liberalism, from faith in the federal government's effectiveness in securing equality, that government was finally prepared at least to try to keep what Johnson described as "The American Promise."

The president's response to Selma had been swift. In a nationally broadcast address, he spoke of the American commitment to and defense of "the dignity of man and the destiny of democracy," and drew events in Selma into the orbit of those at Lexington and Concord (when the Revolutionary War broke out) and at Appomattox (when the Civil War ended); all, he asserted, represented turning points "in man's unending search for freedom." In an echo of King's speech in 1963, Johnson reminded Congress that a "century has passed, more than a hundred years, since equality was promised. And yet the Negro is not equal." "There is no cause for pride in what has happened at Selma," Johnson declared. "There is no cause for self-satisfaction in the long denial of equal rights of millions of Americans. But there is," he asserted, "cause for hope."[3]

With the passage of the Voting Rights Act (1965) and the Twenty-fourth Amendment abolishing poll tax restrictions on the franchise, the United States had completed a cycle of civil rights reforms that had begun with *Brown vs. Board of Education* in 1954. The civil rights in question, however, had never just pertained to the African-American freedom struggle in the South. When Johnson assumed power, the nation, largely driven by the Supreme Court under Chief Justice (1953–1969) Earl Warren, was already in the process of reinterpreting its constitution in the context of the American creed, broadly defined, as that applied to the changing circumstances of the twentieth century and to changing meanings of citizenship. The results have been termed by some the "rights revolution," and much of the impetus for this derived from the New Deal, the second period, following the Reconstruction amendments of the nineteenth century, of America's history when the relationship between the federal government and the people shifted toward the idea of the federal protection of individual and group rights and expanded freedom.

The most obvious of these new rights related to not just racial equality and the franchise, but to law enforcement; no minor issue given how many black and white civil rights activists were being thrown in jail in the South in this period. Four cases specifically were intended to address inequality before the law: *Mapp vs. Ohio* (1961), *Gideon vs. Wainwright* (1963), *Escobedo vs. Illinois* (1964), and *Miranda vs. Arizona* (1966). Each involved the arrest of an individual in circumstances deemed by the court to be unfair in some respect. *Mapp* established that prosecution be based on reasonable evidence acquired within the Fourth Amendment's restrictions on search and seizure; *Gideon* had no attorney, being unable to afford one, and the ruling was that in such cases the state must provide counsel; and in *Escobedo* and *Miranda*, the court went furthest of all. It established not only that an attorney must be present during interrogation, but that the suspect must be informed of his or her constitutional rights; hence the "Miranda warning." These were landmark cases for citizenship rights, but they did little at the time to assure some Americans, and especially some African Americans, that discrimination in all its forms – racial, sexual, or judicial – was either dying out or could be forcibly eradicated.

Exacerbating the rise of black radicalism was the fact that on the other side of the country, the situation was little better than in Selma. In the summer of 1965, race riots broke out in the predominantly African-American Watts area of Los Angeles. Again, the National Guard was sent in, and again American television audiences were confronted with images of violence rending their nation. *Life* magazine later singled out the Watts riots as the "dividing line" of the 1960s, an outburst that "ripped the fabric of lawful democratic society and set the tone of confrontation and open revolt so typical of our present condition."[4]

Yet the Watts uprising was a dividing line only in the sense that confrontation and open revolt moved out of the South; after 1965, urban unrest affected many northern cities, notably Newark, New Jersey, and Detroit, Michigan. In that sense, there had been a shift away from consensus over the meaning of the American creed and its connection with American citizenship and toward disenchantment with democratic society more widespread than that prior to the 1964 election. The usual explanation for this lies in America's escalating involvement in Southeast Asia, but viewing the 1960s as a whole from the perspective of the Vietnam War is apt to mislead as much as it informs. What became known as the "Vietnam syndrome," a term used to insinuate American reluctance to commit to foreign involvement and to face up to the persistent communist challenge after 1975, applies equally to the still early – historically speaking – assessment of the political, cultural, and military impact of that conflict. That it had an impact, of course, is unquestionable.

Not the least important element of the legacy that Kennedy bequeathed his successor was the war in Vietnam, one that he had, in turn, inherited from the Truman and Eisenhower doctrines on containment and on the commitment to aid other nations in the fight against communism that had grown out of World War II and been honed in the context of the Cold War that followed. Allied to that was the fact that, although America had not endured the physical devastation experienced by the European nations in World War II, weapons technology generally, and the nuclear threat specifically, nevertheless rendered her vulnerable to the threat of future destruction. America's response was to reinforce the national security state – and in the process its own military-industrial complex – both in the form of the bureaucracies that controlled and directed this – the Department of Defense, the CIA, and the National Security Council (NSC) – and by growing the areas of civil defense, intelligence, and counterintelligence and military research and development.

From a defense perspective, post–World War II America was caught in a cleft stick. On the one hand, she believed that in communism she faced an enemy that, in Eisenhower's words was "global in scope, atheistic in character, ruthless in purpose, and insidious in method." Further, the threat posed by it promised "to be of indefinite duration." On the other, the danger of becoming too similar to that which she most feared was also a risk. As Eisenhower noted in his farewell address to the nation in 1961, the "conjunction of an immense military establishment and an arms industry is new in the American experience," and, although necessary, this had "grave implications." American government, he warned, "must guard against the acquisition of unwarranted influence, whether sought or unsought, by the military-industrial complex. . . . Only an alert and knowledgeable citizenry can compel the proper meshing of the huge industrial and military machinery of defense with our peaceful methods and goals," he advised, "so that security and liberty may prosper together."[5]

As farewell addresses went, this may be regarded as something of a conundrum. Effectively it advised Americans to develop the nation's defense capacity and simultaneously defend against it. Yet it was fully in keeping with American tradition. After all, in 1796, George Washington had warned Americans not just of the threat of foreign entanglements but of the dangers of internal dissent. By the dawn of the 1960s, America could no longer avoid foreign involvement, but the threat of the nation being undermined from within, whether by forces antithetical to the American creed, such as communism, or by those rather too rigorously dedicated to its protection and through it their own aggrandizement, remained a risk. Indeed, the military-industrial complex did, in the aftermath of Vietnam, become something of a sinister specter in its own right. Yet that was the problem with the Cold War; it fed on fear,

fear of an insidious and "indefinite" threat, one located in the Soviet Union only up to a point, and the fear in turn fed the faith that the United States could, indeed must, win a war waged, in part at least, against no tangible foe but in defense of a national identity long grounded in, and defined through, conflict.

Of course, the United States did not wage the Cold War alone, and at least some of the danger was far from imaginary. Nevertheless, in the case of Vietnam, although communism was perceived to be the threat, too soon America's military credibility became the main issue. The decision, taken in 1950, to aid the French in their battle to retain control of Indochina was made mainly in the context of containment, or what became known as the "Domino Theory," the fear that the "loss" of one nation to communism would swiftly ensure the fall of many more across Asia and the Middle East. Even so it was not a decision that America reached unaided. Indeed, America was initially uncertain that French colonial rule in Indochina was desirable in the wake of World War II, but both British and French interests were bound up in France's retaining her position as a global player – something that, absent American support, was unlikely. American caution on the matter gave way only gradually. Yet by the time that Eisenhower handed over to Kennedy, America was both funding and "advising" (the advice was armed) the pro-American government headed by Ngo Dinh Diem in South Vietnam against the encroachment of the North Vietnamese "Viet Cong."

For Kennedy, the success of American counterinsurgency in Vietnam was partly bound up in his desire to avoid a similar accusation to that leveled at Truman by his Republican opponents that he had somehow "lost" China to communism in 1949, and largely constrained by his own unwillingness to commit American forces to a conflict with rather messy origins and no obvious end point. Kennedy's advisor, General Maxwell Taylor, was dispatched to assess the situation in the fall of 1961. Taylor's opinion was that without American ground troops, South Vietnam could not hold out against the North, but Kennedy was uncertain. "The troops will march in; the crowds will cheer; and in four days everyone will have forgotten," Kennedy observed to the historian Arthur M. Schlesinger. "Then we will be told we have to send in more troops. It is like taking a drink, the effect wears off, and you have to take another."[6] The troops were, nevertheless, sent in, soon to be followed, as Kennedy had feared, by more; from some 900 at the end of 1961 to more than 11,000 a year later, to more than half a million by 1968. It soon became obvious that the cost of American commitment to the containment of communism

FIGURE 11.2. The Secretary of Defense, Robert McNamara, referring to a map of Vietnam at a press conference in April 1965 (Photo by Marion S. Trikosko, April 26, 1965). The previous month had seen American attacks on North Vietnam and its defense of South Vietnam take off in earnest with three main military operations: Rolling Thunder, Flaming Dart, and Arc Light. Image courtesy of the Library of Congress Prints and Photographs Division (LC-USZ62-134155).

in South Vietnam was and would be high. "By the end of 1965," *Life* magazine recalled, "Vietnam had become a real war – and a national trial" (Figure 11.2).

Even as Johnson was campaigning in the months leading up to the election of 1964, the war was already in the process of escalation. In August, an incident in the Gulf of Tonkin, when North Vietnamese ships possibly fired on an American vessel, enabled Johnson to assert that an act of aggression against the United States had occurred. In response, Congress passed the Gulf of Tonkin resolution; this was not an official declaration of war, but it might as well have been, permitting as it did "all necessary measures" to be taken against North Vietnam. In March of the following year, American bombers attacked the North in Operation Rolling Thunder, and within days the Marines arrived in the South. Only a week later, Johnson stood before Congress to remind it of the "American Promise." "This is the richest and most powerful country which ever occupied the globe. The might of past empires is little compared to ours. But," Johnson concluded, "I do not want to be the President who built empires, or sought grandeur, or extended dominion... I want to be the President who helped to end hatred among his fellow men and who promoted love among the people of all races and all regions and all parties. I want to be the President who helped to end war among the brothers of this earth."

The Haunted Generation

It has been said that if you remember the 1960s then you probably were not there – a quip that is more accurate than it seems. It was not just America's military might but her moral imperative that took a beating in Vietnam, and in part the persistent popular perspective on the period as one dominated by antiwar demonstrations reflects that. When *Life* magazine, in 1969, presented its overview of a decade that it chose to label one of "Tumult and Change," it did so not just in the context of the still ongoing war in Vietnam, but in the more specific context of the assassination, the previous year, of both Martin Luther King, Jr. and, just two months later, Robert Kennedy, brother of John F. Kennedy and, at the time of his death, the Democratic candidate for the presidency in the election that year. This combination of events shocked the nation as much, possibly even more, than the killing of the president almost five years before. Yet in common with much media meditation on this period of America's history, *Life* was less than informative about the actual "tremendous forces and changes" that the nation experienced. Hyped to within an inch of its life at the time, it is hardly surprising that the decade of the 1960s seemed, with hindsight, to have somehow fallen short of those ideals identified with it.

Certainly neither the idealism of the 1960s nor the disillusionment that followed could ever have been so potent without the challenge posed by the Vietnam War. What was perceived as radical, at the time and since, relied to a great extent on oppositional forces that did not grow out of the war but were intensified both by it and by the broader cultural context of the Western world as a whole at this time. The soundtrack both to Johnson's election in 1964 and the escalation of the war in 1965 was provided by bands that seemed to exemplify rebellious (although financially astute) youth; both the Beatles and the Rolling Stones toured America for the first time in 1964, and the hysteria their appearance produced seemed to set the tone for a generation prone to such outbursts on matters musical and moral. "The Times They Are a-Changin," Bob Dylan told America in that same year, and his lyrics posited a generational divide that has since come to define the decade. As "mothers and fathers throughout the land" were advised not to criticize what they could not "understand," not a few of them must have contemplated hurling both the album and the turntable out of the window.

The Vietnam generation has come to be called the "haunted generation." How that idea played out with the generation that witnessed firsthand the results of the "Final Solution" or fought in Korea may not be hard to imagine, especially given that in the early years of the Vietnam conflict it was America's youth, and not its parents, who supported the war most strongly. With only one-tenth of 1 percent of the population as a whole demonstrably opposing the war in its early stages, hostility to military involvement in Vietnam was, initially, a minority position. In this respect, the antiwar movement bears comparison with the abolition movement of the nineteenth century. Both were fringe movements driven by a moral imperative that became mass movements as the political, cultural, and military context shifted. For the Civil War generation, the shift had been toward a war that began "a new birth of freedom." For the Vietnam generation, the shift had taken them closer to that freedom promised a century before, and away from war.

In 1964, however, few Americans questioned either the military might or moral authority of their nation. As late as the fall of the following year, indeed, some 20,000 turned out for a prowar march in New York, and they were not atypical – except in terms of American history as a whole. Intervention in Vietnam, at the outset, garnered a greater degree of consensus from the American public than almost any previous conflict, the exceptions being World War II and the Civil War. Washington had always struggled to attract, and retain, troops for the Continental Army; some 64 percent of Americans expressed unease over America's involvement in World War I; some 62 percent did the same over the war in Korea. By contrast, some 85 percent of Americans supported America's intervention in Vietnam in 1964, and some 65 percent still backed it in 1969.[7]

Neither urban unrest nor rock-and-roll, it seemed, translated into a marked deviation from faith in America in the early 1960s. With the focus on Johnson's ambitious plan to eradicate poverty, it seemed that the promise of America was on the verge of being fulfilled. Even those more cynical about how much remained to be done in terms of civil rights could hardly have quibbled with Johnson's assessment of America as not just the wealthiest but the "most powerful" nation on earth. And so much of that power derived from its armed forces, from the military power they could wield in war, and the economic power that victory brought the nation.

In 1964, less than two decades after the end of World War II, and in the context of its economic impact, the war on poverty seemed equally winnable. Couched in the language of freedom derived from the New Deal – freedom from want, from inequality – the "Great Society" program comprised a combination of employment, educational, environmental, and health initiatives that may have had their roots in the reform past but very much addressed contemporary concerns. Work experience programs were offered under the auspices of the Economic Opportunity Act (1964), developmental initiatives, notably Head Start, a pre-school educational program for children, were reinforced by the Higher Education Act (1965), and health care provided via the Medicare and Medicaid programs that sought to ensure medical insurance provision for the elderly and the poor, respectively. There was even a domestic variant of Kennedy's international Peace Corps, Volunteers in Service to America (VISTA), along with a range of measures designed to protect and enhance the environment, whether that be slum clearance in the inner cities or legislation to ensure that rural rivers and waterways remained unpolluted.

At the same time, and in the context of these initiatives, the old certainties also began to give way. Perhaps inevitably, the impetus toward social and economic change at the federal level encouraged rather than muted the reform impulse at the grassroots. Individually, each reform agenda, be it focused on gender, race, sexuality, the environment, politics, or foreign policy, had a potential impact in its own sphere, but the 1960s witnessed a confluence of what might otherwise have been conflicting, or at least competing, agendas that loosely connected in what became known as the "counterculture." The counterculture was far from a coherent movement; indeed, elements of it were very far from coherent, period, but it did posit a sustained and multifaceted challenge not to the American creed, but to the inadequacies of its implementation. The counterculture, too, was aimed at the creation of a "Great Society," if not quite in the way Johnson had in mind.

Not everyone involved in the counterculture would necessarily have seen it this way at the time. Some did. The rise of the New Left, and organizations such as Students for a Democratic Society (SDS), carried a serious political message, one very much grounded in American tradition, in the perennial question of what it meant to be an American citizen, of what the nation stood for. SDS was inspired to challenge what it perceived as the "ruling myths" of its age by a combination of civil rights protests and the Cold War. It identified the "decline of utopia and hope" as one of "the defining features of social life" in the 1960s, and sought to establish what it called "a democracy of individual participation" in which "power rooted in possession, privilege, or circumstance" would be replaced "by power rooted in love, reflectiveness, reason, and creativity." In short, SDS promulgated sentiments strong enough to appeal to the moral-minded and vague enough to apply to almost anyone. "A new left," the SDS declared, unsurprisingly, because it was a student body, "must consist of younger people."[8] Presumably, its potency would decline as these "younger people" aged; but for too many Americans in the 1960s, ageing was not an option.

In 1965, almost 1,500 Americans died in Vietnam. By 1966, this figure had risen to more than 5,000; by 1967, it was 9,000. Yet the Harris Poll of July of that year found that 72 percent of Americans still supported the war. By October, that figure had fallen to 58 percent, but by Christmas it was back up again, with some 60 percent in favor of escalation. Clearly, any causal relationship that may have existed between casualties and public condemnation of the war was a confused one. In this regard, 1967 was a case in point.

The year 1967 was the one in which *Time* magazine first identified – or classified – the "hippie." It had begun with a mass counterculture celebration, the "Human Be-In" in the Golden Gate Park, San Francisco, followed by the "Summer of Love" that focused on the city's Haight-Ashbury district. In other cities, notably Boston, Detroit, and Newark, love was in rather short supply, and race riots had to be quelled by the National Guard (Figure 11.3), which prompted *Newsweek* to rebrand the "Summer of Love" the "Summer of Discontent." October saw "Stop the Draft Week" followed by the antiwar March on the Pentagon, the inspiration for author and journalist Norman Mailer's meditation on literature, history, and Mailer – *The Armies of the Night* (1968) – but again, the impact of the demonstration was perhaps disproportionate to its media image: at the end of that year, 70 percent of Americans expressed their disapproval of antiwar demonstrations, at least to the Harris Poll.

Appalled by the urban rioting, Johnson established a commission under the chairmanship of the governor of Illinois, Otto Kerner, to explore the causes of inner-city unrest. The Kerner Report, published the following year, reached some worrying conclusions, not least that America was "moving toward two societies, one black, one white – separate and unequal." "Discrimination and segregation have long permeated much

FIGURE 11.3. The aftermath of the Washington, DC, riot in 1968 (Photo by Warren K. Leffler, April 8, 1968). The DC National Guard patrolled the streets of the capitol in the wake of five days of race riots that followed the assassination, on April 4, of Martin Luther King, Jr. Riots broke out in cities across the nation in direct response to King's murder, but by 1968, many of these had already become used to the sight of armed forces in their streets, especially in the wake of the "Summer of Discontent" the previous year, the stimulus for the establishment, in 1967, of the National Advisory Commission on Civil Disorders (the Kerner Commission). Image courtesy of the Library of Congress Prints and Photographs Division (LC-DIG-ppmsca-19734).

of American life," it noted, and "they now threaten the future of every American.... To pursue our present course will involve the continuing polarization of the American community," it argued, "and, ultimately, the destruction of basic democratic values." The immediate cause of many of the riots, it found, was African-American violence, not against white Americans, but "against local symbols of white American society," and the stimulus comprised a combination of police tactics, unemployment, and the "inadequacy" of federal employment, educational, and welfare programs. "What white Americans have never fully understood but what the Negro can never forget," it concluded, "is that white society is deeply implicated in the ghetto. White institutions created it, white institutions maintain it, and white society condones it."[9]

For the increasingly beleaguered Johnson, this sobering assessment hardly reflected well on the success of his "Great Society" program, one already compromised by the military situation abroad. The year in which the Kerner Report appeared – election year – began badly for American forces in Vietnam. The Tet Offensive, launched in January, saw North Vietnamese (Viet Cong) forces penetrate the U.S. embassy grounds in Saigon while simultaneously besieging American troops at the American air base at Khe Sanh, near Laos – all events that the American public could track through extensive television and media coverage. American casualty rates were higher than ever, and opinion polls suggested that Johnson was losing the support of the American public. He had certainly lost the support of his party. For the first time since 1912, the Democrats mounted an internal challenge – two, actually – in the form of Minnesota Senator Eugene McCarthy and Robert Kennedy. Johnson left them to battle it out. At the end of March, he announced "I shall not seek, and I will not accept, the nomination of my party for another term as your president." Only days later, Martin Luther King, Jr. was assassinated in Memphis, Tennessee.

Yet neither King's or Robert Kennedy's murder nor Democratic division and the persistent racial gulf exacerbated by a war in which a disproportionate number (relative to population percentages) of frontline troops were black caused cracks sufficient to fissure into American foreign policy, to end American support for the Vietnam War. There was protest, but not sustained and certainly not always on the scale of the March on the Pentagon in 1967. When the iconic singer, Eartha Kitt, was indiscrete – or incensed – enough to criticize the administration's foreign policy at a White House luncheon, her actions garnered her support and censure in equal measure (Figure 11.4). Similar hostility met actress

FIGURE 11.4. An antiwar protest in front of the White House following singer Eartha Kitt's criticism of the Vietnam War (Photo by Warren K. Leffler, January 19, 1968). Image courtesy of the Library of Congress Prints and Photographs Division (LC-DIG-ppmsca-24360).

Jane Fonda's opposition to the war, even before she posed atop a North Vietnamese anti-aircraft battery in Hanoi in 1972. Clearly, even in the endgame, many Americans would not tolerate criticism of their nation's actions in Vietnam. And yet, in the war's aftermath, almost nothing but self-criticism seemed to appear.

Comprehending the lack of opposition to the Vietnam War in the 1960s is perhaps more straightforward than understanding the longer-term response to it. In total, some 2.3 million troops served in Vietnam between 1963 and 1975; some 58,000 of them died (2.5 percent). Yet despite media coverage of students burning their draft cards before the Pentagon, in fact, the Vietnam War witnessed no mobilization on the scale of previous conflicts, certainly not that of World War II. Of the 27 million men who reached draft age between 1964 and 1973, some 2 million were drafted, some 9 million enlisted, and of all these, slightly more than 1.5 million saw combat; in short, some 6 percent of the Vietnam generation fought in Vietnam, so it may not be surprising that either opposition to the war was not sustained or that support of it remained relatively constant.

As Americans looked back on this period of their history, 1968 seemed to be the year not of decision, but the year when a decision failed to be made, and it was that failure that haunted the "Vietnam generation" then, and to an extent continues to haunt it still. The year 1968 seemed to be that point – but only in hindsight – when America turned a corner, away from the liberal consensus and toward the Right. At the time, however, as the 1960s – that decade of "tumult and change" – drew to a close, there was still consensus of a kind, one forged in the context of an American nationalism predicated, in part at least, on the military strength of the nation and on the idea, whose origins lay in the Revolution and in the Civil War but that was promulgated most widely during World War II, that Americans always – with the implication only – fought for freedom, whether on their own streets or on those of others. Only when that freedom failed to materialize did disenchantment and self-doubt creep in. As far as the 1960s were concerned, the change, both in terms of reform and the reaction against the war, only came once the tumult was over.

As the Johnson era drew to a close and Richard Nixon, the new Republican president, prepared to assume power, the eyes of the world were not on Southeast Asia; they were on space. In December 1968, the Apollo 8 mission achieved the first manned lunar orbit and beamed a bible message back from the darkness of space, on Christmas Eve; the opening verses of Genesis, suitable enough, perhaps, for a nation on the brink of a new decade and a new political direction. In the summer of the following year, on July 20, 1969, Neil Armstrong became the first man to set foot on the Moon. Yet, ironically, by that point, the pieces were already in place that would result in the downsizing of the American Space Program – the downsizing, indeed, of the Cold War.

There was little hint of the former, but hope for the latter, in the president's inaugural address. "In throwing wide the horizons of space," he asserted, "we have discovered new horizons on earth." Yet he acknowledged that America was "rich in goods, but ragged in spirit; reaching with magnificent precision for the Moon, but falling into raucous discord on earth."[10] The discord did not dissipate after 1969. Indeed, in some respects it worsened; but like every president before him, Nixon had a program for the nation's ills. This one was rather different, however, from what had gone before. It was called the New Federalism.

To the dismay of some conservatives in Congress, however, the New Federalism under Nixon did not translate into a wholesale dismantling of the liberal New Deal state. Indeed, appropriately for a presidency begun in the year that experienced the pinnacle of the counterculture,

Woodstock (the "Aquarian Exposition," as its organizers entitled it), under Nixon, many of the initiatives begun in the 1960s took more concrete form. A tranche of federal bodies was established to address issues such as environmentalism (the Environmental Protection Agency [EPA]) and health and safety at work (the Occupational Safety and Health Administration [OSHA]), and these were supported by legislation, such as the Clean Air Act and the Endangered Species Act. Nixon could not solve all the nation's problems, but he did go some way toward ensuring that the new horizons on earth that he had identified were cleaner and greener.

In fiscal terms, however, Nixon was limited by the combination of rising inflation and unemployment, and by his own inability to control the huge inflationary pressures caused by the nation's spending on space, on defense, and on the still ongoing war in Vietnam. His proposed solution to unemployment, and to the financial distress it caused, the Family Assistance Plan – essentially a welfare program that would guarantee a minimum level of income for all – failed to get through Congress. His proposed solution to Vietnam, a program termed "Vietnamization" – the gradual transference of responsibility to the Army of the Republic of Vietnam (ARVN), conceived as the means whereby America might effect a gradual withdrawal from the war – proved equally problematic. The timescale proposed was too short to bring the ARVN up to speed and too long to satisfy an increasingly impatient American public. It was undermined, too, by Nixon's contradictory approach to the war that, it seemed, might never go away.

The man who had once indicated that he might "crawl to Hanoi" to secure a settlement initiated, as soon as he was in office, extensive air attacks on North Vietnam and the invasion, in 1970, of a neutral nation, Cambodia. Neither did much for the peace process, but both certainly stimulated domestic opposition to the war, with terrible consequences. The killing of four students at Kent State University by members of the Ohio National Guard during an antiwar protest on campus horrified a nation already stumbling not just over the invasion of Cambodia but over the reports beginning to filter through the media of American atrocities in Vietnam, specifically an event that came to be known as the My Lai massacre, which had taken place on March 16, 1968.

The brutal maiming and slaying of more than 400 unarmed civilians – women, children, and old men – in the village of Son My by Charlie Company, 11th Light Infantry, under Second Lieutenant William Calley seemed to confirm to the world, and to America itself, that the nation had lost its moral compass. Yet if the media, at the time and since, presented My Lai as the nadir of American involvement in Vietnam, it did so from the perspective of the perpetrators. As the story broke, and as its aftereffects continued to contaminate American culture, a great many Americans would come to remember the name of Lieutenant Calley, but forget, if they ever knew it, that of the helicopter pilot, Hugh Thompson, who witnessed the event, and who intervened to rescue survivors, ordering his men to open fire on any American soldiers who might hamper the rescue effort. Encapsulated in that potential standoff between Americans at My Lai was a reiteration of the fact that a nation as powerful as the United States held an enormous power for good but an equally immense capacity for destruction.

Even the events at My Lai, however, were overshadowed by domestic politics, by the leaking to the media, in 1971, of the Pentagon Papers, and by the Watergate scandal that resulted in the first-ever abdication of a president. The Pentagon Papers – Defense Department documents on the early period of America's involvement in Vietnam – were passed to the *New York Times* by Daniel Ellsberg. Irritated by the leak, and already hostile to a media that he felt compromised American negotiations in Vietnam, Nixon set up a Special Investigations Group within the White House – the "plumbers" (they were meant to prevent leaks) – which focused on attempting to undermine Ellsberg's credibility by breaking into his psychiatrist's office in the hope of finding evidence (of what was never entirely clear). The following year saw the creation of the corporate-funded Committee to Re-Elect the President (with the unfortunate acronym CREEP), whose more ambitious remit was to uncover dirt on the Democrats. A foiled break-in at the Democratic Party headquarters in the Watergate building in Washington, DC, in June revealed one of the burglars to be the security chief of CREEP.

The Watergate affair seemed faintly ridiculous at first, but subsequent investigations by two *Washington Post* journalists began to peel away the layers of what became a complex story of abuse of political power. Under pressure from the Supreme Court, the president was forced to release secret tape recordings he had made of conversations in the Oval Office; the revelation that he had been making secret recordings at all was bad enough, but what was on the tapes destroyed his reputation forever. And much more was at stake than one man's reputation. As Watergate unfolded, a whole raft of illegal wiretapping, bribes, and backhanders came to light; it was not the crime, if crime there had been, it was the cover-up that did the most damage, the realization that the president was prepared to subvert the democratic process, to lie about doing so, and to attempt to block the judicial investigation that followed. Calls for Nixon's impeachment, and his resignation in 1974, marked the end of an era that had begun with Franklin D. Roosevelt, that had promoted the federal government, the interventionist state, as the means through which the promise of America could be defined and defended. In the aftermath of Watergate, and in the context of the final debacle that was the American withdrawal from Saigon in 1975, many Americans lost their faith in government, in American military supremacy, almost in America itself.

It is nevertheless important not to exaggerate the extent to which the national mood shifted toward being receptive to the Right to the exclusion of what remained of its liberal ideology, or to dismiss America's continuing international significance. The Pentagon Papers and the Watergate break-in shared the headlines with reminders that America at this time was still reaching for the stars, and for a settlement with the Soviets. Apollo 12 landed men on the Moon once more in November 1969, and in 1971, Americans drove across the Moon's surface for the first time. The following year, however, was the final time that Americans would set foot on the Moon in the twentieth century. It was also the year that saw the Nixon-Kosygin summit agreement on cooperation in space, an agreement that would result, only three years later, in the Apollo-Soyuz Project, the first joint U.S./USSR space venture.

By 1975, indeed, the wheel seemed to have come full circle from 1957, from the launch of *Sputnik*, the wake-up call for Americans that forced them to reconsider their influence in the world and their reality at home. The Cold War, of which *Sputnik* was a symbol, had ushered in a new way of thinking: about government, society, race, the economy, the military, and technology. As Lyndon Johnson had put it, the American Space Program was "the beginning of the revolution of the '60s."

And in the 1960s, America had had ambitious plans. Kennedy had envisaged a "New Frontier," Johnson a "Great Society." Both aimed to solve American domestic and foreign policy problems and simultaneously assert American superiority in space, the new Cold War battlefield. All these initiatives, indeed, proved to have a high cost, economically and ideologically. Until 1975, the American story could be seen as one of success. Here was a nation, the first to break away from colonial rule and establish a republican government; a nation that had conquered its own western frontier and held itself together through a brutal Civil War; a nation that Europe was forced to turn to not once, but twice, when warfare threatened the free institutions of the Western world; a nation that others looked to for practical support and intellectual and ideological guidance.

At the end of April 1975, that nation was forced to flee, in some disarray, from Saigon as North Vietnamese forces closed in on the American embassy. Despite desperate attempts to get as many of their South Vietnamese allies onto the evacuation helicopters, even pushing the helicopters off the decks of the evacuation vessels waiting offshore to make room for more people was not enough; indeed, those they left behind – in every sense, dead and alive – was what really haunted the Vietnam generation.

Third Century

As Saigon fell to communist forces in April 1975, America's bicentennial celebrations, announcing the third century of the nation's existence, had already begun. At the start of the month, America's second "Freedom Train" set off from Wilmington, Delaware, on what would be an almost two-year trip through the states. It had already been preceded by what was known as the "Preamble Express," which had traveled the route the previous year to prepare for the official visit of the American Freedom Train. The only nationwide commemoration – apart from televised celebrations, of course – of the bicentennial, the American Freedom Train carried a similar selection of Americana as the 1940s version, but with additions, including Martin Luther King, Jr.'s pulpit and a rock from the Moon landings.

There was another difference between the train of the 1940s, however, and that of the 1970s. Whereas the former had been the brainchild of a federal employee, had the support and assistance of the National Archives, and president Truman's endorsement, the latter was a private endeavor by a businessman and train enthusiast Ross Rowland, Jr., and was supported by, among others, the singer Johnny Cash, who gave a benefit concert for it. It is doubtful that Rowland intended to make the point that freedom, by the 1970s, was in the process of shifting, not just symbolically but in a very real sense, from the public to the private sphere; but it was. Toward the end of 1975, *Harper's Magazine* had identified "the new narcissism" as the source of individual unease and isolation in a nation that appeared to have come adrift from its moral and material moorings, one still stunned by the resignation of the president, staggering under the stagflation produced by the energy crisis of the 1970s, and shocked by the fall of Saigon. For all these reasons, the bicentennial was a muted affair, and its version of the American Freedom Train traversed what was, for the nation, a very different landscape from that of the 1940s; it followed a track headed toward what is sometimes termed the conservative counterrevolution, the final rejection of liberalism that was deemed to culminate with the election, in 1980, of Ronald Reagan.

It has been argued that Reagan personified, in many respects, the shift in direction in American politics and society that occurred in his own lifetime. He had graduated from college in the year when Franklin D. Roosevelt was first elected president (1932), and the trajectory of his career tracked that of the nation from the New Deal liberalism to the new conservatism that he was deemed to exemplify, away from "Big Government" and back toward individualism. Yet this apparently dramatic change of philosophical direction continued to operate within the context of what was still understood as the American creed; indeed, it was to a great extent the fear of its dissolution that drove the conservative culture. On the one hand, it could celebrate the nation's multiethnic makeup and highlight the expansive expression of liberty and civic nationalism that this implied. On the other hand, it feared that too great an emphasis on ethnic difference might produce a twentieth-century tribalism around which the American national center could not hold. It harked back, in many respects, to eighteenth- and nineteenth-century understandings of the limitations of liberty, the rights and the responsibilities of freedom, albeit no longer positioned in the Anglo-Saxon context.

"Government," Ronald Reagan famously declared upon being elected, "is not the solution to our problem. Government *is* the problem." This had more than a faint whiff of Thomas Paine about it, one that the rest of his inaugural developed with its invocation of the "special interest group" that was "'We the people'" – its reminder that the United States was "a nation that has a government – not the other way around" – and that this fact made it "special among the nations of the Earth. Our government has no power except that granted it by the people," Reagan asserted. "It is time to check and reverse the growth of government, which shows signs of having grown beyond the consent of the governed."[11] He did not actually say that government in its best state is but a necessary evil, in its worst an intolerable one; yet one suspects that that is what many of his listeners actually heard.

However, 1981 was not 1776. By the late twentieth century, a far greater number of rights associated with the individual had been invoked and implemented, and this consequently imposed a far greater range of responsibilities on the federal government – ones that, in practice, it could neither void nor avoid. The backlash against the counterculture, which had been at best a loose collection of ideas and interest groups, produced a New Right that itself covered a wide spectrum of opinion, social, political, religious, and moral. It did draw a great deal of its momentum from religious revivalism, and the increasingly close link between politics and religion challenged what had been, until the later twentieth century, a wholly secular political culture. Aspects of the conservative counterculture sought to rebuild the Puritan village on a grand scale and hammered away at deviation from this ideal with an evangelical fervor. Yet the movement as a whole never succeeded in completely deconstructing the rights revolution that really was the nation's birthright. What Nixon had begun with his environmental policies in terms of securing the legacy of the 1960s in the 1970s held true in many other areas of American political and legal life in the years that followed. The Vietnam era had introduced new voices into the national dialogue about freedom, notably the student voice, and had amplified those of more traditional participants, notably civil rights activists and women. As the excitement of the 1960s died down, or faded out against the backdrop of Vietnam, the decline of the counterculture, and the revelations over Watergate, some of the forces that had driven that decade but had been drowned out by the sheer volume of voices finally made themselves heard.

The women's movement was a case in point. Although suffrage rights had been secured by the Nineteenth Amendment in 1920, and although women's workplace participation had increased during and after World War II, by the 1960s, few women held senior corporate positions or political office in the United States. And there were signs that things were not moving in a forward direction. In 1961, there were twenty women in Congress; by 1969, there were eleven. For most women, the home remained the focus of their lives. Few women in the early 1960s would have described themselves as feminists. And when it came to the antiwar movement, the approach women frequently took – when they consciously acted as women, rather than as, say, African Americans – echoed that of a much earlier generation of female activists, whose opposition to slavery, or to racial division in the later nineteenth century, was predicated on the platform of the woman as the moral heart of the home and, by extrapolation, the nation.

The publication, in 1963, of Betty Friedan's *The Feminine Mystique* took the debate over women's place in society to a whole new level. Along with the Equal Pay Act of that year, and the establishment of the Equal

Employment Opportunity Commission, it initiated a sea change in how women approached employment and how employers treated women. The creation in 1966 of the National Organization for Women (NOW), headed by Friedan, copied both the approach and the rhetoric of civil rights activist to demand full equality for women in all areas of American life. Gender and race were, in this sense, frequently reinforcing as far as equality went, but they could also be divisive.

In the mid-1960s, and in the context of seeking to address the problem of African-American poverty rates in the inner cities, sociologist Daniel Patrick Moynihan produced *The Negro Family: The Case for National Action* (the Moynihan Report, 1965). This report attracted a great deal of criticism in the years since its publication from those who perceived it as seeking to impose white middle-class norms on black families, and especially on black single mothers. The debate remains a potent one in America today, with many conservative voices advocating a reemphasis on the nuclear family that may, or may not, solve all societal ills but that certainly has implications for women within such families. Then, as now, it is a debate that sometimes crosses the color and gender lines, but sometimes simply shouts across the no man's land between them. Indeed, where women's rights are concerned, controversy continues to be the norm, in part because full equality was never asserted via a constitutional amendment and in part because rights that were asserted are in the process of being unpicked.

In 1967, NOW had pushed for two main developments in the area of women's rights: an Equal Rights Amendment (ERA), which had first been mooted in the 1920s, and abortion rights. Both seemed set to be a success. Congress sent the ERA down to the states, fully anticipating ready ratification by the requisite three-quarters of the states required to pass it; by 1973, thirty-six states had done so. It was confidently assumed that the ERA would pass. It failed. And it failed because women opposed it. A grassroots campaign led by Phyllis Schlafly, the National Committee to Stop ERA, argued that the supporters of ERA were antifamily, a position that garnered it support from other somewhat intimidating-sounding groups such as "Mothers on the March." Congress, by contrast, remained keen for the ERA to succeed, so keen that it extended the deadline for its ratification until 1982; but after 1977, no state would touch it, let alone ratify it.

Abortion rights, by contrast, had been recognized in a landmark Supreme Court ruling, *Roe vs. Wade* (1973). Yet this, too, had been (and continues to be) the subject of immediate challenge (Figure 11.5).

FIGURE 11.5. A demonstration at the Democratic National Convention in New York in 1976 in support of the "pro-choice" lobby and against the anti-abortion presidential candidate Ellen McCormack, whose platform was firmly pro-life (Photo by Warren K. Leffler, July 14, 1976). Image courtesy of the Library of Congress Prints and Photographs Division (LC-DIG-ppmsca-09733).

In the same year as it was passed, the National Right to Life Committee was formed. Then in 1989, in *Webster vs. Reproductive Health Services*, the Supreme Court backed a Missouri law that prevented any medical institution in receipt of state funding from offering abortions. The issue was, and still is, divisive; the battle between pro- and anti-abortion activists goes on in many countries, of course, but in America, members of the medical profession willing to carry out abortions have been murdered, abortion clinics picketed, and both staff and patients abused. On this issue, many Americans remain prepared to invoke the First Amendment in their own cause and deny it to others.

More than women's rights versus those of the unborn child are involved in the abortion debate; which is, of course, why it is so very contentious an issue, in the United States as elsewhere. When the White House, in 1989, entered an *amicus curiae* brief for a case seeking to overturn *Roe vs. Wade*, the Supreme Court ruled against this, but did stipulate that states might restrict the availability of abortion in publicly funded clinics – a middle-of-the-road solution that risked satisfying no one, but certainly made it clear that the religious right could not set the agenda on abortion entirely. Indeed, both the ERA and the abortion debate highlighted not just the influence of the conservative counterrevolution, but the persistence of opposition to this.

Since ERA and *Roe vs. Wade*, there has been an expansion of the terms of the rights debate to include other so-called minority groups and attack discrimination, whether that be via the Americans with Disabilities Act (1990) or state legislation designed to secure equal rights for lesbian, gay, bisexual and transgender (LGBT) Americans. Again, these rights remain the subject of ongoing legal and cultural challenges, but the momentum, begun in the 1970s, to end discrimination on the grounds of sexual orientation is unlikely to dissipate or diminish (Figure 11.6). While elements of the religious right continue to rail against same-sex relationships, the broader public perspective, especially in the aftermath of the AIDS epidemic of the 1980s, is inclusive rather than exclusive as far as equal citizenship rights are concerned.

Yet if legal and cultural inclusiveness was extended across hitherto marginalized groups in the United States in the later twentieth century, the debate – indeed the row – over the contents of that culture took on a force of its own in the context of the growth, after 1970, of immigration once again, following the passage of the Immigration and Nationality Act (1965), which abolished the National Origins Quota System that had operated since 1924. The number of immigrants increased from

FIGURE 11.6. A gay rights demonstration at the Democratic National Convention in New York in 1976 (Photo by Warren K. Leffler, July 11, 1976). The Supreme Court ruled in 2003 that criminalizing homosexual acts was unconstitutional. Image courtesy of the Library of Congress Prints and Photographs Division (LC-DIG-ppmsca-09729).

just below 9 million in the 1980s to some 13.5 million in the 1990s, and a significant proportion of these immigrants were either Hispanic (mainly from Mexico) or Asian (mainly from China, Korea, and Vietnam). This exacerbated conservative fears of American cultural disintegration and simultaneous intercultural discord between distinct ethnic and racial groups. When Bill Clinton assumed the presidency, he addressed this issue in an inaugural that stressed both diversity and the unity that came from the "idea of America," an idea that the "nation can summon from its myriad diversity the deepest measure of unity."

Clinton's address, indeed, had a decidedly spiritual spin in its invocation of "the mystery of American renewal," which he described almost as a rite of spring for a nation moving into a post–Cold War world and toward a new century, a nation no longer separated from that world but, through the technological development of the previous few decades, at the heart of it once again. It was "a world warmed by the sunshine of freedom but threatened still by ancient hatreds and new plagues. Raised in unrivalled prosperity," Clinton observed, "we inherit an economy that is still the world's strongest but is weakened by business failures, stagnant wages, increasing inequality, and deep divisions among our own people."[12]

Some of these divisions deepened on Clinton's watch. Bookended as it was between two Bush administrations, the Clinton era can seem like a liberal oasis amid the conservative counterrevolution. To see it as such may be a mistake. The Right did not get all that it wanted, any more than the Left got all that it feared, from the Reagan and George H. W. Bush administrations. Yet in the 1990s, one aspect of the United States that had nothing to do with individual freedom, indeed quite the opposite, came to the fore: crime.

America has the highest incarceration rate in the world, and this has remained the case through the two previous Republican and Democratic administrations. By the end of the Clinton presidency, indeed, more than 5.6 million Americans either were or at some point had been in prison; in short, 1 in every 37 adults in America had some experience of incarceration, but the chances of being the 1 in the 37 varied depending on race. Whereas some 16.6 percent of African-American men were or had been in prison by the end of 2001, that figure was lower for Hispanics (7.7 percent) and still lower for white males (2.6 percent). "If the 2001 rates of incarceration were to continue indefinitely," a Bureau of Justice report concluded, then "a black male in the United States would have about a 1 in 3 chance of going to prison during his lifetime, while a Hispanic male would have a 1 in 6 chance and a white male would have a 1 in 17 chance of going to prison." By the middle of 2009, there were more than 1.6 million Americans in prison.[13]

While these statistics certainly help explain the modern fascination with crime dramas, they highlight a worrying trend not just toward the widespread criminalization of the American population, but the increasing potency that crime and fear of crime has had, and may continue to have, on the United States. In large part this trend derives from the relationship between conflict and identity in the United States, and comprises elements present at the nation's inception, namely the persistent fear that the world's first republican experiment was especially susceptible to attack from forces, both external and internal, with the potential to undermine it. Until the end of the Cold War, the sum of American fears could actually be summed up and categorized, if not contained, as coherent challenges to the "American creed." These fears mainly derived from the threat from what were perceived to be coherent, if not entirely coordinated, groups: Britain, the "South," communism, or

FIGURE 11.7. World Trade Center after its collapse during the 9/11 terrorist attack. Photo by Andrea Boohers/Rex Features.

even "Big Government." The Cold War itself, of course, provided the meta-framework within which these fears could be articulated and on which a distinct American identity could be constructed in response to them. Within it, complexity became simplified, and America's main threat came from what Reagan termed the "Evil Empire" – the Soviet Union. The disintegration of the Soviet Union in 1991 destroyed that framework and opened the way toward what George H. W. Bush optimistically called a "new world order" – which, perhaps inevitably, turned out to be one of disorder.

The full extent of global disorder hit the United States in the first year of George W. Bush's presidency in the attacks on the World Trade Center in New York and on the Pentagon in Washington, DC, on September 11, 2001 (Figure 11.7). Terrorism, of course, by its nature is designed to spread fear. The destruction of the World Trade Center Twin Towers, however, attenuated the fear in a nation already primed to be fearful. The shock and the horror of the event was itself heightened by the ability of the media to transmit events in real time to a stunned world that could only look on, impotently, at the initial, frantic rescue attempts and the sudden disappearance of the towers themselves, and of thousands of lives, in a billow of smoke and ash.

The sense of fear in the wake of the September 11 attacks was palpable. Certainly Americans had experienced domestic terrorism before, and terrorists associated with Al Qaeda had attacked the World Trade Center in 1993; but nothing on such a scale as 9/11 had ever been experienced by the United States. The response on the part of the Bush administration was to declare a "war on terror," but such a war, from the outset, risked chasing shadows. Terror was an ephemeral enemy, and critics of the Bush administration have often pointed out the benefits that accrue from designating oneself a "war president," the civil liberties issues that it raises, the opportunities it creates for those liberties to be compromised. And in the case of a war with no obvious enemy beyond terror – although Al Qaeda was identified by the administration as the culprit – the possibility of such a conflict turning on the United States itself seemed, to some, a very real risk.

Although derived from the specific circumstances of 9/11, the creation of the Department of Homeland Security, followed by the passage of the USA PATRIOT Act, seemed to some, both within America and beyond, the consolidation of the conservative counterrevolution, the victory, indeed, of a more dangerous "neoconservative" cabal that envisaged nothing short of an American empire; an empire of liberty, certainly, but one constructed to an American template that not every nation welcomed wholesale. Bush's rhetoric sometimes gave the world pause as he outlined and then enacted his plans to attack the "axis of evil," overthrow the Taliban in Afghanistan (Operation Enduring Freedom), end Saddam Hussein's dictatorship in Iraq (Operation Iraqi Freedom), and effect "regime change" there. Yet in both cases, in Iraq and Afghanistan, although America had identified enemies that at least had some substance, they have proved no easier to defeat.

On the domestic front, the aftermath of 9/11 produced an upsurge of patriotism that Bush certainly capitalized on. Just as after World War II, the American flag was everywhere. It was planted in the ruins at Ground Zero, where the Twin Towers had once stood; it was displayed from every conceivable structure, from cars, and in windows; rescue dogs were wrapped in it, children were wrapped in it. It became a symbol of defiance and a comfort blanket. War, of course, tends to produce such patriotic reactions, just as it serves to pull populations together, to reinforce a nationalism that, in America's case prior to 2001, had been in some danger of fragmenting. Yet for the United States, the fact that this new nationalist upsurge was the result of conflict served, in some sense, as a form of closure for a nation still haunted by its defeat in Vietnam. Whether terror will prove to be an easier foe to pin down and defeat than communism, however, remains to be seen; whether, indeed, the new Democratic Obama administration can achieve either a peace with honor or a withdrawal without embarrassment from Afghanistan remains to be seen.

Inevitably, 9/11 did not eradicate all those divisive issues that the United States continues to struggle with and against. When nature, in the form of Hurricane Katrina, turned against the nation in 2005, it revealed to the world the persistence of both class and racial divisions in America; divisions that had, since 2001, perhaps been less visible, to outsiders at least. The victory of Barack Obama in the 2008 election owed something to those divisions, but a great deal more to the American urge to overcome them.

As Obama assumed the leadership of the United States, it was in the context of a world that had begun to wonder, indeed worry, about the role of America in the world, the ways in which it seemed to veer between an introverted isolationism and a sometimes aggressive messianic impulse to impose global order, the juxtaposition of its rhetoric of freedom and the reality of Guantánamo Bay. Obama promised a different future, one in which the United States would not compromise its ideals to consolidate its safety, one in which the American civic national ideal would be forged out of the "patchwork heritage" of the nation's history. "This," he asserted, "is the price and the promise of citizenship. This is the source of our confidence – the knowledge that God calls on us to shape an uncertain destiny. This is the meaning of our liberty and our creed."[14] Some expressed disappointment at Obama's inaugural address. They seemed to have been expecting more, but what?

In part, the election of Obama was symbolic – or, rather, many wanted it to be symbolic – on many levels. Obama's was not just the election of a Democrat after two terms of Republican rule, but the apparent end of the dominance of the so-called neocons, the new conservatives, a term that became popular during George W. Bush's administration, one deemed to describe the former liberals of the 1960s, converts to the conservative cause in the 1980s and 1990s, and as deadly serious and committed to their new faith as any kind of convert is apt to be. Disenchanted with the perceived anti-Americanism expressed by some within the nation in the 1960s, and concerned over the levels of anti-Americanism expressed abroad ever since, the domestic and foreign policy of the supposedly new conservatism sought a return to "traditional" values and reasserted religion (via the "theocons") as the fulcrum of the secular faith in the nation.

How new all this was is a moot point; as early as 1920, the English author G. K. Chesterton had described the United States as "a nation with the soul of a church," but the merging of religion (or religious faith) with patriotism (or national faith) was present at the creation, in John Winthrop's sermon in which he assured the colonial ancestors of the twentieth-century evangelicals that their nation was to be a "city on a hill." As far as American nationalism was concerned, the notion of Americans being God's chosen people was pretty much a given from the start; it was just that in the later twentieth century, an increasing number of the people began to choose God, even if, as Obama suggested, the destiny He had in mind for the United States was rather more uncertain than some previous presidents had believed.

Yet on an important level, the election of Obama, the first African-American president, seemed to represent the fulfillment of at least one part of America's destiny, the resolution of the one issue that had compromised the city on a hill since its inception: race. The Founding Fathers had prevaricated on the subject, and much of what followed stemmed from that initial inability to make the nation match its mission statement in 1776. In the middle of the nineteenth century the republican experiment had almost imploded over the issue of slavery and race, and the images of Abraham Lincoln beamed onto the Mall at Obama's inauguration, and Obama's decision to take the oath of office on the very bible Lincoln himself had used, made it clear that a point was being made, a memory invoked of the president who issued the Emancipation Proclamation in 1863. And how many Americans viewing these images would think back, not quite so far back as the Civil War, but to 1963, to Martin Luther King, Jr.'s address on the steps of the Lincoln Memorial, and the faith that he invoked that "this nation will rise up and live out the true meaning of its creed." The election of Obama seemed confirmation that, finally, it had.

Of course, no single individual could hope either to sustain or fully satisfy the degree of expectation that met Obama's election, which came at a bad time for the world's banks. The United States, in common with many other nations, faces both domestic, fiscal difficulties and foreign-policy challenges susceptible to no easy solution. Yet any discussion of the United States today will tend to include two words: globalization and hegemony (or, sometimes, global hegemony), as if this, too, was something new under the sun, as if the Great Depression had affected only America rather than representing a global economic crisis. As far as America specifically was concerned, the financial meltdown that began in 2008 certainly prompted comparisons with the 1930s, just as American troop commitment in Afghanistan and Iraq evoked memories of the war in Vietnam. History, it seemed, was repeating itself, and in ever-expanding global circles.

As globalization has made the world's populations susceptible to market forces and terrorism to military ones, the relationship between these, and America's role in this relationship, occupies many column inches and Web blogs. America as a nation comprises 4.6 percent of the world's population but consumes some 33 percent of the world's resources, and because of its vast consumption it is now in a class of its own as far as economic, military, and arguably political power is concerned. Yet it has become clear, to Americans as to others, that American power without purpose is meaningless and, further, that such purpose can be neither defined nor defended, as Bush tried to do, by America alone. Obama seeks a greater degree of international cooperation and accommodation, but this is surely a process that will work both ways. Some have questioned whether American national ideals, whether American national identity, can survive the pressures of globalization that impact on it from abroad and those of multiculturalism that impact internally. The answer to that is surely affirmative, given that the nation that some argue is no nation at all, the nation that has frequently been described as a "republican experiment," has held together remarkably well since its inception. The experiment is not yet over; indeed, given how brief many consider its history to be, the story of the United States of America could perhaps more accurately be described as having only just begun.

Notes

Chapter 1: New Found Land: Imagining America

1 Thomas Churchyard, *A Generall rehearsal of warres and joined to the same some tragedies and epitaphs* (London, 1597), quoted in Canny, "Ideology of English Colonization," 582 (see Further Reading).

2 The patent granted to Ralegh in 1584 is included in Arthur Barlow, *The First Voyage to Roanoke, 1584: The First Voyage Made to the Coasts of America, with Two Barks, wherein Were Captains M. Philip Amadas and M. Arthur Barlowe, Who Discovered Part of the Countrey Now Called Virginia, anno 1584. Written by One of the Said Captaines, and Sent to Sir Walter Ralegh, Knight, at Whose Charge and Direction, the Said Voyage Was Set Forth* (Boston, 1898) 12–17.

3 Barlow, *First Voyage to Roanoke, 1584*, 3, 7, 5.

4 Hakluyt's *Discourse* can be read in full in Richard Hakluyt, *The Voyages of the English Nation to America* (Edinburgh, 1889) Vol. II, 175–276.

5 Thomas Hariot, *A Briefe and True Report of the New Found Land of Virginia : of the Commodities and of the Nature and Manners of the Naturall Inhabitants: Discouered bÿ the English Colonÿ There Seated by Sir Richard Greinuile Knight In the ÿeere 1585 . . .* Illustrations by John White. Translated out of Latin into English by Richard Hackluyt (New York: J. Sabin & Sons, 1871) 6–7, 25.

6 *The Records of the Virginia Company*, Vol. II, *The Court Book* (Washington, DC: Government Printing Office, 1906) 527.

7 Robert Johnson's *Nova Britannia: Offering most excellent fruites by Planting in Virginia* (1609), American Colonial Tracts Monthly, No. 6 (Rochester, NY: George P. Humphrey, 1897) 6, 10.

8 Smith, *Generall Historie of Virginia . . .* in *Travel and Works of Captain John Smith* (Edinburgh: John Grant, 1910) Part I, 378, 360; descriptions of Virginia after Smith left in *The Life and Adventures of Captain John Smith* (New York; H. Dayton, 1859) 185–7.

9   Thomas More, *Utopia* (Harmondsworth, Middlesex: Penguin, 1986) 79–80.

10 Hakluyt quoted in A.L. Rowse, *The Elizabethans and America* (New York; Harpers, 1959) 51.

11 Johnson, *Nova Britannia*, 10.

12 Johnson, *Nova Britannia*, 11.

13 Instructions quoted in Alden T. Vaughan, *Transatlantic Encounters: American Indians in Britain, 1500–1776* (Cambridge and New York: Cambridge University Press, 2006) 51; see also the *Records of the Virginia Company*, Vol. III, 13–15.

14 *Records of the Virginia Company*, Vol. II, *The Court Book*, Part A, 256, 269, 566.

Chapter 2: A City on a Hill: The Origins of a Redeemer Nation

1   *Records of the Virginia Company (RVC)*, Vol. III, 307–9.

2   Yeardley to Sandys, June 7, 1620, *RVC* III 297–9; "Instructions to the Governor and Council of State in Virginia," June 24, 1621, *RVC* III, 469–73.

3   "Letter to Governor and Council in Virginia," September 11, 1621, *RVC*, III, 504–5.

4   T.S. Arthur and W.H. Carpenter, *The History of Virginia from its Earliest Settlement to the Present Time* (Philadelphia: Lippincott, 1858) 123.

5   *RVC*, IV, 140, 145.

6   Edward Waterhouse, *A Declaration of the State of the Colony and . . . A Relation of the Barbarous Massacre* (1622), *RVC*, III, 556–7.

7   Waterhouse, *Declaration, RVC*, III, 557–8.

8   Waterhouse, *Declaration, RVC*, III, 558.

9   *Relation of What Occurred Most Remarkable in the Missions of the Fathers of the Society of Jesus in New France in the Years 1647 and 1648* (Paris, 1649) 252.

10 http://avalon.law.yale.edu/18th_century/maryland_toleration.asp (November 10, 2009).

11 Robert C. Winthrop, *Life and Letters of John Winthrop* (Boston: Ticknor and Fields, 1867) 5.

12 William Bradford, *History of Plymouth Plantation* (Boston, 1856) 90.

13 Bradford, *Plymouth Plantation*, 78.

14 Winthrop, *Life and Letters of John Winthrop*, 19.

15 Winthrop, *Life and Letters of John Winthrop*, 184.

16 Roger Williams, *The Bloudy Tenent of Persecution for Cause of Conscience discussed in a Conference between Truth and Peace* (1644) 3; Winthrop, *Life and Letters of John Winthrop*, 18.

17 Thomas Hutchinson, *History of the Colony and Province of Massachusetts Bay* (Boston: 1767).

18 Thomas Wiggin to Sir John Cooke, November 19, 1632, in Winthrop, *Life and Letters of John Winthrop*, 31.

19 Bradford, *Plymouth Plantation*, 357; John Mason, *A Brief History of the Pequot War* (1736) 14; Winthrop, *Life and Letters of John Winthrop*, 195.

20 John Winthrop, General Considerations for the Plantation in New England, with an Answer to Several Objections, in Winthrop Papers (Boston: Massachusetts Historical Society, 1931) 2: 120.
21 Bradford, *Plymouth Plantation*, 385–6.
22 The full text is available in several edited editions, but can be read on-line at: http://www.history1700s.com/etext/html/blcrmmr.shtml (November 20, 2009).
23 Berkeley quoted in Wilcomb E. Washburn, "Governor Berkeley and King Philip's War," *New England Quarterly*, 30:3 (September 1957): 363–77, esp. 366.
24 Berkeley quoted in Warren M. Billings, *Sir William Berkeley and the forging of colonial Virginia* (Baton Rouge: Louisiana State University Press, 2004) 236.
25 This analysis of tobacco advertising is derived from Catherine Molineux, "Pleasures of the Smoke: 'Black Virginians' in Georgian London's Tobacco Shops," *William and Mary Quarterly*, 2 (April 2007): 327–76.

Chapter 3: The Cause of All Mankind: From Colonies to *Common Sense*

1 De Champigny, quoted in Saliha Belmessous, "Assimilation and Racialism in Seventeenth and Eighteenth-Century French Colonial Policy," *The American Historical Review*, 110:2 (April 2005): 322–49, 354.
2 Quoted in Bruce P. Lenman, "Lusty Beggars, Dissolute Women, Sorners, Gypsies, and Vagabonds for Virginia," *Colonial Williamsburg Journal* (Spring 2005): http://www.history.org/Foundation/journal/Spring05/scots.cfm (November 28, 2009).
3 *The Friend* (Philadelphia), Vol. 1, No. 1 (October 1827): 27.
4 Penn's charter can be read in full at: http://www.quakerinfo.org/history/1701%20charter/1701Charter.html (November 24, 2009).
5 J. Hector St. John de Crèvecoeur, *Letters from an American Farmer* (1782) (London: Penguin, 1983) 69–70.
6 Aphra Behn, *The Widow Ranter, or, The History of Bacon in Virginia* (1690), ed. Paul Royster (Lincoln: University of Nebraska, 2008) 3.
7 Mary Cooper diary entries from Field Horne (ed.), *The Diary of Mary Cooper: Life on a Long Island Farm, 1768–1773* (New York: Oyster Bay Historical Society, 1981).
8 Gabriel Thomas, *An Account of Pennsylvania and West New Jersey* (1698: Reprint: Cleveland: The Burrows Brothers Company, 1903) 70. Moraley quoted in Susan E. Klepp and Billy G. Smith, eds., *The Infortunate: The Voyage and Adventures of William Moraley, an Indentured Servant* (University Park: The Pennsylvania State University Press, 1992) 89.
9 Reverend Solomon Stoddard to Governor Joseph Dudley, October 22, 1703, quoted in John Demos, *Remarkable Providences: Readings on Early American History*, Revised Edition (Boston: Northeastern University Press, 1991) 372–4.
10 Alexander Medlicott, Jr., "Return to This Land of Light: A Plea to an Unredeemed Captive," *New England Quarterly*, 38:2 (1965): 202–16, quotation

206. There is a detailed entry on Eunice in the *Canadian Dictionary of Biography*.

11 Benjamin Franklin, "The Interest of Great Britain Considered With Regard to Her Colonies and the Acquisition of Canada and Guadaloupe [sic]" (1760), in Ralph Louis Ketcham (ed.), *The Political Thought of Benjamin Franklin*, New Ed. (Indianapolis: Hackett Publishing Company, 2003) 155–6.

12 Franklin to Peter Collinson, May 9, 1753, in Ketcham, *Political Thought*, 73.

13 Jonathan Mayhew, *A Discourse Concerning Unlimited Submission* (1750) is available as an electronic text at: http://digitalcommons.unl.edu/etas/44/ (December 5, 2009): 1, 40, 54.

14 Thomas, *Account of Pennsylvania*, 42; Benjamin Franklin, *Poor Richard's Almanac* (New York: Peter Pauper Press, 1994) 5.

15 Patrick Henry quoted in Bernard Bailyn, *The Ideological Origins of the American Revolution*, Second Revised Edition (Cambridge, MA: Harvard University Press, 1992) 253.

16 *Journal of the First Congress of the American Colonies, in Opposition to the Tyrannical Acts of the British Parliament. Held at New York*, October 7, 1765 (New York, 1845): 27–9; *Statutes at Large* (London, 1767) XXVII, 19–20.

Chapter 4: Self-Evident Truths: Founding the Revolutionary Republic

1 Abraham Lincoln, *Address at Sanitary Fair, Baltimore, Maryland*, April 18, 1864, in Roy Basler (ed), *The Collected Works of Abraham Lincoln*, 11 Vols. (New Brunswick, NJ: Rutgers University Press, 1953) VII, 301–2.

2 Thomas Jefferson, *A Summary View of the Rights of British America* (1774), available at, among others: http://libertyonline.hypermall.com/ Jefferson/Summaryview.html (December 2, 2009).

3 Thomas Jefferson, *Notes on the State of Virginia* (London: John Stockdale, 1787) 270, 271–2.

4 Declaration of Independence (draft), in Julian P. Boyd (ed), *The Papers of Thomas Jefferson*, Vol. 1, 1760–1776 (Princeton, NJ: Princeton University Press, 1950) 246–7.

5 Samuel Johnson, "Taxation No Tyranny: An Answer to the Resolutions and Address of the American Congress," in *The Works of Samuel Johnson* (New York: Pafraets & Company, 1913) Vol. 14, 93–144.

6 Phillis Wheatley, *Poems on Various Subjects, Religious and Moral* (London, 1773) 7.

7 John Woolman, *Journal of John Woolman*, available at: http://etext. lib.virginia.edu/toc/modeng/public/WooJour.html (November 29, 2009) chapter VII, 251; Woolman, "Considerations on Keeping Negroes," Part II (1762) quoted in David G. Houston, "John Woolman's Efforts in Behalf of Freedom," *Journal of Negro History*, 2 (April 1917): 126–38, 135, n. 24.

8 Eliza Lucas Pinckney to Mr. Morley, March 14, 1760; to Mrs. Evance, March 15, 1760, in William A. Link and Marjorie Spruill Wheeler, *The South in the*

History of the Nation, Vol. I (Boston and New York: Bedford/St. Martin's, 1999) 72, 74–5.

9 Daniel Boorstin, *The Americans: The Colonial Experience* (New York: Random House, 1958) 351.

10 Ebenezer Baldwin, *The Duty of Rejoicing Under Calamities and Afflictions* (New York: Hugh Gaine, 1776) 21–22.

11 Samuel Ward to Henry Ward, November 11, 1775, in *Letters of Delegates to Congress*, available at: http://memory.loc.gov/cgi-bin/query/r?ammem/hlaw:@field(DOCID ± @lit(dg002322)) (December 20, 2009).

12 Joseph Doddridge, *Notes on the Settlement and Indian Wars of the Western Parts of Virginia and Pennsylvania from 1763 to 1783* (Pittsburgh, PA: Ritenour and Lindsey, 1912) 142.

13 George Washington to Meshech Weare et al., "Circular Letter on Continental Army," October 18, 1780, in *The George Washington Papers*, Library of Congress, available at: http://memory.loc.gov/ammem/gwhtml/gwhome.html (December 27, 2009).

14 George Washington to Continental Congress, December 16, 1776; to Meshech Weare et al., October 18, 1780, in *Washington Papers*.

15 George Washington to Continental Congress, December 23, 1777, in *Washington Papers*.

16 George Washington to Henry Laurens, November 14, 1778, in *Washington Papers*.

17 George Washington to Continental Congress, December 20, 1776; to John Sullivan, December 17, 1780, in *Washington Papers*.

18 Clinton, memo of conversation on February 7, 1776, quoted in Stephen Conway, "To Subdue America: British Army Officers and the Conduct of the Revolutionary War," *William and Mary Quarterly*, 43:3 (July 1986): 381–407, quote 381.

19 George Washington to John Banister, April 21, 1778, in *Washington Papers*.

20 Benjamin Rush, "Address to the People of the United States," *American Museum*, Philadelphia, January 1787.

21 Joseph Story, *Commentaries on the Constitution of the United States, a Preliminary Review of the Constitutional History of the Colonies and States, before the Adoption of the Constitution* (Boston: Hilliard, Gray and Company; Cambridge: Brown, Shattuck, and Co., 1833) 3: 1120.

22 Noah Webster, *American Magazine*, 1788; quoted in Hans Kohn, *American Nationalism: An Interpretative Essay* (New York: Collier Books, 1961) 57.

23 Benjamin Rush to Dr. John Coakley Lettsom, September 28, 1787, quoted in John P. Kaminski, *A Necessary Evil? Slavery and the Debate over the Constitution* (Lanham, MD: Rowman and Littlefield, 1995) 117.

Chapter 5: The Last, Best Hope of Earth: Toward the Second American Revolution

1 Gouverneur Morris to the Federal Convention, July 5, 1787, in Max Farrand, *The Records of the Federal Convention of 1787*, Vol. I (New Haven, CT: Yale University Press, 1911) 531.

2 Alexander Hamilton, Federalist No. 6, "Concerning Dangers from Dissensions between the States," and Federalist No. 9, "The Union as a Safeguard against Domestic Faction and Insurrection," both published in the *Independent Journal*. The *Federalist Papers* can be accessed through the Library of Congress, available at: http://thomas.loc.gov/home/histdox/fedpapers.html (January 18, 2010).

3 James Madison, Federalist No. 10, "The Same Subject Continued: The Union as a Safeguard Against Domestic Faction and Insurrection," first published in the New York *Packet*, Friday, November 23, 1787.

4 The sixteen "Anti-Federalist" papers were not titled; they appeared in the New York *Journal* between October 1787 and April 1788, over a variety of pseudonyms, including "Brutus," chosen for the allusion to Caesar's assassin. The author was most likely Richard Yates, a New York judge and delegate to the Federal Convention. This quotation is from the second essay, which appeared at the start of November 1787.

5 James Wilson in *The Debates in the Convention of the State of Pennsylvania, on the Adoption of the Federal Constitution*, [Elliot's Debates, Volume 2] 526–7, available at: http://memory.loc.gov/cgi-bin/query/D?hlaw:1:./temp/~ammem_V2sd (January 20, 2010).

6 James Madison, Federalist N. 48, "These Departments Should Not Be So Far Separated as to Have No Constitutional Control over Each Other," first published in the New York *Packet*, Friday, February 1, 1788.

7 Alexis de Tocqueville, *Democracy in America*, ed. Phillips Bradley, 2 Vols. (New York: Vintage Books, 1945), Vol. 2, Book II, V: 114–5, 118.

8 *The Rules and By-laws of the Charlestown Library Society* (1762), available at: http://nationalhumanitiescenter.org/pds/becomingamer/ideas/text4/charlestownlibrary.pdf (January 20, 2010).

9 Sydney Smith quoted in Alan Bell, *Sydney Smith: A Biography* (New York: Oxford University Press, 1982) 120; Ralph Waldo Emerson, "The American Scholar" (1837), available at: http://www.emersoncentral.com/amscholar.htm (January, 20, 2010); Margaret Fuller, "Things and Thoughts in Europe," *New York (Daily) Tribune*, January 1, 1848.

10 Jefferson to Madison, Papers of Thomas Jefferson, *The Papers of Thomas Jefferson*, ed. Julian P. Boyd (Princeton, 1950–) 12: 442; to Washington, *The Writings of Thomas Jefferson*, Memorial Edition, 20 Vols. (Washington, 1903–04) 6: 277.

11 George Washington to Patrick Henry, October 9, 1795.

12 Jefferson and Hamilton quoted in Noble E. Cunningham, *Jefferson vs. Hamilton: Confrontations That Shaped a Nation* (London: Palgrave Macmillan, 2000) 102–3.

13 Washington's Farewell Address (1796) is provided online via the U.S. Congress, available at: http://www.access.gpo.gov/congress/senate/farewell/sd106-21.pdf (January 21, 2010).

14 Philip L. Barbour (ed.), *The Complete Works of Captain John Smith, 1580–1631*, 3 Vols. (Chapel Hill: The University of North Carolina Press, 1986) III, 274–5; Gouverneur Morris, speaking to the Federal Convention,

July 5, 1787, in Max Farrand, *The Records of the Federal Convention of 1787, 4 Vols.* (New Haven, CT: Yale University Press, 1911) Vol. I, 529–31.

15 Tocqueville, *Democracy in America*, Vol. I, 401–2.

16 William Wells Brown, *Narrative of William W. Brown, A Fugitive Slave* (Boston: Anti-Slavery Society, 1847), 41–3.

17 For example, Orlando Patterson, *Slavery and Social Death: A Comparative Study* (Cambridge, MA: Harvard University Press, 1982).

18 Thomas P. Kettell, *On Southern Wealth and Northern Profits* (1860).

19 Ralph Waldo Emerson, *Address Delivered in Concord on the Anniversary of the Emancipation of the Negroes in the British West Indies*, August 1, 1844, in Edward Waldo Emerson (ed.), *The Complete Works of Ralph Waldo Emerson* (Boston: Houghton Mifflin, 1911) II, 125–6.

20 Thomas Jefferson to John Holmes, April 22, 1820.

21 Abraham Lincoln, "Speech at Springfield, Illinois," June 16, 1858, in Basler (ed.), *Collected Works of Abraham Lincoln*, II, 461.

22 John C. Calhoun, *Exposition and Protest*, in W. Edwin Hemphill, Robert L. Meriwether, and Clyde Wilson (eds.), *The Papers of John C. Calhoun* 27 Vols. (Columbia: University of South Carolina Press, 1959–2001) Vol. 10, *1825–1829*, 447.

23 President Jackson's *Proclamation to the People of South Carolina* of December 10, 1832 can be accessed online at: http://www.yale.edu/lawweb/avalon/presiden/proclamations/jack01.htm (January 26, 2010).

24 Tocqueville, *Democracy in America*, Vol. I, 418, 420–1.

25 *Papers of John C Calhoun*, Vol. XIII (1980) 394–5.

26 James Henry Hammond, *Selections from the Letters and Speeches of the Hon. James H. Hammond, of South Carolina* (New York: John F. Trow & Co., 1866) 311–22.

27 "Appeal of the Independent Democrats in Congress to the People of the United States," *Congressional Globe*, 33rd Cong., 1st Session, 281–2.

28 *Dred Scott v. Sandford* (60 U.S. 393 (1856)) can be accessed online at: http://supreme.lp.findlaw.com/supreme_court/landmark/dredscott.html (January 25, 2010).

29 Abraham Lincoln, "Second Inaugural Address," in Basler, *Collected Works*, VIII, 332.

30 Emerson, *Address Delivered in Concord on the Anniversary of the Emancipation of the Negroes in the British West Indies*.

31 Abraham Lincoln, "Speech at Chicago, Illinois," July 10, 1858, in Basler, *Collected Works*, II, 484–500.

Chapter 6: Westward the Course of Empire: From Union to Nation

1 Seward's 1858 address can be read in full at: http://www.nyhistory.com/central/conflict.htm (February 10, 2010).

2 Morse and 1861 message both quoted in Jill Lepore, *A is for American: Letters and Other Characters in the Newly United States* (New York: Alfred A. Knopf, 2002) 10, 154.

3   Abraham Lincoln, "Message to Congress in Special Session," July 4, 1861, in Roy Basler (ed.), *The Collected Works of Abraham Lincoln*, 11 Vols. (New Brunswick, NJ.: Rutgers University Press, 1953) Vol. IV, 438.

4   *New York (Daily) Tribune*, November 27, 1860.

5   New Orleans *Daily Picayune*, June 29 and 26, 1861.

6   William Howard Russell, *My Diary North and South* (Boston: T.O.H.P. Burnham, 1863) 467–8, 470.

7   Joseph E. Johnston quoted in John G. Nicolay, *The Outbreak of Rebellion* (1881. Reprint. New York: Da Capo Press, 1995) 211.

8   Samuel Fiske (14th Connecticut) and diarist from 9th Pennsylvania, both quoted in Stephen Sears, *Landscape Turned Red: The Battle of Antietam* (1983. Paperback Reprint. New York: Warner Books, 1985) 347.

9   Seward's speech was delivered on March 11, 1850. It can be accessed at: http://www.senate.gov/artandhistory/history/common/generic/Speeches_Seward_NewTerritories.htm (February 20, 2010).

10 George Templeton Strong's diary entry March 11, 1861, in Allan Nevins and Milton Halsey Thomas (eds.), *The Diary of George Templeton Strong*, 4 Vols (New York: The Macmillan Company, 1952) III, 109.

11 Howell Cobb to James A. Seddon, January 8, 1865, "Georgia and the Confederacy," *The American Historical Review*, Vol. 1, 1 (October 1895): 97–102, 97–8.

12 John Murray Forbes to Charles Sumner, December 27, 1862, in Sarah Forbes Hughes (ed.), *Letters and Recollections of John Murray Forbes*, 2 Vols. (Boston and New York: Houghton, Mifflin and Company, 1899) I: 350–1.

13 Eva B. Jones to Mrs. Mary Jones, July 14, 1865, in Robert Manson Myers, *The Children of Pride: a True Story of Georgia and the Civil War*, Abridged Edition (New Haven and London: Yale University Press, 1984) 554.

14 *Niles' Weekly Register*, November 28, 1835.

15 Nicholas Faith, *The World the Railways Made* (London: Pimlico, 1990) 67.

16 Ralph Waldo Emerson, "The Young American," 1844, in Joel Porte (ed.), *Essays and Lectures by Ralph Waldo Emerson* (New York: Library of America, 1983) 211, 213–4.

17 George Berkeley, "Verses on the Prospect of Planting Arts and Learning in America," written in 1726, published 1752, in Rexmond C. Cochrane, "Bishop Berkeley and the Progress of Arts and Learning: Notes on a Literary Convention," *The Huntington Library Quarterly*, 17:3 (May, 1954): 229–49, 230.

18 Henry Benjamin Whipple, *Lights and Shadows of a Long Episcopate* (New York: The Macmillan Company, 1912) 105.

19 Whipple, *Lights and Shadows*, 124.

20 Lincoln, "Second Inaugural Address," March 4, 1865, in Basler (ed.), *Collected Works of Abraham Lincoln*, VIII, 333.

21 Lincoln, "Address Delivered at the Dedication of the Cemetery at Gettysburg," November 19, 1863, in Basler (ed.), *Collected Works of Abraham Lincoln*, VII, 19.

22 Kimball H. Dimmick, September 5, 1849 in *Report of the Debates in the Convention of California on the Formation of the State Constitution* (Washington: John H. Towers, 1850) 23.

23 Bayard Taylor, "What is an American?" *The Atlantic Monthly*, Vol. 35, No. 211 (May 1875) pp. 561–567, quotations pp. 562, 565–6.

24 Oliver Wendell Holmes, *The Autocrat of the Breakfast-Table* (1858): 18.

Chapter 7: A Promised Land: Gateway to the American Century

1 *New York Times*, May 15, 1864.

2 John Murray Forbes to Charles Sumner, August 10, 1872, in Sarah Forbes Hughes (ed.), *Letters and Recollections of John Murray Forbes*, 2 Vols. (Boston and New York: Houghton, Mifflin and Company, 1899) II: 178–9.

3 Hiram C. Whitley, *In It* (Cambridge, MA: Riverside Press, 1894) 104.

4 J. S. Pike, *First Blows of the Civil War: The Ten Years of Preliminary Conflict in the United States, From 1850 to 1860* (New York, 1879) 481, 511; *The Prostrate State: South Carolina under Negro Government* (New York: D. Appleton and Co., 1874) 12–13.

5 Horace Bushnell, *Barbarism the First Danger* (New York: American Home Missionary Society, 1847) 16–17.

6 Whitley, *In It*, 5, 174–5.

7 U. S. Grant to the Senate, January 13, 1875, *The Papers of Ulysses S. Grant*, John Y. Simon (ed.), Vol. 26: 1875 (Carbondale, Ill: Southern Illinois University Press, 2003) 6–7, xi–xii.

8 United States vs. Cruikshank (92 U.S. 542 (1875), available at: http://supreme.justia.com/us/92/542/case.html (March 20, 2010).

9 Ida B. Wells-Barnett, *Lynch Law in Georgia* (1899) 7, 10. For a modern assessment of the Hose case, see Edwin T. Arnold, *What Virtue There is in Fire: Cultural Memory and the Lynching of Sam Hose* (Athens: The University of Georgia Press, 2009).

10 Ida B. Wells-Barnett, *Southern Horrors: Lynch Law in all its Phases* (New York, 1892).

11 *New York Times*, February 24, 1884.

12 John Greenleaf Whittier to John Murray Forbes, June 12, 1891, in Hughes (ed.), *Letters and Recollections of John Murray Forbes*, II, 227.

13 Abraham Lincoln to Joshua Speed, August 24, 1855 in Basler (ed) *Collected Works of Abraham Lincoln*, II, 323.

14 Roger Daniels and Otis L. Graham, *Debating American Immigration, 1882–Present* (Lanham, MD: Rowman and Littlefield, 2001) 7.

15 James Bryce, *The American Commonwealth*, 2 Vols. (1888. Revised Edition. New York: The Macmillan Company, 1923) II, 472.

16 Josiah Strong, *Our Country: Its Possible Future and its Present Crisis* (New York: The American Home Mission Society, 1885) 40–41.

17 Lincoln Steffens, *The Shame of the Cities* (1902. Reprint. New York: Hill and Wang, 1957) 7–8. 18.

18 Marcus Eli Ravage, *An American in the Making: The Life Story of an Immigrant* (New York and London: Harper and Brothers, 1917) 60.

19 Grover Cleveland, *Veto Message*, March 2, 1897. available at: http://www.
    presidency.ucsb.edu/ws/index.php?pid=70845 (April 20, 2010).

20 Ravage, *An American in the Making*, 156–7.

21 Owen Wister, "The Evolution of the Cow-Puncher," *Harper's Magazine*,
    Vol. 91 (September 1895) 602–17, quotations 603–4.

22 Rockefeller quoted in Richard Hofstadter, *Social Darwinism in American
    Thought*, Revised Ed. (Boston: The Beacon Press, 1955) 45–6.

23 Abraham Lincoln, "Annual Message to Congress," December 3, 1861, in
    Basler (ed), *Collected Works of Abraham Lincoln*, V, 52.

24 Simon Nelson Patten, *The Theory of Social Forces* (Philadelphia: The Amer-
    ican Academy of Political and Social Science, 1896) 143.

25 Strong, *Our Country*, 41, 48, 44.

26 Henry Benjamin Whipple, Preface to Helen Hunt (Jackson)'s, *A Century of
    Dishonor* (New York: Harper and Brothers, 1881) vi.

Chapter 8: The Soldier's Faith: Conflict and Conformity

 1 *Official Proceedings of the Democratic National Convention Held in
    Chicago, Illinois, July 7, 8, 9, 10, and 11, 1896* (Logansport, Indiana, 1896)
    226–34, 230.

 2 J.B. Henderson speech, Wilmington, Delaware, October 19, 1896, quoted
    St. Louis Post-Dispatch, October 30, 1896.

 3 Roosevelt quoted in H. W. Brands, *The Reckless Decade: America in the
    1890s* (New York: St. Martin's Press, 1995) 258.

 4 *New York Mail and Express* quoted in Jonathan Auerbach, "McKinley at
    Home: How Early American Cinema Made News," *American Quarterly*,
    51, 4 (December 1999) 797–832, 806.

 5 McKinley's first inauguration can be viewed via YouTube, available at:
    http://www.youtube.com/watch?v=F4uOmSEw5-U.

 6 James Monroe, Annual Message to Congress, Senate, December 2, 1823,
    Annals of Congress, 18th Congress, 1st Session, 13–14.

 7 Alfred Thayer Mahan, "The United States Looking Outward," *The Atlantic
    Monthly*, 66: 398 (December, 1890) 816–34, 817, 819.

 8 Josiah Strong, *Our Country: Its Possible Future and Its Present Crisis*
    (New York: The American Home Mission Society, 1885) v, 218, 165, 177,
    218.

 9 "Platform of the American Anti-Imperialist League," in Frederick Bancroft
    (ed.), *Speeches, Correspondence, and Political Papers of Carl Schurz*, Vol. 6
    (New York: G.P. Putnam's Sons, 1913) 77; Erving Winslow, *The Anti-
    Imperialist League: Apologia Pro Vita Sua* (Boston: Anti-Imperialist League,
    1908) 14.

10 Oliver Wendell Holmes, Jr., "The Soldier's Faith: An Address Delivered on
    Memorial Day, May 30, 1895, Harvard University," in Richard A. Posner
    (ed.), *The Essential Holmes: Selections from the Letters, Speeches, Judicial
    Opinions, and Other Writings of Oliver Wendell Holmes, Jr.* (Chicago and
    London: Chicago University Press, 1992) 87–8, 92.

11 Pershing quoted in Gary Gerstle, *American Crucible: Race and Nation in the Twentieth Century* (Princeton and Oxford: Princeton University Press, 2001) 35.

12 Theodore Roosevelt, *Ranch Life and the Hunting Trail* (1888. Reprint. New York: The Century Company, 1911) 2.

13 Theodore Roosevelt, "The Strenuous Life," in Roosevelt, *The Strenuous Life: Essays and Addresses* (New York: Cosimo, 2006) 1, 3.

14 Josiah Strong, *Expansion: Under New World-Conditions* (New York: Baker and Taylor Co., 1900) 18–19.

15 Arthur S. Link, *Woodrow Wilson and the Progressive Era, 1910–1917* (New York: Harpers, 1954).

16 Rudyard Kipling, "The White Man's Burden," *McClure's Magazine*, February 12, 1899; "The Brown Man's Burden" first appeared in *Truth* and was later reprinted in the *Literary Digest*, February 25, 1899.

17 Theodore Roosevelt, "True Americanism," *The Forum Magazine* (April, 1894), available at: http://www.theodore-roosevelt.com/trspeeches.html (June 20, 2010).

18 Schlosser's *Fast Food Nation* originally appeared as a series in *Rolling Stone* in 1999. Upton Sinclair, *The Jungle* (1906. Harmondsworth: Penguin Books, 1984) 129.

19 Theodore Roosevelt, "The New Nationalism," Osawatomie, Kansas, August 31, 1910, available at: http://www.theodore-roosevelt.com/trspeeches.html (June 20, 2010).

20 Woodrow Wilson, "Address at Gettysburg, July 4, 1913," available at: http://www.presidency.ucsb.edu/ws/index.php?pid=65370 (June 20, 2010).

21 Theodore Roosevelt, "Case Against the Reactionaries," Chicago, June 17, 1912.

22 Woodrow Wilson, Second Annual Message to Congress, December 8, 1914.

23 S. Margaret Fuller, *Woman in the Nineteenth Century* (1845. London: George Slater, 1850) 27, 21.

24 Elizabeth Cady Stanton, *A History of Woman Suffrage*, Vol. 1 (Rochester: Fowler and Wells, 1889) 70–71.

25 Mary Church Terrell, "The Justice of Woman Suffrage," *The Crisis*, September 1912, quoted in Marjorie Spruill Wheeler (ed.), *Votes for Women: The Woman Suffrage Movement in Tennessee, the South, and the Nation* (Knoxville: The University of Tennessee Press, 1995) 152, 154.

26 Woodrow Wilson, Address to a Joint Session of Congress, April 2, 1917.

27 *The Crisis*, June 1918, 60.

28 *[To the] French Military Mission. stationed with the American Army. August 7, 1918*, published as "A French Directive," *The Crisis*, XVIII (May, 1919) 16–18, available at: http://www.yale.edu/glc/archive/1135.htm (June 22, 2010).

29 W.E.B. Du Bois, "Returning Soldiers," *The Crisis*, May 1919, 13, available at: http://www.yale.edu/glc/archive/1127.htm (June 22, 2010).

30 Edward L. Bernays, "The Engineering of Consent," *Annals of the American Academy of Political and Social Science*, 250 (March 1947): 113–20, quotation 114.

Chapter 9: Beyond the Last Frontier: A New Deal for America

1   The description of the ceremonies attending the return and burial of the Unknown Soldier are taken from the *New York Times*, November 9–11, 1921.

2   Holmes's opinion can be accessed at: http://caselaw.lp.findlaw.com/scripts/getcase.pl?court=US&vol=249&invol=47 (July 10, 2010).

3   *The Big Money* forms the concluding part of the trilogy that also included *The 42nd Parallel* (1930) and *Nineteen Nineteen* (1932) that was published together in 1938 as *U.S.A.* Quotation from John Dos Passos, *U.S.A.* (Harmondsworth: Penguin Books, 1986) 1105.

4   An audio recording of Harding's speech, delivered in Boston on May 24, 1920, is available via the Library of Congress at: http://memory.loc.gov/ammem/nfhtml/nfexpe.html (July 10, 2010).

5   Sheldon Cheney quoted in Robert Hughes, *American Visions: The Epic History of Art in America* (New York: Alfred A. Knopf, 1997) 405.

6   Sheldon Cheney, *An Art-Lover's Guide to the Exposition* (Berkeley: Berkeley Oak, 1915) 7.

7   Calvin Coolidge, "Whose Country Is This?" *Good Housekeeping*, 72:2 (February 1921): 13–110, 109.

8   James J. Davis, *The Iron Puddler: My Life in the Rolling Mills and What Came of It* (Indianapolis: The Bobbs-Merrill Company, 1922) 27, 60.

9   Purnell quoted in Gary Gerstle, *American Crucible: Race and Nation in the Twentieth Century* (Princeton and Oxford: Princeton University Press, 2001) 105.

10   Harry Hamilton Laughlin, *Eugenical Sterilization in the United States* (Chicago: Published Psychopathic Laboratory of the Municipal Court, 1922).

11   *Buck vs. Bell* (1927), available at: http://caselaw.lp.findlaw.com/cgi-bin/getcase.pl?court=us&vol=274&invol=200 (July 18, 2010).

12   Herbert Hoover, "Address of the 50th Anniversary of Thomas Edison's Invention of the Incandescent Electric Lamp," October 21, 1929, available at: http://www.presidency.ucsb.edu/ws/index.php?pid=21967&st=&st1= (July 20, 2010).

13   Herbert Hoover, Inaugural Address, March 4, 1929, available at: http://www.presidency.ucsb.edu/ws/index.php?pid=21804 (July 22, 2010).

14   Herbert Hoover, campaign speech, New York, October 22, 1928; Annual Message to Congress on the State of the Union, December 2, 1930.

15   Franklin D. Roosevelt, Commonwealth Club Address, September 23, 1932.

16   Raymond Gram Swing, *Forerunners of American Fascism* (New York: Julian Messner, 1935).

17   Herbert Hoover, "The Challenge to Liberty," *Saturday Evening Post*, September 8, 1934; Roosevelt, Fireside Chat, September 30, 1934, available at: http://www.presidency.ucsb.edu/ws/index.php?pid=14759 (July 22, 2010).

18   Raymond Chandler, "The Simple Art of Murder," *The Atlantic Monthly*, *1944; reprinted in The Chandler Collection*, Vol. 3 (London: Picador, 1984) 191.

19 John Dos Passos, *Three Soldiers* (1921. Reprint. California: Coyote Canyon Press, 2007) 282.
20 Hoover, "The Challenge to Liberty."

Chapter 10: A Land in Transition: America in the Atomic Age

1 Anonymous (300 soldiers) to the Editor, *Baltimore Afro-American*, November 23, 1942; Pvt. Norman Brittingham to Truman K. Gibson, Jr., July 17, 1943, both in Phillip McGuire (ed), *Taps for a Jim Crow Army: Letters from Black Soldiers in World War II* (1983. Reprint. Lexington: The University Press of Kentucky, 1993) 11, 18; Anonymous Maryland Black Soldier to the Secretary of War, October 2, 1865, in Ira Berlin et al. (eds.), *Freedom: A Documentary History of Emancipation, 1861–1867, Series II, The Black Military Experience* (New York and Cambridge: Cambridge University Press, 1982) 654; James Henry Gooding to Abraham Lincoln, September 28, 1863, in Corporal James Henry Gooding, *On the Altar of Freedom: A Black Civil War Soldier's Letters from the Front*, ed. Virginia M. Adams (Amherst: The University of Massachusetts Press, 1991) 120.
2 Anonymous, to Mr Carl Murphy, June 26, 1943, in McGuire, *Taps for a Jim Crow Army*, 42–44.
3 Franklin D. Roosevelt, State of the Union Address, January 6, 1942, available at: http://www.presidency.ucsb.edu/ws/index.php?pid=16253 (August 1, 2010).
4 Roosevelt, Annual Address on the State of the Union, January 6, 1941; and Inaugural Address, January 20, 1941.
5 Philip Van Doren Stern (ed.), *The Pocket Book of America* (New York: Pocket Books, 1942), Introduction by Dorothy Thompson, v, vii.
6 Edward Everett Hale, "The Man Without a Country," in *The Man Without a Country and Other Stories* (Hertfordshire: Wordsworth Editions, 1995) 7–8.
7 Langston Hughes, "My America," *Journal of Educational Sociology*, 16:6 (February, 1943) 334–6, quotations 336.
8 General George C. Marshall, "Speech to the Graduating Class, United States Military Academy, May 29, 1942," available at: http://www.marshall foundation.org/Database.htm (August 10, 2010).
9 GI quoted in Paul Fussell, *The Boys' Crusade, American G.I.s in Europe: Chaos and Fear in World War Two* (London: Weidenfeld & Nicolson, 2004) 41.
10 *New York Times*, August 8, 1943.
11 "Defeat at Detroit," *The Nation*, July 3, 1943: 4.
12 Henry R. Luce, "The American Century," *Life*, February 17, 1941, reprinted in Michael J. Hogan (ed.), *The Ambiguous Legacy: U.S. Foreign Relations in the 'American Century,'* (Cambridge and New York: Cambridge University Press, 1999) 12, 20, 26.
13 Henry A. Wallace, "The Price of Free World Victory," in Russell Lord (ed.), *Democracy Reborn* (New York: Reynal and Hitchcock, 1944) 190.

14 Franklin D. Roosevelt, "Fireside Chat 36," June 5, 1944, available at: http://www.presidency.ucsb.edu/ws/index.php?pid=16514   (August   20, 2010).

15 Harry S. Truman, "Special Message to Congress," March 12, 1947, available at: http://www.presidency.ucsb.edu/ws/index.php?pid=12846&st= &st1= (August 20, 2010).

16 Gunnar Myrdal, *An American Dilemma: The Negro Problem and Modern Democracy* (1944. Reprint. New Brunswick, NJ: Transaction Publishers, 2003) 562.

17 *To Secure These Rights: The Report of the President's Committee on Civil Rights* (1947), available at: http://www.trumanlibrary.org/civilrights/ srights1.htm (August 22, 2010):) 80, 82, 87, 139.

18 *Brown v. Board of Education*, 347 U.S. 483 (1954), available at: http: //caselaw.lp.findlaw.com/scripts/getcase.pl?court=US&vol=347&invol= 483 (August 22, 2010).

19 Dwight D. Eisenhower, "Special Message to Congress on the Situation in the Middle East," January 5, 1957, available at: http://www.presidency.ucsb. edu/ws/index.php?pid=11007&st=&st1= (August 23, 2010).

20 Dwight D. Eisenhower, "Annual Message to Congress on the State of the Union," January 9, 1958, available at: http://www.presidency.ucsb.edu/ws/ index.php?pid=11162 (August 23, 2010).

21 John F. Kennedy, "First Inaugural Address," January 20, 1960, available at: http://www.presidency.ucsb.edu/ws/index.php?pid=8032 (August 23, 2010).

Chapter 11: Armies of the Night: Counterculture and Counterrevolution

1 Johnson, quoted in Robert Dallek, *Lyndon B. Johnson: Portrait of a President* (New York and Oxford: Oxford University Press, 2004) 170.

2 The commercial can be viewed via the Lyndon Baines Johnson Library and Museum, available at: http://www.lbjlib.utexas.edu/johnson/media/ daisyspot/ (September 1, 2010).

3 Lyndon B. Johnson, "Special Message to Congress: The American Promise," March 15, 1965, available at: http://www.presidency.ucsb.edu/ws/index .php?pid=26805&st=&st1= (September 3, 2010).

4 'A Divided Decade: The "60s," *Life*, Vol. 26 (December 26, 1969): 8–9.

5 Dwight D. Eisenhower, "Farewell Radio and Television Address to the American People," January 17, 1961, available at: http://www.presidency.ucsb .edu/ws/index.php?pid=12086&st=&st1= (September 3, 2010).

6 Kennedy, quoted in Arthur M. Schlesinger, Jr., *Robert Kennedy and His Times* (1978. Reprint. New York: Houghton Mifflin, 2002) 705.

7 The reaction to the Revolutionary War and World War I are discussed in previous chapters. Figures for American attitudes toward Vietnam are taken from Rhodri Jeffreys-Jones, *Peace Now! American Society and the Ending of the Vietnam War*, New Edition (New Haven: Yale University Press, 2001) 14–15.

8   Tom Hayden et al., "The Port Huron Statement," (1962), available at: http://
    www2.iath.virginia.edu/sixties/HTML_docs/Resources/Primary/Manifestos/
    SDS_Port_Huron.html (September 4, 2010).

9   Report of the National Advisory Commission on Civil Disorders
    (1968), available at: http://www.eisenhowerfoundation.org/docs/kerner.pdf
    (September 4, 2010).

10 Richard M. Nixon, "Inaugural Address," January 20, 1969, available
    at: http://www.presidency.ucsb.edu/ws/index.php?pid=1941 (September 4,
    2010).

11 Ronald Reagan, "Inaugural Address," January 20, 1981, available at:
    http://www.presidency.ucsb.edu/ws/index.php?pid=43130 (September 5,
    2010).

12 William J. Clinton, "Inaugural Address," January 20, 1993, available
    at: http://www.presidency.ucsb.edu/ws/index.php?pid=46366 (September 5,
    2020).

13 Thomas P. Bonczar, "Prevalence of Imprisonment in the U.S. Populations,
    1974–2001" (NCJ-197976); Bureau of Justice, available at: http://bjs.ojp.
    usdoj.gov/index.cfm?ty=pbdetail&iid=2200 (September 5, 2010).

14 Barack Obama, "Inaugural Address," January 20, 2009, available at:
    http://www.presidency.ucsb.edu/ws/index.php?pid=44 (September 5, 2010).

Guide to Further Reading

All the works in this selective guide to further reading contain substantial bibliographies for readers wishing to pursue any topic(s) in depth.

Colonial America

Victoria De John Anderson, *New England's generation: the great migration and the formation of society and culture in the seventeenth century* (New York: Cambridge University Press, 1991)

Bernard Bailyn, *The New England merchants in the seventeenth century* (Cambridge, MA: Harvard University Press, 1955)

Bernard Bailyn, *Atlantic history: concept and contours* (Cambridge, MA: Harvard University Press, 2005)

T.H. Breen, *Puritans and adventurers: change and persistence in early America* (New York: Oxford University Press, 1980)

Francis J. Bremer, *The Puritan experiment: New England society from Bradford to Edward* (Hanover, NH: University Press of New England, 1995)

Francis J. Bremer, *John Winthrop: America's forgotten founding father* (Oxford: Oxford University Press, 2003)

Carl Bridenbaugh, *Jamestown 1544–1699* (New York: Oxford University Press, 1980)

Jon Butler, *Becoming America: the revolution before 1776* (Cambridge, MA: Harvard University Press, 2001)

Elaine Forman Crane, *Ebb tide in New England: women, seaports, and social change, 1630–1800* (Boston: Northeastern University Press, 1998)

William Cronon, *Changes in the land: Indians, colonists, and the ecology of New England* (New York: Hill and Wang, 1983)

John Putnam Demos, *A little commonwealth: family life in Plymouth Colony* (New York: Oxford University Press, 1982)

John Putnam Demos, *The unredeemed captive: a family story from early America* (New York: Random House, 1994)

J.H. Elliott, *Empires of the Atlantic world: Britain and Spain in America, 1492–1830* (New Haven, CT: Yale University Press, 2006)

David Hackett Fischer, *Albion's seed: four British folkways in America* (New York: Oxford University Press, 1989)

Stephen Foster, *The long argument: English Puritanism and the shaping of New England culture 1570–1700* (Chapel Hill: The University of North Carolina Press, 1991)

Kimberly S. Hanger, *Bounded lives, bounded places: free black society in colonial New Orleans, 1769–1803* (Durham, NC and London: Duke University Press, 1997)

Francis Jennings, *The ambiguous Iroquois empire* (New York: W.W. Norton and Co., 1984)

Francis Jennings, *Empire of fortune: crowns, colonies, and tribes in the seven years war in America* (New York: W.W. Norton and Co., 1988)

Edward Douglas Leach, *Roots of conflict: British armed forces and colonial Americans, 1677–1763* (Chapel Hill: The University of North Carolina Press, 1986)

Jill Lepore, *The name of war: King Philip's War and the origins of American identity* (New York: Alfred Knopf, 1998)

John Frederick Martin, *Profits in the wilderness: entrepreneurship and the founding of New England towns in the seventeenth century* (Chapel Hill: University of North Carolina Press, 2001)

Richard Middleton, *Colonial America: a history, 1565–1776* (Oxford: Oxford University Press, 2002)

Edmund S. Morgan, *American slavery, American freedom: the ordeal of colonial Virginia* (New York: W.W. Norton and Company, 1975)

Gary B. Nash, *Red, white, and black: the peoples of early America* (Englewood Cliffs, NJ: Prentice Hall, 1974)

Mary Beth Norton, *Founding mothers and fathers: gendered power and the forming of American society* (New York: Alfred Knopf, 1996)

Anthony S. Parent, Jr., *Foul means: the formation of a slave society in Virginia, 1660–1740* (Chapel Hill: University of North Carolina Press, 2003)

William D. Piersen, *Black Yankees: the development of an Afro-American subculture in eighteenth-century New England* (Amherst, MA: University of Massachusetts Press, 1988)

James Pritchard, *In search of empire: the French in the Americas, 1670–1730* (Cambridge: Cambridge University Press, 2004)

Neal Salisbury, *Manitou and Providence: Indians, Europeans, and the making of New England, 1500–1643* (New York: Oxford University Press, 1982)

Laurel Thatcher Ulrich, *Good wives: image and reality in the lives of women in northern New England 1650–1750* (New York: Oxford University Press, 1982)

Laurel Thatcher Ulrich, *A midwife's tale: the life of Martha Ballard, based on her diary, 1785–1812* (New York: Random House, 1990)

Alden T. Vaughan, *Roots of American racism: essays on the colonial experience* (New York: Oxford University Press, 1995)

Revolution and Independence

David Armitage, *The Declaration of Independence: A global history* (Cambridge, MA: Harvard University Press, 2007)

Bernard Bailyn, *The ideological origins of the American Revolution* (Cambridge, MA: Belknap Press of Harvard University Press, 1967)

Bernard Bailyn, *Faces of revolution: personalities and themes in the struggle for American independence* (New York: Alfred A. Knopf, 1990)

Bernard, Bailyn, *To begin the world anew: the genius and ambiguities of the American founders* (New York: Alfred A. Knopf, 2003)

Colin Bonwick, *English radicals and the American Revolution* (Chapel Hill: The University of North Carolina Press, 1977)

Colin Bonwick, *The American Revolution* (Charlottesville: University Press of Virginia, 1991)

Pauline Maier, *From resistance to revolution: colonial radicals and the development of American opposition to Britain, 1765–1776* (New York: Alfred A. Knopf, 1972)

Pauline Maier, *American scripture: making the Declaration of Independence* (New York: Alfred A. Knopf, 1996)

Robert Middlekauff, *The glorious cause: the American Revolution, 1763–1789*. Rev. ed. (New York: Oxford University Press, 2005)

Edmund S. Morgan, *The birth of the republic, 1763–89*. 3rd ed. (Chicago: University of Chicago Press, 1992)

Gary B. Nash, *The urban crucible: social change, political consciousness, and the origins of the American Revolution* (Cambridge, MA: Harvard University Press, 1979)

Charles Royster, *A revolutionary people at war: the continental army and American character* (Chapel Hill: The University of North Carolina Press, 1979)

John Shy, *A people numerous and armed: reflections on the military struggle for American independence* (Ann Arbor: The University of Michigan Press, 1976)

Gordon S. Wood, *The creation of the American republic, 1776–1787* (Chapel Hill: University of North Carolina Press, 1969)

Gordon S. Wood, *The radicalism of the American Revolution* (New York: Alfred A. Knopf, 1992)

Gordon S. Wood, *The American Revolution: a history* (New York: Modern Library, 2002)

The Early Republic and Antebellum America

Joyce Appleby, *Inheriting the revolution: the first generation of Americans* (Cambridge, MA and London: The Belknap Press of Harvard University Press, 2000)

John Ashworth, *Slavery, capitalism, and politics in the antebellum republic, Vol. 1, commerce and compromise, 1820–1850* (New York and Cambridge: Cambridge University Press, 1996)

John Ashworth, *Slavery, capitalism, and politics in the antebellum republic, Vol. 2, the coming of the civil war, 1850–1861* (New York and Cambridge: Cambridge University Press, 2007)

Joseph P. Ferrie, *Yankeys now: immigrants in the antebellum United States, 1840–1860* (New York and Oxford: Oxford University Press, 1999)

Marshall Foletta, *Coming to terms with democracy: federalist intellectuals and the shaping of an American culture* (Charlottesville and London: University Press of Virginia, 2001)

Eric Foner, *Free soil, free labor, free men: the ideology of the Republican Party before the civil war* (New York: Oxford University Press, 1970)

Susan-Mary Grant, *North over south: northern nationalism and American identity in the antebellum era* (Lawrence: University Press of Kansas, 2000)

John Higham, *Strangers in the land: patterns of American nativism* (New York: Athaneum Press, 1971)

Reginald Horsman, *Race and manifest destiny: the origins of American racial Anglo-Saxonism* (Cambridge, MA: Harvard University Press, 1981)

Winthrop D. Jordan, *White over black: American attitudes toward the Negro 1550–1812* (Chapel Hill: The University of North Carolina Press, 1968)

John Lauritz Larson, *The market revolution in America: liberty, ambition, and the eclipse of the common good* (New York: Cambridge University Press, 2010)

Simon P. Newman, *Parades and the politics of the street: festive culture in the early American republic* (Philadelphia: University of Pennsylvania Press, 1997)

Leonard L. Richards, *The slave power: the free north and southern domination, 1780–1860* (Baton Rouge: Louisiana State University Press, 2000)

Charles G. Sellers, *The market revolution: Jacksonian America, 1815–1846* (New York: Oxford University Press, 1991)

Jay Sexton, *The Monroe doctrine: empire and nation in nineteenth century America* (New York: Hill and Wang, 2011)

David Waldstreicher, *In the midst of perpetual fetes: the making of American nationalism, 1776–1820* (Chapel Hill: The University of North Carolina Press, 1997)

Gordon S. Wood, *Empire of liberty: a history of the early republic, 1789–1815* (New York: Oxford University Press, 2010)

Slavery and the South

Robert E. Bonner, *Mastering America: southern slaveholders and the crisis of American nationhood* (New York and Cambridge: Cambridge University Press, 2009)

Catherine Clinton, *The plantation mistress: woman's world in the old South* (New York: Pantheon Books, 1982)

Carl N. Degler, *The other South: southern dissenters in the nineteenth century* (1974. Paperback Reprint. New York: Harper and Row, 1975)

William Dusinberre, *Them dark days: slavery in the American rice swamps* (New York and Oxford: Oxford University Press, 1996)

William W. Freehling, *The road to disunion, Vol. I, secessionists at bay, 1776–1854* (New York and Oxford: Oxford University Press, 1990)

William W. Freehling, *The road to disunion, Vol. II, secessionists triumphant, 1854–1861* (New York and Oxford: Oxford University Press, 2007)

J. Matthew Gallman, *Northerners at war: reflections on the civil war home front* (Kent, OH: Kent State University Press, 2010)

Elizabeth Fox-Genovese and Eugene D. Genovese, *The mind of the master class: history and faith in the southern slaveholders' worldview* (New York: Cambridge University Press, 2005)

Thavolia Glymph, *Out of the house of bondage: the transformation of the plantation household* (New York: Cambridge University Press, 2008)

Michael A. Gomez, *Exchanging our country marks: the transformation of African identities in the colonial and antebellum South* (Chapel Hill: The University of North Carolina Press, 1998)

John McCardell, *The idea of a southern nation: southern nationalists and southern nationalism, 1830–1860* (New York and London: W.W. Norton and Company, 1979)

William Lee Miller, *Arguing about slavery: the great battle in the United States congress* (New York: Alfred A. Knopf, 1996)

Franny Nudelman, *John Brown's body: slavery, violence, and the culture of war* (Chapel Hill: The University of North Carolina Press, 2004)

Manisha Sinha, *The counterrevolution of slavery: politics and ideology in antebellum South Carolina* (Chapel Hill and London: The University of North Carolina Press, 2000)

Larry E. Tise, *Proslavery: a history of the defense of slavery in America, 1701–1840* (Athens and London: The University of Georgia Press, 1987)

The Civil War Era

Melinda Lawson, *Patriot fires: forging a new American nationalism in the civil war North* (Lawrence: University Press of Kansas, 2002)

Stephen V. Ash, *When the Yankees came: conflict and chaos in the occupied South, 1861–1865* (1995. Reprint. Chapel Hill: The University of North Carolina Press, 2002)

Richard Franklin Bensel, *Yankee leviathan: the origins of central state authority in America, 1859–1877* (New York and Cambridge: Cambridge University Press, 1990)

David W. Blight, *Race and reunion: the civil war in American memory* (Cambridge, MA and London: The Belknap Press of Harvard University Press, 2001)

Gabor Boritt, *The Gettysburg gospel: the Lincoln speech that nobody knows* (New York: Simon and Schuster, 2006)

Michael Burlingame, *The inner world of Abraham Lincoln* (Champaign: University of Illinois Press, 1994)

Orville Vernon Burton, *The age of Lincoln* (New York: Hill and Wang, 2007)

William L. Burton, *Melting pot soldiers: the Union ethnic regiments.* 2nd ed. (New York: Fordham University Press, 1998)

Jacqueline Glass Campbell, *When Sherman marched north from the sea: resistance on the Confederate home front* (Chapel Hill and London: The University of North Carolina Press, 2003)

Richard Carwardine, *Lincoln: a life of purpose and power* (New York: Knopf Publishing Group, 2006)

Christopher Clark, *Social change in America: from the revolution through the civil war* (London: Ivan Dee, 2006)

Robert Cook, *Civil War America: making a nation, 1848–1877* (London: Pearson/Longman, 2003)

Laura F. Edwards, *Scarlett doesn't live here anymore: southern women in the civil war era* (Champaign: University of Illinois Press, 2000)

Drew Gilpin Faust, *This republic of suffering: death and the American civil war* (New York: Alfred A. Knopf, 2008)

Eric Foner, *Reconstruction: America's unfinished revolution, 1863–1877* (New York: Harper and Row, 1988)

Eugene D. Genovese, *A consuming fire: the fall of the Confederacy in the mind of the white Christian South* (Athens and London: The University of Georgia Press, 1998)

William E. Gienapp, *Abraham Lincoln and civil war America: a biography* (Oxford University Press, 2002)

Joseph T. Glatthaar, *Forged in battle: the civil war alliance of black soldiers and white officers* (New York: Meridian, 1991)

Susan-Mary Grant, *The war for a nation: the American civil war* (New York: Routledge, 2006)

Daniel Walker Howe, *What hath God wrought: the transformation of America, 1815–1848* (New York: Oxford University Press, 2008)

Robert Hunt, *The good men who won the war: Army of the Cumberland veterans and emancipation memory* (Tuscaloosa: The University of Alabama Press, 2010)

Caroline E. Janney, *Burying the dead but not the past: ladies memorial associations and the lost cause* (Chapel Hill: The University of North Carolina Press, 2008)

Robert Walter Johannsen, *The frontier, the Union, and Stephen A. Douglass* (Urbana: University of Illinois Press, 1989)

Bruce Levine, *Confederate emancipation: southern plans to free and arm slaves during the civil war* (New York and Oxford: Oxford University Press, 2006)

Chandra Manning, *What this cruel war was over: soldiers, slavery, and the civil war* (New York: Vintage Books, 2007)

Russell McClintock, *Lincoln and the decision for war: the northern response to secession* (Chapel Hill: University of North Carolina Press, 2008)

Stephanie McCurry, *Confederate reckoning: power and politics in the civil war South* (Cambridge, MA: Harvard University Press, 2010)

James M. McPherson, *Battle cry of freedom: the civil war era* (New York and Oxford: Oxford University Press, 1988)

James M. McPherson, *What they fought for, 1861–1865* (Baton Rouge: Louisiana State University Press, 1994)

James M. McPherson, *For cause and comrades: why men fought in the civil war* (Oxford and New York: Oxford University Press, 1997)

Michael A. Morrison, *Slavery and the American west: the eclipse of manifest destiny and the coming of the civil war* (Chapel Hill: University of North Carolina Press, 1997)

John R. Neff, *Honoring the civil war dead: commemoration and the problem of reconciliation* (Lawrence: University Press of Kansas, 2005)

Peter J. Parish, *The American civil war* (New York: Holmes and Meier, 1975)

W. Scott Poole, *Never surrender: Confederate memory and conservatism in the South Carolina upcountry* (Athens and London: The University of Georgia Press, 2004)

David M. Potter, *The impending crisis, 1848–1861* (New York: Harper and Row, 1976)

George C. Rable, *Fredericksburg! Fredericksburg!* (Chapel Hill and London: University of North Carolina Press, 2002)

Brian Holden Reid, *The origins of the American civil war* (Harlow, Essex: Longman, 1996)

Charles Royster, *The destructive war: William Tecumseh Sherman, Stonewall Jackson, and the Americans* (1991. Reprint. New York: Random House, 1993)

Julie Saville, *The work of reconstruction: from slave to wage laborer in South Carolina, 1860–1870* (1994. Paperback Reprint. New York and Cambridge: Cambridge University Press, 1996)

Mark Schantz, *Awaiting the heavenly country: the civil war and America's culture of death* (Ithaca, NY and London: Cornell University Press, 2008)

Harry S. Stout, *Upon the altar of the nation: a moral history of the civil war* (New York: Penguin Books, 2006)

Elizabeth R. Varon, *Disunion!: the coming of the American civil war, 1789–1859* (Chapel Hill: The University of North Carolina Press, 2008)

Bell Irvin Wiley, *The life of Johnny Reb: the common soldier of the Confederacy* (1943. Reprint. Baton Rouge. Louisiana State University Press, 1989)

Bell Irvin Wiley, *The life of Billy Yank: the common soldier of the Union* (1952. Reprint. Baton Rouge: Louisiana State University Press, 1989)

The West

Stephen Ambrose, *Crazy Horse and Custer: the parallel lives of two American warriors* (New York: Doubleday, 1975)

Stephen E. Ambrose, *Undaunted courage: Meriwether Lewis, Thomas Jefferson, and the opening of the American west* (New York: Simon & Schuster, 1996)

Pekka Hämäläinen, *The Comanche empire* (New Haven, CT: Yale University Press, 2008)

Patricia Nelson Limerick, *The legacy of conquest: the unbroken past of the American west* (New York and London: W.W. Norton and Company, 1987)

Dean L. May, *Three frontiers: family, land, and society in the American west, 1850–1900* (New York: Cambridge University Press, 1994)

William G. Robbins, *Colony and empire: the capitalist transformation of the American west* (Lawrence: University Press of Kansas, 1994)

Richard Slotkin, *Fatal environment: the myth of the frontier in the age of industrialization, 1800–1890* (New York: Atheneum Publishers, 1985)

Henry Nash Smith, *Virgin land: the American west as symbol and myth* (Cambridge, MA: Harvard University Press, 1950)

Richard White, *"It's your misfortune and none of my own": a new history of the American west* (Norman: University of Oklahoma Press, 1991)

Donald Worster, *Under western skies: nature and history in the American west* (New York: Oxford University Press, 1992)

The Gilded Age/Progressive Era

Sven Beckert, *The monied metropolis: New York City and the consolidation of the American bourgeoisie, 1850–1896* (Cambridge: Cambridge University Press, 2001)

Edward J. Blum, *Reforging the white republic: race, religion, and American nationalism, 1865–1898* (Baton Rouge: Louisiana State University Press, 2005)

John M. Cooper, Jr., *Pivotal decades: The United States, 1900–1920* (New York: W.W. Norton and Co., 1990)

Steven J. Diner, *A very different age: Americans of the progressive era* (New York: Hill and Wang, 1998)

Judith N. McArthur, *Creating the new woman: the rise of women's progressive culture in Texas, 1893–1918* (Urbana and Chicago: University of Illinois Press, 1998)

Nell Irvin Painter, *Standing at Armageddon: the United States, 1877–1919* (New York: W.W. Norton and Co., 1987)

Stephen Skowronek, *Building a new American state: the expansion of national administrative capacities, 1877–1920* (New York and Cambridge: Cambridge University Press, 1982)

Robert Wiebe, *The search for order, 1877–1920* (New York: Hill and Wang, 1980)

America between the wars

Michael C.C. Adams, *The best war ever: America and World War II* (Baltimore: The Johns Hopkins University Press, 1994)

Anthony J. Badger, *The New Deal: The Depression years, 1933–1940* (Basingstoke: Macmillan, 1989)

John Morton Blum, *V was for victory: politics and American culture in World War II* (New York: Harcourt Brace and Company, 1976)

James MacGregor Burns, *Roosevelt: the lion and the fox* (New York: Harcourt Brace and Company, 1956)

John Diggins, *The proud decades: America in war and peace, 1941–1960* (New York: W.W. Norton and Co., 1988)

David S. Foglesong, *America's secret war against Bolshevism: U.S. intervention in the Russian civil war, 1917–1920* (Chapel Hill: The University of North Carolina Press, 1995)

Ellis W. Hawley, *The Great War and the search for a modern order: a history of the American People and their institutions, 1917–1933* (New York: St Martin's Press, 1979)

David M. Kennedy, *Over here: the First World War and American society* (New York: Oxford University Press, 1980)

David M. Kennedy, *Freedom from fear: the American people in depression and war, 1929–1945*. New ed. (New York: Oxford University Press, 2001)

William Leuchtenburg, *Franklin D. Roosevelt and the New Deal, 1932–1940* (New York: Harper and Row, 1963)

William Leuchtenburg, *The perils of prosperity, 1914–32*. 2nd ed. (Chicago: The University of Chicago Press, 1993)

Michael E. Parrish, *Anxious decades: America in prosperity and depression, 1920–1941* (New York: W.W. Norton, 1992)

Cold War America

Stephen Ambrose, *Nixon, 3 Vols: Vol. 1, the education of a politician; Vol. 2, the triumph of a politician, 1962–1972; Vol. 3, ruin and recovery, 1973–1990* (New York: Simon & Schuster, 1987, 1991)

Larry Berman, *No peace, no honor: Nixon, Kissinger, and betrayal in Vietnam* (New York: The Free Press, 2001)

Irving Bernstein, *Promises kept: John F. Kennedy's new frontier* (New York and Oxford: Oxford University Press, 1991)

John Morton Blum, *Years of discord: American politics and society, 1961–1974* (New York: W.W. Norton and Co., 1991)

Paul Boyer, *By the bomb's early light: American thought and culture at the dawn of the atomic age* (Chapel Hill: University of North Carolina Press, 1994)

Taylor Branch, *Parting the waters: America in the King years, 1954–63* (New York: Simon & Schuster, 1988)

Taylor Branch, *Pillar of fire: America in the King years, 1963–65* (New York: Simon & Schuster, 1998)

Carl M. Brauer, *John F. Kennedy and the second reconstruction* (New York: Columbia University Press, 1977)

Mary Charlotte Brennan, *Turning right in the Sixties: the conservative capture of the GOP* (Chapel Hill: University of North Carolina Press, 1995)

Thomas R. Brooks, *Walls come tumbling down: a history of the civil rights movement, 1940–1970* (Englewood Cliffs, NJ: Prentice-Hall, 1974)

H.W. Brands, *The devil we knew: Americans and the Cold War* (New York: Oxford, 1993)

David Caute, *The great fear: the anti-communist purge under Truman and Eisenhower* (New York: Simon and Schuster, 1978)

Robert J. Cook, *Troubled commemoration: the American civil war centennial, 1961–1965* (Baton Rouge: Louisiana State University Press, 2007)

Alastair Cooke, *A generation on trial: U.S.A. v. Alger Hiss* (New York: Alfred A. Knopf, 1951)

Robert Dallek, *John F. Kennedy: an unfinished life*. Rev. ed. (New York: Penguin, 2004)

Robert Dallek, *Lyndon B. Johnson: portrait of a president* (New York and Oxford: Oxford University Press, 2004)

Robert Dallek, *Nixon and Kissinger: partners in power* (New York: Harper Collins, 2007)

Gareth Davies, *From opportunity to entitlement: the transformation and decline of Great Society liberalism* (Lawrence: University Press of Kansas, 1996)

Robert A. Divine, *Blowing on the wind: the nuclear test ban debate, 1954–1960* (New York: Oxford University Press, 1978)

Robert A. Divine, *The Sputnik challenge: Eisenhower's response to the Soviet satellite* (New York: Oxford University Press, 1993)

Adam Fairclough, *To redeem the soul of America: the Southern Christian Leadership Conference and Martin Luther King, Jr.* (Athens: University of Georgia Press, 1987)

Lawrence Freedman, *The evolution of nuclear strategy*. 2nd ed. (Basingstoke and London: Macmillan Press, 1989)

John Lewis Gaddis, *The United States and the origins of the Cold War* (New York: Columbia University Press, 1972)

John Lewis Gaddis, *We now know: rethinking Cold War history* (Oxford and New York: Oxford University Press, 1997)

David J. Garrow, *Bearing the cross: Martin Luther King, Jr., and the Southern Christian Leadership Conference* (New York: W. Morrow, 1986)

David Halberstam, *The fifties* (New York: Random House, 1996)

Michael J. Heale, *American anticommunism: combating the enemy within, 1830–1970* (Baltimore: The Johns Hopkins University Press, 1990)

Michael J. Heale, *McCarthy's Americans: red scare politics in state and nation, 1935–1965* (London: Palgrave Macmillan, 1998)

Michael J. Heale, *The sixties in America: history, politics and protest* (Edinburgh: University of Edinburgh Press, 2001)

Seymour Hersch, *The dark side of Camelot* (New York: Harper Collins, 1998)

Andrew J. Huebner, *The warrior image: soldiers in American culture from the Second World War to the Vietnam era* (Chapel Hill: University of North Carolina Press, 2008)

Arnold R. Isaacs, *Vietnam shadows: the war, its ghosts, and its legacy* (Baltimore: Johns Hopkins University Press, 1997)

Rhodri Jeffreys-Jones, *Peace now!: American society and the ending of the Vietnam War*, New Edition (New Haven, CT: Yale University Press, 2001)

Philip Jenkins, *The Cold War at home: the red scare in Pennsylvania, 1945–1960* (Chapel Hill: The University of North Carolina Press, 1999)

Zachary Karabell, *Architects of intervention: the United States, the third world, and the Cold War, 1946–1962* (Baton Rouge: Louisiana State University Press, 1999)

Gabriel Kolko, *Anatomy of a war: Vietnam, the United States, and the modern historical experience* (New York: Pantheon, 1985)

Mark Atwood Lawrence, *Assuming the burden: Europe and the American commitment to war in Vietnam* (Berkeley: University of California Press, 2005)

Guenter Lewy, *America in Vietnam* (New York: Oxford University Press, 1978)

Scott Lucas, *Freedom's war: the American crusade against the Soviet Union* (New York: New York University Press, 1999)

David Maraniss, *They marched into sunlight: war and peace, Vietnam and America, October 1967* (New York: Simon and Schuster 2005)

Elaine Tyler May, *Homeward bound: American families in the cold war era* (New York: Basic Books, 1988)

Myra MacPherson, *Long time passing: Vietnam and the haunted generation* (Garden City, NJ: Doubleday, 1984)

Allen J. Matusow, *The unraveling of America: a history of liberalism in the 1960s* (New York: Harper and Row, 1984)

Walter A. McDougall, *The heavens and the earth: a political history of the space age* (New York: Basic Books, 1985)

Lisa McGirr, *Suburban warriors: the origins of the new American Right* (Princeton, NJ: Princeton University Press, 2001)

James T. Paterson, *Grand expectations: The United States, 1945–1974*. New ed. (New York: Oxford University Press, 1998)

Charles M. Payne, *I've got the light of freedom: the organizing tradition and the Mississippi freedom struggle* (Berkeley: University of California Press, 1995)

Howell Raines, *My soul is rested: movement days in the Deep South remembered* (New York: Putnam, 1977)

Ellen Schrecker, *Many are the crimes: McCarthyism in America* (Princeton, NJ: Princeton University Press, 1998)

Neil Sheehan, *A bright shining lie: John Paul Vann and America in Vietnam* (New York: Random House, 1988)

Philip Taubman, *Secret empire: Eisenhower, the CIA, and the hidden story of America's space espionage* (New York: Simon and Schuster, 2004)

Martin Walker, *The Cold War: a history* (New York: Henry Holt and Co, 1993)

James H. Willbanks, *The Tet offensive: a concise history* (New York: Columbia University Press, 2006)

Garry Wills, *The Kennedy imprisonment: a meditation on power* (Boston: Little, Brown and Co., 1985)

C. Vann Woodward, *The strange career of Jim Crow* (New York: Oxford University Press, 1978)

Daniel Yergin, *Shattered peace: the origins of the Cold War and the national security state* (New York: Houghton Mifflin, 1977)

Modern America/General

Stephen Ambrose, *Rise to globalism: American foreign policy since 1938* (New York: Penguin Books, 1997)

Adam J. Berinsky, *In time of war: understanding American public opinion from World War II to Iraq* (Chicago: University of Chicago Press, 2009)

Robert F. Berkhofer, *The white man's Indian: images of the American Indian from Columbus to the present* (New York: Knopf: Random House, 1978)

Jefferson Cowie, *Stayin' Alive: the 1970s and the last days of the working class* (New York: The New Press, 2010)

David Ekbladh, *The great American mission: modernization and the construction of an American world order* (Princeton, NJ: Princeton University Press, 2010)

Adam Fairclough, *Better day coming: blacks and equality, 1890–2000*. Reprint. (New York: Penguin Books, 2002)

Niall Ferguson, *Colossus: the rise and fall of the American empire* (London and New York: Penguin Books, 2004)

Gary Gerstle, *American crucible: race and nation in the twentieth century* (Princeton, NJ and Oxford: Princeton University Press, 2001)

Paula Giddings, *When and where I enter: the impact of black women on race and sex in America* (New York: Morrow, 1984)

Michael J. Heale, *Twentieth-century America: politics and power in the United States* (London: Arnold, 2004)

Rhodri Jeffreys-Jones, *The FBI: a history* (New Haven, CT and London: Yale University Press, 2007)

Linda K. Kerber, *No constitutional right to be ladies: women and the obligations of citizenship* (New York: Hill and Wang, 1998)

Michael Mann, *Incoherent empire* (London and New York: Verso, 2003)

James T. Patterson, *Restless giant: the United States from Watergate to Bush vs. Gore.* New ed. (New York: Oxford University Press, 2007)

Jonathan M. Schoenwald, *A time for choosing: the rise of modern American conservatism* (Oxford: Oxford University Press, 2003)

Michael S. Sherry, *In the shadow of war: the United States since the 1930s* (New Haven, CT: Yale University Press, 1997)

Biographies

Samuel Adams (1722–1803)

One of the Founding Fathers of the American nation, Samuel Adams was born in Quincsy, Massachusetts, and graduated from Harvard College in 1743. He briefly considered a career in the law, and even more briefly, and unsuccessfully, shifted to business, before taking up what would become his permanent career in politics, serving in the Massachusetts House of Representatives and as a member of the Boston Town Meeting in the 1760s. When, in 1763, the British Parliament mooted taxing the colonies to raise revenue to cover the cost of the Seven Years War (or French and Indian War), Adams was instrumental in composing a considered colonial response to this unwelcome suggestion. He argued that

[if] our trade may be taxed, why not our lands? Why not the produce of our lands, and every thing we possess, or use? This we conceive annihilates our charter rights to govern and tax ourselves. It strikes at our British privileges, which, as we have never forfeited, we hold in common with our fellow subjects, who are natives of Britain. If tastes are laid upon us in any shape, without our having a legal representation, where they are laid, we are reduced from the character of free subjects, to the state of tributary slaves. We, therefore, earnestly recommend it to you, to use your utmost endeavours to obtain from the general court, all necessary advice and instruction to our agent, at this most critical Juncture.

It is notable that at this point, Adams located his argument within the context of "British privileges" and used the language – that Thomas Jefferson would also deploy – of enslavement to describe the proposed new financial arrangements that the British sought to establish with regard to their North American colonies. Clearly, although later positioned historically as a radical who acted in defense of his "country," Adams's becoming American was, as for many revolutionaries, not a process that preceded but rather proceeded through the act of rebellion itself. In 1765, Adams was elected as Boston's representative on the general court of Massachusetts, from which position he argued consistently for colonial rights. In 1768, his circular letter in response to the Townshend Duties again proposed that taxation was unconstitutional because the colonies had no parliamentary representative – a position that so irritated the colonial governor, Francis Bernard, that he dissolved the assembly. This act, in part at least, fomented the civil unrest that led to the Boston Massacre of 1770. Two years after the confrontation between colonials and British troops, Adams was instrumental in the establishment of the Committee of Correspondence, a coordinated group of colonial leaders who in time became the leaders of organized resistance to British Crown control. Adams attended the First Continental Congress in Philadelphia in 1774, helping draft both the Articles of Confederation and the Massachusetts Constitution. By 1776, he was fully convinced of the need to declare independence, a position he believed the only logical outcome of the colonial predicament. He retired from Congress in 1781, was elected lieutenant governor of Massachusetts in 1789 and governor in 1794 until his final retirement in 1797. He died some six years later, in 1803, at eighty-two years of age. Historians have portrayed Adams either as a man committed to colonial rights or as a demagogue who inspired violence among the colonials in the cause of independence; in the end, Adams may be just one example of the maxim that one man's radical is another's freedom fighter, but in fact, within the context of his times, Adams was more moderate than extreme.

Jane Addams (1860–1935)

Jane Addams was one of the most prominent reformers of the Progressive Era in the United States, the founder of the Hull House in Chicago and a women's rights and suffrage activist. She was born in Illinois and attended the Women's Medical College in Pennsylvania, but was unable to complete her studies due to ill health. It was when she visited England with Ellen Gates Starr and visited Toynbee Hall, a settlement house in Whitechapel, that she conceived the idea of establishing similar settlement houses in the United States. Her social reform efforts were only part of a broader progressive program that included sanitation and housing reform, workers' and immigrants' rights, the abolition of child labor, and children's and women's education. Her philosophy was perhaps summed up in her observation and question, proposed in 1929, that the "modern world is developing an almost mystic sense of the continuity and interdependence of mankind – how can we make this consciousness the unique contribution of our time to the small handful of incentives which really motivate human conduct? Addams really operated, both personally and professionally, at a time of sweeping changes in American society, when that society was moving from relative homogeneity to heterogeneity, from the country to the city, and from an albeit imperfect isolationism to a global involvement honed and hampered in equal measure through World War I. Her arguments for female suffrage were couched – as many were – in what can today seem very Victorian, traditionalist terms; the woman as the moral heart of the home and, by extrapolation, the nation (much the same argument used to challenge female suffrage then and, in the context of the Equal Rights Amendment [ERA] much later).

John Caldwell Calhoun (1782–1850)

John C. Calhoun was one of the leading spokesmen for the South and regarded as instrumental in the refinement both of the defense of slavery and of states' rights in the years leading up to the American Civil War. He was born in what was then Abbeville District, in upcountry South Carolina, graduated from Yale in 1807, and entered the legal profession in Abbeville at the same time as serving in the state house of representatives. He was elected on the Democratic-Republican ticket to Congress and served from 1811 to 1817. He was the Secretary of War under James Monroe, and then was elected vice president of the United States when John Quincy Adams became president – a post he retained when the presidency was held by Andrew Jackson. Although both came from the slave-owning southern ruling class, the relationship between Jackson (who was from Tennessee) and Calhoun was a stormy one, but Calhoun remained as vice president until 1832, when he resigned to join the Senate. Calhoun began his political career as a strong nationalist, a "War Hawk" during the War of 1812, arguing in favor of protective tariffs as the means to support American business and internal growth. Calhoun was a noted political theorist, and it was his analysis of republican theory, in particular the role of "minority rights" and the need for a "concurrent majority" to protect these, that instigated his move toward the belief in states' rights, limited government, and, in particular, the right of states to nullify such acts of the federal government in which they did not concur – a position that paved the way for the eventual secession of the southern states from the Union in 1860–1861. Historian William Freehling described Calhoun as having "no small talk, only large principle." It was perhaps unfortunate for his nation that the principle revolved around the right to retain chattel slavery, and that one of his most famous utterances (in the Senate in 1837) was to declare that slavery was "a positive good." "We of the South," Calhoun declared, "will not, cannot, surrender our institutions... I hold that in the present state of civilization, where two races of different origin, and distinguished by color, and other physical differences, as well as intellectual, are brought together, the relation now existing in the slaveholding States between the two, is, instead of an evil, a good – a positive good." Calhoun increasingly came to perceive the South as a section more sinned against than sinning, and his move away from his earlier nationalist position was made clear in December 1828, when he penned the "South Carolina Exposition and Protest" in response to the so-called Tariff of Abominations passed that year and argued that under it the individual states risked "being reduced to a subordinate corporate condition" within the federal system. Although published anonymously, Calhoun was known to be its author, and his resignation in 1832 was largely as a result of the widening rift between himself and Jackson over the tariff question. Resigning enabled Calhoun to argue openly in favor of nullification, a position he maintained until his death, from tuberculosis, in 1850. Calhoun's legacy, in the medium term, boosted the secessionist impulse, especially in South Carolina; in the longer term, and with the Civil War long in the past, his defense of minority rights – shorn of its association with the interests of slaveholders – within the federal system remains influential.

Henry Clay (1777–1852)

Like John C. Calhoun, Henry Clay was one of an influential group of nineteenth-century politicians and statesmen known as the Great Triumvirate (Clay, Calhoun, and Daniel Webster). Born in Hanover Country, Virginia, Clay, in common with most politicians of the period, began his career in the law, being admitted to the Virginia bar in 1797. He moved west to Kentucky, as many lawyers did, because the opportunities for a successful career negotiating land settlements were greater on the frontier. Often described as a Jeffersonian Republican on the slavery issue as in other matters (although unlike Jefferson, Clay emancipated his slaves in his will), Clay nevertheless did not envisage a mixed and equal society as being a possibility in the United States. He advocated colonization for the nation's free African Americans, and in 1836 became president of the American Colonization Society. It was not for his advocacy of colonization that Clay came to prominence, but for his support of internal improvements and manufacturing (that came to be termed the American System). He was a member of the Kentucky state house of representatives before being elected on the Democratic-Republican ticket to the United States Senate in 1806. Reelected in 1811, Clay served as Speaker of the House of Representatives and later as Secretary of State under John Quincy Adams. Like Calhoun, at the start of his career, Clay was a War Hawk in the War of 1812, and at that time a strong exponent of nationalist policies for the United States; unlike Calhoun, he retained that position. Indeed, in contrast to Calhoun, who sometimes exacerbated division, Clay came to be known as the Great Compromiser for his efforts to broker deals between the sections over such issues as the tariff, internal improvements, federal banks, and slavery. He supported the Missouri Compromise, which established the representational balance between the slave and free states, and the Compromise Tariff of 1833, which brought the Nullification Crisis to an end. In this regard his support for colonization may have been a factor, given that support for that endeavor, at first popular in the South, gradually – and certainly by the later 1830s – waned, to be replaced with the rather stronger sentiments expressed by Calhoun that slavery was a "positive good," and any attempt to curb its extension an attack on minority rights. Clay's thinking on this matter, and perhaps more his political maneuvering through the moral and material minefield that slavery was becoming, was something that Abraham Lincoln took note of when he, later, was faced with the problem of advocating abolition to an often hostile audience. Clay, like Lincoln, was adamant that slavery was "a curse – a curse to the master, a wrong, a grievous wrong to the slave. In the abstract it is ALL WRONG," he declared in 1836, "and no possible contingency can make it right." Nevertheless, Clay operated within the law and within the Constitution as he understood both, and was able to broker the 1850 Compromise that seemed, on the surface, to have achieved stability between North and South but which turned out to be the beginning of the end for slavery in the United States. Clay died in the year that *Uncle Tom's Cabin* was published (1852), having done as much as possible to hold his nation together long enough that when it did come apart, eight years later, it stood a far greater chance of surviving secession.

Alexis-Charles-Henri Clérel de Tocqueville (1805–1859)

Alexis de Tocqueville was a French aristocrat and political philosopher whose visit to the United States resulted in two volumes on *Democracy in America* (1835 and 1840). America was host to a great array of European visitors at that time, including Charles Dickens, all of whom were keen to see the first republican experiment in action and to report back on its success, or otherwise, to a fascinated and sometimes skeptical world. Specifically – and one must bear in mind that this predates the twentieth century's fascination with Michel Foucault and the social control implications of penitentiaries and asylums – Europeans were interested – not exclusively – with American variants of these, and it was ostensibly to study American prisons and asylums that de Tocqueville was able to visit the United States. Given the political upheavals in France, of course, de Tocqueville was far more interested in the broader implications of democracy in America. As he wrote, "I confess that in America I saw more than America; I sought there the image of democracy itself, with its inclinations, its character, its prejudices, and its passions, in order to learn what we have to fear or hope from its progress." Scholars continue to debate the extent to which de Tocqueville fully understood what he saw, but certain "sound bites" from his work continue to resonate today (and indeed at the time), specifically the phenomenon that he identified (and Calhoun worked so hard to restrain) as the "tyranny of the majority." In de Tocqueville's opinion, the "very essence of democratic government consists in the absolute sovereignty of the majority; for there is nothing in democratic states that is capable of resisting it." Given that de Tocqueville arrived in the United States in the midst of the Nullification Crisis, it is perhaps unsurprising that he should have devoted so much consideration to the matter, nor that Americans pored so carefully over what he wrote about them and their institutions. "When I refuse to obey an unjust law, I do not contest the right of the majority to command," de Tocqueville observed, "but I simply appeal from the sovereignty of the people to the sovereignty of mankind. Some have not feared to assert that a people can never outstep the boundaries of justice and reason in those affairs which are peculiarly its own; and that consequently full power may be given to the majority by which it is represented. But this is the language of a slave."

Stephen Arnold Douglas (1813–1861)

Stephen A. Douglas was born in Vermont and, like so many politicians, studied law (although Douglas was also briefly a teacher in Illinois). After being admitted to the bar, he practiced in Jacksonville, Illinois, where he served in the state house of representatives. He was unsuccessful in his bid for election to Congress in 1838, but was elected as a Democrat to the House of Representatives five years later, and to the Senate in 1847, where he served until his death. He was one of the most influential politicians of his age, nicknamed the Little Giant both because of his height and because of his impact on politics. He was Chairman of the Committee on Territories, and it was through this office that he wielded such influence of the crucial political issue of the day, which was the possible expansion of slavery into the West. Along with Henry Clay, he maneuvered the Compromise of 1850 through Congress, but it was the Kansas-Nebraska Act four years later that really undid all that the Compromise had hoped to achieve. In his support for "popular sovereignty," whereby the settlers of a territory were given the choice of whether it would be slave or free – a solution that should have pleased everyone and in fact satisfied no one – Douglas prompted a split in his own party from which it never recovered, and persuaded many Democrats to change allegiance to the new Republican Party that was in the process of pulling itself together to stand in the 1856 election. Aware of the impact of the Kansas-Nebraska Act, Douglas commented that his way home to Chicago was now lit by his own burning effigies. Nevertheless, he stuck to his political guns and his belief in popular sovereignty. In 1857, Douglas supported the Supreme Court's *Dred Scott* decision that effectively rendered the Missouri Compromise nugatory and opened up not just the Western territories but every existing state to the possibility of becoming "slave" rather than "free." Douglas's views on the matter were aired extensively in 1858, when his Republican opponent for the Senate seat for Illinois, Abraham Lincoln, engaged him in a series of debates – the Lincoln-Douglas debates – that addressed popular sovereignty and the future of slavery in the nation. In what became known as the Freeport Doctrine (as it was in the course of the debate at Freeport that Douglas articulated it), Douglas proposed the optimistic position that the *Dred Scott* ruling need not open up former free states to slavery if the population of those states refused to support legislation in favor of slavery. No "matter what the decision of the Supreme Court may be on that abstract question," Douglas asserted, "still the right of the people to make a Slave Territory or a Free Territory is perfect and

complete under the Nebraska bill." The people did not concur. By the
1860 election, the Democrats split with Douglas, achieving the nomination, but a pro-Southern faction fielded their own candidate, John C.
Breckinridge, creating a fissure that allowed the Republican candidate,
Lincoln, to win. This precipitated the secession of several Southern states
and a four-year Civil War that Douglas did not live long enough to
endure.

Frederick Douglass (1818–1895)

Born a slave in Maryland, Frederick Douglass escaped the South's "peculiar institution" in 1838, traveling first to New Bedford, Massachusetts.
He became a prominent abolitionist speaker and author – he published
a newspaper, *The North Star*, and penned no fewer than three auto-
biographies – and regularly lectured on behalf of the Massachusetts
Anti-Slavery Society. His *Narrative of the Life of Frederick Douglass, an
American Slave* (1845), his first and best-known autobiography, proved
a powerful counterargument to slaveholders' assertions regarding the
capabilities of African Americans, and a potent propaganda publication
for abolitionists both North and South. Douglass traveled widely, at
home and abroad, to spread his message. He consistently challenged the
United States to live up to its stated civic ideas, and in one famous speech
reminded his audience that national celebrations held little meaning for
African Americans; held little meaning, indeed, so long as slavery existed. "What to the slave is the fourth of July?" he demanded in 1852.
"The existence of slavery in this country brands your republicanism as
a sham, your humanity as a base pretence, and your Christianity as a
lie. It destroys your moral power abroad; it corrupts your politicians at
home." Slavery, he went on, "is the antagonistic force in your government, the only thing that seriously disturbs and endangers your Union.
It fetters your progress; it is the enemy of improvement, the deadly foe
of education; it fosters pride; it breeds insolence; it promotes vice; it
shelters crime; it is a curse to the earth that supports it; and yet, you
cling to it, as if it were the sheet anchor of all your hopes." When the
Civil War came, Douglass saw the conflict not just as an opportunity to
end slavery, but a chance for African Americans to prove their patriotism by fighting for the Union. He was appalled that, at first, they were
denied the right to do so. After the Emancipation Proclamation in 1863,
and the official raising of black regiments, Douglass's sons, Charles and
Lewis, joined the North's most famous African American regiment, the

54th Massachusetts Colored Infantry (although Charles transferred to the 5th Cavalry). After the war, Douglass continued to speak out for the rights of African Americans, and was dismayed at the growing tendency to downplay the significance of emancipation in the public evocations of the war. "We are sometimes asked in the name of patriotism," he reminded Americans in 1871, "to forget the merits of this fearful struggle, and to remember with equal admiration those who struck at the nation's life, and those who struck to save it." The Civil War, as Douglass realized, was fast becoming the exception to the rule that history is written by the winners.

William Edward Burghardt (W.E.B.) Du Bois (1868–1963)

W.E.B. Du Bois represented a new generation of African-American spokesmen to follow men like Douglass, and in *Black Reconstruction* (1935), he echoed Douglass's 1871 comments by noting that America had fallen "under the leadership of those who would compromise with truth in the past in order to make peace in the present." His entire career was devoted to challenging and seeking to eradicate what he identified, in *The Souls of Black Folk* (1903), as the "problem of the twentieth century," the "color-line." Born in Massachusetts, Du Bois was educated at Fisk and at Harvard (he was the first African American to gain a doctorate from Harvard), and was professor of history and economics at Atlanta University. His perspective was that of the Progressive era in which he grew up, as he believed that through education, social reform might be effected and racism eradicated, and he argued that the educated elite – what he termed the "talented tenth" of the African-American population – should lead the way. In 1905, he organized a meeting of black leaders in Canada (or rather, the Canadian side of Niagara Falls, where the hotels accommodated blacks; hence the group came to be known as the Niagara Movement), out of which emerged a "Declaration of Principles" that called for franchise reform (many African Americans had been effectively disenfranchised under the so-called Jim Crow laws of the South) and the ending of racial segregation. Together with white Progressive reformers, and in a reaction against a lynching, one that took place not in the South but in Illinois, Du Bois founded the National Association for the Advancement of Colored People (NAACP) that remains active today. In the early twentieth century, the NAACP pushed hard for the implementation of both the Fourteenth and Fifteenth Amendments, but with little success. With the outbreak of World War I, and

America's commitment of troops in 1917, Du Bois, like Douglass in the case of the Civil War, encourage African Americans to join up to fight, to establish their claim to equal citizenship rights. In 1919, when the troops were returning home, Du Bois considered the implications for these black "Returning Soldiers" in *The Crisis*, the NAACP's monthly journal, whose return to a country that disenfranchised and lynched African Americans held out hope that blacks would return "fighting" for equality. "Make way for Democracy," Du Bois declaimed. "We saved it in France, and by the Great Jehovah we will save it in the United States of America, or know the reason why." Over the course of a very long life, Du Bois would challenge both the social and scientific arguments that supported racism, although his perceived radicalism and support for communism attracted both criticism and the attention of the FBI. He was one of the few African-American spokesmen to challenge the forced internment of Japanese Americans during World War II.

Benjamin Franklin (1706–1790)

One of America's Founding Fathers, Benjamin Franklin seemed to exemplify what came to be called the American Dream over the course of a life that saw him rise from poverty to international prominence and a career that covered printing, publishing, and politics, and combined science with statesmanship. Famous for his many inventions, including the lightning rod (devised after his famous kite-flying experiment), the Franklin stove (or circulating stove, as it was designed to circulate hot air around a room) and bifocal spectacles, perhaps his greatest invention was himself and, through that, the nation that became the United States. Franklin's career began in printing, but from the start he was driven to publish his ideas on social and individual progress, at first under pseudonyms, Silence Dogood, and later the persona of Poor Richard (Richard Saunders) of *Poor Richard's Almanack* fame, published from 1732 to 1758. The *Almanack* contained pithy pieces of wisdom concerning the efficacy of frugality and hard work, collected together in as *The Way to Wealth* (1758). Perhaps the best-known of these is the "early to bed, and early to rise, makes a man healthy, wealthy, and wise" maxim. Although a little too relentlessly upbeat for some tastes – both at the time and since – Franklin's advice resonated in a colonial setting in which the possibility of reinvention of both self and society seemed real enough to many. At the very least, the opportunity existed in the colonies to critique the elite, which Franklin did via the pages of the *Pennsylvania Chronicle and*

Universal Advertiser, founded in 1767 and largely devoted to challenging the influence both of the Penn family and perceived British intrusion into colonial affairs. At this point, of course, Franklin positioned himself in a British context; he was clearly an individual born with a determination to succeed (being one of twenty children may have fomented that ambition) but not necessarily in a new national context. Ten years before he became involved with the *Chronicle*, Franklin had been sent to Britain to represent Pennsylvania, and took the opportunity to promote the idea of increased self-government for the colony, but with little success. On his return to the colonies, consequently, he increasingly advocated colonial unity and opposition to what he regarded as overbearing dominance of colonial affairs by a parliament 3,000 miles away. The *Chronicle* reflected the growing radicalism of the day in its publication of John Dickinson's *Letters from a Pennsylvanian Farmer*, which argued against overtaxation. As a member of the Second Continental Congress, Franklin contributed to, and was a signer of, the Declaration of Independence, and in the year that it appeared (1776), he was dispatched to France to persuade the French to aid the American colonies in their conflict with Britain. Franklin returned to the by then United States two years after the signing of the Treaty of Paris (1783) that ended the American War of Independence.

Sarah Margaret Fuller Ossoli (1810–1850)

Margaret Fuller was born in Massachusetts and, as was and remains the fate of many educated women, her career began in teaching, largely because, after her father's death, she had to support her younger siblings. However, active in journalism (she edited the transcendentalist journal *The Dial* and wrote for the then-moderately radical New York *Tribune*, edited by Horace Greeley), she was able to access a broader constituency beyond the classroom, and actively promoted not just women's rights but equality more generally. Many of the arguments that appeared in her book, *Woman in the Nineteenth Century* (1845), were outlined two years previously in a long essay published in *The Dial*, "Man versus Men, Woman versus Women," in which she emphasized the national promise inherent in the Declaration of Independence. "Though the national independence be blurred by the servility of individuals," she wrote, "though freedom and equality have been proclaimed only to leave room for a monstrous display of slave dealing and slave keeping," nevertheless the idea that all men are created equal remained "a golden certainty, wherewith to encourage the good, to shame the bad." Sent to Europe by Greeley in

1846, Fuller furnished a series of "dispatches" published in the *Tribune*, in which she detailed the events of what she described as the "sad but glorious days" of the Italian revolution and the importance of the leading revolutionaries, notably Guiseppe Mazzini, and their ideals to the United States. "The cause is OURS, above all others," she wrote to her country, a nation she believed to be "not dead" but sleeping through the issue of slavery, and one in which "the spirit of our fathers flames no more but lies hid beneath the ashes." When in Italy, Fuller met and (possibly) married the revolutionary Marchese Giovanni Angelo d'Ossoli, with whom she had a son, Angelo. As they returned to the United States in 1850, their ship was wrecked off the coast of New York and all three perished. Fuller was not well served by her contemporaries as far as her lasting legacy was concerned, and her dispatches from Europe, although available in the *Tribune*, of course, were published as *At Home and Abroad* (1856), edited (and modified) by her brother, Arthur. The fame that she eventually was accorded as a women's rights advocate has tended to overshadow the much broader importance of her analysis not just of women's rights but of citizenship rights in the United States in the mid-nineteenth century.

Alexander Hamilton (c. 1755–1804)

Alexander Hamilton, another of America's Founding Fathers (and another lawyer), was actually born in the West Indies and was sent to the American colonies (to New Jersey) for his education in 1772, which he then continued at King's College (now Columbia) in New York, where he became a strong supporter of the colonial cause and soon captain of an artillery company raised by the New York Providential Congress. He announced himself in print with the publication of "A Full Vindication of the Measures of Congress," which defended the Continental Congress from Loyalist attack, but his route to fame really began when he was appointed aide-de-camp to George Washington in 1777, a position he held for four years. Hamilton's experiences during the war, and especially over the terrible winter at Valley Forge when the revolutionary army was at its lowest point – both in terms of morale and men – is often cited as a factor in his later arguments in favor of a strong centralized federal state. Like Washington, Hamilton perceived that individual state concerns and loyalties operated against the efficient conduct of the war, and would most likely have the same effect on the (still putative) nation. He argued for a revision of the Articles of Confederation, and found he had common cause with others, such as future president James Madison and John Jay and, together with them he would compose and publish what became known as *The Federalist Papers* (originally *The Federalist*). This was a series of constitutional essays that appeared in the New York press between 1787 and 1788, and which was devised to support the case for a revised Constitution for America. It remains of relevance, and is sometimes cited, in contemporary Supreme Court rulings. One of Hamilton's most notable contributions (*Federalist* 84) to the constitutional debate was his objection to the inclusion of the Bill of Rights on the grounds that to enumerate a series of rights risked restricting those rights already enjoyed by "the people." A separate Bill of Rights, Hamilton, believed, would be "not only unnecessary in the proposed constitution, but would even be dangerous." Why, he asked, "declare that things shall not be done which there is no power to do?" In 1789, Hamilton was appointed the first Secretary of the Treasury under George Washington, a post he held until 1795. In this capacity, Hamilton was instrumental in establishing the fiscal framework of the nation, its banks, revenue, national debt and credit systems, and the rules governing manufactures.

Oliver Wendell Holmes, Jr. (1841–1935)

Oliver Wendell Holmes was born in Massachusetts, the son of doctor and author Oliver Wendell Holmes, and attended Harvard. When the Civil War broke out, he joined up to fight for the Union, and was wounded and left for dead after the Battle of Antietam in 1862 (his father recounted the experience of traveling to the battlefield to look for his son in an *Atlantic Monthly* article, "My Hunt after 'The Captain'"). The war is usually deemed to have been the formative event in Holmes, Jr.'s life, the origin of what is sometimes described as his moral skepticism, largely because, toward the end of the century, he delivered two notables addresses on the subject of war and the life struggle. In 1884, in a Memorial Day Address delivered to the Union veterans' association, the Grand Army of the Republic, Holmes argued that "the generation that carried on the war has been set apart by its experience. Through our great good fortune, in our youth our hearts were touched with fire. It was given to us to learn at the outset that life is a profound and passionate thing." A decade later, speaking before the graduating class at Harvard on Memorial Day, 1895, he urged the students "to keep the soldier's faith against the doubts of civil life." Holmes was certainly not unusual in evincing, in his later years, a robust and possibly slightly romanticized recollection of a conflict faced in his youth. By that time he was already very well established in his legal career, which he had taken up after the Civil War. He edited the *American Law Review* from 1870 to 1873, and in 1880 delivered a series of lectures at the Lowell Institute, which began with the observation that the "life of the law has not been logic; it has been experience." Holmes was briefly professor of law at Harvard Law School but was appointed as associate justice of the Supreme Judicial Court of Massachusetts in 1883 and became chief justice in 1899. As a former soldier, he naturally appealed to Theodore Roosevelt who appointed him to the U.S. Supreme Court at the end of 1902. His most famous ruling was perhaps in *Schenck vs. United States* (1919), in which he established that the First Amendment did not protect an individual if they posed a "clear and present danger" to society (the individual in question had been encouraging Americans to avoid the draft). In *Abrams vs. United States* (1919), he argued – in what some interpreted as a contradiction to his previous judgment – that there was no "clear and present danger" (the individuals in this case had been distributing leaflets denouncing the war effort). There was no contradiction, because the crucial part of Holmes's 1919 decision was that the words "are used in such circumstances and are of such a nature as to create a clear and present danger." In fact, Holmes was consistent throughout his career in his emphasis on the importance of free speech as underpinning American liberties.

Andrew Jackson (1767–1845)

The seventh president of the United States, who gave his name to the "Age of Jackson," and whose nickname, Old Hickory, implied toughness, was at the time, and has largely remained, hugely symbolic in a nation that emphasizes self-help, frontier vigor, and determination. Although there was no widespread extension of the franchise, and certainly no dramatic upward social mobility during the Age of Jackson, his image was that of a common man who would extend the democratic process and the economic opportunities of the nation to common men generally. For an individual who, if nothing else, was a loner, he came across as a man of the people. Some of his popularity at the time derived from the fact that he had served (as a courier, as he was barely a teenager at that point) in the Revolutionary War. His childhood was resolutely grim; he had lost both parents by the age of fourteen. He studied law and, as many others did, moved to the frontier – to the territory that would become the state of Tennessee – for the opportunities that offered. When Tennessee was admitted to the Union in 1796, Jackson became the state's representative in Congress. Land speculation enabled him to become a wealthy man, a cotton planter and a slave owner, but it was the War of 1812 that brought him to national prominence and, ultimately, the presidency, in particular his victory over British forces at New Orleans in 1815. When Alexis de Tocqueville visited the United States during Jackson's second term of office, he was critical of a man he described as "of violent character and middling capacities," and one unpopular with "the enlightened classes of the Union." Yet Tocqueville understood that it was "the memory of a victory he won twenty years ago under the walls of New Orleans" that maintained his public popularity. The victory alone was not in itself sufficient; it was the war, too, that played its part in securing Jackson's image, his immediate financial future, and eventually executive office. The War of 1812, a second conflict with the British, was not just symbolically significant but, in practical terms, it removed many native peoples from both the South and the Northwest and opened up vast tracts of land to white settlers (and their slaves). New opportunities on a new frontier seemed to be opening up, and Jackson was well placed to exploit these. He first stood for election in 1824, but with four candidates in that election, and none with an overall majority, it fell to the House of Representatives to select the president, and it chose John Quincy Adams. In 1828, Jackson was elected president in an election that really witnessed party politics come into operation for the first time in America; elections became mass entertainment, and if image was not quite yet everything, it was definitely moving in that direction. In that respect, Jackson was a foretaste of things to come in American politics.

John Fitzgerald Kennedy (1917–1963)

The election of John F. Kennedy, America's first Catholic president, seemed at the time and since as promising a new start for America, as a moment when, as Kennedy himself put it, the torch was passed "to a new generation of Americans." It was also one of the closest elections in American history, and one in which the media was deemed to have played a crucial role. In the televised debates between Kennedy and his Republican rival, the then-Vice President Richard Nixon, Kennedy was quite literally seen to be the more persuasive candidate (it is often observed that radio listeners tended to consider Nixon's the stronger performance). Both this, and the tragedy of Kennedy's assassination by Lee Harvey Oswald in Dallas, Texas, in November 1963, have heavily influenced the public perception of America's thirty-fifth president, and a 2011 televised miniseries on the Kennedys will doubtless reinforce the reverence with which the Kennedy name is treated, or sometimes mistreated, in the United States. For the pre-9/11 generation, often a crucial historical marker in their lives was that they always remembered where they were and what they were doing when they heard that JFK had been assassinated. Kennedy's brief presidency was itself overshadowed by the Cold War, in some respects defined by the Cuban Missile Crisis in 1962, and was a time when the domestic program took second place to a vigorous prosecution of an anti-communist agenda. This drove the Kennedy administration to compete, globally and in space, with the Soviet Union. Prompted by the "Sputnik Challenge" in 1961, Kennedy committed America to achieving a Moon landing within the decade, but said little, and did less, about the growing racial problems that were more down to earth and, in states such as Mississippi, were becoming acute. Yet the Kennedy legacy was not so much in what the president himself did, or did not do, but in the symbolism and in the rhetoric provided by a leader who promised new frontiers for a nation that, in the aftermath of World War II and the McCarthy era, and in the context of the ongoing Cold War, wanted something, if not necessarily someone, to believe in.

Abraham Lincoln (1809–1865)

As the president who held the American Union together in the mid-nineteenth century, Abraham Lincoln's legacy might seem secure, but in recent years, concerted efforts to challenge the Lincoln legend have been launched; to very little effect, it must be said, since the scholarship on Lincoln is voluminous – it used to be the case that only Napoleon had more books written about him, but that may no longer be true – and shows no signs of diminishing. The focus of much of the debate (and sometimes diatribe) tends to revolve around Lincoln's decision for emancipation, although there has been a move to critique Lincoln's suspension of certain civil liberties in the Border States, especially, and with regard to the press, during the Civil War. Given that the Civil War is central to the national narrative (no Union victory, no nation), and Lincoln central to the Civil War, the understanding of the individual cannot be divorced from that of the war. Lincoln was a man of his time. Like Henry Clay, he was a frontier lawyer and, like Clay, he loathed slavery but was not convinced that a color-blind society was an option, and he also supported the idea of colonization for free African Americans. Much of what Lincoln said and did with regard to slavery and secession derived from the fact that he was a committed constitutionalist and operated within the assumption (and the legal position that implied) that secession represented a rebellion in, but not of, the South. He was also a pragmatist. Just as Clay had found that direct attacks on slavery stood little chance of success in an environment where slaveholding was entrenched, so Lincoln found that direct attacks on the institution were worse than useless and potentially damaging to the Union war effort in a nation where racism was not a sectional sin but a national outlook. Yet from the outset, what came to be called the Civil War (but not until 1912; before that point, it was the War of the Rebellion) was not clear-cut legally or constitutionally (for example, one of the first acts of the Union was to blockade Southern ports; yet in international law, no nation could blockade itself). In this context, whatever Lincoln did about emancipation had to be done in such a way as to make it binding on the nation once the war was over, and assuming the Union won. Not the least of his frustrations at the time was fielding the strident demands from radicals and reformers that he end slavery in a part of the country that the Union no longer controlled. In addition, the Civil War was waged by a Union in which the two-party system continued to function (it did not in the Confederacy), so both presidential actions and words had to be carefully considered in an environment where the maintenance of support for a war fought not by a regular army but mainly by volunteer troops depended on the continuing support at the polls. It is often assumed that the Union, with more men and a stronger economy, more munitions and a more robust transport network, was bound to win the Civil War, but that perspective ignores the real world in which Lincoln operated and the fact that all the power in the world (as Vietnam surely made evident) is worse than useless if not harnessed effectively. Lincoln's assassination by John Wilkes Booth in 1865, at the end of the Civil War, has produced even more "what ifs" than the death of Kennedy in 1963. The period of Reconstruction (to 1877) has been regarded as a missed opportunity to consolidate the emancipation momentum that Lincoln had built up over the course of the conflict (the leading historian of the era has termed Reconstruction "America's unfinished revolution"), necessitating the so-called "Second Reconstruction" of the 1960s.

Ronald Reagan (1911–2004)

Ronald Reagan was born and educated in Illinois and moved to California in 1937 where he had a successful career as an actor and as president

of the Screen Actors' Guild (making him the only union leader so far
to hold executive office) and where, in the 1950s, he became a spokesman for the General Electric Corporation. It was his speech in support
of Barry Goldwater's 1964 presidential bid that brought him national
attention, and in 1966, he was elected governor of California. His own
bid for the presidency failed in 1968 and again in 1976, but the third
time was a charm in 1980. Reagan's victory in 1980 was regarded as
a turning point, not just in the narrow sense of the rising fortunes of
the American Right, but more generally for a nation still smarting from
the debacle that had been the Vietnam War. With his emphasis on government as the problem, Reagan both harked back to Thomas Paine
and to the tradition that developed along with the nation itself of individual entrepreneurship as the driver both of the American economy and
of individual American lives although, as was the case with the Age of
Jackson, the rhetoric of inclusivity disguised the exclusivity enjoyed by
a fairly narrow and mainly business elite. The post-1980 retreat from
perceived liberal values, from the active state solutions represented by the
New Deal and the Great Society, was also accompanied by the rise of a
moralistic right intent on directing the lives of others to a degree that no
state – in its most intrusive imaginings – could ever conceive or achieve.
In some respects, fear was the motivating ideology that drove the rise
of the "New Right" after 1980, fear of disintegration at home and the
dangers of the "evil empire" abroad. In this context, Reagan offered a
deceptively straightforward solution to America's problems at home and
abroad. His economic program moved the American economy away from
its pre-1980 Keynesian (in brief, government or public-sector spending as
economic driver) toward supply-side (sometimes termed "trickle-down")
economics ("Reaganomics") and drove through tax cuts via the Emergency Recovery Tax Act (1981) in an attempt to reduce the deficit. At
the same time, because Reagan believed that defense was not a "budget
item," American military spending rose by 40 percent between 1980 and
1984. Reagan's reelection in 1984 saw the president increasingly involved
in foreign affairs, most notably the beginning of the end of the Cold War.
Reagan's efforts to improve relations with the Soviet Union were generally deemed successful, but in 1986, the revelation that the United States
had been secretly supplying the Contras in Nicaragua – in defiance of
the Congressional decision to suspend such aid – exposed (or not, given
that both files and memories conveniently disappeared) the extent of the
shadow state behind Congress. Ultimately, Reagan's success with regard
to the Soviets counterbalanced what was known as the Iran-Contra Affair

(the funds for the Contras had come from arms sales to Iran negotiated in return for American hostages seized by Shi'ite groups), and Reagan left office as one of America's most popular presidents.

Theodore Roosevelt (1858–1919)

Theodore Roosevelt, the twenty-sixth president of the United States, was born in New York. Early childhood illness produced in him a determination to overcome his weak health with a robust physical fitness regime (he later praised what he termed the "strenuous life") that came to define his political outlook, a regenerative impulse that grew from his own personal experience into a progressive program for the nation. He was educated at Harvard, and after this was elected to the New York State Assembly. His interest in America's naval power saw him publish *The Naval War of 1812* (1882). He came to presidency as the youngest man to hold the executive office with the assassination of William McKinley in 1901. By that time, Roosevelt already had a reputation as a man of action, a reputation partly forged at San Juan Hill on Cuba during the Spanish-American War of 1898. As president, Roosevelt sought to promote broadly progressive values, and his economic program, the Square Deal, sought to ensure that the interests of "Big Business" in the form of the U.S. Steel and Standard Oil did not operate against those of the public, or the nation. He was a strong proponent of antitrust legislation and of the conservation of the great American wilderness. Roosevelt was instrumental in protecting the nation's natural resources from economic exploitation and secured millions of acres with the intention that the land be used for new national parks. The United States, by the time of Roosevelt's presidency, had already designated Yellowstone (1872) and Yosemite (1890) as federally protected National Parks, so Roosevelt was developing, rather than instigating, a policy of environmental protection. In terms of foreign policy, just as Roosevelt divided corporations into those he deemed beneficial to the nation and those whose power threatened it, abroad he tended to see a juxtaposition between civilized and uncivilized, and to extend his progressive domestic politics onto the world's stage by attempting to intervene in the internal affairs of several Central American nations, inaugurating the idea of America as "the world's policeman." Having served two terms, Roosevelt left office, but in 1912 he sought to return, and established a new Progressive Party whose platform, the New Nationalism, advocated control of business and the expansion of social justice achieved via greater government intervention. Although not successful – he was defeated by Woodrow Wilson – Roosevelt's general ideology proved influential in American economic, political, and social development in the twentieth century.

Franklin Delano Roosevelt (1882–1945)

Franklin D. Roosevelt (FDR), America's thirty-second president, was one of the nation's most – if not the most – popular leaders, both in his lifetime and since. He remains the only president to have been elected to serve more than two terms in office. He guided the United States through the Great Depression, implemented the New Deal, and led the nation through World War II. His presidency began with an election that represented a decisive rejection of the old political order in the form of the Republicans, and established the Democratic Party in control of both the Senate and the House of Representatives. The New Deal that he brought to the American people went far beyond the domestic economic and social programs of the 1930s; the New Deal persisted, both in its economic implementation and in the ideology behind it, well into the 1960s, and the Democrats became the default party of government, holding the executive office for twenty-eight of the following thirty-six years. Much of FDR's success rested on the creation of what became known as the "New Deal coalition," his bringing together of organized labour (in the form of the newly created Congress of Industrial Organizations [CIO]) that supported the Democratic Party and brought much of the urban vote with it, African Americans (some three-quarters of northern African Americans supported FDR for reelection in 1936), intellectuals, and the white South. The New Deal also represented a secular shift in a nation that had seen the influence of the religious right rise: one of the FDR administration's first acts was the repeal of Prohibition – not an overtly secular act in itself, but definitely a rejection of one example of the extremes of right-wing morality. Over the course of his "First Hundred Days," FDR began the implementation of the relief programs that would constitute the economic heart of the New Deal, at the same time keeping an eye on global events, which were building toward World War II. When the war did break out, his emphasis on America as the "Arsenal of Democracy" was an important step between neutrality and commitment, merging as it did the practical economic benefits of weapons production with a much larger idea of what the nation stood for, and might fight for. After Pearl Harbor was attacked, FDR placed the American economy on a war footing, which saw its industrial productivity skyrocket, with all the benefits accruing from that and from mass mobilization of the population. FDR died in the final year of World War II, and the new world order that he had begun to broker at Yalta and Tehran would fall to others to accomplish. Yet FDR's lasting legacy was that through his presidency, the American people – a people traditionally suspicious of government – were encouraged to have faith in that government, an outgrowth of their faith in FDR himself. It was this that really distinguished this era of America's history, a faith in the efficacy of government that FDR's cousin, the progressive Theodore Roosevelt, shared but had never been able to convince the electorate of wholeheartedly, and a faith that the nation relinquished in the election of Ronald Reagan in 1980.

Benjamin Rush (1745–1813)

Benjamin Rush, perhaps today a less well-known Founding Father of the United States, was born near Philadelphia, and in 1759 attended the College of Physicians in that city. His medical training progressed at Princeton and then abroad, in Edinburgh, Scotland, and in continental Europe. In 1769, Rush opened a private practice in Philadelphia, and also taught as Professor of Chemistry at the College of Philadelphia, publishing the first American textbook on the subject. Yet Rush did not confine himself to matters medical, but wrote a series of editorials on behalf of the Patriot cause in the years preceding the American Revolution, and was actively involved in the Sons of Liberty organization in Philadelphia. In 1776, he represented Philadelphia at the Continental Conference and was a signatory to the Declaration of Independence. Appointed surgeon-general of the Continental Army in 1777, but his opposition both to the Army Medical service at that time and to George Washington himself forced his resignation. In 1789, he was a member of the Pennsylvanian convention that adopted the new Constitution, and was later appointed as treasurer of the U.S. Mint, a post he held from 1797 until his death. Before that he had been appointed professor of medical theory and clinical practice at the University of Pennsylvania, and throughout his life he sustained a wide variety of social activist interests, including abolition, the broadening of access to education for all, including women (on the grounds that a republic required an educated citizenry), and for medical clinics to treat the poor. Although a slave owner himself (he had one slave), in 1773 Rush published "An Address to the Inhabitants of the British Settlements in America, upon Slave-Keeping," in which he argued that slavery "and Vice are connected together, and the latter is always a source of misery," and reminded his readers of "the Rod which was held over them a few years ago in the Stamp, and Revenue Acts." In a precursor of the argument that Abraham Lincoln would use in his second inaugural address, Rush stressed "that national crimes require national punishments, and without declaring what punishment awaits this evil, you may venture to assure them, that it cannot pass with impunity, unless God shall cease to be just or merciful." Rush also described the yellow fever epidemic of 1793, and was ahead of his time in his interest in mental as well as physical disease. His *Medical Inquiries and Observations upon the Diseases of the Mind* (1812) was the first American textbook on the subject.

Margaret Sanger (1879–1966)

Margaret Sanger (nee Higgins) was born in New York, one of eleven children born to a woman who had endured eighteen pregnancies. She was a contentious figure in her day, a day not fully comfortable with the dissemination of birth-control literature, which it tended to designate as "obscene" (under the terms of the Comstock Law – named for social reformer Anthony Comstock – of 1873), and has remained a controversial one since. Sanger trained as a nurse and worked for a time on Manhattan's Lower East Side, at the same time being involved in the radical culture that concentrated on Greenwich Village and included such figures as social reformer and author Upton Sinclair and the anarchist Emma Goldman. In 1912, Sanger began writing a regular column for the *New York Call*, entitled "What Every Girl Should Know," about sex education and contraception. The particular column on venereal disease was suppressed on the grounds of obscenity. In 1914, she published the first issue of the feminist publication, *The Woman Rebel*, but it, too, ran afoul of the censors who were unhappy with Sanger's advocacy of contraception, and so great was the furor – and the risk of imprisonment accompanying this – that Sanger was forced to leave for England. In her absence, her associates disseminated some 100,000 copies of her pamphlet on contraception, *Family Limitation*. Sanger returned to New York for trial in 1915, which never happened, rather to her dismay as she had hoped that the publicity would raise awareness of the issues. Sanger opened the first birth control clinic in Brooklyn in 1916, which led to her conviction and imprisonment but did raise public awareness and, crucially, funds for the cause for birth control reform. In 1923, she opened another clinic, the Birth Control Research Bureau, making use if a legal loophole that permitted physicians to prescribe contraception. She had, in 1917, begun publication of the *Birth Control Review*, and three years later opened the American Birth Control League, to be followed, in 1929, by her formation of the National Committee on Federal Legislation for Birth Control. Sanger at least lived long enough to see birth control become legal (for married couples only, in *Griswold vs. Connecticut* [1965]). Sanger's advocacy of birth control has been variously described as deriving from her experiences among poorer women whose health inevitably suffered during pregnancy but was also jeopardized by the widespread recourse to illegal and sometimes self-induced abortion, or as having a rather more eugenicist purpose in an era when population control carried overtones of racial control and national improvement. Certainly her reputation was affected by the impact of the eugenics movement and by her own support for the sterilization of the mentally ill, a subject ruled on by Oliver Wendell Holmes in *Buck vs. Bell* (1927).

Index

Other Titles in the Series (continued from page iii)

A Concise History of Greece, 2nd Edition
RICHARD CLOGG

A Concise History of Hungary
MIKLÓS MOLNÁR, TRANSLATED BY ANNA MAGYAR

A Concise History of Modern India, 2nd Edition
BARBARA D. METCALF AND THOMAS R. METCALF

A Concise History of Italy
CHRISTOPHER DUGGAN

A Concise History of Mexico, 2nd Edition
BRIAN R. HAMNETT

A Concise History of New Zealand
PHILIPPA MEIN SMITH

A Concise History of Poland, 2nd Edition
JERZY LUKOWSKI AND HUBERT ZAWADZKI

A Concise History of Portugal, 2nd Edition
DAVID BIRMINGHAM

A Concise History of South Africa, 2nd Edition
ROBERT ROSS

A Concise History of Spain
WILLIAM D. PHILLIPS JR. AND CARLA RAHN PHILLIPS

A Concise History of Sweden
NEIL KENT

A Concise History of Wales
GERAINT H. JENKINS